BVR's Guide to Intellectual Property Valuation

Second Edition

Mike Pellegrino

BVR
What It's Worth

1000 SW Broadway, Suite 1200, Portland OR 98205
(503) 291-7963 • www.bvresources.com

BVR
What It's Worth

Managing Editor: Janice Prescott

Publisher: Sarah Andersen

Chair and CEO: David Foster

President: Lucretia Lyons

Vice President of Sales: Lexie Gross

Customer Service Manager: Jasmine Pearsall

ISBN: 978-1-935081-60-9
Library of Congress Control Number: 2012931900

Table of Contents

ABOUT THE AUTHOR **8**

ACKNOWLEDGMENTS **9**

CHAPTER 1: ABOUT THIS GUIDE **11**

The Growing Importance of IP 11

Why Is This Guide Needed? 15

What This Guide Is Not 16

CHAPTER 2: IP VALUATION OVERVIEW **19**

About Patents 19

The Advantages of Patents 20

The Disadvantages of Patents 20

About Copyrights 24

The Advantages of Copyrights 24

The Disadvantages of Copyrights 26

About Trademarks 26

The Advantages of Trademarks 27

The Disadvantages of Trademarks 28

About Trade Secrets 29

The Advantages of Trade Secrets 29

The Disadvantages of Trade Secrets 31

CHAPTER 3: ABOUT IP VALUATION **33**

Applying the Science 33

Practicing the Art 38

The Science-Art Continuum 62

CHAPTER 4: USING VALUATION APPROACHES 63
The Cost Approach 63
The Market Approach 67
The Income Approach 67
The Assignment-Approach Match 68
Common Pitfalls of the Various Approaches 84
Reconciling Several Valuation Approaches 105
Valuation Method Selection Summary 110

CHAPTER 5: GENERAL DUE DILIGENCE 113
Performing Initial Interviews 114
Analyzing Historical Financials 117
Understanding the IP 119
Verifying IP Ownership 132
Commissioning Independent Counsel Review 134
Reviewing Enforcement History and Ability 143
Performing Market Analysis 148
Evaluating the Regulatory Environment 156

CHAPTER 6: PATENT DUE DILIGENCE 159
The Invention Status 161
Current Art 163
Patent Utility 167
Patent Quality 172
Patent Age 175
The Administrative House 178
Blocking Patents 184
Status of Active Administrative or Legal Actions 188
Outstanding Contractual Provisions Affecting Value 194

CHAPTER 7: COPYRIGHT DUE DILIGENCE 195
Nature of the Copyrighted Material 196
Verifying the Nature of Rights to Value 199
Administrative Issues That Can Impair Copyright Value 200
Registration 201
Factual Works 201
Fair Use Value Erosion 203
Work Made for Hire 205
Copyright Notice 207
Ease of Duplication 208
Mechanical Rights for Nondramatic Musical Works 209
Termination of Transfers 210
Public Domain 211
Visual Artists Rights Act of 1990 212
Special Considerations for Computer Software 213
Easier to Avoid Infringing Activity 215
Disclosure 216
The Rule of Doubt 218
Special Considerations for Semiconductor Designs or Masks 218

CHAPTER 8: TRADEMARK DUE DILIGENCE 221
What Is Trademark Due Diligence? 225
Maintenance Fees 232
Owner of Record 233
Pending Trademark Challenges 233
Continued Use 234
Public Notice 236
Durability 237
Incontestability 240
Interference 241
Standards of Use 241
Trademark Strength 244
Dilution 246
Counterfeit Risk 247
Market Dynamism 250
Fair Use Value Impacts 252

CHAPTER 9: TRADE SECRET DUE DILIGENCE 255
Trade Secret Value Sources 258
Trade Secret Floor Value 260
Factors That Prolong Trade Secret Value 263
Factors That Kill Trade Secrets 264
Litigation Effects 265
Inadvertent Disclosures 265
Trade Secret Agreement Terms 266
Publication as Patent or Copyright 268

CHAPTER 10: DISCOUNT RATE DEVELOPMENT 269
Accounting for IP Risk 270
Deeper Analysis of Current Methods 273
An IP Discount Rate Estimation Model 276
Target Rate of Return 277
Holding Period 278
Success Rates 280
Target Returns 281
Investment Expenses 281
What About Empirical Evidence of Support? 283
Proving the Model 285
Model Extensions 287
Back to the Roots 289
Real-World Examples 289

CHAPTER 11: DETERMINING ROYALTY RATES 293
Royalty Rate Considerations 295
Royalty Rate Magnitude 296
Common Royalty Rate Determination Methods 300
Analytical Royalty Rate Determination Process 321
Calculating the Value Proposition 323
Determining Licensor and Licensee Contributions 326
Analytical Method Attack Points 329

CHAPTER 12: CASE STUDY IN IP VALUATION 333
A Poor Example of Celebrity Valuation 333
A Credible Approach to Celebrity Valuation 339

CHAPTER 13: MANAGING AN ENGAGEMENT 343
Project Preparation 344
Initial Due Diligence 345
IP Analysis 346
Market Analysis 349
Valuation Modeling 351
Valuation Reporting 353
Project Support 354

CHAPTER 14: AUDITOR'S REVIEW GUIDE 355
Analyzing the Analyst 355
Analyzing the Due Diligence 357
Report Boilerplate 359
Economic Conditions and Nature of the Industry 360
IP Utility 361
Government Protections 361
Functional Realization 362
Demand Analysis 363
Financial History 363
Chronology 364
Royalty Rate Analysis 364
Income Approach Using Reasonable Royalty Method 366
Consideration of Cost Approach 366
Use of Market Methods for IP Valuation 366
Use of Valid and Reliable Inferential Statistics 367
Repeatability 367

About the Author

Mike Pellegrino is the founder and president of Pellegrino & Associates. He is a former practicing software engineer, chief finance officer, and accountant. This diverse background gives Mike the requisite experience to credibly and defensively value intellectual properties that include best-selling books, top-selling branded products, cutting-edge software, patents that drive many of today's high-tech products, and even John Dillinger's publicity rights. An unconventional valuation analyst, Mike plays no favorites when it comes to valuation. With a strong emphasis on the economic fundamentals of the assets he values, he has developed a reputation for asking penetrating questions that can get right to the heart of an asset's value. Mike has successfully defended his value opinions in state and federal court actions as well as with state and local tax authorities and the Internal Revenue Service.

Mike is a prolific writer and an energetic and frequent speaker on software and intellectual property valuation, delivering practical seminars and boot camps regularly that integrate many valuation examples drawn right from the headlines. Having graduated from Indiana Tech summa cum laude with a Bachelor of Science in computer science, he earned a Master of Business Administration from Ball State University, went back to school a third time for accounting at Indiana Tech, and attended the Center for Creative Leadership's flagship Leadership Development Program. Mike is a member of the editorial board for BVR's *Intellectual Property Management & Valuation* newsletter. He also serves on the board of The Villages of Indiana. Mike is a former board member of Techpoint, the Techpoint PAC, the Indiana Venture Club, Early Childhood Alliance (executive secretary), and Pathways, a not-for-profit organization that helps runaway teens.

Acknowledgments

The intellectual property landscape has changed dramatically in the three years since we published the previous version of this book. The U.S. Congress took up the issue of patent reform for the first time in 50 years—resulting in passage of the America Invents Act, which moved the U.S. to a country that awards patents on a first-to-file basis from a first-to-invent basis. The U.S. Supreme Court weighed in on the patentability of business method processes in *Bilski v. Kappos*. The U.S. Supreme Court reinforced the presumption of patent validity in *Microsoft Corp. v. i4i Limited Partnership*. Perhaps most interesting is that the most valuable U.S. patent ever issued (in my opinion) expired on June 28, 2011. That was U.S. patent #5,273,995, which describes the calcium salt of atorvastatin, also known as Lipitor. Information within the intellectual property landscape changes at a dizzying pace, and it takes significant effort just to keep up.

A good support network makes writing a book easier. Fortunately, I have a great team to work with at my firm, Pellegrino & Associates, LLC. Despite having a robust level of projects to address, the team has answered the call of duty to help with research, test theories, double-check my math, and ensure that my thoughts and ideas make their way to these pages in a coherent form. I offer special thanks to Jill Starbuck, who has been editing my work professionally for more than eight years and whose eagle eye always seems to catch things that I miss. You have done more to improve my writing than anyone has.

I have had the honor and opportunity to interact with a great many professional people in the IP valuation field. I would especially like to thank the great efforts of Neal Beaton, Ryan Brewer, Jeff Champa, Emad Isaac, Chad Kellar, Gary Lipson,

Rob Schlegel, and Kevin Yeanoplos who have been kind enough to discuss or debate valuation issues, especially in public forums and conferences. I would like to thank our hundreds of clients who have honored us with the pleasure of valuing their intellectual properties. While we did not always meet our clients' valuation expectations, I appreciate their understanding of our approach and the acceptance of our results. I would like to thank the Internal Revenue Service, local tax jurisdictions, and all opposing counsel for hiring competent valuation analysts to challenge our valuation work. The fruits of our ability to defend our work soundly to those challenges have made their way right into this guide.

I would also like to thank the kind people at BVR who have withstood the countless broken promises of chapter delivery dates and kept the faith. David Foster, Blake Lyman, Sherrye Henry, Randy Cochran. Thanks also to Colin Murcray, who served as my main champion for this and my other guides. His patience regarding this update has been phenomenal. I would also like to send a special thank you to Kevin Yeanoplos, who took the time to read my early drafts of this guide and provide meaningful suggestions for improvement.

Mike Pellegrino

Chapter 1
About This Guide

The Growing Importance of IP

Market trends underscore companies' new focus on exploiting intangible assets such as patents, copyrights, trade secrets, trademarks, brands, and technical know-how. Patent licensing revenues have soared to $110 billion from $15 billion in just the last 10 years.[1] A 2001 survey of 272 senior executives from across North America showed that protecting proprietary research, valuing intellectual property, and extending patent protection are top concerns.[2] In addition, new accounting rules require companies to more accurately calculate and report the value of their intangible assets.

Empirical evidence suggests that IP today drives a significant portion of the market value of companies. The most compelling evidence of this is the wide disparity between the market value and book value of publicly traded companies. Companies that derive a substantial portion of their income from IP (e.g., software companies) may have price-to-book value (PBV) ratios remarkably in excess of traditional industries. The primary reason is that these companies rely on a significant amount of intellectual property to generate revenues, yet the companies' balance sheets do not reflect that intellectual property properly.

For example, according to Yahoo! Finance, as of June 2011, the application software industry PBV ratio was 11.7, indicating that the market priced the value of the average application software company at 11.7 times the value recorded on its balance

1 "The Online Agora: Licensing or Selling Intellectual Property," PricewaterhouseCoopers, accessed on June 20, 2011.

2 "Patients or patents? New Andersen Survey Reveals What Matters Most to the 21st Century Healthcare Community," Arthur Andersen press release, April 24, 2001.

sheet. Unrecognized intellectual property explains a substantial portion of the excess market value of a company above its book value. For example, compare the application software industry with a more traditional, conservative industry such as lumber and wood production (e.g., Georgia Pacific). The PBV of the lumber and wood production industry is 2.4, owing to a much lower reliance on intellectual property to drive company value.

The number of U.S. patents issued is growing at an exponential rate. Exhibit 1 demonstrates the accelerated pace of patent application filing.

Exhibit 1. U.S. Patent Growth Over Time

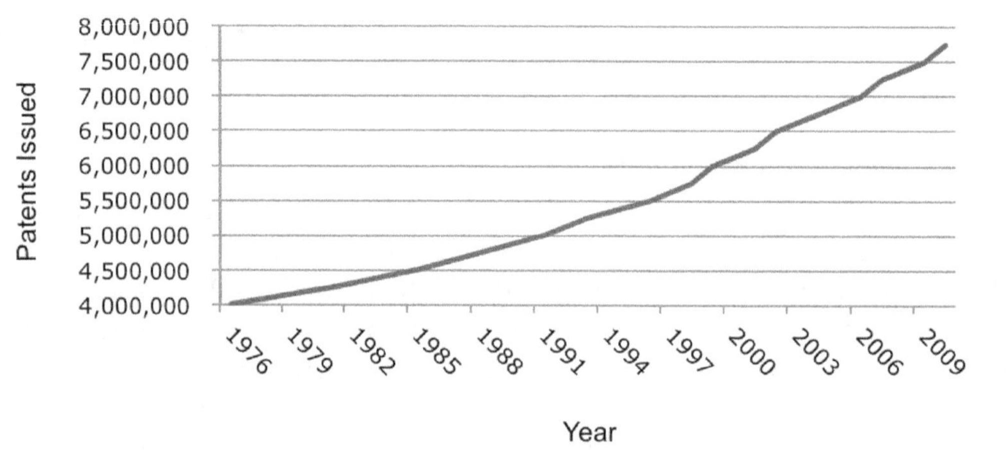

While the total growth represents a modest compound annual growth rate (CAGR) of 1.96%, the graph demonstrates that rate of growth is nonlinear and has been increasing since 1976. Between 1999 and 2010, the CAGR rate for patents issued in the United States was 2.35%. Empirical evidence suggests a strong relationship between the growth in U.S. patents and the growth in the U.S. knowledge economy. Evidence suggests that the growth in U.S. patents has a strong relationship with the increases in PBV ratios over the same period as companies invest less in bricks and mortar and more in intellectual assets.

An additional metric to demonstrate the increasing pace in intellectual property growth, besides cumulative patent filings, is the interval between successive patent filings. Exhibit 2 demonstrates the rate of change in time between each set of 250,000 patents that the United States has issued since 1976.

Exhibit 2. Average Days Between Every 250,000 Patents Issued

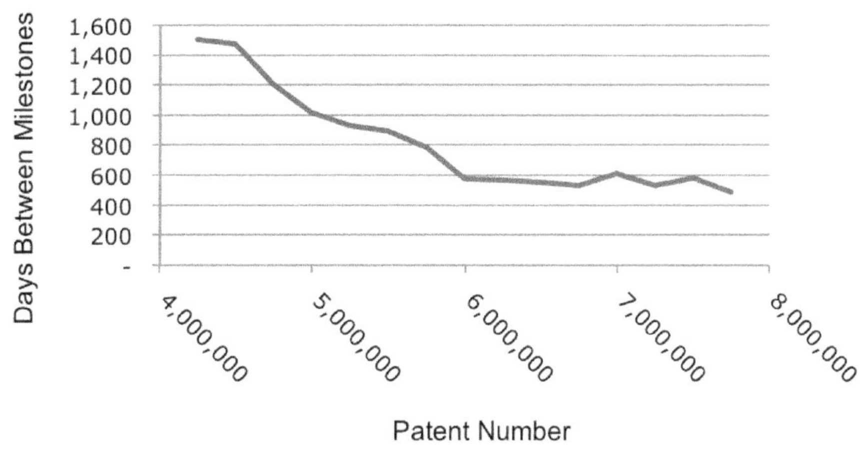

As Exhibit 2 demonstrates, the date interval between every 250,000 patents filed since 1976 shrank at a remarkable rate. In 1976, the United States issued patent number 4,000,000; it issued patent number 4,250,000 on February 10, 1981, or 1,505 days later. By 2010, the interval between every 250,000 patents issued was 490 days. The United States Patent and Trademark Office (USPTO) granted 121,238 patents in the first half of 2011—compressing the time line even further! The United States is creating an increasing number of patents, and it is issuing them at three times the rate it did in the late 1970s and early 1980s.

A primary driver for this patent growth is that companies are finding it imperative to patent inventions. Companies do this not only for direct exploitation, but also as a means of defensive posturing. For example, companies may prosecute new patents to protect against competitors patenting technologies underneath them, thus blocking them from their own markets. The impact of defensive posturing has been remarkably large for Microsoft, one of the largest software development companies in the world. Microsoft historically has not filed for many patents. However, Exhibit 3 on the following page captures Microsoft's patent binge remarkably well.

What is the key reason for Microsoft's growth in patent activity? Litigation. Between 2004 and 2009, Microsoft was party to more than 115 lawsuits regarding patent infringement matters (indicated by the solid line in the chart). Over that same period, its patent activity grew 351% on an annual basis, from 148 patents in 2004 to 668 patents in 2010 (indicated by the dashed line in the chart). Microsoft's record in court exacerbates the pain of its increased litigation frequency. The number of cases that Microsoft litigates that reach final decision in court is greater than four times

Exhibit 3. Microsoft's Recent Patent Scorecard

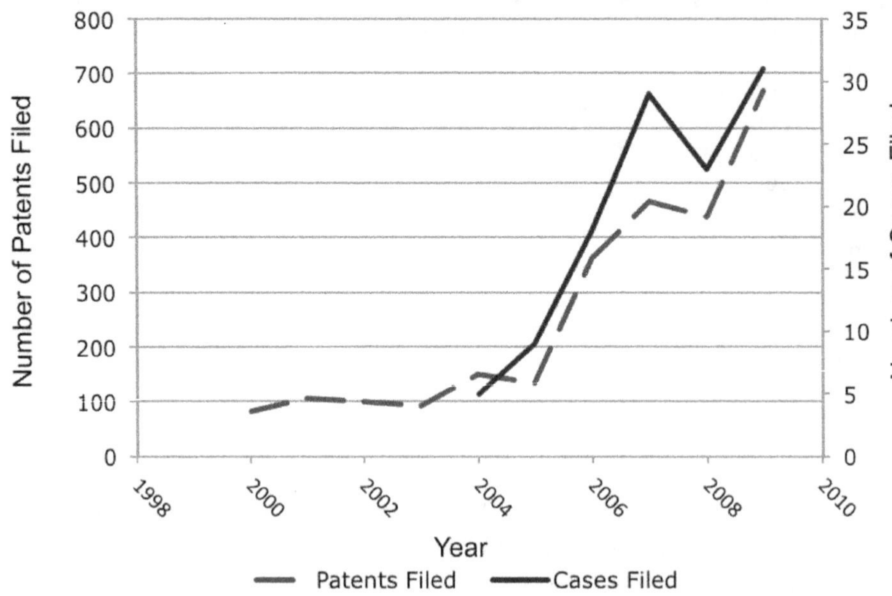

that of the general industry. Microsoft's patent application activity appears to have increased directly because of its increased patent lawsuit headaches. For example, there is a remarkably strong correlation between Microsoft's increased litigation activity and its increased patent activity, as Exhibit 4 demonstrates.

Exhibit 4. Correlation of Microsoft's Patent Infringement Lawsuits and Patent Filings

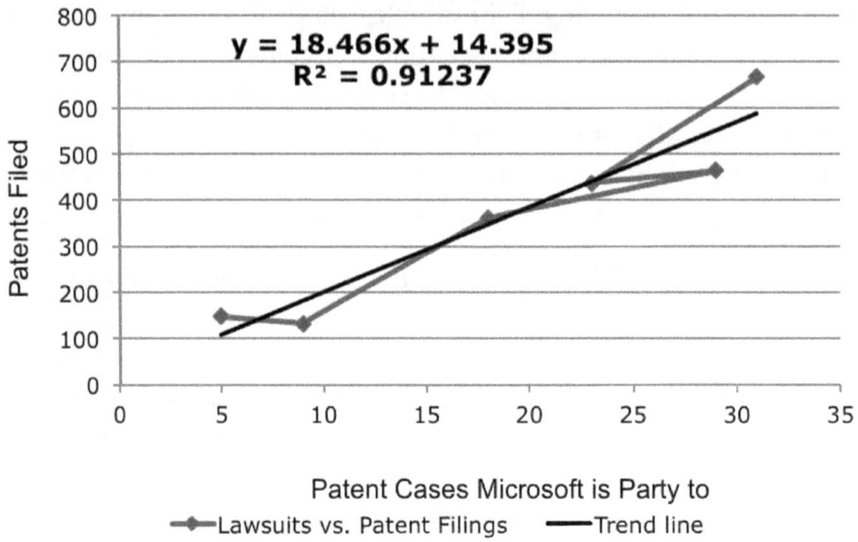

As the chart demonstrates, Microsoft's patent litigation record explains some 91.24% of the increase in Microsoft's patent activity. Microsoft appears to have adopted an aggressive patent position out of necessity and for defensive reasons.[3]

Such trends indicate the continuing strong importance of IP and strong growth opportunities for IP valuation needs.

Why Is This Guide Needed?

This guide is intended to serve a niche in the IP valuation space that I believe current and historical authors have underserved. Many authors today focus their texts on the basics of IP valuation, theoretical models, and, to a certain extent, accounting procedures (e.g., cost accounting). However, IP valuation requires a much deeper practical analysis, which, in my opinion, current texts largely do not address. Much of this practical analysis focuses on the actual analysis of the IP in question and the rights that present the IP owner with a value proposition. IP represents an owner's set of legal rights that may generate economic advantage, primarily in the form of preventing others from doing the same thing as the IP owner, provided the correct combination of talent, finances, market dynamics, IP features, cost, and many other factors exist. Yet, few published texts focus on how to perform this practical analysis or on how to apply valuation techniques to real-world problems. This guide will present an objective means to perform the due diligence of IP rights and reflect the impact of that due diligence on IP value.

This guide presents a set of due diligence procedures and considerations that practical IP valuation analysts can use to create credible, defensible IP valuations. It fills in many of the blanks left open by other IP valuation authors, particularly with respect to performing credible due diligence of IP protections. After all, what good is accounting for the value of IP if the valuation analyst cannot establish that the IP rights exist in the first place? This guide serves as a real-world walk-through of the due diligence for an IP valuation analysis from start to finish for each of the primary IP types: patents, copyrights, trademarks, and trade secrets. It is a practical guide for people working in the trenches of IP valuation, who I presume are already well versed in the basics of valuation theory.

3 There is remarkable validation in the procurement of IP as a defensive measure. In 2011, a consortium including Microsoft, RIM, Apple, Ericsson, and Sony outbid Google for a collection of over 6,000 patent and patent applications owned by the bankrupt Nortel Networks. To help bolster its own defensive posturing, Google bought more than 1,000 patents from IBM a short while later to build out its patent portfolio.

What This Guide Is Not

I do not rehash topics already covered quite thoroughly in IP valuation books by other authors. Those authors have done a fine job introducing such topics and providing meaningful examples. You will not find in-depth introductions to topics such as basic valuation theory, standards of value, discounting cash flows, and other like concepts in this guide.

Instead, the focus will be on fundamental analysis of the value drivers for IP. Fundamental analysis has tremendous bearing on the valuation approaches I use in this guide. I focus on methods that have a strong theoretical foundation provable mathematically or empirically beyond mere correlation. As such, this guide does not present dot-com valuation metrics—such as price per clicks to a website or price per eyeballs on a website—or other valuation metrics such as lifetime customer value or customer acquisition costs. There is also little material on the relative valuation metrics common in business valuation methods, such as price-to-earnings or price-to-sales multiples. IP is unique by definition. This means that such relative valuation metrics are largely meaningless. I also do not proffer empirical valuation models built on multiple regression analysis and the law of averages. Again, IP is unique, so extrapolated values attributable to empirical models based on averages and multiple regression analysis may be spurious. Additionally, this guide does not present any specific format for calculating damages for lawsuits. Damages engagements often comprise performing forensic analysis, and this analysis may take many forms, requiring due diligence that is outside the scope of this guide or a normal IP valuation engagement. Further, many damages engagements may not have to consider the impact of future events (e.g., lost profits damages calculations); yet much of the content in this guide focuses on future events.

Examples are a point of consternation in guides such as this one. They make for challenging situations. For brevity, the examples cannot be too long; however, the author must still structure them well to provide a window into how valuation works in practice, not in some fabricated, Petri dish environment. In general, this guide does not present a set of contrived examples to demonstrate concepts. Such examples suspiciously indicate values created using the cost, market, and income approaches, which all magically fall within 10% of each other. Valuation results simply do not occur like this in practice. I have never had any value indication generated by differing methods (such as the market or income approaches) come even remotely close to each other unless by pure accident or happenstance.[4] While simple examples show the theory cleanly, the examples do not match reality. More

4 In fact, I am quite suspicious of value conclusions that I have reviewed in practice that line up so neatly.

importantly, they do not bring much clarity or value to the reader as to how a real project works or how to reconcile widely disparate results. Value inputs and indications do not neatly stack up as they do in textbooks. Requisite information is often discontinuous, nonlinear, not available, or plain nonsensical, yet observable (e.g., an uninformed buyer overpaying for an asset by a wide margin just because of associated hype). Thus, this guide demonstrates real-world examples as much as possible to explain and demonstrate various IP valuation concepts.

Practitioners in the trenches performing IP valuation should find this guide useful, as it presents real-world examples of the valuation of IP and the myriad problems that arise, particularly with respect to valuation considerations. This guide is a tool to help direct the practitioner around the land mines typical in an IP valuation engagement. Since I generally use real-world data in the examples in this guide, I do not round much of the data in the examples. The world does not deliver data to IP valuation analysts in a neat, rounded form. In the interest of authenticity, I did not round them in this guide either.

The concept of legal jurisdiction has an important impact on an IP valuation engagement. The presumption in this guide is that all matters of the law, particularly for patent, copyright, and trademark issues, occur within the U.S. jurisdiction. There may generally be strong similarities between legal protections and procedures in different legal jurisdictions (e.g., Japan versus the United States); however, in this guide, all statutory references point to the United States Code.

Finally, I do not present valuation topics already covered well in other sources. Instead, I cover certain topics that current valuation texts do not already cover well. As such, readers with a firm understanding of key valuation concepts and theories will gain the maximum benefit from this guide. Readers should be familiar with the main ways that one values IP (i.e., cost, market, and income approaches), standards of value, the Uniform Standards of Professional Appraisal Practice (USPAP), remaining economic life analysis, market analysis, and other general valuation concepts. Readers may also find it useful to have a strong understanding of forecasting technologies (e.g., exponential smoothing, linear regression analysis) and Monte Carlo and statistical analysis, as this guide does not introduce such concepts.

Chapter 2
IP Valuation Overview

There are four generally accepted types of IP.[5] They include the following:

- Patents;
- Copyrights;
- Trademarks; and
- Trade secrets.

The first three IP types come with formal and explicit government protections. Trade secrets—which may encompass organizational or personal expertise or knowledge, such as formulas, processes, devices, or other proprietary information—are not subject to traditional government protection. With or without government protections, all IP forms may have economic value. Each of the various IP types provides both advantages and disadvantages.

About Patents

At the most basic level, patents are nothing more than a set of exclusive rights granted by a government to an inventor or the inventor's assignee for a fixed period in exchange for the disclosure of an invention. Patents represent the legal right to exclude others from the market and generally cover the discovery of a new and useful process, machine, manufactured article, composition of matter, or any new

5 Some practitioners consider rights of publicity as an additional intellectual property type. State law typically defines rights of publicity, and some states have stronger rights of publicity statutes than others (e.g., Indiana). While economic value models for rights of publicity can mirror those of copyrights and trademarks, damage models for rights of publicity tend to mirror that of copyrights.

and useful improvements thereof. Importantly, patents are not guarantees to make money. In some situations, patents may indeed be liabilities instead of assets (e.g., a recent spate of lawsuits related to expired patent marketing created millions of dollars in liabilities for some companies).

The Advantages of Patents

Patents provide several distinct advantages among IP types. First, patents protect a design of something functional or utilized. The government provides patent owners with monopoly protection for up to the statutory life of the patent. The monopolistic nature of patents creates an artificial market limitation or shortage in the market for technology that embodies the claims of the patent. As we know from classic economic theory, artificial limitations to the market allow the patent owner to raise prices higher than the market clearing price, providing the patent owner with abnormal profits. The patent owner can continue to increase prices to a point where the market seeks substitute technologies, if available. Other IP types do not offer such benefits for something that is functional or utilized.

Next, patents offer superior rights when willful infringement does occur. Under 35 U.S.C. §284, the patent owner may receive up to treble damages for infringement that a competent authority determines as willful. Of course, the economics of such a proposition are obvious: if the court finds a competitor has willfully infringed and that infringement created damages of $1 million to the patent owner, then the patent owner would be entitled to $3 million in damages from the competitor.

The Disadvantages of Patents

Patents have several associated disadvantages, which relate to cost, a relatively short economic life, and a disclosure requirement. The next sections cover these concepts in greater detail.

Cost

Patents are expensive to acquire, oftentimes costing tens of thousands of dollars to prosecute. Costs involve direct costs for legal services as well as soft costs (i.e., costs that do not include hard dollars, such as inventor's time) to describe the technology to the patent attorney and patent offices. These costs increase dramatically if the application includes foreign jurisdictions. Once a patent owner receives a patent, the patent owner then has to maintain the patent with the patent office. Maintenance generally includes the completion of some standardized forms and the periodic payment of a fee that may range from hundreds to several thousands of dollars, depending on the company size of the patent owner. Failure to pay maintenance fees has serious consequences, up to and including loss of patent protection (more on this later in Chapter 6 regarding patent specific due diligence).

Short Economic Life

Time has an immense impact on patent value in particular. Patents provide for only a relatively short economic life compared with other IP types. Copyrights generally provide protection for an author, extending for the author's life plus 70 years. Trademarks and trade secrets have possibly infinite economic lives. Under 35 U.S.C. §154(a)(2), the statutory life for a patent is 20 years from the earliest effective filing date of the patent application. Since the earliest effective filing date is the trigger point for starting the statutory clock, patents are unique among IP types in that the award process consumes a significant portion of the patent's economic life. This has administrative and value impacts.

Patents that have a longer economic life will have monopoly protection for a longer period. Thus, owners of patents with longer economic lives will be able to extract abnormal profits from the market for a longer period than patents with shorter economic lives. The present value of a patent with a constant income stream as it relates to its remaining economic life is shown in Exhibit 5.[6]

Exhibit 5. Patent Value Over Time

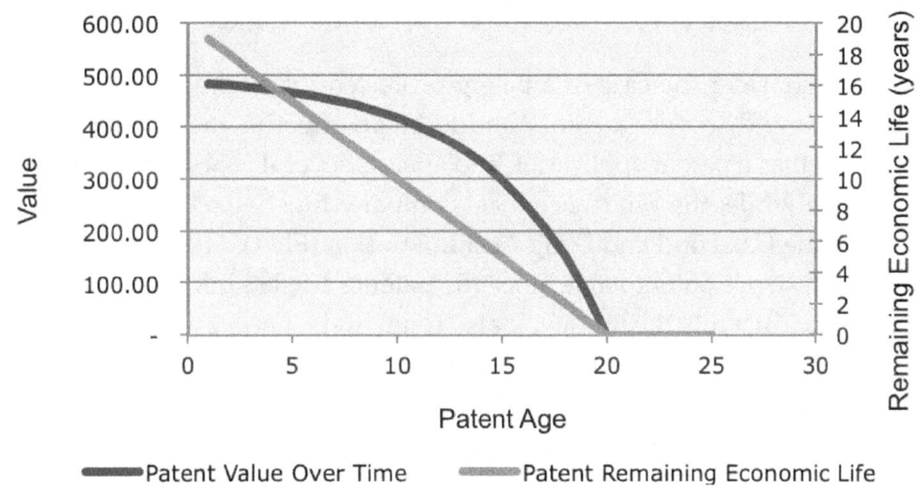

6 This of course ignores the fact that a patent owner can pursue an infringer for damages going back six years prior to the filing of a complaint, which may contribute additional value sources not considered for this example. Moreover, it may take some time for inventions claimed in a patent to gain traction in the market; thus, revenues associated with patents are not static, but instead tend to start small and grow over time. Further, the risk profile changes over time as the market accepts the inventions claimed in a patent. Thus, the actual value for the patent can fluctuate over time, reflecting both a change in the revenues attributable to the patent and the associated risk for generating those revenues.

As Exhibit 5 demonstrates, time has an important value impact for patents. The newer the patent, the more valuable it is, all else equal. The older the patent, the less valuable it is, all else equal. Note that the value drops to zero when the patent runs out of statutory protection, because there is no legal stick the patent owner can swing to prevent anyone from using the patent to build a competing product once the patent expires. Practically, the patent may have little economic life in the last one or two years in certain circumstances, indicating an even shorter economic life, as companies generally would not go through the time and expense to purchase or sell a patent that will expire in a year or two without significant mitigating circumstances. The buyer could instead simply wait, provided the waiting costs are reasonable, and then use the patented invention without any legal risk.

It takes time to proceed through the patent award process. In many cases, it may take three or four years before the patent office awards a patent to an inventor. The nature of the patent governs how long it may take the patent to proceed from initial application to award. Mechanical patents may typically take three years to process from application to award, whereas software patents may take four years or longer to process from application to award. Before the patent publishes, the patent applicant must protect the patent with trade secrets to prevent a third party from filing a competing or blocking application with an earlier priority date. During the patent prosecution period, the patent loses value because the patent owner consumes valuable life of the patent readying the product for the market.

For example, consider the case of a patent-protected drug compound. A pharmaceutical company discovers a compound to be an effective therapy for a disease. The company files a patent application and spends several years in the prosecution phase. All the while, the pharmaceutical company must also certify the product for sale with the U.S. Food and Drug Administration (FDA). The certification takes time, which destroys patent value since the patent's life begins at the file date, not the date the product hits the market. It also reduces the period with which a patent owner can recoup nonrecurring engineering costs to develop the pharmaceutical. The net effect of this reduction in the protection period is either an increase in the price of the product, or a decrease in the margin available for profit.

If it cost $100 million to develop the drug and the pharmaceutical company took 10 years to bring the product to market, then the pharmaceutical company has a total of 10 remaining years left to recoup the $100 million in development costs and make a profit as well. The company will recapture the nonrecurring engineering costs typically as an amortization expense of $10 million per year over the 10-year period.[7] Now consider if the pharmaceutical company had 15 years left to recoup the $100 million in development costs. In this scenario, the pharmaceutical company will incur an amortization expense of approximately $6.7 million, improving the profitability of the firm. While seeming small, this difference may affect the price of the product when sold in the market, as the cost structure would be lower. Price affects the demand for the product in the market. Demand for the product ultimately affects the value of the product in the market. If the price were low enough to spur additional demand, then the product may in fact be more valuable than it would be otherwise, because the increased volume would make up for lost value associated with a lower selling price. Further, the extended economic life will have a direct impact on the value of the patent as the patent owner has greater duration of monopoly protection.

Disclosure

An important distinction for patents is the contingencies that are inherent in patent law. Governments grant patents to foster investment in research and development and provide monopoly protection for a certain period, allowing the inventor to recoup the initial research costs and earn a profit on such efforts. In exchange for the monopoly protection, the government requires that the inventor disclose the exact nature of the inventions described in patents, including how the inventions work, what problems the inventions address, and how the designs differ in a novel way from prior art. Further, the disclosure requirement is specific, requiring enough detail so that anyone of ordinary skill in the art can reproduce the inventions claimed within the patents. The purpose of the disclosure requirement is to educate the public to the invention so that the public can learn from and possibly extend the current state of the art.

Of course, the downside to this disclosure requirement is that competitors have exact and specific knowledge of how inventions described within the patents work. The disclosure requirement makes it easy for those competitors to use the designs without fear of legal repercussions in jurisdictions that do not have patent protection. For example, if a company develops a new technology for an efficient engine but files a patent only in the United States, then any engine company can use that exact design in Japan without any threat of legal action from the U.S. patent owner, as U.S. law does not maintain jurisdiction in Japan. Either the company can lose the Japanese market to a competitor, or it must expend the additional, sometimes significant, funds it would take to prosecute the patent in all jurisdictions that provide

7 $100 million / 10 years = $10 million/year.

a material economic opportunity. This is not necessarily affordable for small or early-stage companies. It can also be quite expensive for a company to monitor the market to find companies that might infringe on the patented invention.

About Copyrights

At the most basic level, copyrights are like patents in that copyrights represent nothing more than a set of exclusive rights granted by a government for a creation. Unlike patents, which focus on an invention or something of function or utility, copyrights apply to works of authorship. With copyrights, the author gains the exclusive rights to creations for a fixed period. Unlike patents, copyrights do not require disclosure, though disclosure generally is desirable for copyrighted works, as visibility to copyrights may drive a higher valuation.[8] Like patents, copyrights represent the right to exclude others from the market. Under 17 U.S.C. §102, common works of authorship fall into one of the following categories:

- Literary works;
- Musical works, including any accompanying words;
- Dramatic works, including any accompanying music;
- Pantomimes and choreographic works;
- Pictorial, graphic, and sculptural works;
- Motion pictures and other audiovisual works;
- Sound recordings; and
- Architectural works.

The Advantages of Copyrights

Copyrights have several advantages over other IP types, including a significantly longer statutory life, higher statutory damages, circumvention difficulty, low cost, and registration simplicity. The next sections cover these concepts in greater detail.

Long Statutory Life

Under 17 U.S.C. §302(a), the statutory life for copyrights created on or after January 1, 1978, is the life of the author plus 70 years. This would indicate that, as of the effective date of many copyright valuation engagements, there are at least 70 years of

8 For example, a movie protected by a copyright may be of little value if an audience never sees the movie.

additional statutory life for copyrighted works created on or after January 1, 1978. Several acts of Congress have brought works created before January 1, 1978, in line with works created after January 1, 1978, thus normalizing the statutory life for all works. For joint works, under 17 U.S.C. §302(b), the statutory life consists of the life of the last surviving author plus 70 years. In many circumstances, the protected life of an author's work may extend well past 100 years.

Many copyrights will not generate economic activity for anywhere near the statutory life of the author or beyond. Further, the later years of copyrights valued using an income approach will have little to no impact on the value of said copyrights, as the effects of the discount rate will erode any present value economic benefits attributable to the copyrights. For example, the present value of $100 received 70 years in the future at a 15% discount rate is less than one cent.

Higher Statutory Damages

Under 17 U.S.C. §504(a), a copyright owner is entitled to actual damages and any additional profits enjoyed by the infringer, or statutory damages. The calculation of damages can be easier for a copyright litigation as opposed to a patent litigation. This is because the valuation analyst needs to consider only gross revenues in the damages calculation (the defendant must prove deductible expenses). The statute 17 U.S.C. §504(c) includes a provision to make damage valuation calculations easier still. Specifically, that section allows the copyright owner to recover statutory damages that can range from $750 to $150,000, depending on the facts of the situation and whether a court determined that willful infringement occurred. Other intellectual properties do not provide such explicit, absolute damages in the statute of the magnitude of those associated with copyrights.

Design Circumvention Difficulty

Copyright law provides the primary weapon a copyright owner has to enforce copyright value: unauthorized use. Copyright law does not allow for easy circumvention of the copyright. In accordance with 17 U.S.C. §106(2), the copyright owner has the exclusive rights to authorize one "to prepare derivative works based upon the copyrighted works." These rights increase the risk for a third party to face repercussions from the copyright owner for the unauthorized extension of the original works. This enforcement mechanism differs from patent law, for which patent claims provide explicit direction to the protected subject matter. In general, one cannot design around a copyrighted work's subject matter. The effect is that a copyright may have more sustainable value for an asset than other intellectual property types.

Low Cost and Registration Simplicity

Under 17 U.S.C. §101, authors gain protection and ownership for copyrightable works at the point authors fix the work in a tangible medium. Thus, the copyright owner receives protection immediately after that point without any explicit action with a government agency. However, registration becomes important with respect to copyright litigation. In accordance with 17 U.S.C. §411(a), an author may bring action against a party for infringement of the author's copyrighted works. However, §411(b) limits such power to authors who register such works with the U.S. Copyright Office. Thus, copyright owners who wish to bring action against potential infringers must first register these works with the U.S. Copyright Office and must do it in a timely fashion (more on this later).

The good news is that copyrights are relatively inexpensive to register. To register a copyright, the copyright owner has to fill out a one-page form and send in a nominal registration fee (amounting to $35 at the time of this writing for an online filing and $45 for a paper-based filing). Thus, the cost of entry for copyright protection is low. Unlike patents, the U.S. Copyright Office does not perform a prior art search with copyright registration. The U.S. Copyright Office is merely the librarian for copyrighted works.

The Disadvantages of Copyrights

The primary disadvantage for copyrights is that copyrights protect the expression of an idea, but copyrights do not protect the idea itself. Patents and trade secrets typically protect ideas. The difference may be subtle, but it is an important distinction. For example, an inventor publishes an article describing a new disk drive technology. Copyright law protects the way the author expressed the invention in the article; however, the actual invention described in the article does not receive copyright protection. To receive protection of the invention, the inventor would have to file a patent for the disk drive technology.

About Trademarks

Trademarks provide explicit protections for brands, slogans, logos, and other similar items. Generally speaking, trademarks represent the most valuable types of IP in the market. While it is not uncommon for patents to be worth hundreds of millions of dollars or even several billion dollars, the market has valued many brands at literally tens of billions of dollars. Icons such as Coca-Cola (widely thought to be the most valuable brand in the world), Marlboro, or Nike's swoosh all represent brands that command a market premium, despite seemingly nonexistent or minimal functional differences among nonbranded products.

The Advantages of Trademarks

Trademarks have some advantages that other IP types, such as patents and copyrights, lack. First, there are no statutory limitations for the life of trademarks. The maximum statutory life for patents is 20 years. The maximum statutory life for many copyrights is the natural life of the author plus 70 years. Trademarks have a statutory life as long as the trademark owner maintains registration of the trademark, keeps the trademark in continued use, and enforces the trademark owner's rights.

Second, registration of a trademark at a trademark office is relatively inexpensive. To register a trademark, the trademark owner has to fill out a form and send in a registration fee ($275 to $375 per international class, depending on a paper or electronic filing, at the time of this writing). Thus, while the cost to register the trademark is more than the cost to register a copyright, it is still relatively inexpensive compared to patent prosecution costs. Of course, it may take substantial financial resources to generate a brand that has reverence, which would compel a buyer to pay a premium for a product that is otherwise undifferentiated (more on this shortly). These additional resources represent an additional cost, whether direct (e.g., marketing fees) or indirect (e.g., opportunity costs), to build trademark value.

Third, trademarks are unique in that one can use them to brand and create demand for otherwise uninteresting or commodity products, inducing a buyer to pay a premium for something that could otherwise be purchased at less cost. The fragmented psychology of brand-induced demand is amazing to witness, yet it happens very often, whether it relates to everyday commodities or items unique in design. For example, consider common household table salt—sodium chloride by chemical name. It is a naturally occurring commodity in wide abundance around the world. No amount of product branding will remove the fact that table salt is sodium chloride. That said, Morton International Inc. (Morton) has created a brand and demand for its branded version of sodium chloride (i.e., table salt). People are willing to pay a premium to acquire Morton's branded sodium chloride. Empirically, it is easy to verify the value of the brand that Morton was able to create. At one local grocery in Indianapolis, one can buy the generic store brand of sodium chloride and spend $0.44 for a 26-ounce carton. The same size carton of Morton's sodium chloride costs $0.52, representing a premium of $0.08 or 18%. Despite the price premium, the ingredients are identical. There is nothing else of material difference in either carton with the granulated sodium chloride. Yet, people pay a premium for Morton's product on a daily basis. The brand value drives the reason people pay more for Morton's salt. Establishing the market value of the brand is relatively straightforward (more on this in Chapter 8), but the psychology behind consumers' preference for Morton's carton of sodium chloride over the generic container of sodium chloride is amazing. Consumer preferences can drive tremendous value potential for a brand owner.

The Disadvantages of Trademarks

Trademarks represent some of the largest brands in the world. However, like boxers and wrestlers, the bigger they are, the harder they fall. Trademarks can possess a remarkable amount of volatility in the market. Markets and perceptions change on a whim and such changes can impair value in dramatic ways. For example, ChiChi's Mexican restaurant experienced a Hepatitis A outbreak in its Pittsburgh locations in 2004. The outbreak scared the public enough that people stopped eating at ChiChi's restaurants across the country. ChiChi's ultimately went out of business and it took only a few months to kill the business. This type of volatility transcends businesses and products, as the following examples demonstrate:

- Wendy's restaurant claimed lost revenues of more than $2.5 million because of an alleged food tainting involving a woman planting a severed human fingertip in a cup of chili.[9]
- Taco Bell estimated an operating profit loss of $20 million surrounding a case of contaminated lettuce.[10]
- Atlanta Falcons quarterback Michael Vick lost $142 million, including $71 million in salary, $50 million in endorsement income, and $20 million in bonuses already paid, after his indictment and conviction for dog fighting activities.[11]

In addition to volatility, it takes significant financial resources to build major brands. Broad-based consumer brands may require tens or hundreds of millions of dollars to launch and maintain. Much of the brand expenditures focus on building buyer awareness, generating interest, formulating desire, and ultimately compelling buyers to purchase the branded product. Given the myriad sources for marketing today, an effective campaign, particularly for a consumer-oriented product, must cover all popular mediums including television, print, Internet, and radio. Though marketing campaigns can vary by product and purpose, typical national marketing campaigns for consumer products exceed $50 million. Building the brand can also take significant time. The epidemiology of brand awareness follows dissemination patterns consistent with a virus (hence, the term "viral marketing"). Depending on

9 http://www.sfgate.com/cgi-bin/article.cgi?f=/c/a/2005/05/18/FINGER.TMP
10 Strott, Elizabeth, "Taco Bell and KFC: Not so YUM-my?" MSN, February 23, 2007.
11 http://sports.espn.go.com/nfl/news/story?id=3148549, accessed on September 24, 2011.

the resources allocated to the brand, the brand strength can take months or years to develop.[12]

Popular trademarks are also at risk for genericide, which occurs when the public begins to associate a brand as a representation of common products of the same utility. Xerox, Escalator, Kleenex, and many others never began as common words. They began as branded products that ultimately the public associated with more general products. These brands lost value because of genericide.

About Trade Secrets

Trade secrets are explicit protections that accrue to inventors or creators of some intangible asset. 18 U.S.C. §1839(3) defines trade secrets as follows:

> (3) the term "trade secret" means all forms and types of financial, business, scientific, technical, economic, or engineering information, including patterns, plans, compilations, program devices, formulas, designs, prototypes, methods, techniques, processes, procedures, programs, or codes, whether tangible or intangible, and whether or how stored, compiled, or memorialized physically, electronically, graphically, photographically, or in writing if—
>
> > (A) the owner thereof has taken reasonable measures to keep such information secret; and
> >
> > (B) the information derives independent economic value, actual or potential, from not being generally known to, and not being readily ascertainable through proper means by, the public.

Common examples of trade secrets include customer lists, chemical formulas, manufacturing processes, business plans, inventions, and so on. A key tenet of trade secrets is that there is no public disclosure of the asset. The primary means with which one protects trade secrets is with contracts (typically non-disclosure agreements), which disallow disclosure of the trade secrets; and non-competition agreements, which disallow parties with knowledge of the trade secrets from creating competing products or services in the market using those trade secrets.

The Advantages of Trade Secrets

Trade secrets carry several distinct advantages over other intellectual properties. First, trade secrets can cover any type of design, information, or other knowledge

12 Technology companies from the dot-com era spent millions of dollars to build brand awareness (e.g., Super Bowl commercials), though many were ultimately unsuccessful in generating sustainable traction.

that may also otherwise be protectable with other intellectual property forms. In fact, it is quite common that companies protect other intellectual property types, such as patents and trademarks, with trade secrets before they receive formal protections from the government. For example, suppose an inventor has discovered a new design for reducing friction in a worm gear assembly for a car's transaxle. The inventor plans to file a patent for the new design. The inventor will protect the invention using trade secrets until the point where the patent publishes with the government. It is imperative to protect the invention before publication—the inventor risks usurpation with the USPTO by a possible competitor if the invention is not protected with trade secrets beforehand. Further, many patent jurisdictions require that inventions not be disclosed prior to the patent application process. If there were documented disclosure, then those jurisdictions would not grant the patent. Thus, even though the eventual protections may manifest as a patent, trade secret protections provide all initial protections for the patent. These initial trade secret protections have important valuation impacts, depending on whether a patent is pending or awarded. A valuation analyst needs to consider such impacts in a patent analysis.

Second, unlike copyrights, trade secrets can cover functional items or items of utility, such as a chemical formula or a method to solve a problem with a computer and software. Unlike patents, trade secrets can cover the expression or concatenation of data, such as a customer data list or a process for compiling competitive market intelligence.

Third, trade secrets can present a competitive advantage that may be difficult to reverse engineer or reproduce. Patents require full disclosure in exchange for the limited monopoly protection that they afford. However, there is no disclosure requirement for trade secrets. While surrendering the limited monopoly protection a patent may afford, the inventor also may be able to extract sustainable value from the invention for many more years than with a patent because competitors cannot reverse engineer the invention. Thus, trade secret values can weather the effects of time if parties with access to the trade secret can manage access to it. For example, few people in the world know the complete formula for Coca-Cola and it has been that way for more than 100 years, despite repeated attempts by competitors to reverse engineer the formula. To this day, that original formulation is still quite valuable to Coca-Cola.

Fourth, trade secrets are generally easy and low cost to create. Trade secrets require no formal registration or approval process with a regulatory entity, which is common for copyrights, trademarks, and patents. The trade secret inventor merely guards access to the secret data. Moreover, trade secrets require no continued maintenance fees and do not expire on some statutorily defined date—they persist as long as the trade secret owner protects them.

The Disadvantages of Trade Secrets

Trade secrets maintain several disadvantages that are unique to their intellectual property type. First, nothing prevents one from independently deriving the same or similar design for an invention protected with a trade secret. The fact that others can independently develop the same or similar design allows a competitor the possibility to design a competing product that is the same or substantially similar, patent it, and then block the original inventor from selling embodiments of the trade secret in the open market. This naturally has a value impact, as the original inventor could no longer generate cash from the original product's design. Such a situation is not possible if the original inventor had a patent on the design or priority rights for a patent application.

A second disadvantage of trade secrets is that they may be subject to key person discounts. Key person discounts are value impairments. They apply when certain individuals or groups of individuals have a material impact on the success or failure of a given asset based on their participation. In cases where such participation is no longer possible (e.g., employee attrition, project reassignment), there is a cost to replace the key persons. This cost may include hiring or training replacement staff, lost market opportunities due to the loss of the key staff, and others. Copyrights do not maintain such risk, as an intrinsic property of copyrights is that the owner affixes the expression in a tangible form—something that is not a requirement of a trade secret. Awarded patents do not generally maintain such risk either, as the law requires that an inventor disclose the complete design in sufficient detail so that one of ordinary skill in the art can reproduce the intellectual property described by the patent and monetize it.

A third disadvantage of trade secrets is that trade secrets require diligent attention to the administration and enforcement of non-competition and non-disclosure agreements, the marking of documents, limiting information access, and consistent enforcement. Administratively, tending to agreement administration can be cumbersome and expensive to enforce and sometimes inefficient (e.g., what steps does the company need to take to ensure business continuity while the key person goes on vacation?). Moreover, the nature of trade secrets may preclude disclosure to potential partners who are generally unwilling to execute non-disclosure agreements (such as large corporations and venture capital firms). In these situations, trade secrets may lose value from a loss of opportunity that may be greater than the potential value losses associated with disclosure.

Finally, trade secrets receive no formal federal protections like a patent, copyright, or trademark does. Thus, the jurisdiction for a trade secret lawsuit will generally vary by the state where a company transacts its business and any governing law clauses in trade secret owner agreements. These variations make it more difficult to determine value, particularly in valuations for damages, as statutory provisions may limit damages to certain circumstances, monetary caps, or other factors. They also may make it more difficult and expensive to enforce legally as the trade secret owner may need to contract with local counsel in jurisdictions all around the country or the world.

Chapter 3
About IP Valuation

IP valuation is not easy, and it requires a broad range of expertise. It represents the integration of a set of skills that requires the valuation analyst to have more than a cursory understanding of marketing, accounting, finance, scientific and/or applied science, the applicable intellectual property law, statistics, financial modeling, and report writing. Continual changes in each of these fields present a high barrier to an IP valuation analyst seeking to perform IP valuation credibly. To the extent possible, the IP valuation analyst must keep up with the state of the art for all of these knowledge areas concurrently. In the end, intellectual property valuation is similar to other valuation forms in that it is part science, part art. It is important that a valuation analyst maintain a mastery of both the science and the art to generate credible, repeatable results.

Applying the Science

The science in IP valuation relates to the fundamental mathematics that surrounds the quantification and distillation of the value proposition into dollars and cents. It includes things such as financial formulas and the ability to perform quantitative analysis. Proper knowledge of basic math, discounting, calculating revenues, calculating profits, and calculating cash flows are all important. Quantitative analysis also requires the valuation analyst to perform meaningful statistical analysis to support an engagement. Statistical analysis may include seemingly complex mathematical operations such as linear regression computations, linear programming, or Monte Carlo-type simulations. The science results are unequivocal and should be exactly repeatable, regardless of the valuation analyst. Further, the science is independent of the analyst's background, certifications, education level, schooling, or other factors.

For example, a $100 cash flow received one year from today is worth $80 today with a 25% discount rate. Every valuation analyst should come to the same conclusion given these inputs. It does not matter where the analyst went to school, whether it was Harvard, a community college, or even no college. It does not matter if the valuation analyst has an accounting certification, a finance certification, or even no certification. That said, a valuation analyst's improper use of the science could lead to erroneous valuation conclusions.

For example, consider a cell phone that contains some new, patented technology for handing calls off between cell phone towers such that the phone never drops a call again. It is straightforward to calculate that if one sells one million cell phones at $200 per phone, the total revenue would be $200 million.[13] However, this revenue model includes many different valuation assumptions. For example, the valuation analyst would at least have to know that the technology works, that it is durable in the market (i.e., difficult to design around), that the market is willing to buy at $200 per phone (if at all), and how aggressively the market will adopt the technology. If the market will buy only 100,000 units and it refuses to pay more than $50 per unit, then the total revenue, which drives the valuation, would be $5 million or about 2.5% of the other revenue indication. Even though the valuation analyst initially applied the science correctly to arrive at a $200 million revenue indication, the science might not detect whether the parameters used were reasonable or achievable. Further, the valuation analyst may have to anticipate changes that could render the technology obsolete. Only the art of IP valuation would illuminate such issues. Thus, the art of how to apply the science becomes very important in an IP valuation engagement.

This is not to say that a valuation analyst can produce a valuation free of scientific defects. With today's technological solutions (e.g., spreadsheets), it is relatively easy to produce a scientific and sophisticated valuation model that looks impressive, yet generates a wrong value indication because there is an error in a formula. There is a simple correlation between model complexity and the possibility for model errors: the more formulas and cells in a spreadsheet, the greater the likelihood that the valuation analyst will introduce an error into the spreadsheet. Consider Exhibit 6 as an example.

In Exhibit 6, the model is relatively simple. Yet there are six different formulas in the model (indicated by the boxed text), meaning six cells where a valuation analyst can enter a wrong formula. There are five additional places for data entry errors in the total sales for the U.S. market. In short, even if the science is unequivocal, the

13 1 million phones x $200 per phone = $200 million.

Exhibit 6. Example of Spreadsheet Errors	
	Year 1
Total units sold in the U.S. market	8,536,312
Net revenues (reachable market * $117.50 price per unit)	1,003,016,660
Less Research & Development Costs at 15% of revenues	(150,452,499)
Less General & Administrative Costs at 5% of revenues	(50,150,833)
Earnings before income taxes (EBIT)	802,413,328
Less income taxes at 45% of EBIT	(361,085,998)
After tax net income	441,327,330

valuation analyst must ensure that the science is operating correctly for the engagement. Model checks and audits by valuation analysts that are independent of the valuation model's creator will help reduce the types of valuation errors that result from incorrect application of the science.

Some simple audit checks that a valuation analyst may want to make before the delivery of any valuation models for review include the following:

- Does the value result calculate correctly (i.e., no #DIV/0!, #NAME, or #REF errors)?
- Are the formulas correct (i.e., parentheses in correct places, logic statements correct)?
- Are cross-worksheet references correct (i.e., do worksheets refer correctly to the cells on other worksheets that hold values of interest)?
- Does the balance sheet balance?
- Does the income statement include all revenues and expenses?
- Does the valuation model capitalize a negative free cash flow number (which would be nonsensical)?
- Does the valuation model account properly for income taxes?
- Does the valuation model account properly for loss carry-forwards and carry-backs?
- Does the valuation model capitalize a free cash flow amount that includes depreciation in excess of net capital reinvestment (which would mean that, eventually, accumulated depreciation would exceed total acquisition cost of assets)?

- Does the valuation model account properly for the timing and magnitude of planned expenditures (i.e., are salaries coming in at the correct months, are monthly payroll costs calculating correctly)?
- Does the valuation model calculate depreciation correctly for the various asset classes (which affects non-cash expenses added back to after-tax net income to determine free cash flow)?
- Does the valuation model use the appropriate discount rate (i.e., using an annual discount rate when looking at annual free cash flows, using a quarterly discount rate when looking at quarterly free cash flows)?

An average valuation model may have more than 10,000 cells containing formulas. That means that there may be more than 10,000 ways that a valuation analyst can introduce an error into a valuation model that results in an improper value conclusion! So how does one reasonably defend against seemingly innocent errors that nonetheless generate catastrophic results? A valuation analyst typically employs several defensive measures to reduce the risk of such errors:

- *Keep it simple:* Contemporary modeling tools can be remarkably powerful. With this power comes responsibility to use the tools properly. Sometimes, valuation analysts generate extremely complex models. For example, they may generate complex expense allocation algorithms or revenue calculations that may not effect a material change in valuation outcome. Yet, with this complexity comes the increased chance to introduce valuation model error. Formulas may be more complex to debug or understand. Further, it may be difficult to revisit a complex model six months later or more and understand quickly what the formulas are doing. Keeping the models simple reduces error potential.
- *Automated checks:* One way to protect against possible math errors is to develop automatic dashboards to verify proper model calculation. For example, if every valuation model includes a balance sheet, an appropriate check is to verify whether the balance sheet balances in each period modeled. If the valuation model has five years under consideration, then the valuation check should test each year's calculation independently. A sophisticated valuation model may include a dashboard that tests hundreds of different value conclusions to ensure internal model consistency. Exhibit 7 is an example of what an automated valuation model consistency check dashboard might look like:

Exhibit 7. Example of an Automated Valuation Model Consistency Check Dashboard

Number of Issues Diagnostic Checklist Indicates: 14

Calculation Checks

Check	Status	Check	Status
The value is calculating correctly (i.e., no #REF, etc.)	Check	Year 1 total expenses match on SoOE and PIS	Okay
Revenues are positive in at least one year	Okay	Year 2 total expenses match on SoOE and PIS	Okay
There is net income in year 10	Check	Year 3 total expenses match on SoOE and PIS	Okay
There is positive gross margin in year 10	Okay	Year 4 total expenses match on SoOE and PIS	Okay
There is positive free cash flow in year 5	Okay	Year 5 total expenses match on SoOE and PIS	Okay
Capitalized growth rate less than WACC	Check	Year 6 total expenses match on SoOE and PIS	Okay
		Year 7 total expenses match on SoOE and PIS	Okay
Lack of marketability discount value is set	Check	Year 8 total expenses match on SoOE and PIS	Okay
Lack of marketability discount mean value is set	Okay	Year 9 total expenses match on SoOE and PIS	Check
Lack of marketability discount median value is set	Check	Year 10 total expenses match on SoOE and PIS	Okay
Minority interest discount value is set	Okay		
Minority interest discount mean value is set	Okay	3-year fixed assets match on SoFA and SoCA	Okay
Minority interest discount median value is set	Okay	5-year fixed assets match on SoFA and SoCA	Okay
		7-year fixed assets match on SoFA and SoCA	Okay
PIS revenue wired for at least 1 product in for all years	Check	10-year fixed assets match on SoFA and SoCA	Okay
		15-year fixed assets match on SoFA and SoCA	Okay
		39-year fixed assets match on SoFA and SoCA	Okay
		Land fixed assets match on SoFA and SoCA	Okay
		Model has been checked and verifited by analyst	Check
		Model has been checked and verifited by reviewer	Check
		Model reviewer name is set	Okay
		Amortized SoFA costs match capitalized SoOE costs	Okay

General Configuration Checks

Check	Status	Check	Status
Fixed asset upgrade path is not empty	Check	Primary valuation analyst is not empty	Okay
Long-term debt and capital is fully allocated to 100%	Okay	Primary valuation analyst office street is not empty	Okay
Inventory on cash flow statements is not empty	Okay	Primary valuation analyst city/state/ZIP is not empty	Check
Monthly operating contingency is not empty	Check	Primary valuation analyst phone is not empty	Okay
Federal income tax rate is not empty	Okay	Primary valuation analyst fax is not empty	Okay
State income tax rate is not empty	Okay	Primary valuation analyst email is not empty	Okay
SIC code for project is not empty	Okay	Valuation model type is set	Okay
Useful life for the valuation is not empty	Check	Inflation rate is set	Check
		Interest income rate is set	Okay

- *Use style guides:* Ralph Waldo Emerson wrote, "a foolish consistency is the hobgoblin of little minds." While Emerson's point may have been that the mundane is boring, the mundane can be the savior of a valuation analyst. Consistency works. Walk into a McDonald's restaurant and the experience is, on average, consistent regardless of the restaurant's location. Work product consistency is a remarkable defensive measure against valuation calculation error. Tools like Microsoft Excel provide features to apply consistent formatting to all cells of a particular type in a valuation model. Strategic use of cell formatting (fonts, colors, etc.) may provide quick visual indication of what a cell's contents should be. For example, a valuation analyst may code all user-changeable cells with a yellow background, making it easy to determine visually which cells the valuation analyst should modify. The valuation analyst may use other cell colors to differentiate between calculated cells, total rows, total columns, etc. The goal of using such styles is to make it easy for reviewers (and the valuation analyst) to recall the intended purpose of the cell in question.
- *Peer review process:* Regardless of how good a valuation analyst may be, a valuation analyst is human. Humans make mistakes. An inadvertent

keystroke; an improper cell reference; transposed numbers all create conditions that one may reasonably miss in reviewing one's own work. The ideal solution is to have an independent party perform an objective peer review of the valuation model. This independent party does not have to be outside of the valuation analyst's firm; rather, the reviewer only needs to be independent of the original valuation model creation activity. The sometimes obvious items that a peer review process may discover can save a valuation analyst embarrassment and preserve the valuation analyst's credibility and reputation. Further, if the valuation analyst does use a valuation model style guide, the peer review process may discover violations of the style guide.

Granted, a valuation analyst can employ all of these strategies and still introduce errors into the final work product (again, it is a human process); however, such strategies have proven to reduce the impacts of any possible residual errors.

Practicing the Art

The art in IP valuation relates to the qualitative judgments a valuation analyst renders to generate a final result. It is not a "gut" feeling a valuation analyst relies upon to render a conclusion in a valuation engagement. Frankly, clients would likely find little solace knowing their value opinion depends on what the valuation analyst had for lunch that day. Further, "gut" feelings do not stand up well to cross-examination (more on this in a Chapter 4 discussion of *Daubert* considerations). Thus, the artful application of valuation principles becomes crucial to generating a credible valuation report. Several important principles include the following:

- Understanding and scoping the valuation engagement correctly;
- Selecting appropriate valuation methods for the engagement;
- Performing credible due diligence;
- Properly constructing the valuation models;
- Picking the appropriate time horizon for consideration;
- Generating a credible, professional valuation report; and
- Knowing and admitting when you are in over your head.

The next sections explore these principles in detail as well as the value impacts of artfully performing the valuation engagement.

Understanding the Valuation Engagement

While a seemingly simple thing to "get right" in a valuation engagement, coming to a mutual understanding of what exactly constitutes the valuation engagement between the client and the analyst is not necessarily as simple as it seems. The client and the valuation analyst need to understand and agree on several factors to scope the IP valuation engagement correctly. This is where generic business valuation and IP valuation engagements diverge. Business valuation engagements typically constitute consideration of the entire enterprise, including all historical and reasonably prospective value propositions. For example, a business owner wants to have a gas station appraised for estate planning purposes. It is straightforward to specify this job and come to a mutual understanding of the work effort. For IP valuation, the specification of the engagement can be more difficult.

Problem specification for IP is more difficult because IP represents a right that may comprise a unique set of restrictions. Restrictions may include a geographic restriction (a national border at the broadest level or a geographic region at a contractual level), a market restriction (perhaps through a trademark specification), or a product restriction (perhaps through a patent specification), among others. For example, U.S. patent #6,082,054 relates to a retractable-roof sports stadium that opens during good weather and closes during inclement weather. The patent for this valuation engagement inherits a natural geographic restriction (only in the United States), which occurs because the patent is a U.S. patent, which has no jurisdiction outside of the United States. Further, the patent represents a product restriction, which limits protected usage of the invention, as it applies to sports stadiums. Thus, applying a retractable roof to a commercial office building would not create enforceable value for the patent owner, as the patent's claims provide the patent owner with no coverage for commercial office buildings. This naturally limits the market analysis as well to that of stadiums. However, the valuation of a broader patent, perhaps filed under the Patent Cooperation Treaty (PCT) or a global brand, is decidedly more complex to digest.

Consider the example where one is valuing a global brand for a fictitious company, Global Electric, a conglomerate that builds a variety of products in consumer, transportation, and heavy industrial markets across 10 different countries. For the purposes of this example, assume Global Electric manufactures 100 different products for the consumer market, 20 different products for the transportation market, and 50 different products for the heavy industrial market. The engagement is to generate a value for the Global Electric brand. For brevity, assume the average brand valuation per target market, defined by product type and geography, will require 100 hours of

Exhibit 8. Total Project Hours for Global Electric					
	Consumer Products	Transport-ation Products	Heavy Industrial Products	Total Market Analyses	Total Project Hours
Country 1	100	20	50	170	17,000
Country 2	100	20	50	170	17,000
Country 3	100	20	50	170	17,000
Country 4	100	20	50	170	17,000
Country 5	100	20	50	170	17,000
Country 6	100	20	50	170	17,000
Country 7	100	20	50	170	17,000
Country 8	100	20	50	170	17,000
Country 9	100	20	50	170	17,000
Country 10	100	20	50	170	17,000
Totals	1,000	200	500	1,700	170,000

work to perform. How many hours will it take to generate a comprehensive, credible valuation for the Global Electric brand? The answer may be shocking, but it is 170,000 hours, as Exhibit 8 demonstrates

Why does the project require so many hours to complete? The answer is simple and a function of the labor hours the valuation analyst needs to value the brand with the greatest confidence and credibility. The valuation analyst must study the specific application of the Global Electric brand for each product, in each market segment, for each country where Global Electric sells its products. Perhaps the value of the Global Electric brand is very high for consumer products in Country 1. However, suppose the Global Electric brand commands no premium for transportation products in Country 10. The only way to make such a determination with any measure of confidence is to perform a thorough market analysis for each application of the brand in each market, in each target country. Global Electric may require the level of analysis just described, but Global Electric may be unwilling to pay the valuation analyst to perform that level of analysis. This can create problems for the valuation analyst's delivery of a final valuation work product that meets Global Electric's expectations.

Further, suppose Global Electric needs the valuation completed in 90 days. To meet that delivery schedule, a valuation analyst who works 200 hours per month will be able to handle six of the 1,700 total required market analyses. Thus, the project would require a team of 284 analysts to perform the work. At an average billing rate of $200 per hour, Global Electric may expect to spend $34 million to have this analysis performed, which may be well outside its budget. Establishing these facts early in the engagement is important, so Global Electric and the valuation analyst can come to some mutual understanding of the project scope, schedule, and cost.

As the example demonstrates, it becomes very important to gain quickly an exact understanding of the valuation engagement and its specific scope. One who can appropriately apply the art of IP valuation will avoid misunderstandings that lead to an erroneous value conclusion or to a value conclusion that does not match the client's understanding of the engagement, project timing, or budget.

Selecting Appropriate Valuation Methods

Selecting the appropriate valuation method for an IP engagement is not necessarily as easy as it is with other types of valuation engagements. IP generally belongs in a class of its own for several reasons. First, intellectual property is intangible and has no intrinsic value in a fixed form like other assets one may value, which negates the applicability of asset- or cost-based approaches for IP valuation. For example, an inventor may attempt to build a continuous steel casting machine and fail miserably in its creation. Yet there is still intrinsic value in the steel and other components the inventor could sell for scrap in liquidation. In many instances, there is no such recourse for intellectual property, particularly IP with no working prototype. However, a novice valuation analyst may mistakenly assume that an asset approach, such as tabulating accumulated costs, is an appropriate value indication for intellectual property.

The selection of the appropriate valuation method relies in part on the experience of the valuation analyst. Novice intellectual property valuation analysts may immediately jump to traditional business valuation methods, such as the market approach, for valuing intellectual property. These novice analysts may decide, erroneous as it may be, that intellectual property is "comparable" to other products already in the market. However, intellectual property is unique and novel by definition. Thus, in many instances, using a comparable is not an appropriate course of action for generating a credible value indication. The artful application of an IP valuation process would avoid such errors.

Alternatively, a valuation analyst may choose to use an income-based approach to value, yet fail to apply it in a manner that is appropriate to the engagement. For example, suppose an analyst is valuing a patent for a new molecule used in a therapy for attention deficit hyperactivity disorder (ADHD) for a large, publicly traded pharmaceutical company named PharmaCo. The new therapy is at a discovery stage and PharmaCo has not yet initiated its preclinical studies. PharmaCo's weighted average cost of capital (WACC) in the public markets is 15%. A novice may think it appropriate to use PharmaCo's WACC for the discount rate for future income attributable to the therapy or perhaps an average of the WACC of several companies that offer ADHD therapies. This is an erroneous valuation assumption to make because the company that owns the ADHD therapy under consideration, in this case, PharmaCo, achieves portfolio diversification through other income sources. Except for platform technologies, IP typically does not have multiple disparate income sources—IP is typically a single-source income model.[14]

A skilled artisan in IP valuation would not make the WACC determination described above, as the risk profile for the new therapy is much higher than that of a diversified pharmaceutical company such as PharmaCo. The lower discount factor for PharmaCo reflects this diversification. A skilled artisan would use a discount factor higher than the parent company's WACC, adjusted to account for the relative riskiness of the investment in the new therapy.

Chapter 10 explores in detail the impacts of risk analysis on the discount rate, and Chapter 4 provides a thorough discussion of appropriate valuation methodologies.

Performing Credible Due Diligence

The art of performing due diligence for an IP valuation engagement is crucial to generating a credible work product. Yet, a preponderance of the education and analysis common to IP valuation reports focuses on performing forensic analysis of the historical income-generating ability of the intellectual property. In doing so, the valuation analyst misses many of the key value-creating considerations for the IP. This can lead a valuation analyst to the wrong IP valuation conclusion.

Consider that the company ValveCo owns a U.S. patent for a valve train mechanism for a car. The company has been monetizing that patent for five years and it has 10 years remaining for patent protection. ValveCo licenses the rights to produce embodiments of the patent to the top six automobile original equipment manufacturers in the U.S. market. These top six OEMs comprise 85% of the cumulative market share and consist of General Motors, Toyota, Ford, Chrysler, Honda, and Nissan. The OEMs each pay ValveCo a 5% royalty on the value of the total engine system, which, according to a 2007 study by Merrill Lynch, has a nominal value of $2,350

14 To make the analysis more complex, which is what happens in practice, IP exploitation strategies may generate income from several sources for the same IP, each with a different risk attribute. In such cases, the valuation analyst should use a different, risk-adjusted discount rate for each income source or a composite discount rate based on the weighted average risk of the investment, perhaps weighted by contribution margin from each income source.

per vehicle. Thus, each OEM pays ValveCo a royalty of $117.50 per vehicle for the rights to use ValveCo's design. Industry watchdog Frost & Sullivan indicated engine sales from 2003 to 2007 in the U.S. market are shown in Exhibit 9.[15]

ValveCo is an IP holding company. It does not make products itself. Instead, it maintains its IP portfolio and expends 15% of revenues per year on research and development for new products. All other expenses represent a de minimis impact, amounting to less than 5% of total revenues. Thus, ValveCo is highly profitable (as many IP holding companies are) generating a pre-tax net margin of 80%. ValveCo is in a tax jurisdiction that has a combined effective income tax rate of 45%. Exhibit 10 is a summary of the historical financial performance of ValveCo from 2003 to 2007.

Exhibit 9. Engine Sales from 2003 to 2007

Research Source	2003	2004	2005	2006	2007
Frost & Sullivan	8,536,312	8,449,473	8,588,244	8,758,010	8,940,376

Exhibit 10. Historical Financial Performance of ValveCo

	2003	2004	2005	2006	2007
Total units sold in the U.S. market	8,536,312	8,449,473	8,588,244	8,758,010	8,940,376
Top 6 OEM market share of 85% (total reachable market)	7,255,865	7,182,052	7,300,007	7,444,309	7,599,320
Net revenues (reachable market * $117.50 price per unit)	852,564,138	843,891,110	857,750,822	874,706,249	892,920,053
Less research & development costs at 15% of revenues	(127,884,624)	(126,583,667)	(128,662,630)	(131,205,937)	(133,938,008)
Less general & administrative costs at 5% of revenues	(42,628,208)	(42,194,556)	(42,887,543)	(43,735,312)	(44,646,003)
Earnings before income taxes (EBIT)	682,051,329	675,112,893	686,200,696	699,764,999	714,336,042
Less income taxes at 45% of EBIT	(306,923,098)	(303,800,802)	(308,790,313)	(314,894,250)	(321,451,219)
After-tax net income	375,128,231	371,312,091	377,410,383	384,870,749	392,884,823

15 *Advances in Engine Technologies*, Frost & Sullivan, San Antonio, Texas, 2007.

As the financial data suggest, ValveCo has been a huge success, generating revenues of nearly $2 billion from 2003 to 2007 from the top six automobile OEMs at an average after-tax net income rate of $380,321,255. Suppose a valuation analyst looks at this income stream and determines that ValveCo may receive an average future income stream of $380,321,255 for the next 10 years. At a 25% discount rate, the present value of the after-tax cash flows for those 10 years is $1,357,938,286. If due diligence consisted merely of measuring historical performance and projecting it forward with some nominal macroeconomic and marketing analysis, then the valuation analyst would render a value indication of about $1.3 billion. There is one problem, however, and it will only become apparent with a credible due diligence process. ValveCo did not pay its periodic maintenance fees three and a half years after the patent award, as is required under 35 U.S.C. §41(b) to keep the patent in effect. Further, ValveCo missed the grace period to pay its fees after the statutory requirement of three and a half years. The result is that ValveCo inadvertently abandoned its patent, effectively releasing it to the public domain. As such, ValveCo's licensees are no longer required to pay ValveCo a royalty for the use of ValveCo's design. The bottom line: ValveCo's patent is worthless, despite a forensic, historical review, which would have otherwise indicated that the patent was worth $1.3 billion. Further, there is no residual value to the patent. GM, Toyota, and all the other OEMs can now use ValveCo's design without fear of legal recourse. Patent owners abandon patents continually, sometimes intentionally and sometimes accidentally. Patent abandonment, whether deliberate or inadvertent, also happens at large companies. For example, Fields Hybrids, LLC sued Toyota Motor Corp. and Toyota Motor Sales, U.S.A. Inc. for infringement of Fields Hybrids' hybrid engine patents. Fields Hybrids inadvertently abandoned its patents in the process and ultimately lost its infringement suit against the two Toyota corporations.[16] It is up to the valuation analyst to verify that patent rights are in force. A credible due diligence process is essential to that verification.

Such administrative oversights are not unique to patents. Consider the registered trademark for the phrase "A diamond is forever." At the time of this writing (September 2011), diamond company De Beers registered two different standard character marks with the USPTO related to this phrase. De Beers registered its marks in U.S. classes 002, 021, 023, 026, 027, 028, 036, 038, 050, 100, 101, 102, 103, 106, and 107. Most of these classes deal with jewelry and diamond processing. However, suppose that a new company called Diamond Tool manufactures forged hand tools with unlimited lifetime warranties. Diamond Tool decides to use the phrase "A

16 *Field Hybrids, L.L.C. v. Toyota Motor Corp.*, 2005 WL 189710 (D. Minn. 2005).

diamond is forever" and registers it under U.S. class 029. A valuation analyst hired by De Beers to quantify possible damages for the use of the phrase "A diamond is forever" will not have a viable damage model.[17] Diamond Tool happens to use its trademark selling forged hand tools, not jewelry and diamond-processing equipment. Thus, trademark law does not provide any relief, as sales of Diamond Tool's wares would not create confusion among buyers with respect to De Beers' products, unless De Beers' mark was famous, since the buyer knows beforehand if he or she is buying diamonds or hand tools.

Empirically, this distinction with consumers about the goods or services they are buying is visible in practice. Caterpillar Inc., a Peoria, Illinois-headquartered company, is one of the largest producers of heavy equipment, selling products across the world that range from common bulldozers to generator sets. It uses the registered trademark "CAT" with its products regularly and uses the colors black and yellow routinely to designate its products. The following is a sample of the wordmark "CAT" that Caterpillar has filed under IC 007, US 013, 019, 021, 023, 031, 034 and 035, which relates generally to earth moving, earth conditioning, and materials handling equipment:

Cat Scale Company is an Iowa-based company that operates one of the largest truck scale networks in the world. Cat Scale maintains more than 1,000 locations where over-the-road truck drivers can go to weigh their loads to ensure compliance with road weight restrictions imposed by government law. It uses the registered trademark "Cat Scale" with its products regularly and uses the colors black and yellow routinely to designate its products. The following is a sample of the wordmark "CAT SCALE" that Cat Scale registered under IC 042, US 100, which relates generally to weighing vehicles:

17 This would be true unless De Beers can prove that its trademark is famous, as defined in 15 U.S.C. §1125, which it may likely attempt to do. Interestingly, another company, Ecommerce Innovations LLC, registered the trademark "A Diamond May Be Forever But a Cubic Zirconia Is for Right Now" for use in jewelry stores and retail stores selling jewelry. There is no record of De Beers contesting this trademark.

By inspection, it is obvious that both companies are using similar words and colors, yet both can participate in unrelated markets without creating confusion because of the difference in application. This is where skillful application of IP valuation principles is crucial. A novice may mistakenly form a value conclusion for damages where such damages do not exist. This guide explores many more of the nuances in IP research that materially affect IP value during the due diligence process for each of the primary IP valuation types. A skilled artisan considers these factors, as failure to consider them may lead a valuation analyst to a wrong conclusion.

Properly Constructing the Valuation Models

Constructing an appropriate IP valuation model is as much an artistic creation as a painting by Van Gogh or a book by Mark Twain. Constructed properly, a valuation model will reflect a reasonable and probable reality of value for the value standard and premise for the engagement. An improperly constructed valuation model will be as much a work of fiction as *Moby Dick*.

IP valuation is difficult. An IP valuation analyst must consider many value drivers, sometimes consisting of hundreds or thousands of exogenous inputs. This is not to say valuation models need to be complex. To the extent possible, the valuation analyst should follow the KISS principle (Keep It Simple, Stupid!), as doing so reduces the chance of mathematical or other propagation errors. Parsimony, as long as it is appropriate for the valuation engagement, is a good thing. However, insisting on simplicity in the face of a complex problem is unacceptable. A quote widely attributed to author H. L. Mencken captures it best, "For every complex problem, there is a solution that is simple, neat, and wrong."

What are some examples of improper valuation models? Using an income-capitalized valuation approach (e.g., Gordon Growth Model) for a patent valuation that has a 15-year remaining economic life is not appropriate, as income capitalization determines value of a perpetuity, which clearly does not apply to patents. Patents have finite economic lives (in many cases, shorter than their statutory lives) and no residual value beyond the statutory life. Consider top-down revenue models, which make the gross assumption that a company will capture a certain percentage of the market. These revenue models actually capture what one may call the "China Syndrome." With the China Syndrome, an analyst projects some infinitesimally small percentage of the total market capture of a large market, like China's billion-plus population. The revenue models indicate that the inventors are fantastically wealthy. It is easy to diagnose entrepreneurs, inventors, and valuation analysts who suffer from the China Syndrome.

Contemplate an example in the commercial lawnmower industry with the fictitious company MowerCo, which manufactures midsize zero-turning-radius (ZTR) commercial-grade mowers. A quote from MowerCo's principals usually sounds something like this:

> The projections by Outdoor Power Equipment Institute (OPEI), an international trade association representing the manufacturers and suppliers of consumer and commercial outdoor power equipment, forecast positive sales for ZTR mowers up to 2009, despite a downturn in the housing market. OPEI projects a contraction in sales for all other comparable products, such as walk-behind mowers, riding garden tractors, and lawn tractors. OPEI estimates annual shipments between 2005 and 2009 of 203,271; 201,615; 180,518; 176,793; and 190,527 units, respectively, for a total of 952,724 units. Assuming that we capture just 5% of this market and we sell our commercial mowers at $9,000 per unit wholesale, we will generate revenues of $428 million over the next five years. We project a conservative pre-tax net income of 19%, and a total value of $24 million, as the revenue model in Exhibit 11 demonstrates.

On paper, the idea looks to generate a value indication for MowerCo of $24 million (with the simplifying assumption of no segregation of value components for intellectual property and other assets). However, the valuation model is fundamentally wrong for several reasons. First, it is rare that a company will achieve its target market share in the first year. Market share builds over time, typically along a sigmoid curve of the general shape in Exhibit 12.

Exhibit 11. Revenue Model					
	2005	2006	2007	2008	2009
Total units sold in the U.S. market	203,271	201,615	180,518	176,793	190,527
Market share of 5% (total reachable market) (rounded figure)	10,164	10,081	9,026	8,840	9,526
Net revenues (reachable market *$9,000 price per unit)	91,471,950	90,726,750	81,233,100	79,556,850	85,737,150
Less direct and indirect costs at 81% of revenues	(74,092,280)	(73,488,668)	(65,798,811)	(64,441,049)	(69,447,092)
Earnings before income taxes (EBIT)	17,379,671	17,238,083	15,434,289	15,115,802	16,290,059
Less income taxes at 45% of EBIT	(7,820,852)	(7,757,137)	(6,945,430)	(6,802,111)	(7,330,526)
After-tax net income	9,558,819	9,480,945	8,488,859	8,313,691	8,959,532
Discount rate	25%				
Net present value of after-tax net income	24,402,303				

Exhibit 12. Market Share Builds Over Time

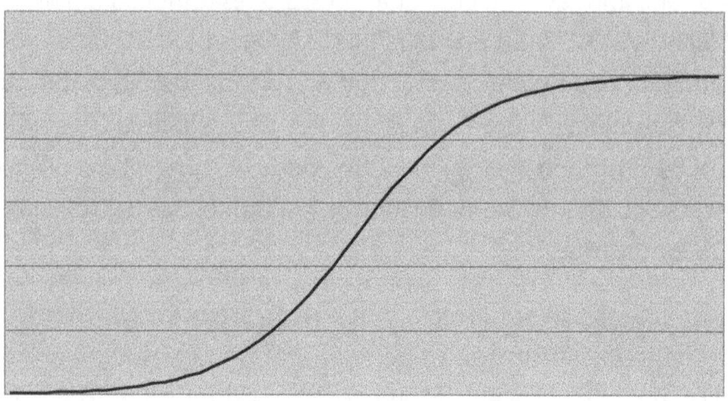

Thus, while MowerCo might actually capture a market share of 5% by the end of Year 5, a proper accounting for the time it takes to reach that market share has a dramatic effect on the value. Exhibit 13 is a more reasonable approximation of how long it may take for MowerCo to ultimately achieve its 5% ending market share.

Exhibit 14 demonstrates the impact.

Exhibit 13. How Long for MowerCo to Achieve 5% Market Share

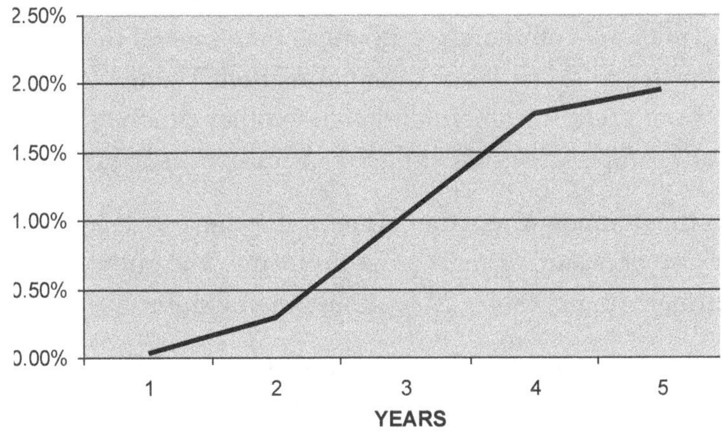

Exhibit 14. Updated Valuation Model

	2005	2006	2007	2008	2009
Total units sold in the U.S. market	203,271	201,615	180,518	176,793	190,527
Market share % (total reachable market)	2.00%	15.00%	52.00%	89.00%	98.00%
% of total market share captured in each year	0.10%	0.75%	2.60%	4.45%	4.90%
Total reachable market	203	1,512	4,693	7,867	9,336
Net revenues (reachable market * $9,000 price per unit)	1,829,439	13,609,013	42,241,212	70,805,597	84,022,407
Less direct and indirect costs at 81% of revenues	(1,481,846)	(11,023,300)	(34,215,382)	(57,352,533)	(68,058,150)
Earnings before income taxes (EBIT)	347,593	2,585,712	8,025,830	13,453,063	15,964,257
Less income taxes at 45% of EBIT	(156,417)	(1,163,571)	(3,611,624)	(6,053,879)	(7,183,916)
After-tax net income	191,176	1,422,142	4,414,207	7,399,185	8,780,342
Discount rate	25%				
Net present value of after-tax net income	9,231,034				

As Exhibit 14 demonstrates, merely accounting properly for the time it takes to get to market share impaired value in this example by almost $15 million. But wait, there's more. At $9,000 wholesale, MowerCo is one of the most expensive providers of commercial, midsize mowers on the market. At that pricing structure, even the best-run companies are commanding no more than several thousand mowers per year, which equates to about 1% of the total market. The market sees little incremental value from premium pricing relative to other products. At 1% of the total market, the value drops off significantly to $1.8 million, as Exhibit 15 demonstrates.

Next, consider the situation where the company may have to delay its product launch by a year because of design or marketing problems. The one-year delay generates a value impairment of more than 20%, as shown in Exhibit 16.

One can even consider the situation that MowerCo is projecting a net income that is more than four times that of the market in general. Perhaps it is possible because MowerCo has some IP that allows it to operate more efficiently (not likely, since most of the value in a mower is in the engine and hydrostatic motors and pumps,

Exhibit 15. Valuation Model at 1% of Total Market

	2005	2006	2007	2008	2009
Total units sold in the U.S. market	203,271	201,615	180,518	176,793	190,527
Market share % (total reachable market)	2.00%	15.00%	52.00%	89.00%	98.00%
% of total market share captured in each year	0.02%	0.15%	0.52%	0.89%	0.98%
Total reachable market	41	302	939	1,573	1,867
Net revenues (reachable market * price per unit)	365,888	2,721,803	8,448,242	14,161,119	16,804,481
Less direct and indirect costs at 81% of revenues	(296,369)	(2,204,660)	(6,843,076)	(11,470,507)	(13,611,630)
Earnings before income taxes (EBIT)	69,519	517,142	1,605,166	2,690,613	3,192,851
Less income taxes at 45% of EBIT	(31,283)	(232,714)	(722,325)	(1,210,776)	(1,436,783)
After-tax net income	38,235	284,428	882,841	1,479,837	1,756,068
Discount rate	25%				
Net present value of after-tax net income	1,846,207				

Exhibit 16. Value Impairment After 1-Year Delay					
	2005	2006	2007	2008	2009
Total units sold in the U.S. market	-	203,271	201,615	180,518	176,793
Market share % (total reachable market)	0.00%	2.00%	15.00%	52.00%	89.00%
% of total market share captured in each year	0.00%	0.02%	0.15%	0.52%	0.89%
Total reachable market	-	41	302	939	1,573
Net revenues (reachable market * price per unit)	-	365,888	2,721,803	8,448,242	14,161,119
Less direct and indirect costs at 81% of revenues	-	(296,369)	(2,204,660)	(6,843,076)	(11,470,507)
Earnings before income taxes (EBIT)	-	69,519	517,142	1,605,166	2,690,613
Less income taxes at 45% of EBIT	-	(31,283)	(232,714)	(722,325)	(1,210,776)
After-tax net income	-	38,235	284,428	882,841	1,479,837
Discount rate	25%				
Net present value of after-tax net income	1,476,965				

and in steel, which provides little opportunity for cost reductions, but let us assume this is the case).

What is the value impact if MowerCo understates its expenses by 15% of revenues and overstates its profit expectation by 15% of revenues? The only way to establish the value impact is to model it. As the following valuation model in Exhibit 17 demonstrates, the value impact was about $1.1 million, indicating that MowerCo is now worth $388,000, as opposed to $24 million as the initial valuation model indicated.

Finally, consider that MowerCo's management is not sure it is right on any of these value drivers. After all, each value driver represents MowerCo management's best guess of how MowerCo will perform, and these guesses carry the baggage of management or market biases. Accounting for the uncertainty in key valuation assumptions, such as ending market share, the wholesale price, operating margin, and time has a huge value impact.

Exhibit 17. Value Impact Model					
	2005	2006	2007	2008	2009
Total units sold in the U.S. market	-	203,271	201,615	180,518	176,793
Market share % (total reachable market)	0.00%	2.00%	15.00%	52.00%	89.00%
% of total market share captured in each year	0.00%	0.02%	0.15%	0.52%	0.89%
Total reachable market	-	41	302	939	1,573
Net revenues (reachable market * price per unit)	-	365,888	2,721,803	8,448,242	14,161,119
Less direct and indirect costs	-	(347,593)	(2,585,712)	(8,025,830)	(13,453,063)
Earnings before income taxes (EBIT)	-	18,294	136,090	422,412	708,056
Less income taxes at 45% of EBIT	-	(8,232)	(61,241)	(190,085)	(318,625)
After-tax net income	-	10,062	74,850	232,327	389,431
Discount rate	25%				
Net present value of after-tax net income	388,675				

An IP valuation analyst typically captures the complex model interactions in the face of uncertain estimating assumptions in the valuation model using simulation methods. Doing so does not constrain the valuation model to any single value prediction of key values such as ending market share, wholesale prices, or time variance. The valuation analyst would program the valuation model to recalculate itself repeatedly to create a distribution of outcomes to then analyze and interpret. With a sample size that large, the value indications that the valuation model generates can turn out statistically significant results. In complex situations that involve uncertainty, this simulation methodology allows the valuation model to generate meaningful estimates that would otherwise be impossible to model using discrete methods such as best-, expected-, and worst-case modeling. The histogram in Exhibit 18 captures the results of performing such a simulation analysis on the MowerCo valuation model.

At a 90% confidence interval, the valuation model indicates a value between $101,000 and $4.3 million. Yet the central tendency in the data is around $1.2 million (thus nullifying the simple solution common among business valuation analysts of using the average of minimum and maximum value indications to arrive at a value conclusion). A stepwise linear regression analysis of the four factors modeled is equally illuminating, as the tornado chart (so named for its general shape) in Exhibit 19 demonstrates.

As the chart suggests, managing expenses should be the number one priority for MowerCo, as expenses have the largest value impact. Expenses have an inverse relationship with value, as one would expect. A lower expense ratio yields a higher after-tax net income and ultimately results in a higher value. The chart also suggests that maintaining market share is the second most important factor for MowerCo to

Exhibit 18. Distribution for Net Present Value/B92

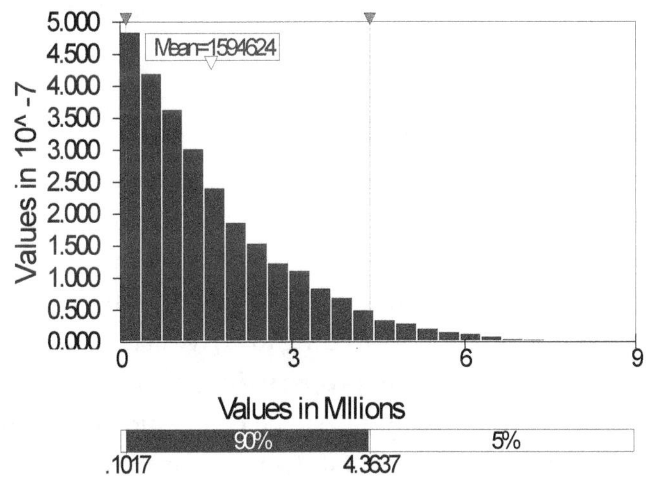

Exhibit 19. Regression Sensitivity for Net Present Value/B92

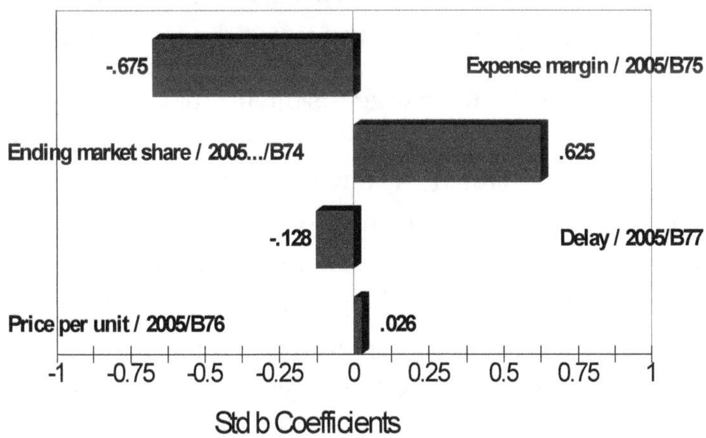

consider. It has a direct relationship with value, as one would expect. The greater the market share, the greater the net income that is available, resulting in a higher value. It is interesting to note that price is the least important in the sample. Thus, MowerCo could likely lower its prices to generate a higher demand and market share and drive a higher value than that it would obtain by sticking with its premium-pricing model and limited market share.

While this example somewhat simplifies what a true analysis entails, it is emblematic of the types of considerations a valuation analyst should model to reflect a truer picture of the IP's value prospects. In the end, it is important to get the valuation model right. If the valuation model is wrong, then the value conclusion will be wrong. Despite the added complexity, the artful and careful design of the valuation model should generate more credible and defensible results, particularly for contested situations.

Picking the Appropriate Time Horizon for Consideration

IP valuation differs from many engagements, such as real estate or business valuations, in that the selection of the appropriate time horizon has a material value impact. Oftentimes, business valuation analysts calculate a perpetual value for the business as a going concern. Commercial real estate appraisers do the same thing when they capitalize earnings from a building to arrive at a value determination. Yet it is erroneous to do so for intellectual property in general. Patents and copyrights have defined statutory lives. In many cases, the economic life of the IP will be less than its statutory life. For example, the statutory life for the copyright on this guide is the life of the author plus 70 years. Yet this guide will likely be out of print long before its statutory life expires. Trademarks and trade secrets do not necessarily have defined statutory lives, meaning they could persist perpetually. However, practically, this may be rare as market preferences and tastes change over time.

Much in current valuation literature suggests intellectual property may retain some type of residual value. For example, use of a market approach or a market multiple may assign a perpetual life to the IP. A valuation analyst that uses a yield capitalization method for an income approach valuation makes the same presumption. This is confusing in general to a novice, because the IP's time horizon depends on the definition of life the valuation analyst considers (e.g., statutory, technological, etc.). Take for example a patent that has a remaining economic life of five years. As the current theoretical residual value models suggest, the residual value would account for value that a patent owner would have after the statutory period, which is Year 6 and beyond. Unfortunately, residual valuation analysis is pointless for IP types such as patents and copyrights, which have defined statutory lives. There are fundamental flaws in the theoretical basis for residual valuation models for several reasons.

First, recall that a patent or copyright is nothing more than a legal right to prevent others from exploiting the same property in the market. Thus, a patent provides the patent owner with the legal right to sue someone who is using a product in the market without authorization. The teeth in the laws provide statutory damages and injunctive relief. However, once beyond the statutory life of the intellectual property, there is no further value proposition derived from the legal protection. Thus, there is no sustainable value proposition the moment a patent or copyright expires. This is why companies with sustainable intellectual properties fight hard to maintain and extend statutory protections for their products. For example, the Walt Disney Co. lobbied Congress on behalf of the Copyright Term Extension Act of 1998 to extend the statutory life for copyrights to preserve Mickey Mouse and other Disney creations because they were due to come off copyright protection. Without the protection, the patent or copyright owner has no legal rights to sue or seek injunctive relief from a competitor. Thus, the patents and copyrights, which are nothing more than legal enforcement rights, become worthless when the statutory life ends. Any attempted dispute of the claim that the economic life ends when the statutory life ends is trivial to dismiss in practice. One can merely attempt to enforce an expired patent or copyright in court. The likely outcome is that the action would not survive summary judgment.

Second, residual value analysis confuses the things that drive value for a product, which change over time. Consider a new drug that the pharmaceutical company PharmaCo has developed to address hypertension, which we will call NewDrug. Initially, the value source for the drug is patent protection, since the patent provides PharmaCo with the right to sue any competitor that builds a competing product based on information from PharmaCo's FDA filings and published clinical trials. Recall that patent value declines each day on a present value basis until the patent expires. Yet, NewDrug maintains its value. Why? Brands and other tangible and intangible factors provide the continued value proposition for NewDrug once patent protection ends. Exhibit 20 depicts the theoretical basis for NewDrug's value sources over the duration of the patent (assuming a constant value over the life of the patent).

Empirically, this theoretical model is easy to prove in the market. Consider Prozac, a former blockbuster drug for Eli Lilly & Co. (Lilly) used to treat depression. Lilly had patent protection for Prozac under two different patents and sold Prozac on

Exhibit 20. Patent Value Sources Over Time

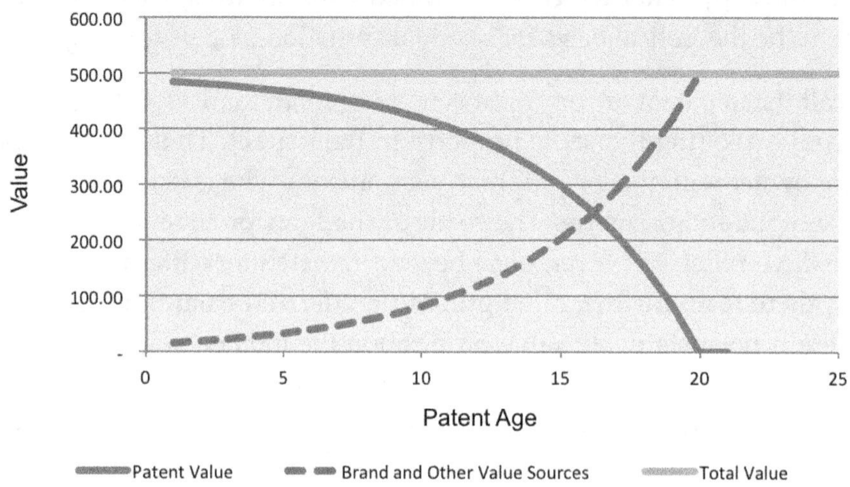

the market for years. Its patent protection was in two forms: one patent covered the compound that Lilly created (U.S. patent #4,314,081), which expired in 2001. The second patent (U.S. patent #4,626,549) covered the use of the compound as a mechanism of action (i.e., the method for how the drug worked), which was set to expire in December 2003. In 2001, Lilly lost its protection for the '549 Prozac patent two years prematurely. The impact for Prozac sales was immediate and unequivocal, with sales dropping off more than 80% within a year as consumers flocked to generic substitutes that had the same active ingredients.[18] However, Lilly did still maintain some sales level for Prozac, though those sales did not relate to patent protection, since Lilly lost that. Lilly unwillingly had a new, different business model for Prozac—namely selling a branded product against generic competition. Its business model is much like that of selling branded aspirin against the generic version in a CVS drugstore (more on this subject in Chapter 8). The source for Lilly's continued sales related to the Prozac brand and other value sources that Lilly possesses (e.g., weekly reformulation, sales and distribution networks, low required rate of investment return, etc.). Exhibit 21 outlines the value impact for Prozac before and after Lilly's patent protection loss.

A valuation analyst valuing the Prozac product would naturally study the after-tax free cash flows before and after the loss in patent protection. The difference between the two clearly indicates the patent's value to Lilly. For brevity, the valuation model in this example is necessarily simpler than what a real-world USPAP-compliant

18 Gardiner Harris, "Market Place: Despite Missteps, Lilly Remains a Hard Stock to Bet Against," *The New York Times*, February 25, 2004.

Exhibit 21. Total Combined Prozac Revenues

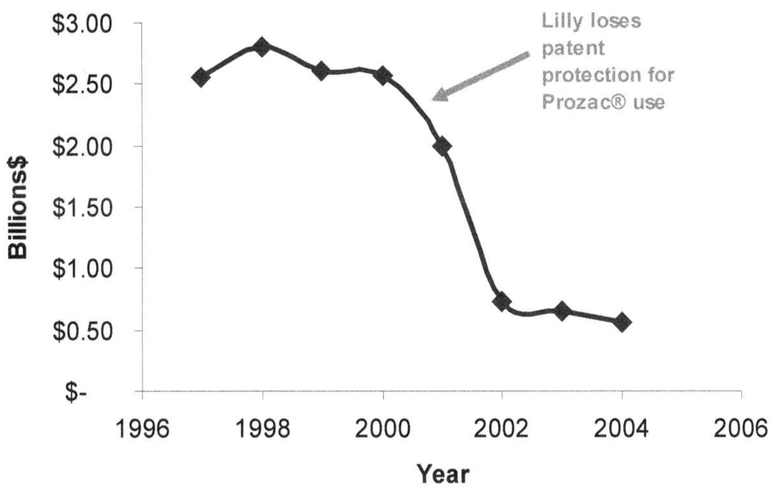

appraisal would require. However, this simplification does not affect the credibility of the example. The simplifying assumptions are as follows:

- A discount rate of 15%;
- A variable revenue stream calculated using a linear regression forecasting algorithm based on 1997-2000 Prozac revenues for the duration of the remaining economic life for the Lilly patent, which generated revenues of $2.59 billion, $2.57 billion, and $2.56 billion for years 2001, 2002, and 2003, respectively;
- A 64.8% expense ratio consistent with that reported in Lilly's annual report for the last full year before the loss of patent protection for Prozac;
- A 20.77% income tax ratio consistent with that reported in Lilly's annual report for the last full year before the loss of patent protection for Prozac; and
- A consideration of after-tax net income as opposed to free cash flow to avoid having to determine allocated interest, depreciation, amortization, and changes in working capital and investment.

Exhibit 22 is the hypothetical valuation model for Prozac before Lilly lost patent protection.

Exhibit 23 is the hypothetical valuation model for Prozac after Lilly lost patent protection.

Exhibit 22. Hypothetical Valuation Model for Prozac Before Lilly Lost Patent Protection			
	2001	2002	2003
Prozac revenues	$2,595,000,000	$2,578,000,000	$ 2,561,000,000
Less direct and indirect costs	($1,681,560,000)	($1,670,544,000)	($1,659,528,000)
Earnings before income taxes (EBIT)	$913,440,000	$907,456,000	$901,472,000
Less income taxes at 20.77% of EBIT	($189,721,488)	($188,478,611)	($187,235,734)
After-tax net income	$723,718,512	$718,977,389	$714,236,266
Net present value of after-tax net income	$1,642,592,583		

Exhibit 23. Hypothetical Valuation Model for Prozac After Lilly Lost Patent Protection			
	2001	2002	2003
Prozac revenues	$1,990,000,000	$730,000,000	$650,000,000
Less direct and indirect costs	($1,289,520,000)	($473,040,000)	($421,200,000)
Earnings before income taxes (EBIT)	$700,480,000	$256,960,000	$228,800,000
Less income taxes at 20.77% of EBIT	($145,489,696)	($53,370,592)	($47,521,760)
After-tax net income	$554,990,304	$203,589,408	$181,278,240
Net present value of after-tax net income	$755,736,491		

Exhibit 24. Differences Between the Two Valuation Models	
	Value Indication
Prozac value with patent protection	$1,642,592,583
Prozac value without patent protection	$755,736,491
Prozac patent value	$886,856,092

Exhibit 24 captures the summary differences between the two valuation models.

The difference between the value indications for Prozac before and after patent protection indicates the value of the patent as well as the value of the brand and other intangibles.[19] The total value of patent-protected Prozac in this model was $1.642 billion. The patent value was 53.99% of the total, or $886 million, with the Prozac brand and other factors explaining the balance of the difference. If one were interested in the value of the brand, he or she could then compare the market premium for Prozac to the generic comparables (see examples of how to do this in Chapter 8).

19 The analysis is slightly more complicated, as Lilly had more than seven months of sales in 2001 and launched Prozac weekly. Both items tend to inflate the value without patent protection (thus understating value slightly). However, for the purposes of this example, such a transgression is acceptable.

Exhibit 25. Total Combined U.S. Flonase® Revenues

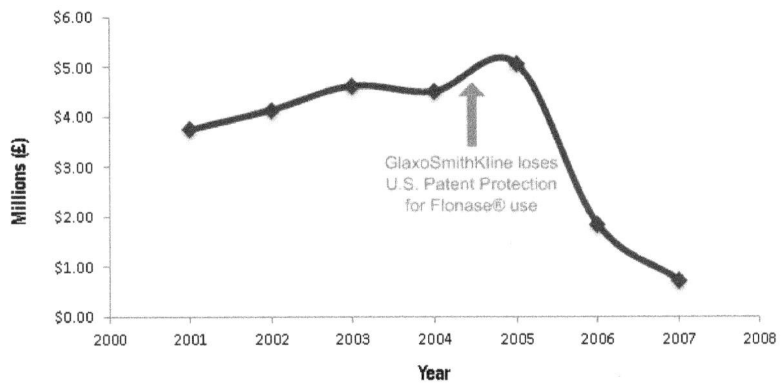

As an aside, it is interesting to note that Lilly lost nearly $35 billion in market value in one day when its stock crashed on the day of the adverse Prozac patent announcement, or about 40 times the simplified total intrinsic value of the patent to Lilly at the time. The market overreacted to the adverse ruling with the precipitous drop in Lilly's market value, overselling the stock by a wide margin, in part because it did not understand the true economic value impact of the ruling for Lilly.

A skilled IP valuation artisan considers the appropriate economic life for the IP and the associated rights unique to that IP and nothing more. As seen in our analysis, Prozac does retain value on a forward basis; however, none of this continued value relates to Lilly's patent since there is no residual value associated with expired patents. Any continued value for Prozac relates to the strength of its brand and other factors that Lilly brings to bear selling Prozac in the market. The trend is similar for other products that have lost patent protection. For example, GlaxoSmithKline experienced a similar value drop when it lost patent protection for its Flonase product, as Exhibit 25 demonstrates.

Generating Credible, Professional Valuation Reports

The skilled master approaches the professional valuation report as Michelangelo approached the canvas, *not* as one approaches a wall to slap on a coat of generic latex paint. The professional valuation report is a work of art that needs deliberate painting with care and professionalism. The IP valuation analyst should articulate key parts of the valuation process in a form so obvious that one skilled in the art could reasonably reproduce the same results given the same inputs. This can only occur when the valuation analyst expresses all aspects of the valuation development process fully.

Valuation analysts must be sensitive to the intended use and the intended users of the report. In many cases, the report is an integral part of a formal set of proceedings, such as a lawsuit or a tax proceeding. Thus, there will be critical review of the report from the moment the IP valuation analyst delivers it. Weak reports, typical of the novice valuation analyst, do not have the credibility or integrity to stand up to such critical review. As such, the valuation analyst must transparently state and quantify all assumptions and describe all methods, tools, and analytical processes in the report. Detailed description of data collection methods must be included. The report must share entire series of data collection methods, data analysis methods, and inferences made without opacity so that other valuation analysts may be able to repeat the study for reliability purposes. Without such transparency, the valuation report cannot stand alone, and reviewers may question any conclusions.

Authoring professional valuation reports is not for the faint of heart. It takes a strong command of writing skills and a creative mind to digest the very complex technical and financial details of IP valuation engagements into comprehensible, concise, and defensible prose. While it can be tempting to take the easy or short route and produce a work product representing the absolute minimum (what one may produce under the summary format described by USPAP), such a work product lacks the depth and breadth to convey a strong and confidant message that the valuation analyst has competence to perform the analysis. This means that most IP valuation reports should not conform to the summary format, but should instead be self-contained, explaining fully all relevant and material aspects of the engagement. With considerable sums of money oftentimes at stake, the report must stand on its own and its valuation processes must be repeatable.

Are You in Over Your Head?

IP valuation, especially patent valuation, is hard. In most cases, to perform an IP valuation engagement competently, a valuation analyst must demonstrate aptitude in science or engineering, as well as in finance, accounting, marketing, operations, and intellectual property law. Despite such heady competence requirements, some who practice in the profession unfortunately do not have the technical competence to perform an IP valuation engagement. Worse, they sometimes are not aware of what is required in performing the engagement and wind up committing to a project for which they cannot meet competence provisions inherent in valuation standards. Part of this unfortunate state of affairs relates to a body of knowledge that has, to date, largely ignored major components of IP valuation analysis, such as legal, scientific, engineering, and marketing analyses. Another part of it relates to a basic lack of understanding of key technical concepts. As a result, using current analytical methods, such as the comparable profits method specified in 26 U.S.C. §482, a valuation analyst concludes that a patent accounts for some portion of a company's market value, when it in fact may not for several reasons.[20]

For example, consider a company that owns two related software patents. The first patent (Patent A) describes a method for speaking by a computer to a remote user by way of an Internet connection. The second patent (Patent B) describes a software application for speaking using a computer to a remote user by way of an Internet connection. To the untrained, nontechnical valuation analyst, the patents appear to be "comparable" under conditions described in 26 U.S.C. §482 and an analysis based on comparables is acceptable. However, to the trained valuation analyst, the patents are starkly different.

It is important to note that Patent A excludes unauthorized use of the technology described in Patent A by end users. Patent B excludes unauthorized use of the technology described in Patent A by companies that will sell products or services in the market. This is a subtle, yet important distinction. For example, Patent B would apply to a software company that authors and markets a product that allows one to speak to a remote user by way of an Internet connection (e.g., Skype). Patent A would apply to customers who purchase software sold by vendors that implement claims described by the second patent.

As a practical matter, Patent A would be much more difficult and expensive for a company to enforce. Identifying possible infringers for products that mimic the functionality described by Patent A could number literally millions of people. Further, it would be extraordinarily difficult and expensive to do unless the company had access to or knowledge of the operations of many companies and households. Further, possible infringers may be casual users or those who have no assets to make an infringement pursuit worthwhile. This type of challenge mirrors that of the recording industry in enforcing copyright protections for illegally downloaded music. It would be substantially easier for the company to defend Patent B, as fewer companies author such software and detection of infringing companies and their products is easier.

To demonstrate further the subtlety in the analysis process that a valuation analyst may have to consider, suppose that Patent C describes a method for speaking using a computer to a telephone exchange of a phone company user by way of an Internet connection. Patent C is identical to Patent A except for the audience at the other end

20 There are a variety of theoretical errors with methods that 26 U.S.C. §482 prescribes for IP valuation; however, a discussion of these theoretical errors is beyond the scope of this guide.

of the connection. Yet Patent C may be quite valuable. First, Patent C represents a much smaller applicable market, as a relatively small number of owners of telephone exchanges exist. Thus, the prospects of enforcing Patent C are much brighter than they are for Patent A. It is easier to identify possible infringers and the patent owner will have fewer infringers to sue. Second, the incremental cost savings for a telephone company multiplexing thousands of conversations over a single connection could be huge, establishing a large economic income base to use as a royalty base. Such qualitative analysis is generally outside the expertise of the traditional valuation analyst who lacks a formal technical education.

IP valuation difficulties do not end there. Valuation analysts often consider statistics and parameters in IP valuations, including simulations where a model containing dozens of independent variables generates thousands of data points. These cases are likely to prompt statistical or econometric considerations, such as heteroskedasticity, skewness, multicollinearity, or nonrandom samples, which can threaten the validity of the results. Using large amounts of data in formulating valuation conclusions requires a level of statistical and mathematical seasoning that transcends the capabilities of many traditional valuation analysts who have formal education only in accounting.

In short, the details matter in IP valuation and existing methods. Those prescribed in the current body of knowledge can lead a valuation analyst to erroneous results. Without offense to those in the esteemed CPA profession, who at times face engineering-related IP valuation engagements, IP valuation has less to do with accounting and more to do with science, engineering, marketing, and logic. To avoid unforeseen liability from errors and omissions, CPAs without demonstrated technical competence should seek help with technology-heavy IP valuations.

The Science-Art Continuum

When it comes to IP valuation, the question is "which is more important, the science or the art?" One may argue that both are equally important. If the science is wrong, then the ending value indication is not going to be correct. However, applying the science in an artful manner is not easy. As the various examples in this chapter demonstrate, seemingly innocuous items or oversights can have a material value impact. So the art of rendering qualitative judgments to arrive at an appropriate valuation demands—as with any art— imagination and skill.

Chapter 4
Using Valuation Approaches

Valuation analysts use three well-known valuation approaches today to calculate a value. These include the cost approach (sometimes called the asset approach), the market approach (sometimes called the sales comparison approach), and the income approach. Each has an appropriate use, depending on the context of the IP valuation engagement at hand. The challenge for a valuation analyst is to know when to use the various valuation approaches, as few current references explain why a valuation approach is reasonable for a particular assignment. For example, why is the cost approach a generally terrible indication of value for intellectual property, and under which circumstances is it the only reasonable approach to use? Alternatively, why is the income approach generally the preferred way to value a patent? This chapter will help illuminate such situations.

The Cost Approach

A valuation analyst who values intellectual property using the cost approach looks at what it would cost to produce the IP, or what it would cost to reproduce the IP as of a given effective date. The cost would include things such as labor, materials, applied overhead, and capital charges. Depending on the effective date of the valuation, the valuation analyst may trend costs from a historical reference point to the effective date. For example, if the IP owner has cost data from five years ago and wants a value using the cost approach in today's dollars, the valuation analyst may grow the cost at the rate of inflation over those five years to arrive at the cost in today's dollars. Once the valuation analyst accumulates all factors of the cost, he or she adjusts the final tally for obsolescence to arrive at a final value opinion.

There are several methods to establish value using the cost approach. The first is the reproduction cost new method. Under this method, the valuation analyst looks to re-create the concept using the same or similar development methods and materials as the original effort. The reproduction cost new method does not account for changes in technology, higher utility from other materials, and other factors. The second method is the replacement cost new method of the cost approach. Using this method, the valuation analyst considers what it would take to re-create the concept, but takes into account the impact of new technology and development on the concept re-creation effort.

Consider an example to determine the reproduction cost and replacement cost of a software application. Suppose that a software author created a program in the C programming language in 1993 to sort a list of addresses and broadcast those addresses over the Internet. It cost $100,245 at the time ($55 per labor hour) to develop the software. The assignment is to find the value in 2008 dollars for the software, assuming that it is not obsolete. Using the reproduction cost new method, one assumes that the developers in 2008 would use the same software development language to develop the application. Using an inflation calculator or current market rates for software developers, the valuation analyst determines the cost per labor hour in 2008 is $81.41 and the total reproduction cost is $148,381.

What is the answer using the replacement cost new method? The simple answer is that "it depends," because it can quickly turn into a deep analytical exercise. Keeping it simple for the moment, assume the valuation analyst determines that it is more efficient to develop the same software in Microsoft's C# programming language. Using the same labor cost per labor hour of $81.41, the valuation analyst determines the value to be $62,883, indicating that using new tools of similar utility would reduce the value by $85,498, or about 57%. However, calculating the replacement cost in 2008 dollars has many permutations and considerations. Here are just some of the factors the valuation analyst must consider. Will the replacement cost effort consider:

- Offshore labor to reduce the blended labor rate?
- Programming toolsets or widgets to reduce the number of required engineering hours?
- Using source code under an open source license, thereby reducing the number of required engineering hours?

- Conformance with any particular software development standard, perhaps not available at the time?
- Any new software development techniques not necessarily developed in 1993?

The replacement cost for the software can vary materially just by changing any one of those factors. By using a more experienced team, perhaps staffed offshore, the value may be even lower.

Once the IP valuation analyst establishes value using the reproduction or replacement cost new method, he or she adjusts the value for obsolescence. Valuation analysts consider four types of obsolescence factors: physical deterioration and functional, technological, and economic obsolescence.

Physical deterioration generally has no tangible impacts on IP value because IP is generally intangible. Its physical manifestation on mediums such as paper or electronic media physically deteriorates, but the IP itself never physically deteriorates. For example, consider some Ada computer source code that represents software that a defense contractor authored to control a cruise missile system. That software never deteriorates, even though Ada's use is not as prevalent as it once was. The nature of software drives this fact. Fundamentally, software is nothing more than a high-level abstraction that humans use to represent a predetermined way to transfer voltages in a microprocessor. This high-level abstraction makes it easy for humans to use and program computers. Nevertheless, the reality is that software represents nothing more than human knowledge and is thereby intangible, being something that you cannot touch, see, or feel directly. Further, software does not have any physical form of its own. Software, on things such as hard drives and printouts of source code, has physical manifestations, but these physical manifestations are incidental to the inherent value of software.

This is not to say that physical manifestations are unimportant in certain cases. For a work of authorship to have copyright protection, the creator must affix the work in tangible form. Without it, there is no copyright value under U.S. law, as the copyright owner has no enforcement ability. The value of an original painting vanishes if the painting burns in a fire (though the original work may still have value in copied form as a lithograph or an artist's copy). Some software may be worthless or very valuable depending on physical form. An old computer tape with an important product algorithm is worthless if nobody has hardware that can read the tape. A printout of a software algorithm may be very valuable, especially if it describes something central to a patent claim.

Functional, technological, and economic obsolescence do affect the value of intellectual property more directly. Functional obsolescence occurs when the IP user must incur excess operational costs to use the IP versus current alternatives, which may be state of the art. For example, manufacturing Company A uses a patent under license from Company B and pays Company B a royalty of 5% of gross revenues for use of the patent. However, Company A determines that new technology would allow it to sell equivalent functionality in the market with new technology that it has developed for lower cost. Thus, Company A is experiencing functional obsolescence using the patent under license from Company B, as there is newer technology that can provide the same utility for lower cost.

Technological obsolescence occurs when technological forces render the intellectual property worthless. For example, patents for a next-generation computer floppy disk drive may likely be very effective and have the fastest seek time and greatest data recovery rate ever known to man. Yet the technology is largely worthless because there are better technological options already on the market, such as high-capacity flash memory, which provides more utility in a much more efficient and superior manner. The impact of technological obsolescence varies by industry. In relatively old-line industries, such as the insurance industry, a company uses an IBM AS400 for its policy administration system and may run such a setup for decades and continue to operate without interruption.[21] However, cellular telephone technology changes continually as carriers race in a hyper-competitive market to introduce the latest product features. Thus, state-of-the-art telephones developed in 2004 are largely worthless today, rendered ineffective by technological obsolescence. Palm, Inc. introduced the Treo Smartphone in early 2005 and listed it for a suggested retail price of $549 ($449 with a two-year contract). As of this writing, such phones are selling for as low as $30 for unopened phones and $10 for opened/gently used phones on eBay. Technological obsolescence drives this value impairment.[22]

Economic obsolescence occurs when the use of the intellectual property in its highest and best form cannot provide an adequate return on investment (ROI). This can occur easily because intellectual property is generally unique and may have little utility outside of a particular function. This tends to limit the value of the IP economically, especially compared to newer IP. Going back to the Prozac example in Chapter 3, Eli Lilly & Co. could continue to invest heavily in Prozac marketing efforts after it

21 This was in fact the case for IBM, which had a hard time moving users from the obsolete AS400 platform to its iSeries hardware because of the overall stability and reliability of the AS400 platform.

22 In the most extreme of circumstances—such as with Palm, Inc., which for all intents and purposes created the smartphone category with the Palm VII in the late 1990s—the creator of the intellectual property does not even exist anymore. HP acquired Palm in April 2010.

lost patent protection. However, if Lilly could invest comparable dollars into its next blockbuster—Zyprexia—and generate a higher economic return, then Prozac would be economically obsolete compared with other investment alternatives.

The Market Approach

Using the market approach, an IP valuation analyst looks for comparable transactions in the same industry and of the same relative size and form that recently occurred in the open market. The valuation analyst determines value indirectly using the comparable intellectual property transaction as a value proxy for target intellectual property. The reasoning seems logical: If the market paid $X for rights to use or own that intellectual property once, then one would expect that the market would reasonably pay a similar amount again, all else being the same.

Establishing value using the market approach has several methods, depending on the desired value standard and value purpose. For example, if one desires the fair market value for licensing intellectual property to another company, the valuation analyst would look to other recent licensing transactions in the same industry and use a similar royalty rate. Another market approach to valuation of intellectual property is to use a gross multiplier such as a cash flow multiplier. For example, an intellectual property generates $1 million of free cash flow in Year 5 and the valuation analyst uses a cash flow multiplier of eight, so the intellectual property is worth $8 million.

Valuation analysts commonly use other multiplier factors as well, and these factors are usually ratio-based. Once the valuation analyst arrives at a value, he or she then adjusts the intellectual property's value to account for identifiable differences, such as the market power of a comparable intellectual property. While IP valuation analysts typically use the market approach to establish reasonable royalty rates for intellectual property-licensing transactions, using the market approach to value IP in general carries substantial challenges to generating a credible value opinion (more on this shortly).

The Income Approach

Valuation analysts typically use the income approach for intellectual property valuation engagements. A valuation analyst using the income approach bases his or her opinion on the intellectual property owner's business plan, marketing and operational inputs, and other external references. Using this method, the valuation analyst projects the economic income generated solely from the intellectual property over a discrete period, known as the remaining economic life (REL).

The REL is generally one of the most difficult attributes of the intellectual property's value to determine when using the income approach. It is also one of the most significant drivers for the intellectual property's value. All else the same, intellectual property with a long REL is worth more than intellectual property with a shorter REL. The REL will vary based on the intellectual property under review. Certain intellectual property may have a longer REL than others (e.g., a patent for a truck gas tank mount versus a patent on a software search algorithm) because of technological risk or the potential for substitutions.

To determine economic income, the valuation analyst projects the revenue (or cost savings or other economic benefit) generated from the intellectual property over the REL, and then offsets that revenue with costs related directly to the intellectual property's exploitation, such as labor, materials, required capital investment, and any appropriate economic rents or capital charges. IP valuation analysts employ several methods to measure economic income associated with a given piece of intellectual property.

The income discount rate that the valuation analyst uses has, aside from the REL, one of the largest value impacts. There is an inverse relationship between the discount rate and the value. Higher discount rates lower value, and vice versa. This is desirable, as it mirrors classic risk/reward principles when determining an appropriate discount rate. Early-stage intellectual property with little proven market power commands a higher discount rate than proven intellectual property because the risk of the early-stage intellectual property generating no economic income is higher than with proven intellectual property.

The Assignment-Approach Match

In many of the examples presented in Chapters 2 and 3, the cost and market approaches both would have failed to account with any measure of precision or defensibility the value of the intellectual property. And in our examples, neither of these approaches can account for the value loss of the Prozac patent to Eli Lilly, the loss in value associated with ValveCo failing to pay patent maintenance fees, the value of the Morton Salt brand, or the patent value associated with MowerCo's sales.

In the simplest sense, the IP valuation engagement encompasses consideration of a variety of factors that dictate the appropriate valuation method to use. The following questions deserve consideration:

- Does the valuation engagement require consideration of a historical valuation date, and is all relevant data available?[23]
- Are the incremental economic benefits determinable?
- Does empirical evidence suggest a value proposition at all (i.e., does someone pay a premium for a branded product, or is it a commodity with little to no pricing power)?
- Is it possible to account for the economic life properly?
- Is it possible to account for the risk attributable to the IP properly?
- Is it possible to account for time delays in the market that may adversely affect IP value?
- Is it possible to represent the unique monopolistic attributes of the IP using the valuation approach?

The following sections review these questions further.

Historical Valuation Date

In intellectual property valuation, especially for tax or litigation purposes, valuation analysts must determine the value of an IP asset as of a given historical date. For example, a company learns of a trade secret misappropriation and needs to understand the value of the trade secret for litigation support. On the other hand, a company elects to change its income tax status from a C corporation to an S corporation, triggering the need to determine the value of the IP as of the effective date of the election to calculate the basis properly. Both cases are reasonable scenarios where it may be appropriate to use a historical valuation date.

The good news about valuing an asset as of a historical valuation date is that the valuation analyst will generally have greater information available. The valuation analyst will already know the revenues because they have already occurred. Also well known are market participants and cost structures, and the impacts of obsolescence and technology; this type of forensic information lends well to a cost-based or an income-based valuation approach. Naturally, valuation analysts may consider additional macroeconomic and geopolitical factors that they may not otherwise reasonably foresee with current or future effective dates (e.g., the economic impact of terrorists flying planes into the World Trade Center on Cantor Fitzgerald, a large

23 Such a situation may arise when considering a model for economic damages for a lawsuit.

trading operation based in the center, and Cantor Fitzgerald's ability to monetize its IP assets).

Because of the broader availability of information inherent to an historical valuation date, there is generally less uncertainty surrounding the final IP value opinion. In the Prozac example in Chapter 3, the determination of the true economic impact to Eli Lilly & Co. was straightforward to calculate and, even in that simplified example, is likely close to the true economic impact that Lilly experienced. However, the market incorrectly ascribed the value of the adverse patent announcement at $35 billion that same day, mostly because it did not have information to work with.

Are Incremental Benefits Determinable?

IP valuation is about determining the incremental benefits attributable to intellectual property. Businesses may operate in a competitive market without the effects of intellectual property. However, intellectual property provides an advantage to a company so that it may compete more effectively and generate an incremental economic profit higher than another market player generates. Because IP valuation focuses on incremental analysis, it dictates that the valuation analyst consider using an income-based approach for the assignment since the measure of incremental value is incremental income. The market approach and the cost approach cannot capture this process adequately.

Consider again the example from Chapter 2 regarding Morton salt. Morton's strong brand in the eyes of consumers provides it with an advantage—to the tune of being able to charge the consumer an additional 18%—for an otherwise completely generic product. Suppose that Morton and a generic salt company each sell 10 million cartons of salt at $0.52 and $0.44 respectively and each generates a 15% after-tax profit. Exhibit 26 is the difference in each company's economic result for one year.

Clearly, both salt companies may generate profits. However, Morton generates incrementally higher benefits ($120,000 in incremental after-tax benefits on $800,000 in

Exhibit 26. Difference in Economic Result

Morton International, Inc.		Generic Company, Inc.	
Per-unit cost	0.52	Per-unit cost	0.44
Units sold	10,000,000	Units sold	10,000,000
Total revenues	5,200,000	Total revenues	4,400,000
After-tax margin	15%	After-tax margin	15%
After-tax earnings	780,000	After-tax earnings	660,000
Incremental benefits	**120,000**		

incremental revenues), which become the focus in an IP valuation engagement. Being able to determine the incremental benefits attributable to the intellectual property is paramount. If the IP valuation analyst cannot discriminate the incremental benefits, then a final value opinion is indeterminate,[24] as there is not enough information to provide a defensible valuation.

Note that incremental benefits do not always manifest in higher revenues. Suppose Morton is able to generate the same volume of sales, yet it can obtain higher operating margins of an additional 3% because it has a strong supplier network.[25] In this scenario, the results are shown in Figure 27.

Clearly, in this case, the incremental benefits relate to the fact that Morton would be able to generate 3% higher margins due to a corresponding incremental drop in expenses to service an equivalent volume compared to the generic market. It generated an additional $132,000 in annual after-tax benefit. However, delineating the source of this benefit may be more complicated than in the prior example, which demonstrated price differentials.

Incremental benefits may also relate to a higher overall market share. In such a case, Morton would generate a higher volume than the generic market, but it would otherwise have constant margins and a price that matched the market. The incremental analysis of such a situation may be described in Exhibit 28.

Again, the results are straightforward to calculate. Morton generates a volume 20% higher when compared to generic competitors equating to an additional after-tax incremental benefit of $132,000. The challenge is getting the information to determine the sources attributable to the difference in market share. Several factors make it

Exhibit 27. Difference in Economic Result, Strong Supplier Network

Morton International, Inc.		Generic Company, Inc.	
Per-unit cost	0.44	Per-unit cost	0.44
Units sold	10,000,000	Units sold	10,000,000
Total revenues	4,400,000	Total revenues	4,400,000
After-tax margin	18%	After-tax margin	15%
After-tax earnings	792,000	After-tax earnings	660,000
Incremental benefits	132,000		

24 It is important to understand that the value is indeterminate, as opposed to having no value. Saying that IP has no value constitutes a value opinion (i.e., zero dollars); however, saying that the IP value is indeterminate allows the valuation analyst to avoid having to render a value opinion when lacking key information.

25 Note that the Morton brand would offer less in the value proposition under this scenario as the supplier network provides the additional value to Morton, allowing it to generate a given equivalent volume for lower cost.

Exhibit 28. Difference in Economic Result, Higher Overall Market Share			
Morton International, Inc.		Generic Company, Inc.	
Per-unit cost	0.44	Per-unit cost	0.44
Units sold	12,000,000	Units sold	10,000,000
Total revenues	5,280,000	Total revenues	4,400,000
After-tax margin	15%	After-tax margin	15%
After-tax earnings	792,000	After-tax earnings	660,000
Incremental benefits	132,000		

difficult to equate market share differences directly with intellectual property. The following are some of the complexities that arise in comparing incremental market shares associated with IP:

- ***Are the companies serving the same markets?*** If not, then any comparisons between Morton and the generic companies would not be appropriate. Further, it may be necessary for a valuation analyst to restrict the analysis to only those markets where Morton and the generics compete, as that subset presents the only means to perform an incremental analysis.

- ***Are there abnormal attributes keeping companies from competing in the market?*** Perhaps Morton owns the largest and broadest array of salt mines across the country, and it can deliver its product to the market in greater volume just because it is in more locations. In such a case, the additional volume attributable to Morton's IP is likely smaller than the volume benefits that Morton enjoys from a geographically dispersed collection of salt mines.

- ***Is the market shrinking or is operating the business economically obsolete?*** Perhaps one of the worst psychological mistakes to make is to feel good about getting an increasing share of a shrinking market. It tricks the business owner into thinking that the market and business are more viable than they are. However, the reality may be that competitors left the market because it no longer generated adequate returns.

- ***Do the competitors run their businesses poorly?*** Never discount the possibility that a competitor has a lesser market share because it runs its business poorly. Perhaps Morton has smart people who know the industry inside and out. Contrast that with the generic competitor: a family-run business handed down to a fourth generation who care more about surfing the Internet than addressing customers. In such a situation, the improper attribution of the incremental market share to some IP aspect may result in a significant valuation misstatement.

Naturally, an IP incremental benefits analysis is challenging because there are as many complicating factors in the analysis as there are companies and people in the world. If the IP valuation analyst cannot determine the incremental benefits attributable to the intellectual property, then any value conclusion will be indeterminate.

Is There a Value Proposition?

A fundamental driver for IP value is the existence of a value proposition. The value proposition varies with the intellectual property type. Exhibit 29 summarizes the types of value propositions that emerge based on the various IP types:

Exhibit 29. Types of Value Propositions Based on IP Types

IP Type	Value Proposition
Patent	Functional utility
Copyright	Pleasure, utility
Trademark	Esteem, trust, market share, lower search costs
Trade secret	Uniqueness, reproduction difficultly, cost savings, revenue generation

While it is tempting to say that intellectual property always has value, in reality, IP may have little or no inherent value in many cases. An inventor does not want to hear that the patent he or she spent $50,000 prosecuting has little marketable value. An author does not want to find that the manuscript he or she spent four years authoring has little marketable value. A business owner does not want to discover that his or her brand has little value in the eyes of the consumer. Yet the IP valuation analyst's reality is to seek out the truth regarding the IP valuation engagement and determine whether a value proposition exists. What's more, and perhaps more difficult, is that the valuation analyst must deliver the bad news to the client.[26]

Certain value propositions are easy to prove with data. If Eli Lilly & Co. can sell Prozac in the market but no other competitor may because of a patent, demonstrating incremental benefits attributable to the patent is straightforward because the Prozac therapy has strong market support. If a consumer is willing to pay $0.08 more for a carton of Morton salt than for a generic counterpart, determining an overall value is straightforward also, because the market indicates strong support

26 This is likely to sting even more for the client because not only does the client learn that his or her prized possession is worth nothing in the open market, the client likely spent thousands of dollars to learn this.

for the Morton brand. However, many times, an IP valuation analyst may not have such a clear-cut value proposition.

Many factors may compound to destroy a value proposition for an IP type, having little to do with the utility of the IP (if it were a patent) or the marketability of the IP asset (if it were a brand). First, an IP owner can destroy any value proposition by not abiding by the law protecting the IP (e.g., not paying patent maintenance fees, using a mark under the wrong class, not protecting trade secrets adequately, etc.). Later chapters explore the dramatic effects of administrative oversights on IP value. Second, the utility of the IP asset may offer no value proposition to an end user in the market. Consider patents for a next-generation computer floppy disk drive. They may be the best-written, broadest, most defensible patents ever authored by man. Yet the technology is largely worthless because there are better technological options already on the market, such as high-capacity flash memory, that provide more utility in a much more efficient and superior manner. Third, the nature of the intellectual property may make any traditional benefit more difficult to calculate. This is particularly common with new technologies that are potentially disruptive in the market. In such a situation, the IP valuation analyst must reasonably estimate as to what the incremental benefits may be, and how the market may value those incremental benefits when the product does eventually reach the market.

For example, consider new drug company NewCo as it launches a product to compete against an incumbent therapy. Suppose that the incumbent drug therapy requires a patient to take two pills per day and each pill costs $5. Thus, the patient will spend $10 per day for that drug therapy. Now suppose that NewCo devises a once-daily formulation that is easier for the patient and will lead to higher overall drug protocol compliance (i.e., the patient will not miss taking the second dose of the drug later in the day). What is that worth to the client? Empirical evidence suggests, in fact, that patients prefer once-daily dosing to multiple dosing. That alone may be worth a price premium, perhaps of $1 per day. Thus, NewCo could sell its therapy for $11, with patients paying 10% more just for the convenience. Convenience aside, the client spends $10 per day for the total therapy. Assuming the manufacturing costs are the same, NewCo could sell its therapy for less than $10 and create instant economic benefit for patients beyond convenience. Suppose that NewCo can sell the drug for $7.50 per daily dose. Even though the unit cost per dose is $2.50 more, the patient has to take fewer doses. Annually, the patient will save $912.50 by switching to the once-daily dosing formulation. Economically, this will drive market demand for the new product and help define a value proposition (further protected, of course, with patents to prevent competitors from re-creating the therapy and competing

head to head). While there is some uncertainty as to how the market will react under this scenario, it is still possible, using empirical evidence, to build a defensible incremental benefit model that ultimately may drive IP value.

How do the market and cost approaches fare in this type of scenario? Not well. Consider the Google brand. Google is the largest Internet search company in the world and commands greater than 60% of the total market for Internet search-related revenues. Now consider a new search technology called Doodle. Is there an incremental benefit associated with the Doodle brand over another generic Internet search company using a market approach? The answer is not likely, particularly if Doodle were a start-up company.[27] The cost approach would not capture the value proposition well either. If Doodle spent $10 million on an advertising campaign, it may not translate well into a persistent value proposition. In fact, evidence suggests this to be the case. Pets.com had a largely famous singing sock puppet as a mascot and part of a multimillion dollar marketing campaign to sell pet food on the Internet. Pets.com shut down its operations after being in business less than three years (and about seven months after raising $82.5 million in an initial public offering).[28] In total, in 2000, more than a dozen Internet companies collectively spent more than $40 million on television ads.[29] Yet that cost never materialized into value for most of these companies because there were no sustainable value propositions.

Accounting for the Economic Life

A key driver for profitability for intellectual property is the economic life over which the company will be able to exploit the IP. IP with a longer economic life has a higher value than IP with a shorter economic life, all things being equal. As Exhibit 30 demonstrates, the cumulative value of an income annuity of $100,000 grows the longer one holds it.[30]

As the example demonstrates, IP that has an economic life of five years is worth $147,922 more than the same IP with an economic life of one year.[31] Thus, consideration of the economic life of the intellectual property is very important.

Each valuation method has a means to account for economic life. Under the cost approach, valuation analysts account for the economic life of a product by applying a depreciation charge against the value. Over time, the value of the asset drops off

27 One may reasonably expect Google's trademark counsel to call on Doodle with some stern cease-and-desist instructions, claiming that Doodle was infringing on Google's brands.
28 Troy Wolverton, "Pets.com latest high-profile dot-com disaster," *CNet News*, November 7, 2000.
29 http://www.msnbc.msn.com/id/6877753/.
30 This calculation assumes a 35% discount rate and an end-of-period discounting convention.
31 $221,996—$74,074 = $147,922.

Exhibit 30. Cumulative Value of an Annuity of $100,000					
Economic life (years)	1	2	3	4	5
Annual cash flows	$100,000	$100,000	$100,000	$100,000	$100,000
Present value	$74,074	$128,944	$169,588	$199,695	$221,996

as the holding period gets shorter and as the accumulated depreciation grows. As the Exhibit 31 demonstrates, the depreciated value of a technology with a five-year economic life in Year 4 is $20,000, assuming a straight-line depreciation and an end-of-year depreciation charge. It is $42,857 using a seven-year economic life and $60,000 using a ten-year economic life.

The only problem here is that the intellectual property has the same starting value, regardless of the IP's economic life. In the example, the value of the intellectual property is $100,000 in Year 0 whether it has an economic life of five, seven, or ten years. This fails the postulate that an income-producing asset with a long economic life is worth more. Thus, one may reasonably conclude that the cost approach will not provide a reasonable mechanism for economic-life accounting in an IP valuation engagement.

The market approach does not do much better because it has the implicit assumption that guideline IP transactions and the subject IP have similar economic lives. The market approach presumes the exit event (i.e., sale) occurs using a given multiple of earnings or sales rate. However, none of the multiples describes the expected

Exhibit 31. Depreciated Value

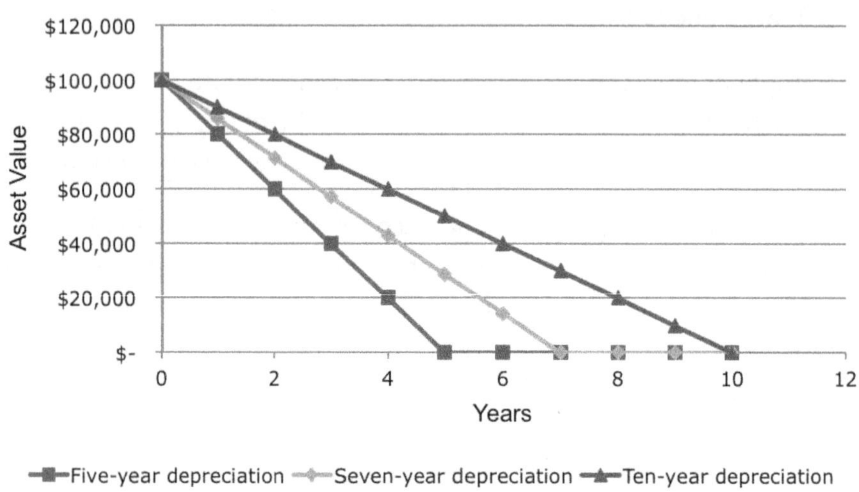

economic life of the intellectual property in the transaction. Thus, when an analyst uses a market multiple, it is with an implicit assumption that the economic lives of the guideline IP transactions and the subject IP are identical. If the economic lives are different and there is no knowledge of that difference, then the value conclusion is essentially meaningless, amounting to nothing more than a random guess. Values as divergent as $1,000,000,000, $0, or -$1,000,000,000 may be equally probable.

The following example valuation model demonstrates that matching economic lives of the intellectual property can have a larger value impact than choosing the appropriate valuation multiples from guideline IP transactions. The valuation example makes the following assumptions:

- Revenues of $10 million in the corresponding exit year;
- Earnings of $1,000,000 in the corresponding exit year;
- It is equally probable that the exit event can occur in year 1, 2, 3, 4, 5, 6, 7, 8, 9, or 10;
- Price/Sales multiples that range from 0.5 to 3 using a triangular distribution and a most likely value of 1.5;
- Price/Earnings multiples that range from 10 to 50 using a triangular distribution and a most likely value of 20; and
- A discount rate of 35%.

In simulating this 10,000 times and analyzing the data with a regression analysis, it becomes obvious that the economic life is the most important value driver, even more important than the market multiples used to calculate the terminal value.

A regression analysis of the economic life and sales market multiple yielded the following coefficients:

Description	Value
Exit year	-0.842
Sales market multiple	0.344

The exit year has an expected inverse relationship to value. A shorter economic life equates to a lower value. The sales market multiple has an expected positive relationship to value. Higher price/sales multiples equate to higher values. What is interesting is that the magnitude of the impact of the exit year is more than twice as large as the impact of the price/sales multiple. This makes sense. If the economic life is zero, then the total revenue is $0. One can multiply $0 in revenues by a 1,000 market multiple and still get a value of $0. However, intellectual property with a long economic life can have a fractional market multiple and retain a value in the millions or more.

A similar regression analysis of the economic life and earnings market multiple yields similar results:

Description	Value
Exit year	-0.834
Sales market multiple	0.350

The exit year exhibits an expected inverse relationship to value, and the market multiple has an expected positive relationship to value. Like the price/sales market multiple analysis, the magnitude of the impact of the exit year is more than twice as large as the impact of the price/earnings multiple.

In short, the simplifying assumption is that the economic lives of guideline IP transactions and the subject IP have a large impact on value. In fact, matching economic lives has a larger impact than any error inherent in the selection of the market multiples. It is generally impossible to know the anticipated economic life a buyer presumes in a transaction because buyers do not generally make public their views on this. The magnitude of this uncertainty attacks the basic premise of the market approach and its effectiveness at valuing IP.

Accounting for the economic life in a valuation model is trivial and something that the income approach handles very well. While the income approach does not absolve the valuation analyst from the need to capture the correct economic life for the IP, the approach can make the economic life consideration explicit because analysts can account for the economic life in valuation models. For example, if the economic life is five years, the valuation model can ignore any economic impacts after Year 5. Thus, there is no need to make any simplifying assumption regarding economic life as one does when using guideline transactions with a market approach.

Accounting for Risk

The concept of risk has a bearing on intellectual property, as events can alter the value of IP. There is an inverse relationship between risk and value. IP that carries higher risk is worth less than IP that carries lower risk. Risk may arrive in many forms, including:

- External factors that affect obsolescence may increase the risk of future IP value impairment as the market switches to other substitutes;
- The IP owner impairs the value of the IP through unrelated actions (e.g., Lindsay Lohan's personal problems and the subsequent impairment of her ability to capture lead roles in motion pictures);
- The IP owner does not have the financial resources to defend the IP in the market; and
- The IP owner receives a rejection from the USPTO on a patent currently under license.

The suitability of accounting for risk varies with the approach used and the purpose of the IP valuation. The cost approach generally has no meaningful way to account for risk, aside from increasing or lowering the cost of the asset to account for the valuation analyst's estimation of the risk impact. There is little empirical evidence in valuation literature to support a methodology for making such adjustments objectively. Further, it is questionable that adjustments would account properly for several types of risk. For many assignments, this risk assessment may not be an issue. For example, if the IP valuation analyst were considering the value of economic damages associated with a patent infringement on a historical basis, there would be no need to account for risk in the valuation, because there was certainty in the outcome (i.e., infringement and subsequent economic damages). Using the cost approach for such an assignment is merely summing the individual elements.

With the market and income approaches, the IP valuation analyst does have more ability to adjust for the risk of the deal using either a market multiple, in the case of the market approach, or the discount rate, in the case of the income approach. Both can capture the risk, as the discount rate serves as an inverse of a market multiple. Thus, a required rate of return net of growth of 20% equates to a market multiple of five, a required rate of return net of growth of 33.33% equates to a market multiple of three, and so on. Exhibit 32 captures the inverse relationship between the discount rate and the market multiple.

Exhibit 32. Discount Rate Relationship to Market Multiple

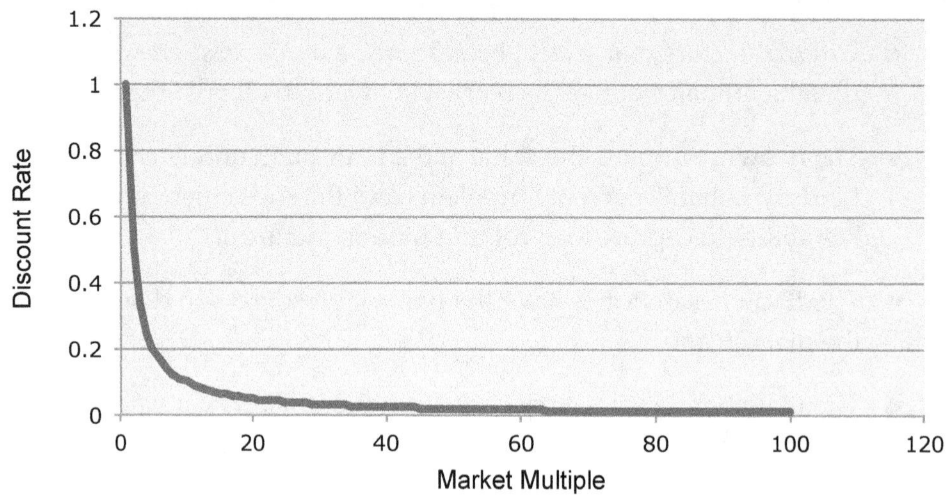

What this chart shows is that as the discount rate (or yield capitalization rate) increases, the market multiple decreases, as does value. This is good. Since the discount rate serves as a proxy for the risk of buying the IP, higher discount rates and risk should indicate lower values. Alternatively, if one were using a market approach, the higher-risk IP transactions would trade at a lower market multiple. For IP valuation jobs with a need to account for risk, the market and income approaches provide the means of doing so.

Accounting for Time Delays

Time has a large impact on intellectual property value, particularly for patents. Consider the typical lifecycle for a patent, as shown in Exhibit 33.[32]

As the patent lifecycle demonstrates, the economic life for the patent is generally going to be less than the statutory life of the patent.[33] Recall that a patent nominally loses value each day it exists until it expires. Thus, patented products that are in the market longer will generate a greater value. Consider the value of a patent that generates a $100,000 annual cash flow stream for five years, as Exhibit 34 demonstrates using a 35% discount rate.

32 This is a somewhat simplified model because the patent value will depend on the perspective of the current holder. A patent may have an economic life that begins well before a product enters the market, such as when a new drug company licenses a patent-pending technology to a major pharmaceutical company for market development.

33 Of course, companies launch products while patents are pending or before even filing a patent application, thereby lengthening the economic life of the product beyond what the chart shows; however, in doing so, the importance of time does not diminish.

Exhibit 33. The Simplified Life of a Patented Product in the Market

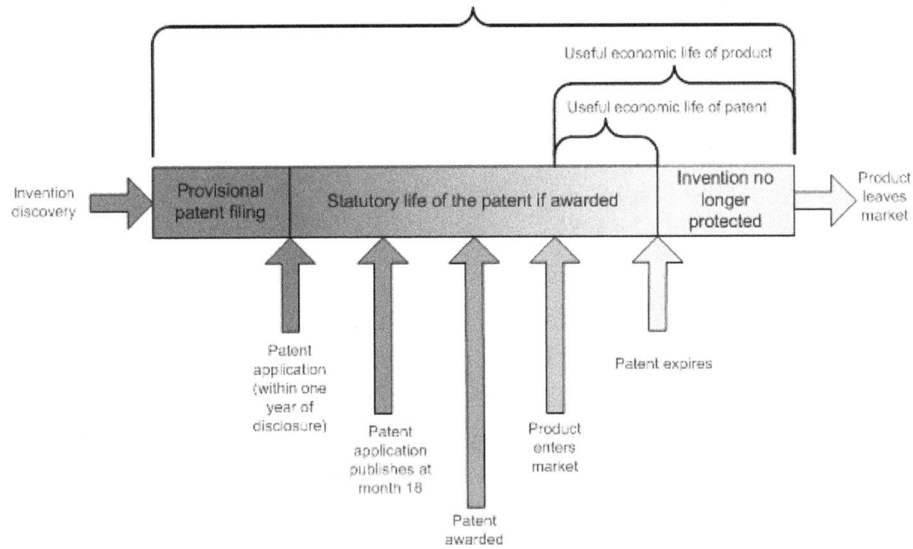

If the patent has a remaining economic life in the market of five years, it will have a value of $221,996. However, suppose the patent owner delays the product launch for two years because of technical difficulties. Exhibit 35 shows the result of this delay.

The IP value would be $93,052, indicating an IP impairment of $128,944.[34] This is proper because the value attributable to the patent subsides as soon as the patent expires, and the IP owner lost two years in the market. Naturally, time is of importance for IP types other than patents; however, given that the statutory lives for these are much longer (copyrights) or possibly infinite (trademarks and trade secrets), it is much more important to account for time in patent valuation models.

Exhibit 34. Value of a Patent, Using a 35% Discount Rate

Economic life (years)	Year 1	Year 2	Year 3	Year 4	Year 5
Annual cash flows	$100,000	$100,000	$100,000	$100,000	$100,000
Present value	$221,996				

Exhibit 35. Value of a Patent After a 2 Year Delay

Economic life (years)	Year 1	Year 2	Year 3	Year 4	Year 5
Annual cash flows	$0	$0	$100,000	$100,000	$100,000
Present value	$93,052				

34 $221,996—$93,052 = $128,944.

The challenge for the IP valuation analyst is representing the effects of time on the value opinion. The cost approach cannot represent the effects of time—it has the same shortcomings reflecting time as it does a differing economic life. The market approach also presents difficulties with reflecting time. Yet accounting for such a value impact as time is a natural fit for the income approach. If the valuation analyst must measure the effects of a time delay (e.g., product launch delay for a damage model) on IP value, the income approach will work well.

Attribute Considerations

Oftentimes in intellectual property valuation, it is important to value certain IP attributes, such as some contractual feature associated with a license. These attributes generally do not form the entire value basis. Rather, they tend to enhance the value of some IP types. For example, a copyright is a basic IP type. However, there are several attributes the copyright owner may choose to license, each having a unique value proposition, such as the right to make copies, the right to sell the work, the right to display the work, or the right to make derivative works.

Other common IP attributes include:

- Geographic restrictions (e.g., can only sell products in the United States);
- Rights to use in a certain application (e.g., rights to use a patent in jet engines, but not in automobile engines);
- Rights to use in certain markets (e.g., rights to use a patent in any engine type, but only for engines in the over-the-road truck market);
- Time boundary (e.g., rights to use IP for a certain period);
- Minimum license fees (e.g., minimum of 5% of revenues, or $50,000 per year);
- Reversionary rights (e.g., the right to cancel a license for nonperformance); and
- Extension options (e.g., the right to extend a license for some additional consideration).

The challenge for the IP valuation analyst is to know the appropriate method to use to value IP attributes. In most cases, the valuation analyst will use an income-based approach to value these attributes because the cost and market approaches cannot fundamentally represent the value contribution of an attribute.

For example, consider a license to use an insurance brand in the state of Florida for a hurricane insurance product. Suppose that the following data are available:

- The brand cost $15 million to date to generate and protect;
- There was a licensing transaction for a similar brand in Ohio, which indicated a value of $1 million for crop insurance in 2002; and
- The brand generates an average of an additional 15% pricing premium over generic products that offer substantially the same features and benefits, and the total market in Florida is $2 billion.

Applying the cost approach to value the geographic attribute will create misleading and irrelevant results because it depends highly on what type of cost allocation strategy one employs. Does the valuation analyst use the number of customers to allocate the cost? Alternatively, does the valuation analyst use a direct written premium (a common industry metric) to allocate cost? The decision is arbitrary because in the end neither metric expresses essentially the value of the brand in Florida. Recall that the value of the brand is the present value of the future benefits one receives from the brand exploitation. The cost approach simply does not capture this geographic attribute adequately.

Applying the market approach, different problems arise when attempting to use the Ohio transaction to value the brand in Florida. First, the Ohio transaction represented a crop insurance product, not a hurricane insurance product. As the financial returns for each product vary by local market, the Ohio transaction is not relevant. Second, even if it were relevant, the timing is different. The comparable transaction occurred in 2002, before a raft of hurricanes hit Florida. Thus, the actuarial tables are different from what they were in 2002. One may argue that some transactions in the market do capture the value adequately, but this guide explores the relevance of those transactions later in this chapter in the discussion of the market approach.

This leaves the income approach. If the valuation analyst knows the market premium for the brand is 15%, the total market is $2 billion, and the brand owner has 10% of the market, then the benefit is $30 million before consideration of any brand-building expenses for Florida.[35] Using the income approach, the valuation analyst is able to arrive concisely at an objective value. The income approach is the preferred and only practical way to value such IP attributes. Here is how a valuation analyst may deal with valuing the following attributes:

35 15% x $2 billion x 10% market share = $30 million.

- *Geographic restrictions:* Measure the present value of the future economic income that one receives from the geographic region over the economic life of the IP.
- *Rights to use in certain applications:* Measure the present value of the future economic income that one receives from the IP application over the economic life of the IP.
- *Rights to use in certain markets:* Measure the present value of the future economic income that one receives from the IP in the target markets over the economic life of the IP.
- *Time:* Measure the present value of the future economic income that one receives from the IP over the allowable time.
- *Minimum license fees:* Measure the difference between the present value of the minimum future license fees and the present value of the future license fees one may have received were it not for the minimum fee requirement.
- *Reversionary rights:* Measure the difference between the present value of the future economic income that one receives from an existing, underperforming licensee and the future economic income that one receives from a new, higher-performing licensee.
- *Extension options:* Measure the difference between the present value of the future economic income that one receives from extending the option to an existing licensee and the present value of the future economic income that one receives from a new, potentially higher-performing licensee.

Common Pitfalls of the Various Approaches

Each valuation approach has its associated shortcomings. Some of these pitfalls are structural and create fundamental valuation problems. Others relate to the improper application of the method by the IP valuation analyst.

Cost Does Not Equal Value

Value and cost are disjointed concepts. The cost of an asset does not relate directly to its value—any similarity is merely accidental. Recall that intellectual property's value is in what future income it will generate. The IP's value is not in what the company invested to develop it, for those are sunk costs. This generally makes it problematic to use the cost approach to generate a credible IP valuation. One author notes that using the cost approach is "useless for making rational decisions."[36] For example, Nike paid Carolyn Davidson $35 in 1971 to purchase the rights to the "swoosh" emblem it puts on all its products.[37] That swoosh is worth substantially more than what it cost Nike to purchase it, even after considering the hundreds of millions of dollars that Nike has spent over the years reinforcing and enforcing its brand. Empirically, it is easy to see the value. Put a Nike swoosh on a golf club and the price of the golf club increases more than the $35 that Nike originally paid to Davidson. Given that future income is what is important for IP valuation, one generally will not use the cost approach for IP valuations because it cannot account for the economic income attributable to the brand over time, only for what it cost to develop.

Next, valuation using the cost approach can reward the wrong behavior. For example, the cost approach can reward inefficiency and penalize efficiency and creativity. A company expends $10 million in resources to generate a given technology that receives a value of $10 million. However, another company generates the same exact technology for $1 million yet receives a lower value of $1 million. The cost approach thus emphasizes expenditures and investment instead of efficiency. Empirically, this was evident during the dot-com boom of the late 1990s and early 2000s. The market valued companies that lost larger sums more highly than it did companies that lost smaller sums.[38] Never mind the fact that the dot-com companies that lost more money and had a higher value are now bankrupt after wasting money on Super Bowl ads, which generated no revenue, as opposed to more fiscally prudent companies still in existence today.

Moreover, the cost approach cannot adequately account for the timing impacts of a product launch or other events. If a patent cost $1 million to develop, this represents an absolute value independent of time and other macroeconomic factors. The only reflection of time is in cases where absolute cost might be the effect of inflation in a trended historical cost model (e.g., the cost was $10 with energy costs at $100 per barrel for crude oil, and $14 with energy costs at $140 per barrel for crude oil). The cost approach to valuation cannot account for delays in timing that do not translate directly into dollars, and it cannot account for the monopolistic attributes of a patent.

36 Robert Pitkethly, "The Valuation of Patents: A Review of Patent Valuation Methods With Consideration of Option Based Methods and the Potential for Further Research," Saïd Business School, University of Oxford, March 1997, p. 6.

37 http://imprint.printmag.com/branding/swoosh-40-years-fly-by/.

38 Tim Koller, Marc Goedhart, and David Wessels, *Valuation: Measuring and Managing the Value of Companies*, John Wiley & Sons, 2005, p. 655.

Lastly, the cost approach is an inappropriate theoretical model for some IP types. For example, it is generally irrelevant for an IP valuation analyst to calculate a reproduction cost for a copyright, as reproduction would constitute a derivative work, still owned by the original IP owner. Thus, one who wanted the benefits of a copyrighted work could not reproduce it. Instead, he or she would have to acquire rights to use the copyrighted work from the copyright owner and pay whatever price the copyright owner demanded. As the copyright owner has protection under copyright law to prevent the proliferation of derivative works, the cost of a buyer reproducing an unauthorized copy is irrelevant.

The Fallacies of Comparability

Inherent in several IP valuation methods is the concept of comparability. Comparability is in fact fundamental to the market approach. Comparability also rears its head indirectly in the income approach to value, as a valuation analyst uses many market-derived factors, such as required rates of return, pricing, and expense data. The idea behind comparability is this: If the market paid $X for a given item, then the market may be willing to pay a similar amount for an item of reasonable comparability, all else being the same.

Do IP Comparables Exist?

With respect to intellectual property, comparable transactions in the market are rare. Therefore, any reference to other IP transactions is at best a crude value approximation. For example, consider a market-based approach where the valuation analyst must normalize the comparables and the subject IP to value. How does that occur? Current literature provides no objective method for comparing company intellectual property portfolios. Nobody recommends doing a patent search for each company to compare the size of the intellectual property portfolios, even though such methods may well provide meaningful results (what if a company owns one valuable patent but another company owns 100 poor ones?). The point is that general industry is lacking altogether in methods to objectively determine comparability. Several key attributes must be identical for a comparison to be meaningful:

- The remaining economic lives would have to be similar;
- Free cash flow generation potential would have to be reasonably similar, which can be difficult to determine for novel products; and
- The timing of the products in the market would have to be similar.

The risks associated with the subject IP and the comparable IP would have to be similar. It is fruitless to value a preclinical pharmaceutical against one already on the market, as the risk associated with just achieving regulatory approval to sell a pharmaceutical product is high.

The comparable IP may have the support and expertise of a proven management team, existing customers, available working capital, and a host of other factors that dictate why the IP sold for the price it did. The candidate IP under valuation would require the same circumstances, or the valuation analyst must make adjustments to account for any dissimilarity. However, these adjustments are generally arbitrary approximations and their use can compound valuation error. Valuation analysts would argue that their "expertise" and "judgment" allow them to make credible value determinations. For example, if one IP asset generates free cash flow with a higher return, perhaps a valuation analyst would account for this benefit with a higher valuation multiple, perhaps from six times cash flow to seven times cash flow. However, a rational buyer would pay the higher multiple only if the intrinsic value commanded such. Objectively proving this valuation is difficult without demonstrating the intrinsic value benefits to the buyer, which would entail using an income-based approach.

This is not to say that looking to the market is a poor practice for IP valuation and comparison. Valuation analysts typically use a variety of market-derived data to arrive at a fair market value for an asset. Commonly used data include interest rates on debt and available cash, discount rates for costs of capital, and costs for professional services. The reasoning is sensible, logical, and objective, thus defensible. If the current market pays X% for a given level of capital, an analyst can make the reasonable inference that the capital needs for a business under valuation would be similar. Examples of common factors that valuation analysts must consider in arriving at a credible, repeatable, and testable fair market value opinion are:

- Communications costs;
- Rental costs for a building;
- Cleaning costs for a building;
- Legal services in a given market;
- Capital costs for a given economic market; and
- Salaries for employees in a given labor market.

These and many other factors have this in common: there are plenty of options for a company to consider. If one law firm charges too much and generates no new client work, that law firm will lower its prices to meet the market, provide a greater value, or go out of business. The same holds true for many other value attributes important to IP valuation.

Next, market approaches fail when applied to valuation of items such as intellectual properties, which are unique and novel by definition (i.e., they have no direct market comparable). No matter how you slice it, comparable circumstances do not exist between the IP items under comparison, as each item is unique. This makes it difficult to compare one item to another with any degree of reliability. For example, suppose one owns a patent for a new algorithm for an Internet search portal. Is it appropriate to use Google as a baseline comparable company to value the new technology? Not likely. Google has many points that dictate its current market valuation, many of which have nothing to do with Google's intellectual property portfolio, such as:

- Does the company have available capital?
- Is there a strong management team?
- Is the company culture attractive?
- Does the company have any strong intellectual property?
- Does the company have a strong product pipeline?
- How well does the company translate resources into free cash flow?
- What is the brand reverence for the target asset versus the comparable asset?
- Where is the company located?

In addition, the value of the IP depends on the application of the IP to the market, and the circumstances need to be similar to serve as a credible value proxy. The value a soft-drink trademark commands may not be near that of a car, but may be similar to that of a fruit-flavor, sugar-sweetened water. To use a soft drink brand transaction as a basis for establishing the value of a car's brand is not appropriate, either—the two are altogether different in their application and industry. Ideally, the IP valuation analyst should not use data when the application differs; however, valuation analysts may use more general and less precise data, when lacking data that are more specific to the item under review.

Does the Market Really Understand IP Valuation?

Much in the IP valuation literature looks to connect stock market valuations with IP valuations. Yet to estimate the value of intellectual property using a stock market valuation implies the assumption that the market has perfect information about the company's IP and resulting rights and can calculate the value accordingly.[39] Evidence suggests that the generalized market, that enigmatic thing to which valuation analysts refer, has demonstrated that it does not understand how to value IP correctly. First, stock analysts who track publicly traded stocks likely have little background in valuing IP directly. The considerations and due diligence for stock valuation differ from IP valuation. Second, few in the market who actually understand and value IP on a daily basis likely have the power to move the market. As of this writing, the American Society of Appraisers has about 5,000 members, of which about 2,000 members focus in generic business valuation. IP valuation, which many consider a subset of general business valuation, has even fewer dedicated practitioners (i.e., IP valuation is all that they do). These few IP practitioners represent the best minds in the IP valuation space, yet they comprise a small portion of the overall population that may participate in the buying and selling of intellectual property in the public market. For example, Rivette and Kline observed the following in their review of the public market's due diligence into IP valuation for mergers and acquisition (M&A) activity:

> ... unfortunately, many managers would be surprised to discover just how abysmal most due diligence efforts regarding intellectual property actually are. "I'd say—and I'm speaking very generally now—that patent analysis is usually just a pro forma component of the due diligence process in most M&As" admits a senior executive at one of Wall Street's leading investment banks. "Most M&A companies, including ours, simply don't look closely at the patent portfolios involved, either for valuation issues or for exploitation possibilities." Most investment banks have teams of accountants, tax advisers, management consultants, and regulatory affairs experts to structure their deals to a company's greatest advantage. But one would be hard pressed to find a major investment bank that employs even one individual with experience in evaluating patent portfolios. Doubtless, this will change as corporate America and Wall Street become more attuned to the financial and strategic value of intellectual property, but as matters stand now, "due diligence" regarding patent assets is usually more myth than reality.[40]

39 Robert Pitkethly, "The Valuation of Patents: A Review of Patent Valuation Methods With Consideration of Option Based Methods and the Potential for Further Research," Saïd Business School, University of Oxford, March 1997, p. 2.

40 K. Rivette and D. Kline, "Discovering New Value in Intellectual Property," *Harvard Business Review*, January-February, 2000.

So when people claim that the "market" is smart about IP valuation, to what are they referring? Dissecting the broad financial market indicates a population that may have little understanding of the IP valuation process and requisite considerations. While the market is composed of smart people, the market's intelligence does not focus on IP valuation. The point is: if the market is so poor or inexperienced at valuing IP, then how can a valuation analyst possibly rely on the market for a value indication and still generate a credible value indication, particularly when performing any of the common market IP valuation approaches such as comparing profits, residual incomes, or business enterprise value? This is where reality and theory clash. The fact is that the market is not good at valuing IP. It is not appropriate to rely on market indications of IP value, especially by people who are not skilled or educated at valuing IP in the first place.

Market participants enter the market routinely with imperfect information, and these investors drive prices sky-high. Market participants also leave the market irrationally and abnormally, depressing market transaction prices. For example, literature suggests the market can indirectly reflect value of intellectual property by changing the market value of companies.[41] On the surface, one may infer that the market value of the Prozac patent to Eli Lilly & Co. was $35 billion because Lilly lost approximately $35 billion in market value on the day it lost its Prozac patent protection. However, as the analysis of this in Chapter 3 demonstrated, the market overreacted in a tremendous way, as the true economic impact to Lilly was less than $1 billion. The Eli Lilly case is not unique. When Phillip Morris announced a 20% price reduction on its Marlboro cigarettes, the company's stock dropped 23.20% and lost $13 billion in market value on the day of the announcement, suggesting an unimpaired brand value of $65 billion.[42] On its face, this sounds like a reasonable assumption. However, further inspection of the data suggests that the indirect value indication from the market was wrong and by a wide margin, just as it was with Eli Lilly and Prozac.

First, within six weeks of the Phillip Morris announcement, and under volatile trading, the stock had instances where it recovered much of the loss in value. What fundamentally changed if the brand was indeed impaired? The price of Marlboro cigarettes was still the same 20% lower per pack that it was when Phillip Morris lowered the pack's price. Consider that the average closing price for the stock was 17.28% lower for the 12 months following the announcement, instead of the initial 23.20% drop. The difference would nominally indicate that Phillip Morris did indeed

41 Gordon V. Smith and Russell L. Parr, *Intellectual Property: Valuation, Exploitation, and Infringement Damages*, John Wiley & Sons, Inc., New Jersey, 2005, p. 171.
42 *Id.*

impair its brand with the announcement; however, a permanent impairment was in reality something more along the lines of \$9.68 billion, suggesting an extrapolated brand value of \$48 billion. This is an indication of an overstatement of value of more than 27%. Further, the error can vary even more than that based on the selection criteria (or selection bias for that matter) for the subsequent market value data and other externalities, which manifested in Phillip Morris' stock price. If one looked two years out, Phillip Morris' stock price was 12.65% higher than on the date of the announcement. The data would perhaps suggest no long-term value impairment to the brand after all, or perhaps the market did not have a clue as to what the brand value was in the first place and gyrated finally to some harmonic balance (or it forgot about the issue altogether).

Lastly, the market simplifies many complex considerations with assumptions about risk, timing, and other intrinsic features. eBay paid \$2.6 billion in cash to purchase Skype in 2005. Others in the market used the Skype transaction to value other related deals. Yet a scant two years later, eBay impaired the value of Skype by \$1.4 billion (indicating an overvaluation of about 54%). In April 2008, eBay indicated its willingness to sell Skype if synergies did not materialize. Thus, valuation analysts who used the Skype transaction as a value proxy perpetuated throughout an industry the bad decision made by eBay to overpay for Skype. Over time, propagation of bad decisions such as those involved in the Skype purchase can permeate an entire industry, creating speculative bubbles in asset classes that have no bearing on the true value of the underlying assets.

The Portfolio Effect

Comparable transactions in an IP valuation engagement may represent a portfolio of intellectual property with a set of conditions that are unique (e.g., strong reversionary rights, preferential rights to derivative inventions, etc.). It is rare to find stand-alone comparable IP transactions that do not include other bundled tangible or intangible assets, or similar contractual arrangements. Suppose a valuation engagement is to value the brand for the breakfast cereal Kellogg's Raisin Bran. Kellogg Company packages the cereal in boxes of the typical form, shown at right.

Under a market-based approach, the valuation analyst might explore the profits associated with

Kellogg and the profits of a generic cereal maker and compare the relative profits, attributing any differences to the brand, typically using what one may call the "excess earnings" method. Several problems immediately emerge from this seemingly trivial analysis. First, Kellogg owns a large number of live registered trademarks[43] including the following:

Snap! Crackle! Pop!®	Livebright®	Honey Smacks®	Raisin Bran®	Cheez-It®
L'eggo My Eggo®	Yogos®	Toucan Sam®	Nutri-Grain®	All Bran®
Orchard Obsession®	Eggo®	Frosted Flakes®	Tony the Tiger®	Pop-Tarts®
Gardenburger Gourmet®	Keebler®	Froot Loops®	Cocoa Krispies®	Special K®

As the sample brand list indicates, Kellogg owns registered trademarks for many well-known product names or slogans. Some of Kellogg's brands likely generate much value and some likely generate little value. If Kellogg does generate excess earnings, how does a valuation analyst attribute the earnings to the Raisin Bran brand alone? What if Kellogg's Keebler brand generates greater excess earnings and bolsters overall corporate earnings? This effect would overvalue the Raisin Bran brand. What if Raisin Bran generates greater excess earnings but weaker brands depress overall corporate earnings? This effect would give the illusion of a lower value for Raisin Bran. The IP valuation analyst has no reasonable or defensible way of knowing if this occurs or not because of both a lack of data fidelity and incremental economic benefits that relate directly to the Raisin Bran trademark. Thus, a gross-level excess earnings approach will not generate credible results for this valuation assignment.

Next, which companies does the valuation analyst compare to determine the "normal" earnings for any possible excess? Kellogg operates primarily in SIC code 2043-01, which covers breakfast cereal manufacturers. A search of generic cereal makers using ReferenceUSA yields less than 10 companies producing products in the primary SIC code; many of those companies do not produce a comparable product and many have strong brands themselves, possibly obfuscating any excess earnings. Thus, an excess earnings method would not capture the true economic value of the brand because not enough data would exist to allow the valuation analyst to generate credible results.

43 There were 436 of them according to the Trademark Electronic Search System at the USPTO at the time of this writing.

Other factors may tend to exacerbate the portfolio effect as well. First, IP valuation literature has little about researching patents of comparable companies to determine if the sizes of the intellectual property portfolios are comparable and what any possible effects on market value would be. This is not necessarily a bad thing, as there is little academic research to suggest that such a method works and that any value conclusion would be reliable. Second, patent quality is a very important factor in a portfolio analysis. A company that owns one strong patent may be worth more than a company that owns 100 weak patents. NTP Inc., a Virginia-based patent holding company, owned several patents relating to electronic mail systems using radio frequency communications. It leveraged its patent portfolio into an ultimate settlement of $612.5 million against Research in Motion Ltd., maker of the BlackBerry personal communication device, even though NTP did not have a product on the market.

Survivorship Bias

Problems surface using market data as a value proxy when analysts move from commodity items that trade frequently on a free, open, active market to items that do not. Factors that valuation analysts routinely use as value proxies include revenue, earnings, or cash flow multiples. When problems arise they all relate to the same fundamental issue—too much market data is missing, whether relating to transactions that close or to those that do not close. Transactions are stored in databases or online websites that analysts can search, yet these locations include only transactions that actually closed successfully. For example, Pratt's Stats does not list the thousands of deals that do not close per year or the companies that go out of business because the owners cannot sell them. Thus, there is a survivorship bias inherent in all of the transaction listings that lack data on unsuccessful transactions.

What is survivorship bias? It is a sampling bias that occurs when valuation analysts use only successful transactions to value a company. Valuation analysts typically provide little consideration for the survivorship bias. This robs the valuation analyst of crucial market data and forces the conclusion that all deals close successfully and transaction databases capture them accordingly. This is a fallacious simplifying assumption, because many businesses fail to reach a transaction.

There is no database showing valuation analysts how many companies never closed on a transaction because the asking price was too high, and no database that valuation analysts can search to determine how many companies went out of business because there was no buyer. Without this data, the valuation analyst is not capturing the full opinion of the market for a fair market value opinion.

Finally, historical market transactions represent just that—history. All asset valuations deserve the same general disclaimer as stock price reporting—past performance is not indicative of future performance. This is because history does not equal market value. However, valuation professionals rely on transaction databases that have years-old data and may have no relevance to current market conditions.

Here are some of the important factors missing from transaction databases (especially private transaction databases):

- Why did the sale occur?
- When did the sale occur?
- How many potential buyers were aware of the sale?[44]
- Was it a forced transaction?
- Was it a hostile transaction?
- Was there a bidding war and, if so, how many bidders?
- What was the range of bids?
- How many bidders dropped out?
- How long did the sale take to close?
- What was the purported value standard?
- What was the effect of the sale later (i.e., was it accretive or destructive to market value)?

The last point deserves extra attention. There is a common post-sale effect known as the "winner's curse." Many transactions never generate the expected value, although sophisticated investors create these deals! However, there is little in the literature about how to adjust down the value of companies in transaction multiples because proposed multiples do not include post-merger value considerations, such as goodwill impairments because the acquirer paid too much for the target company. For example, if it is known that 50% of M&A deals miss initial financial performance targets by 25%, the value of a company should be adjusted down by 12.5%[45] to account for the expected value of the eventual missed performance. The author hypothesizes that this pattern is exponential in nature and is researching this for future publication.

44 It is a much different situation if 100 potential acquirers considered buying a target as opposed to two, lending credence to a more liquid market in the former case.

45 50% failure rate x 25% performance miss.

There are plenty of examples of missed financial expectations for public companies, and they include such deals as KKR/RJR Nabisco, AOL/Time Warner, Sony/Columbia Pictures, Quaker Oats/Snapple, Boston Scientific/Guidant, EBay/Skype, and Daimler/Chrysler. Naturally, these represent only the public companies where the failures are reported and apparent, not IP transactions. Likely, there are many more failures in the private market that go unconsidered, especially IP transactions.

Survivorship Biases on Market Valuations

There is little or no formal discussion of mortality analysis for valuation, particularly in any coursework or prevalent texts in the industry. While mortality analysis is a fundamental part of intangible valuation, such as intellectual property valuation or contractual valuation, there is little literature relating to the failure rates of businesses, mergers, and acquisitions. However, mortality analysis is a highly important consideration for valuation analysts because value generally relates to future economic-generating capability, which is time-bound.

Failure to consider mortality creates sampling error and a survivorship bias. This survivorship bias puts remarkable upward pressure on valuations. Because valuation analysts do not generally account for the probability of nonsuccess exit events, they generate consistently optimistic values. Consider the following example.

An early-stage software company owns a software asset that generates $1 million in net income in 2004. A search using SIC codes 7371, 7372, 7373, 7375, 7376, 7377, 7378, and 7379 in Pratt's Stats yields 99 transactions with a median equity price to net income of 19.966. Thus, an analyst may value this asset at $19,966,000. However, Pratt's Stats represents only transactions that succeeded. What about transactions that never closed? What if some market-derived study indicates that 20% of all M&A activity in the industry is abandoned?[46] The valuation analyst should then reduce the value of the asset because, on average, there is a 20% chance that the assets owner would never close a deal at the price indicated in a database laden with only successful exit events. The expected value for the asset in this scenario would thus be $15,972,800.[47]

There are other considerations, too. What about a transaction that ultimately closed, but subsequently failed, or never met expectations? This is entirely possible, if not probable. In fact, Todd Saxton and Marc Dollinger indicate a greater than 50% failure

46 There is no general repository for such data by industry, although academics have studied this phenomenon in some media industries (e.g., Muehlfeld, Sahib, & Witteloostuijn, 2006) and have suggested between 14% and 25% abandonment of all mergers and acquisitions in those industries.

47 $19,966,000 x (1 - 20%).

rate[48] for M&A activity after transaction completion across different industries in different countries.[49] Does it appear inappropriate to include such discounts because they generate a value that is "too low"? First, recall that valuation analysts should have no opinion on the value itself—but should only follow value development and reporting processes consistent with valuation standards. Next, valuation analysts have a responsibility to consider such value impacts, as they are theoretically sound and empirically testable. To ignore them would be analogous to a pharmaceutical company ignoring detrimental effects of an experimental compound for a new drug protocol, despite indications that 50 patients in 100 died from side effects in a Phase I clinical trial.

For example, consider eBay's 2005 purchase of Skype for $2.6 billion in the related and relevant market. eBay wrote down the value of that acquisition by $1.4 billion in October 2007, indicating an overpayment of 53.84%. Thus, accounting for the probability of post-M&A failure (if it was a similar type of company and there existed enough relevant data), the expected value of the company in the related and relevant market at $15,972,800 is now worth $7,372,061. This same company, using market-derived data, is thus worth 36.9% of the initial value indication. In a perverse twist of events, Microsoft announced in May of 2011 that it was acquiring Skype for $8.5 billion—in *CASH*! Some sources quoted in the news believe that Microsoft made

Exhibit 36. Observed Versus Forecast Skype Revenue Curve

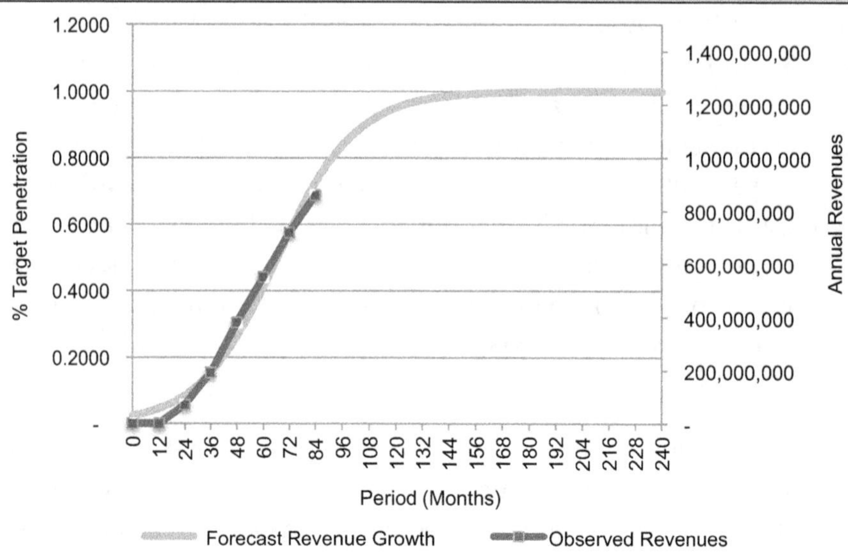

48 The definition of failure varies depending on the source, but nominally, failure would indicate that a buyer fails to meet the financial targets of the transaction by some material margin of error.

49 Todd Saxton and Marc Dollinger, "Target Reputation and Appropriability: Picking and Deploying Resources in Acquisitions," 30 *Journal of Management* 123 (2004).

the purchase to keep Google or Facebook from getting it. From a value perspective, Skype was a loser. According to Skype's amended 2010 S-1, it generated 2010 revenues of $860 million and lost $68 million, losing more than $360 million in the prior two years as well. Assuming a discount rate of 15%, Microsoft would have to generate free cash flows of at least $1.6 billion per year over the next 10 years to break even on the Skype acquisition.[50] Consider Skype's historical revenue performance, as Exhibit 36 demonstrates.

As the data suggests, Skype's revenues follow a Fisher-Pry pattern fairly well. While 2010 revenues were $860 million, Microsoft needs to generate free cash flows of twice that amount each year just to break even on this transaction! Based on the historical financial performance of Skype, it appears improbable that Microsoft will be able to generate the free cash flows that it needs to break even on its Skype acquisition.

Uncertainty

IP valuation analysts who use an income-based valuation approach must consider future events and the value impacts of those events. In doing so, valuation analysts must make forecasts of the timing and magnitude of events that may or may not occur in the future. For many valuation analysts trained in a forensic accounting business, where there is much certainty around all of the data the analysts work with (i.e., income in a cash-based business is determinable by checking the change in the bank balance at the end of the period), this is a hard concept to grasp. Such practitioners may call such valuation methods speculative. Yet patent valuation (and IP valuation in general) involves making judgments about the future, thus, such "speculation" is unavoidable.[51] Further, such "speculation" is arguably better than the implicit speculation built into other valuation methods, such as the market approach, which speculates that factors in other IP transactions are identical to the IP under consideration. Moreover, particularly with income-based models, it is possible to account for the uncertainty surrounding many of the key drivers for an IP valuation model, thereby clearly accounting for the uncertainty surrounding the monetization of the IP. Thus, valuation analysts can account for factors such as time and risk, which an income-based model represents well, explicitly. Author Pitkethly recommends ignoring income-based valuation models that fail to account for such factors explicitly.[52]

50 This is calculated by solving for an annual payment amount that satisfies the present value of a 10-year annuity using a discount rate of 15%.

51 Robert Pitkethly, "The Valuation of Patents: A Review of Patent Valuation Methods With Consideration of Option Based Methods and the Potential for Further Research," Saïd Business School, University of Oxford, March 1997, p. 3.

52 *Id.*, p. 8.

Daubert *Considerations*

While many valuation engagements may never see a courtroom, it is important that the IP valuation analyst perform the assignment using methods that will withstand scrutiny. For all the valuation analyst knows, a report never intended for use in a courtroom may well wind up there if a party sues the valuation analyst. Thus, it is prudent for the valuation analyst to use methods with strong acceptance in the profession. The U.S. Supreme Court's decision in the case of *Daubert v. Merrell Dow Pharmaceuticals* (*Daubert* case) and several related follow-on cases provide helpful guidance.[53] Though the *Daubert* case focused primarily on scientific evidence, later decisions broadened this scope to technical and other specialized knowledge.[54]

The *Daubert* case dealt with pregnant mothers' claims that consumption of a prescription drug, Bendectin, marketed by Merrell Dow, caused serious birth defects in their children. The crux of the case for both sides was testimony presented by well-credentialed experts. The court had to decide whether the testimony was admissible for each set of experts. Ultimately, the court cited Rules 702 and 703 of the Federal Rules of Evidence as providing guidance for the admissibility of expert scientific evidence. Those rules are as follows:

> **Rule 702. Testimony by Experts**
>
> If scientific, technical, or other specialized knowledge will assist the trier of fact to understand the evidence or to determine a fact in issue, a witness qualified as an expert by knowledge, skill, experience, training, or education, may testify thereto in the form of an opinion or otherwise, if (1) the testimony is based upon sufficient facts or data, (2) the testimony is the product of reliable principles and methods, and (3) the witness has applied the principles and methods reliably to the facts of the case.
>
> **Rule 703. Bases of Opinion Testimony by Experts**
>
> The facts or data in the particular case upon which an expert bases an opinion or inference may be those perceived by or made known to the expert at or before the hearing. If of a type reasonably relied upon by experts in the particular field in forming opinions or inferences upon the subject, the facts or data need not be admissible in evidence in order for the opinion or inference to be admitted. Facts or data that are otherwise inadmissible shall not be disclosed to the jury by the proponent of the opinion or inference unless the court determines that their

53 *Daubert v. Merrell Dow Pharmaceuticals*, 509 US 579 (1993); Kumho Tire Co. v. Carmichael, 526 US 137 (1999).
54 *Kumho Tire Co. v. Carmichael*, 526 US 137 (1999).

> probative value in assisting the jury to evaluate the expert's opinion substantially outweighs their prejudicial effect.[55]

In the *Daubert* case, the court went to great pains to define the words "scientific" and "knowledge." That context provides an important backdrop for valuation engagements. "Science," as the court defined, implies grounding in the methods and procedures of science."[56] "Knowledge," as the court defined, "applies to any body of known facts or to any body of ideas inferred from such facts or accepted as truths on good grounds."[57] Importantly, the court did recognize that there is some flexibility in the definitions, as illustrated by the following:

> Of course, it would be unreasonable to conclude that the subject of scientific testimony must be "known" to a certainty; arguably, there are no certainties in science ... indeed scientists do not assert that they know what is immutably "true"—they are committed to searching for new, temporary theories to explain, as best they can, phenomena . . . science is not an encyclopedic body of knowledge about the universe. Instead, it represents a process for proposing and refining theoretical explanations about the world that are subject to further testing and refinement ... in order to qualify as "scientific knowledge," an inference or assertion must be derived by the scientific method . . . proposed testimony must be supported by appropriate validation.[58]

What the valuation analyst may glean from this is: "we understand that there are no absolutes in the presentation of scientific evidence, but so long as the presentation represents a process for proposing, testing, and refining theoretical explanations based on validated principles, then it is okay." This may provide the valuation analyst with a means to use the proper valuation technique, but it leaves open some holes the court filled with what the broader community now knows as the "*Daubert* principles." The intent of the *Daubert* principles is to help filter expert testimony to reduce the possibility of pseudoscience making its way into the courtroom, which could mislead a jury.[59] These principles are:[60]

- The valuation method is testable;
- The valuation method has undergone publication and peer review;

55 Federal Rules of Evidence, Article VII, Rule 702.
56 *Daubert v. Merrell Dow Pharmaceuticals*, 509 US 579 (1993).
57 *Id.*
58 *Id.*
59 Note that these rules apply to cases tried in federal courts; adoption of these principles varies in state courts.
60 Steven Babitsky, Esq., and James Mangraviti, Jr. Esq., *Writing and Defending Your Expert Report*, SEAK, Inc., Massachusetts, 2002, p. 247.

- The valuation method has an acceptable rate of error and maintenance of standards concerning its operation; and
- The valuation community has accepted the valuation method.

The implications of the *Daubert* principles have an important impact on the methods a valuation analyst uses on an assignment, particularly those methods that have little empirical evidence to support usage in a particular context or have empirical evidence that discredits their use. It is common in the industry to pose a "*Daubert* challenge" to an expert witness to ensure that the expert's opinion satisfies the *Daubert* principles.

Testable Valuation Method

The point of this principle is to demonstrate that one can test the valuation method in concert with the scientific method and get a valid result. The court quoted that "scientific methodology is based on generating hypotheses and testing them to see if they can be falsified … the criterion of the scientific status of a theory is its falsifiability, or refutability, or testability."[61] Valuation methods that fail testability under a scientific method would not likely fare well under a *Daubert* challenge.

Many of the basics in the valuation industry pass the testable method. For example, the valuation community uses and accepts the use of valuation methods such as accounting for cash flow timing and summing historical costs. Measurable fundamental economic drivers are the basis for these and other valuation methods; thus, using those methods should meet the criteria for testability. Where it gets sticky is whether the valuation analyst is using the methods in a manner relevant to the valuation assignment; if not, the valuation analyst risks a ruling against admissibility of his or her opinion.

Peer Review and Publication

Publication and peer review carry weight because one may presume the broader community will have reviewed the publication, detecting and publishing any flaws in the methodology the peer review process finds. As it relates to valuation theory, IP valuation analysts use many techniques based on practices outlined in peer-reviewed trade journals such as *Valuation Strategies* magazine, *Business Valuation Update*, and numerous finance and valuation textbooks. Thus, in many cases, a valuation analyst will not have a problem defending the use of a particular approach if the application is reliable and relevant to the assignment.

61 *Daubert v. Merrell Dow Pharmaceuticals*, 509 US 579 (1993).

This does not preclude a valuation analyst from using a non-published theory. In *Daubert*, the court stated "in some instances, well grounded but innovative theories will not have been published," but that publication is a component of "good science" because it may allow the broader community to detect flaws in a particular methodology.[62] Publication is one part of the peer review process, though publication does not necessarily equate to reliability.[63] That said, publication is not a panacea.

Things tend to get dicey when valuation analysts start to depend on published methods that have not undergone an intense peer review process. For example, during the dot-com era, the valuation industry saw a growth in new valuation methodologies, published them, and ultimately applied them without verification. These analysts stated that then-current valuation methods, such as fundamental valuation analysis, no longer worked in the new economy. Instead of academic studies, investment bankers, analysts, and others with stakes in the outcomes (such as contingent fees paid on successful deal financing) proffered these new valuation methods. They offered new relative valuation metrics such as eyeballs or clicks on a web page as means to generate valuations. Consider an example. Company X generates 2 million visits per month to its website and 10% of those visitors make purchases of $10 on average. Company X generates $2 million per month in sales and has a market value of $240 million. Company X thus has a value of $10 per eyeball.[64]

Company Y figures that with the proper advertising and viral marketing it will generate five million visits per month. Using Company X as a proxy for its own expected performance, and considering $10 per eyeball for 60 million eyeballs per year, Company Y would have a valuation of $600 million. Suppose Company Y figures it will close those visitors with revenue per eyeball of $20, expecting higher sales performance to Company X because of Company Y's superior website format. Company Y would then have a market valuation of $1.2 billion.

Valuation analysts employed such methods regularly even though there were many problems with these approaches. First, academics and independent analysts did not validate the new valuation methods. The eventual studies conducted, which disproved some of the methods, occurred after the fact, when there was general availability of data. In fact, one study indicated that earnings from dot-com-era companies accounted for only 3% of the companies' market value.[65] Another reference noted

62 *Id.*
63 *Id.*
64 $240M market value ÷ (2M eyeballs per month x 12 months).
65 Brett Trueman et al., "The Eyeballs Have It: Searching for the Value in Internet Stocks," University of California, Berkeley, 2000, p. 3.

the market viewed companies with larger losses as more valuable.[66] Second, there was little published analysis to correlate the buyers and sellers of various goods and services with retailers. Just because Amazon.com was successful in selling books on the Internet did not mean that Webvan.com would be successful selling groceries (it was not). Product timing needs were different, the distribution infrastructure was grossly different (books would not spoil, but produce would), and the margins were different (much higher for books than for retail grocery sales). Valuation analysts did not consider such correlations or the impact of these correlations on value. Without significant confirming research, valuation analysts cannot assume what works for Amazon.com also correlates to another concept.

A thorough peer review process of these new valuation methods would have likely illuminated the fundamental flaws in the methods and dispelled the notion of using those approaches for any IP valuation engagements. Such a process would have also weeded out the flawed theories.

Acceptable Rate of Error and Maintenance of Standards

In an ideal world, valuation analysts will render an exact amount that truly reflects the economic value of the intellectual property in a given situation. However, valuation analysts must consider many different factors that introduce error into the process. Error may arrive in several forms, including statistical biases, incorrect application of valuation methods, or fundamental flaws in the valuation methodology. An IP valuation analyst must determine what error level is acceptable for the assignment. For the generalized valuation industry, there are no hard rules on what constitutes an acceptable rate of error. The *Daubert* court referenced *U.S. v. Smith* regarding acceptable rates of error, wherein the court noted:

> Of the 35,000 comparisons made in this study, the error rate for false identifications was 2.4% and the error rate for false eliminations was about 6%. This study previously has been cited as authoritative by other federal courts of appeal. See, e.g., Williams, 583 F.2d at 1198; Baller, 519 F.2d at 465. A follow-up to that study conducted by Dr. Tosi involving only actual cases examined by trained voice examiners found no errors whatsoever.[67]

The boundary for error was narrow at 2.4% to 6% in *Smith*; valuation analysts have much more latitude regarding acceptable error rates. For example, consider a valuation for a software asset. Industry literature suggests good software estimation

66 Tim Koller, Marc Goedhart, and David Wessels, *Valuation: Measuring and Managing the Value of Companies*, John Wiley & Sons, Inc., 2005, p. 655.

67 *United States v. Smith*, 869 F.2d 348 (7th Cir 1989).

approaches will provide estimates that are within 25% of the actual results 75% of the time, and that this rate is the most common standard used to evaluate estimation accuracy.[68] The COCOMO II empirical software cost model has an indicated estimation accuracy that will render an estimate within 30% of the actual cost 80% of the time.[69] This falls right within the guidelines of what the industry considers acceptable. As such, a valuation analyst using the COCOMO II valuation model should have the confidence of producing a credible result, based upon a reasonable degree of probability within the valuation industry.

On a practical note, knowing the error rate associated with data usage is important to surviving a *Daubert* challenge. Valuation analysts use averages often in the course of calculating a value. One measure of the possible error associated with the data would be to study the dispersion of the averaged data about the mean (Exhibit 37).

Exhibit 37 demonstrates three distributions that all have the same mean of 50. Yet the dispersion about the mean varies. The flattest line would indicate a data set that has greater dispersion about the mean and fatter tails (hence less reliability)

Exhibit 37. Dispersion of Averaged Data About the Mean

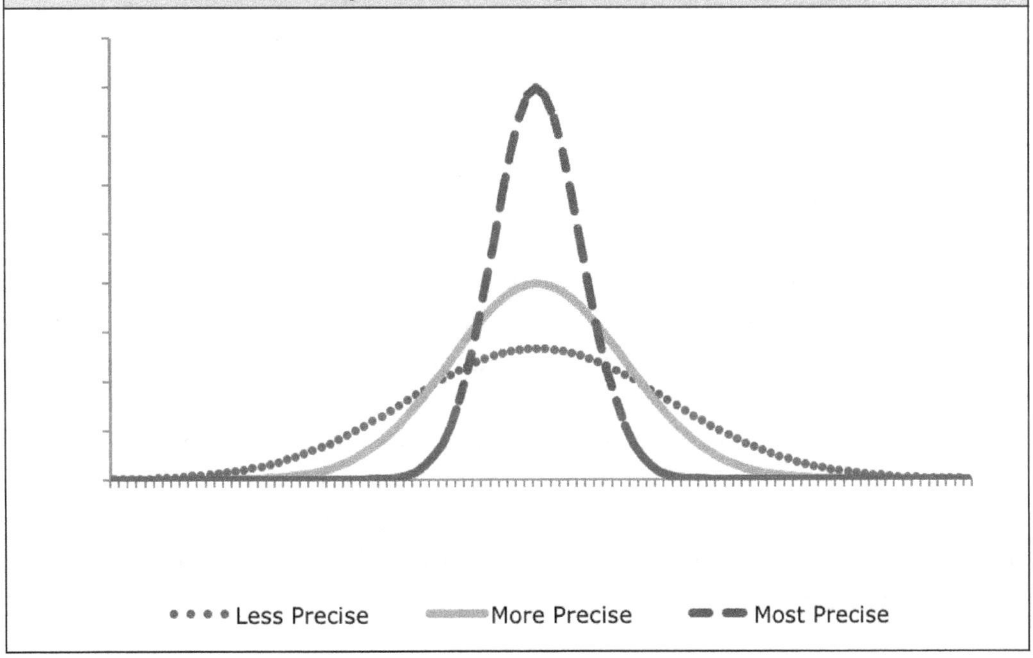

68 Steve McConnell, *Software Estimation: Demystifying the Black Art*, Microsoft Press, Washington, 2006, ISBN 0-7356-0535-1.

69 Barry Boehm, *COCOMO II Overview*, University of Southern California, Center for Software Engineering, California, 2000.

than the most peaked line, which shows less dispersion about the mean and flatter tails (hence more reliability). A common statistical measure of this dispersion is the kurtosis statistic, which measures the "peakedness" of the data.[70] A normal distribution will have a kurtosis of three. Distributions that have a kurtosis less than three are flatter, tending to indicate greater dispersion about the mean, hence less precise indication. Distributions that have a kurtosis greater than three tend to be more peaked, indicating greater clustering about the mean, hence a more precise indication. If one were performing a statistical analysis of a valuation factor, such as pricing, and found that the standard deviation for a set of data exceeds the mean of the data, such information would likely indicate a low confidence level in the data, hence a less reliable conclusion.

Interestingly, suppose that a company can consider three investments, each generating the same mean valuation; however, each of the three investments has a different risk profile, commensurate with the three distributions in the chart. In this situation, the most risk adverse company would select the investment with the greatest precision. With this selection, the company balances both the upside and downside potentials. The company that wants to "swing for the fences" would select the investment with the lowest precision. In this case, the company could have a higher possible failure rate; however, the company could also notch a larger win if it is successful. A variance analysis of the possible investments could add a new dimension to early stage or IP project investments.

Scientific Community Acceptance

The last *Daubert* principle covers the expectation of acceptance of a valuation method by the broader scientific community. The standard of what constitutes scientific community acceptance is broad, providing discretion to the courts. Using methods the greater valuation community accepts as appropriate for a valuation engagement will help the valuation analyst better defend the selected valuation method. For example, returning to the software cost model, companies, including the Internal Revenue Service, the Federal Aviation Administration, IBM, and Xerox, routinely use the COCOMO II. Because government and sophisticated organizations use this tool, it lends strong credence to the notion that this particular tool can produce credible valuation results.

70 David Vose, *Risk Analysis: A Quantitative Guide*, John Wiley & Sons, Ltd., New York, 2001.

Reconciling Several Valuation Approaches

Suppose a valuation analyst values a pharmaceutical patent using the cost, market, and income valuation approaches. The following are the values indicated by the analysis in a real project:

Exhibit 38. Values Indicated by Analysis	
Valuation Approach	**Valuation Conclusion**
Cost Approach	$150,000
Market Approach	$100,000,000
Income Approach	$1,000,000

As the data indicates, the cost to develop the patent was $150,000. There were several transactions in the market that one may consider to be similar (same affliction but different therapeutic protocols) that sold in excess of $100 million. On a risk-adjusted basis, the income approach yielded a value of $1 million.

What is the valuation analyst to do? The simple arithmetic average of the three would yield a value indication of $33.7 million. Yet doing so is improper because it assumes that it is possible to indicate a reasonable patent value using the cost approach or that a market comparable is a reasonable proxy for the value. As noted earlier in this chapter, strong evidence suggests that such situations are rare or nonexistent. Ignore this for the moment. What if the valuation analyst performed a weighted average of the three? In this case, the value indication would be in excess of $98.8 million, as Exhibit 39 demonstrates.

Exhibit 39. Weighted Average			
	Value	**Weight**	**Weighted Contribution**
Cost Approach	$150,000	0.15%	$222
Market Approach	$100,000,000	98.86%	$98,863,075
Income Approach	$1,000,000	0.99%	$9,886
Total	**$101,150,000**	**100.00%**	**$98,873,183**

What if the valuation analyst assigned weights for each approach and applied them to render a final value opinion? For example, suppose the valuation analyst had high confidence in the market approach, followed by high confidence in the cost approach, followed by low confidence in the income approach, and assigned weights of 60%, 30%, and 10% respectively. The results of that exercise are shown in Exhibit 40.

Exhibit 40. Assigned Weights			
	Value	Weight	Weighted Contribution
Cost Approach	$150,000	30.00%	$45,000
Market Approach	$100,000,000	60.00%	$60,000,000
Income Approach	$1,000,000	10.00%	$100,000
Total	**$101,150,000**	**100.00%**	**$60,145,000**

In this case, the value indication was about $60 million. The problem is: what basis did the valuation analyst have to assign those weights to the various approaches? One may argue that a valuation analyst's "experience" is all that one needs to consider in order to reconcile the differences. Unfortunately, some valuation analysts put too much confidence in their abilities to render objective adjustments for comparability. How does experience relate to assigning the proper weights? A weighting methodology represents a completely arbitrary decision and fails all four *Daubert* principles simultaneously. The experience argument is a wishful self-fulfilling prophecy. The duration a valuation analyst uses such a method hardly explains to a target audience any justification for whether the approach is correct—it may just mean that the target audience never knew to challenge the valuation analyst on the errors inherent in the methods. Further, the fact a valuation analyst used such a method is irrelevant in court if the opposing party never challenged the valuation analyst's methods under a *Daubert* hearing.

In practice, there is little in valuation literature to support a scientific weighting of the various approaches to determine a final intellectual property value. As such, an IP valuation analyst has little objective evidence to bring to bear to justify any such use. Instead, the valuation analyst has to consider the facts associated with the IP valuation engagement and the standard of value under which the valuation analyst renders the opinion. To do so requires a fresh look at the meaning of the standard of value.

Consider an IP valuation under the fair market value standard. For the purposes of the assignment, the valuation analyst uses the fair market value standard of value as defined in Revenue Ruling 59-60:

> Fair market value is the amount at which property would change hands between a hypothetical willing buyer and a hypothetical willing seller when the former is not under any compulsion to buy and the latter is not under any compulsion to sell, both parties having reasonable knowledge of relevant facts.[71]

71 Internal Revenue Service, Revenue Ruling 59-60.

Court decisions frequently assume the hypothetical buyer and seller are also willing and able to trade the property and have sufficient information as to the property and the market for such property.

Fair market value, as defined, does not necessarily reflect the actual price that the seller could realize from a true sale of the intellectual property in the real market. Rather, this value standard reflects the notional value of the IP in an assumed market. This assumed market considers the historic and prospective value of the IP in light of the business risk associated with the IP. The notional value does not include possible synergistic benefits or economies of scale that might accrue to the potential purchaser.

In the real market, the IP could generate as many prices as there are buyers in the market, with each buyer having the ability to pay its own specific price based on its own specific set of circumstances. In the end, the final price will be the result of a set of negotiations between buyers and sellers that the valuation analyst cannot ascertain or forecast. However, the IP valuation analyst can test his or her value conclusions to ensure that there is a reasonable economic basis for the value opinion (e.g., the opinion does not rely on market growth rates or risk rates that empirically are nonsensical).

For example, the IP valuation analyst can use the efficient market hypothesis (EMH), cross-referenced with the definition of fair market value in 59-60, to aid in a reasonableness test analysis for the IP. The EMH is an investment theory that reflects the diffusion of information and the integration of it in the value of assets. The EMH provides an important context for understanding the definition of fair market value, particularly with respect to available information and the reflection of such information in value.[72]

The EMH asserts that the market is efficient and rational in the processing of information and that the market reflects such efficiency in the value of a given asset. Empirically, this is an easy concept to test, whether it is for a commercial building or a share of stock in a company. If the market finds a commercial property to have toxic waste, the market will adjust the value of that property to account for the liabilities associated with the cleanup, future lawsuits, and other factors. If a public company misses or exceeds earnings targets, then the market reflects such information in the company's share price. As the market reflects information in the price of

72 Of course, this context comes with the assumption that the market can reflect the value of the information in the asset appropriately in the first place. This author does not believe that this assumption is reasonable for many IP types.

the asset, there exists a fundamental belief in the efficient market hypothesis that the values are unbiased, hence, objective. Of course, the magnitude of the value change is of significant importance, as it drives the ultimate price and market value of the company.

Varying degrees of market efficiency reflect the dissemination of information by the public. The EMH classifies the varying degrees as follows:

- *Weak-form efficient:* The historical prices of securities represent all information with respect to value and no one can earn excess returns in the market (i.e., "beat the market").
- *Semi-strong-form efficient:* The market reflects all information with respect to value within a timely fashion (nearly instant) and no one can earn excess returns in the market.
- *Strong-form efficient:* The market reflects all information both public and private with respect to value and no one can earn excess returns in the market.

One may argue that 59-60 implies that the market is strong-form efficient, as valuation analysts must render a value conclusion with respect to a hypothetical buyer and a hypothetical seller, both having access to relevant information, with equity to both. Such a scenario only exists in a strong-form efficient market. Deviations from the strong-form efficient market would not reflect relevant information or create equity, thus violating the fair market value standard definition in 59-60.

While there has been much empirical analysis both for and against the EMH, what is important is that 59-60 implies the concept of the EMH in its definition of fair market value:

> As a generalization, the prices of stocks which are traded in volume in a free and active market by informed persons best reflect the consensus of the investing public as to what the future holds for the corporations and industries represented.[73]

Because of the implications of 59-60 and the reliance on strong-form efficiency of the EMH, a natural conclusion is that hypothetical rational buyers and sellers would only close a transaction when there is equity to both and access to all relevant information. Merely looking at share prices (or share-price-related multiples, such as revenue, earnings, or cash flow multiples) as a value proxy for other companies does

73 Internal Revenue Service, Revenue Ruling 59-60.

not provide such relevant information (particularly to the buyer). Therefore, it is practically impossible to make a determination as to whether equity exists. This will almost immediately invalidate the use of a market approach for an IP transaction. This analysis naturally gets more complicated if there is a stock swap as opposed to a cash purchase for the company, as selling shareholders assume the risk of the buyer, for which they may have little working knowledge. Further, it gets more complicated still when dealing with collections of assets that have no reasonable comparables in the market, such as is the case with intellectual property portfolios.

Implicit in the definition of buyer and seller equity is that both parties are satisfied with the outcome at the closing of a transaction, considering the relevant economic environment (i.e., the deal meets or exceeds expected returns). Yet one cannot begin to prove equity without performing the due diligence associated with determining the intrinsic value of the asset. The buyer cannot prove buyer's equity until performing a returns-based analysis, which one does by calculating the intrinsic value of the asset to the buyer. The seller cannot prove seller's equity until performing a returns-based analysis, which one does by calculating the intrinsic value of the asset to the seller. Exhibit 41 is a continuum that demonstrates the equity allocation under the fair market value standard.

Exhibit 41. Value Continuum

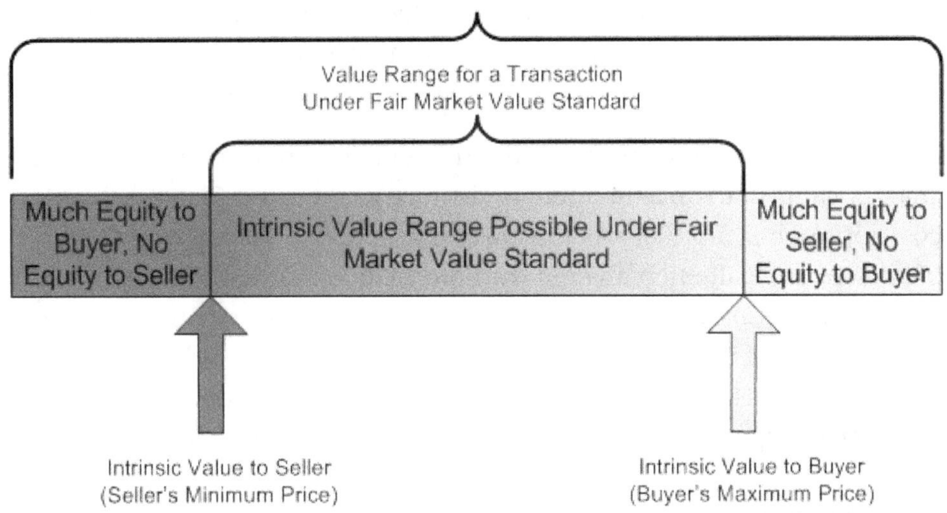

Therefore, if both the buyer and the seller perform an intrinsic value analysis to test equity, the natural result would be something within the range of the seller's intrinsic value, which sets the minimum or "floor" value for the transaction, and the buyer's intrinsic value, which sets the maximum or "ceiling" value for the transaction. Any value within that range will produce equity for both parties and meets the definition of fair market value. Any value outside of this range will not create equity and fails the definition of fair market value. That said, the cost approach to the hypothetical buyer might be appropriate for setting the minimum value for the IP. That is, the hypothetical buyer would not pay more than the total cost, including hard costs, soft costs, and opportunity costs, to redevelop the IP itself, if possible, as it could just do so itself and not close a transaction with the hypothetical seller.

Thus, it is possible that the IP valuation analyst will consider using the lower of the cost or income approaches for a valuation opinion. For example, consider the patent evaluation presented at the beginning of this section, which patent might not have potential infringement risk when redeveloped using the cost approach. The valuation analyst determines value in two ways, using a cost-based approach, and an income-based approach. Under the fair market value continuum, the minimum determined under either the income approach or the cost approach becomes the value of the asset. When the income approach generates a value in excess of the cost, then the cost approach provides the "floor value" for a hypothetical buyer based on the full cost to redevelop (including opportunity costs and capital charges). This is because if a hypothetical buyer can redevelop the patented invention for lower than the cost to purchase it, the buyer would just redevelop it. When the income approach generates a lower value than the cost, that value becomes the value for the patent, because the hypothetical buyer would not pay more to redevelop the patent's utility than what the buyer could generate on a risk-adjusted basis.

As a result, in the original example, the IP valuation analyst determines that the fair market value of the patent under an income approach is $1,000,000 and under the cost approach is $150,000. As the lower of the cost or income will set the value for the patent, the valuation analyst would conclude that the cost approach is the appropriate valuation method for the assignment. However, if the cost approach indicated a value of $1,500,000, then the valuation analyst would conclude that the income approach is the appropriate method to use. At no time would the valuation analyst ever average the two.

Valuation Method Selection Summary

This chapter presents a significant amount of material to aid the IP valuation analyst in selecting the proper valuation approach for a particular engagement. Exhibit 42 summarizes various types of business purposes that may demand creation of

Exhibit 42. Business Purposes and Valuation Methods	
Business Purpose	**Recommended Valuation Method**
Technology License	Royalty rate/profit split determination
Capital Formation	Integrated DCF and real option model
Technology Acquisition	Integrated DCF and real option model
Divesting Technology	Integrated DCF and real option model
Co-development of New Technology	Royalty rate/profit split determination

Exhibit 43. IP Type and Valuation Methods	
IP Type	**Recommended Valuation Method**
Patent	Integrated DCF and real option model
Copyright	Integrated DCF and real option model or cost approach for weak copyrights
Trademark	Integrated DCF and real option model
Trade Secret	Lower of integrated DCF and real option model or cost approach
Software	Lower of integrated DCF and real option model or cost approach

a valuation opinion and the primary valuation methods that valuation analysts should consider.

Exhibit 43 summarizes the various types of intellectual property and the primary valuation methods that valuation analysts should consider for engagements based upon those IP types.

Chapter 5
General Due Diligence

As several examples in this guide have demonstrated thus far, it is the details in due diligence that can make or break an IP value proposition. Yet little in published literature seeks to explain a process for performing IP due diligence with any measure of specificity adequate to confirm facts unique to IP assignments. Much in the current literature's due diligence discussion mirrors that relevant to traditional real estate or business valuation assignments. This includes review of audited financial statements (if available), plant tours, discussions with management, review of business plans, and similar activities. In many ways, IP due diligence involves all of the considerations of a traditional business valuation effort; yet it also includes specific attention to items a traditional business valuation analyst can ignore, such as a deep analysis of IP rights and an engineering analysis. Little in current business valuation literature suggests that valuation analysts expend much effort verifying IP rights for companies they value. Yet it is imperative that an IP valuation analyst perform due diligence of this nature to avoid rendering an incorrect value conclusion.

IP due diligence involves several distinct research areas, including, if applicable, an engineering review to study the utility the intellectual property brings to bear. The research involves an IP review to study current legal protections relating to the IP. Next, the research entails a specific market review to examine historical and prospective evidence and support for a value proposition in a competitive market. Lastly, this research includes a study of general IP value considerations, such as payment policies (e.g., when does a licensee pay royalties?), capital costs, necessary operating expenses, and others. Going through this entire process enables the IP valuation analyst to gain a clear understanding of the nature of the intellectual property.

The due diligence process will typically include the following discrete analysis components:

- Performing initial interviews;
- Analyzing historical financials;
- Understanding the IP;
- Verifying IP ownership;
- Commissioning independent counsel review;
- Reviewing enforcement history and ability;
- Performing market analysis; and
- Evaluating the regulatory environment.

The following is a discussion of these components.

Performing Initial Interviews

As is common in IP valuation assignments, it is important for the valuation analyst to perform upfront interviews to learn more about the intellectual property, the value proposition it offers, and the means that the IP owner will use to monetize the IP. This begins with the IP valuation analyst interviewing all relevant people who have knowledge of the IP and its resulting monetization strategy. These interviews, performed at the beginning of the assignment, will generally comprise onsite interviews with a cross-functional team representing the original inventors or creators (if applicable), and finance, legal, operations, and sales and marketing staffs. Each functional area represents knowledge important to realizing value from the IP. For example, the inventors or creators will best be able to explain the nature of the IP under review and can answer technical questions with a level of detail that others cannot match. This may be particularly important when considering design circumvention strategies for patents, as the inventors may already know the benefits and costs of particular design strategies (e.g., the inventors already tried a given design and it failed for some reason, thus rendering it impotent as a means to circumvent a patent).

Initial interviews will include discussions with finance staff, who will generally know about the costs incurred and the income generated from the IP. This data is important in building a credible set of expenses and a capital budget to monetize the IP. The finance staff will also have in-depth knowledge of the capital structure supporting the project, and the means that the IP owner uses to account for risk among its various capital projects (e.g., the CFO will know and/or set the project hurdle rate for the company's capital projects). The finance staff will have all relevant data regarding income taxes. Recall that when performing IP valuation, the valuation analyst is interested in after-tax cash flows, so the valuation analyst must know the income tax rates to calculate the value correctly. Further, it is important to understand the impacts of any incentives that may affect the effective income tax rate used. For example, if the IP owner can claim income tax credits under Section 41 of the Internal Revenue Code (also known as the research and experimentation tax credit), that may, in effect, reduce the effective income tax rate, thereby increasing the value of the IP. If a state program offers an incentive for investing in early-stage companies that monetize IP, then the value of the IP may be higher, again, because of the lower income tax rate. Deep discussions with the finance staff will help discover these value-adjusting factors.

The legal staff represents one of the most important perspectives in an IP valuation assignment. Recall that protections afforded by intellectual property consist fundamentally of legal rights. Thus, it is imperative that the IP valuation analyst understand the nature of the legal rights surrounding the IP. The legal staff, which consists generally of in-house personnel for larger companies and outsourced personnel for smaller companies, will understand every nuance of the IP and will know and be able to explain the claims structure for a patent. The legal staff will understand the composition of the prior art and possible overlap with the IP, will know and be able to explain any design-around strategies they considered when prosecuting the patent, and will know how to deal with them effectively through the claims construction. The legal staff will also maintain a finger on the pulse of any licensing agreements that may have a value impact, either in an out-licensing situation (value creator) or through a royalty obligation (value impairment). Lastly, the legal staff will know the disposition of any administrative or court proceedings relating to the IP, including any pending lawsuits, patent reexaminations, or formal or informal negotiations surrounding the IP.

The operations staff represents those people responsible for monetizing the IP, particularly in a direct exploitation revenue model (i.e., where the IP owner markets the IP directly without licensing it to a third party). For example, if a copyright owner wants to publish a manuscript, the operations team holds the responsibility for editing, producing, and fulfilling orders for the books. Often with IP, the IP owner has no formal operations team, as the IP owner would be monetizing the IP through a license agreement. For example, NTP, Inc. issued a license to Research In Motion, Ltd. regarding the use of some of its patents concerning wireless email technology. Thus, NTP never practiced its inventions directly, so the concept of NTP fulfilling customer orders was foreign to their specific company, making a deep analysis of NTP's operational capability irrelevant. That said, it is important for the IP valuation analyst to gain confidence that the licensee would be able to monetize the IP, because that forms the basis for a royalty due to the licensor. Lacking the confidence the licensee could execute, the valuation analyst would have a difficult time defending a projected royalty revenue stream for the licensor.

The last staff the IP valuation analyst interviews should come from a company's sales and marketing organization. The sales and marketing staff have the responsibility for creating the demand for the IP in the market. Thus, they are on the front lines and will have the greatest sense of the market's perspective on the value proposition the IP offers. For example, in the case of a patent, the sales and marketing staff will have the best view of how the patented invention's utility stacks up against competing solutions and on the market's perception of that utility. They will also have a reasonable understanding of the relative costs associated with the patented invention and the competing market offerings. Finally, the sales and marketing staff will know the sales cycle well, which will ultimately drive the revenues for the IP, either in a direct or an indirect (through a royalty) form.

While somewhat dependent on the nature of the IP, an IP valuation analyst may expect initial interviews to take anywhere from eight to sixteen hours to complete. For complex IP projects, due diligence may extend well beyond this schedule. Recall the Chapter 3 example regarding the scope of the valuation assignment for Global Electric. In that example, 170 different branded products marketed in 10 countries generated possibly 1,700 different market analyses to perform for the brand valuation. Understanding the value proposition for each branded product in a target country takes time. In such a situation, the initial due diligence may well take a person years to perform to determine the value with the greatest precision.

While IP is intangible, it may be important for the IP valuation analyst to inspect embodiments of the IP, particularly patent-related IP that may describe processes or complex mechanical devices. The IP valuation analyst may benefit from demonstrations of the invention in operation, a forum that will provide a means for the valuation analyst to ask technical questions to confirm key aspects of the invention. Depending on the nature of the valuation assignment, it may be helpful for the valuation analyst to film a movie or capture still images of the invention to aid in understanding the IP, in explaining the IP to the audience for the valuation report, and in performing competitive product benchmarking.

Analyzing Historical Financials

Historical financials, while an important reference point for an IP valuation assignment and a favorite item for the traditional business valuation analyst, are of secondary importance to an IP valuation assignment. As sacrilegious as that sounds, history can be quite irrelevant to an IP valuation assignment. A continuing theme in IP valuation is this: the value of IP is the present value of the future incremental benefits attributable to the IP. History is but a footnote, worthy of quoting for validation of pricing differentials (for brands), manufacturing costs for direct embodiments of IP, and other uses. However, history can be a terrible indicator of the future market potential for IP. Many in the valuation industry find this a difficult concept to grasp, in part because many valuation analysts are accountants by training. Much in the accounting curriculum (auditing, intermediate accounting, and advanced accounting) focuses on studying the past and organizing it into financial statements, on taking historical data and organizing it. While historical financials may be meaningful in a broad business valuation context, oftentimes they are not meaningful for IP valuation assignments because historical financial performance is discontinuous with future expectations.

Nassim Taleb captured the concept well in his book, *The Black Swan*, which studies improbable and unpredictable events that run contrary to historical performance. In it, Taleb discusses the concept of a turkey. A farmer feeds a turkey generously for 1,000 days. Based on historical performance, the turkey has every expectation of eating well and living out the rest of its natural life. Further, history supports this notion well, based on all data available. Yet, on the 1,001st day, the farmer slaughters the turkey and serves it for dinner. History in this case bore little resemblance to

Exhibit 44. Anatomy of a Blowup

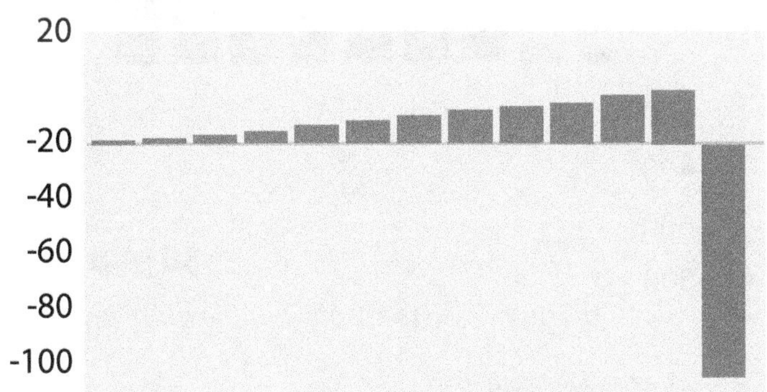

the ultimate outcome, especially for the turkey. Taleb notes that a typical blowup has a profile similar to that shown in Exhibit 44.

As it relates to the economic climate of late 2008, the significance has remarkable relevance. By late 2008, the banking industry had lost more than $1 trillion in profit, which Taleb estimates to be greater than all income ever generated in the history of banking. Consider IndyMac Bank as an example. Exhibit 45 is a summary of IndyMac Bank's annual net income for the last 10 years.

On a historical basis, an analyst would expect that IndyMac would generate profits of approximately $375 million or so. However, it recorded a loss of $614.81 million. An analysis weighted heavily on historical consideration with low or little analysis into future events would not account for such a probability.

What does this have to do with IP valuation? Plenty. First, IP valuation centers on the concept of the legal right to exclude another party from using the intellectual property in the market without authorization. Nevertheless, suppose the legal right disappears, as was the case for Eli Lilly and the Prozac patent (see Chapter 3 discussion of picking an appropriate time horizon). The impact of such an occurrence, however improbable, had a material value impact. Second, IP, especially patents and brands, oftentimes may be at an early stage, perhaps not yet even generating revenue let alone free cash flow. Thus, history would suggest the IP was worthless, which may not be the case for a valuable patent or brand that becomes the next Coca-Cola. It certainly was not the case for NTP, Inc., which took a patent it was generating no income with and leveraged it into a settlement with Research In Motion, Ltd. for $612.5 million.

Exhibit 45. IndyMac's Annual Net Income (in Millions)

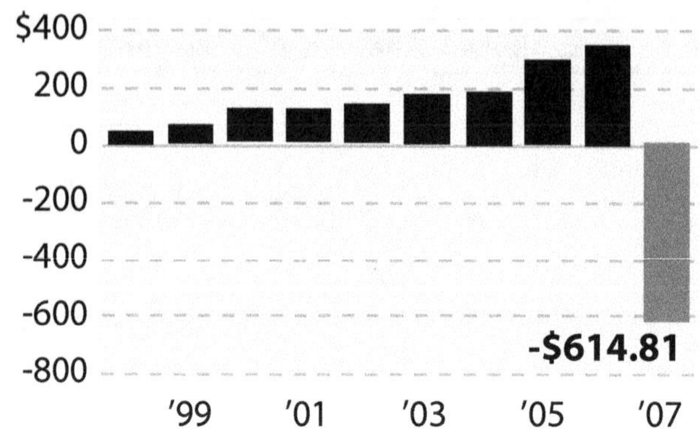

Source: *Bloomberg News*

That is not to say that historical financial statements are without value. Historical data is quite important for evaluating value drivers that serve as inputs to a broader valuation model. For example, evidence of the market's brand predilections for table salt and willingness to pay 18% more per carton for Morton's branded salt may provide reasonable evidence that an IP valuation analyst can use in a brand valuation. However, using historical evidence for the volume of salt that Morton sells (which will help define brand value) by itself may not be adequate without a study of new market entrants, salt substitutes, wholesale shifts in consumer dietary habits, and other external factors.

Understanding the IP

Understanding the IP may seem like an obvious requirement for an IP valuation analyst to accept and perform an assignment. Yet IP valuation, unlike generalized business valuation, generally requires specific market and technical knowledge. The IP valuation analyst must gain an understanding of the IP clear enough to author an appropriate description of the IP in the report. For copyrighted works and brands, this is a straightforward proposition. Copyrights, excluding software, may include a manuscript, a musical recording, or a movie that has an obvious description. Brands may consist of applications to various products that serve a particular niche market. Thus, understanding the form and function of the IP in these examples is relatively easy. However, for patents or trade secrets, where key value-creating concepts may reside in science, engineering, and technology, understanding the technology is much more difficult. In the relatively short space of an IP valuation assignment, the IP valuation analyst needs to gain a clear understanding of the following:

- Technical nature of the IP;
- Sustainable competitive advantages of the IP;
- Where applicable, if the IP works as the inventor envisions;
- Infringement risks; and
- Economic life of the IP.

Ultimately, the IP valuation analyst must generate a suitable understanding of the intellectual property in order to articulate the IP, anticipate and model the value-creating features of the IP, and report the results in a manner consistent with appraisal standards.

Technical Understanding

Understanding patent or trade secret forms of intellectual property can be complex. Patents are complex legal documents that vary in length. Some may have only five or 10 claims and consist of 10 pages total, relatively easy to read. Others may have hundreds of claims and may comprise 60 pages or more, which are not at all easy to read. However, the size of the patent document may also indicate invention complexity, making it more difficult for the IP valuation analyst to understand the nuance of the invention and compare the utility of the invention to market substitutes. Of course, short patents may be difficult to understand by the untrained professional, but at least under that circumstance, the job of understanding the IP is possibly somewhat easier because there is less text to comprehend.

To demonstrate the basic level of understanding a valuation analyst must possess for an IP valuation assignment, consider a random published patent selected for analysis—U.S. patent #6,358,254.[74] The patent is straightforward and relatively short, consisting of about 12 pages including diagrams and 26 claims. The patent describes several inventions related to spinal surgery and addresses spinal stenosis, which is a narrowing of the spinal canal. Acute symptoms include severe back and leg pain because the spinal canal narrows, putting pressure on the nerves in the spinal cord.

Conventional treatment for severe cases requires surgeons to perform a spinal laminectomy, consisting generally of the removal of portions of the spinal column, allowing the nerves additional "breathing room" within the spinal column. While effective, it also has substantial side effects, as the surgeon changes the structural integrity of the spine. The patented invention seeks to address shortcomings in the current surgical solutions by allowing the surgeon to relieve the pressure on nerves in the spinal cord, yet maintain the structural integrity of the vertebra. At the most basic level, instead of cutting and removing the vertebra, the surgeon cuts the vertebra and adds a stent to support the widened position of the vertebra, without ever removing portions of the vertebra. Exhibit 46 shows a picture of the invention the patent describes.

Anticipated benefits of such an invention include the preservation of muscle attachments to vertebra, less chance of spinal instability, less manipulation and scarring around spinal nerves, greater spinal decompression, a quick and safe operation, and a permanent solution requiring no revisions later for recurring spinal stenosis.[75] The

74 At of the time of this writing, the author had no prior knowledge of this patent or the inventions it describes, and never spoke with the inventors about the patent.

75 D. Greg Anderson, "Method and Implant for Expanding A Spinal Canal," U.S. Patent 6,358,254, September 11, 2000, p. 9.

Exhibit 46. Patent Invention

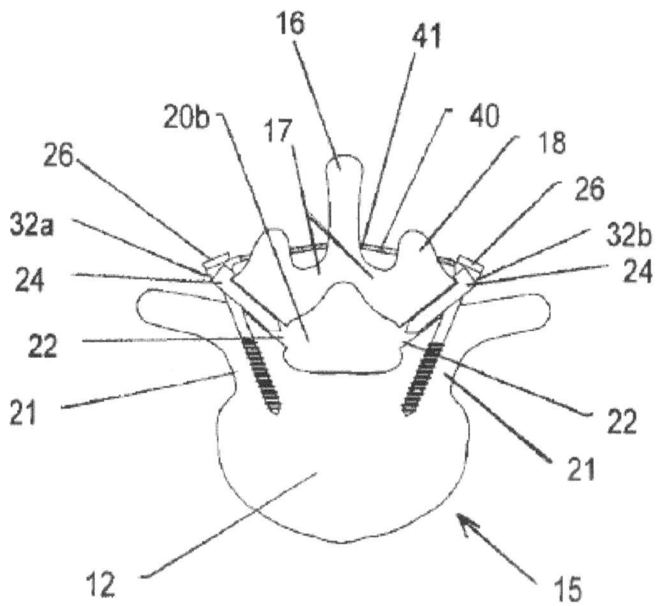

patent describes both a method for performing the new surgical procedure and the actual implants an orthopedic company would produce that a surgeon would install.

In this example, the valuation analyst must have a reasonable understanding of the science to understand the nature of the invention. Not only must the valuation analyst understand the cause and effect of spinal stenosis, but also the current methodologies for treatment to perform a meaningful comparative analysis against competitive product offerings. The valuation analyst must understand the mechanical function of the inventions and possible issues that may arise regarding both treatment efficacy (i.e., does it work?) and regulatory hurdles (i.e., can the manufacturer gain regulatory approval in an abbreviated filing under section 510(k), or must it perform a complete premarket application?). For some types of IP, this sort of analysis may be a tall order for the valuation analyst. Many practitioners may not possess the requisite knowledge to perform the assignment competently under appraisal standards. In such cases, it is important for the valuation analyst to be a quick study, and be able to generate credible results within the parameters of the assignment; otherwise, the valuation analyst must obtain competence with the assistance of an additional professional (e.g., an orthopedic surgeon).

Sustainable Competitive Advantages

For intellectual property to retain value, it is imperative that it maintain certain sustainable competitive advantages. These competitive advantages should be durable and difficult to duplicate in the market. If they were easily duplicable, market forces would erode any economic power of the IP and drive a lower value or no value as the IP owner competes on price in a commodity market as opposed to on value with monopolistic attributes afforded by the IP.

IP in general may have several intrinsic sustainable competitive advantages, such as explicit government protection under patent, copyright, or trademark law and portability (i.e., transferring IP rights is relatively easy to do, as opposed to moving a plant, property, or equipment). Depending on the IP type, it may have a long statutory life (e.g., copyrights) or a perpetual economic life (e.g., Coca-Cola brand).

In addition to intrinsic competitive advantages, the IP must demonstrate additional advantages not easily duplicated in the market. This varies by the nature of the IP under review. For example, one valuing a book for the author John Grisham is not going to see the same types of competitive advantages that accrue to a patented product. Unlike IP valuations that focus on the selling of a product that may generate some utility for a business or consumer, the competitive forces for Grisham's works are more complex; people who seek Grisham's books will buy his books. Purchasing books by John Steinbeck or William Faulkner will not suffice. This eradicates competition through substitute products, as there are no substitute products for Grisham's works if one wants to read his works. Contrast that example with a patented invention to improve the efficiency of the internal combustion engine (ICE). The auto industry spends billions of dollars annually to improve the efficiency of the ICE. Yet basic laws of thermodynamics have plagued the engine designers who for decades have sought to harness greater mechanical energy from conventional engine designs. The company that can patent an invention that meets or exceeds current engine performance requirements, yet achieves a greater power density, could reap tremendous economic rewards. However, the means for reaping those rewards is not prescriptive—the inventor might reap similar rewards with reduced moving parts and friction, new designs, more computerization, or more efficient heat conversion to kinetic energy.

In determining the sustainable competitive advantages, the valuation analyst may use any one of a variety of conventional published methods including SWOT analysis (evaluating Strengths, Weaknesses, Opportunities, and Threats), Michael Porter's five forces model, Martyn Jones' six forces model, and others. Ultimately, the IP valuation analyst needs to estimate the strengths of these competitive advantages and answer the following questions:

- Does the IP have a unique value proposition not easily replicated by substitute products in the market?
- Are there significant barriers to entry not related to the legal IP protections that will prevent a competitor from easily entering the market?
- Will the regulatory framework serve to provide additional value for the IP owner (e.g., if the IP owner has already passed FDA approval on a medical device, competitors must also)?
- Does the IP put the revenues of other companies already in the market at significant risk due to possible infringement?
- Does the company have deep financial resources to help ensure stamina in any protracted IP defense activity?

Functional Realization

Oftentimes a client asks an IP valuation analyst to consider an intellectual property that has yet to make a significant penetration into the market. It may be that a brand does not yet have any reverence or power in the eyes of the market. It may be that a patent owner has not yet proven the utility offered by an invention to an unbiased set of market participants, or that the public has no interest in a manuscript an author shopped to various publishers over several years. As such, it is entirely possible for one to own some IP that one could never monetize. This has a value impact, as it changes the risk associated with future cash flows related to the IP. Intellectual property that has generated economic activity is worth more than IP that has not. Instances of working intellectual property demonstrate that the IP owner has overcome possible scientific and technological or other hurdles and can prove that the IP has some utility beyond mere speculation. Intellectual property that one only supposes will have a favorable market response carries a higher risk profile than IP that describes something in the market that the market finds functionally and economically superior to market alternatives.

If the IP owner is already monetizing the IP in the market, the valuation analyst should have a higher confidence that the IP owner may continue to generate future monetary rewards. Thus, this fact pattern has a lower risk. However, if the IP owner has yet to prove the value proposition to the market (i.e., "proof" means that the market pays to gain access to the IP), then uncertainty is greater for the IP, as is the risk of ever-generating future cash flows. It is important for the valuation analyst to understand what stage of development an intellectual property is at, and how that may influence value.

Infringement Risks

As intellectual property typically represents legal rights to exclude others from the market, companies that can generate abnormal profits by exploiting their IP may find that competitors want to capture the IP owner's market share. Infringement risks will vary by IP, but all have some general features explored later in this chapter. Specifically, the IP valuation analyst is interested in the following:

- How easy is it to infringe on the IP? For patents, the infringement ease may rely on how easy it will be for a competitor to design around a patent's claims, or to break the patent with a declaratory judgment of invalidity, or through the patent reexamination process. For a brand, it may be as easy as labeling a counterfeit product as authentic and putting it for sale on eBay. The harder it is to infringe the IP, the higher the value for the IP.
- How easy is it to detect infringement? IP is worth more if detecting infringement of the IP is relatively easy.
- Can the IP owner survive a protracted IP litigation? IP rights are only good if the IP owner can survive asserting those IP rights financially.

Economic Life Analysis

An important value driver for any intellectual property is the economic life over which the owner can exploit it. The economic life has a direct relationship to value. IP with a longer economic life has a higher value than similar IP with a shorter economic life, all else the same. The economic life for the IP is usually going to be the minimum of the statutory life for the IP, or the IP's economic life in the market. The economic life of the IP cannot extend past statutory boundaries; there is no enforcement mechanism for an IP owner to restrict the use of the IP after the statutory protection expires. However, many intellectual properties have economic lives that are significantly shorter than those afforded in statute.

In considering the economic life of the IP, the valuation analyst should include several factors:

- Historical economic life of similar IP in the market;
- Statutory life of the IP; and
- Contractual terms that may extend the economic life of the IP beyond statutory boundaries.

When considering the historical utility of the IP, it is important to realize that IP is novel by definition. Thus, oftentimes, the valuation analyst will not have a reasonable proxy for the IP based on some historical reference point. Next, even though the IP may exist for some time, embodiments of it may only recently have made their way to the market. Thus, an IP valuation analyst may not find much economic life guidance from similar intellectual properties in the market.

The statutory life for IP varies by the IP type. Under 35 U.S.C. §154(a)(2), the statutory life for a patent is 20 years from the earliest effective filing date claimed by inventors.[76] Under 17 U.S.C. §302(a), the statutory life for a general copyright created on or after January 1, 1978 is the life of the author plus 70 years. For joint works, under 17 U.S.C. §302(b), the statutory life consists of the life of the last surviving author plus 70 years. For anonymous works, pseudonymous works, and works made for hire, under 17 U.S.C. §302(c), the statutory life endures for a term of 95 years from the date of first publication or 120 years from the year of creation, whichever expires first.[77] Trade secrets and trademarks have no statutory life. Trade secrets can persist as long as the information remains generally unknown and of value (e.g., a company may have a trade secret in the number of times it has replaced the weather stripping on its front entrance door, but that is of little general value to the company or its competitors). Trademarks can persist as long as the owner uses them continually.

Companies may engage in contracts that may extend the economic life for IP beyond statutory boundaries. Such contracts would typically involve patents, as trade secrets and trademarks have no statutory life, and a copyright's statutory life is long enough to make such contract negotiations moot. With a contractual term extension, an IP owner would require additional payment for use of the invention even after the patent expires. Companies may employ such a strategy when licensing a bundle of patents, whereby the licensee would pay a royalty until the last patent in the portfolio expires. Thus, the patent owner in effect would extend the economic life of the patents; however, the value to the IP owner would not relate directly to the patents, but instead to the contract requirement extending a royalty requirement beyond the statutory life. If the IP valuation assignment calls for valuing the

76 Patents issued prior to June 8, 1995, however, have a statutory life of 17 years after the issue date.

77 Under normal discounting provisions with risk-appropriate costs of capital (i.e., not the risk-free rate), later years will offer little or no material value contribution.

bundled portfolio, the distinction is unimportant. However, if the assignment calls for valuing the patent and the contract, the patent's value still ends on the patent expiration, because the patent owner has no actionable cause to defend the patent as soon as it expires. Any other value would relate to the economic life-extending contract clause.

The hard part is actually figuring out the economic life to use for the IP, and this depends on the IP type. Exhibit 47 represents a simplified framework to use when determining the economic life for an IP.

Exhibit 47. Framework to Determine Economic Life for an IP

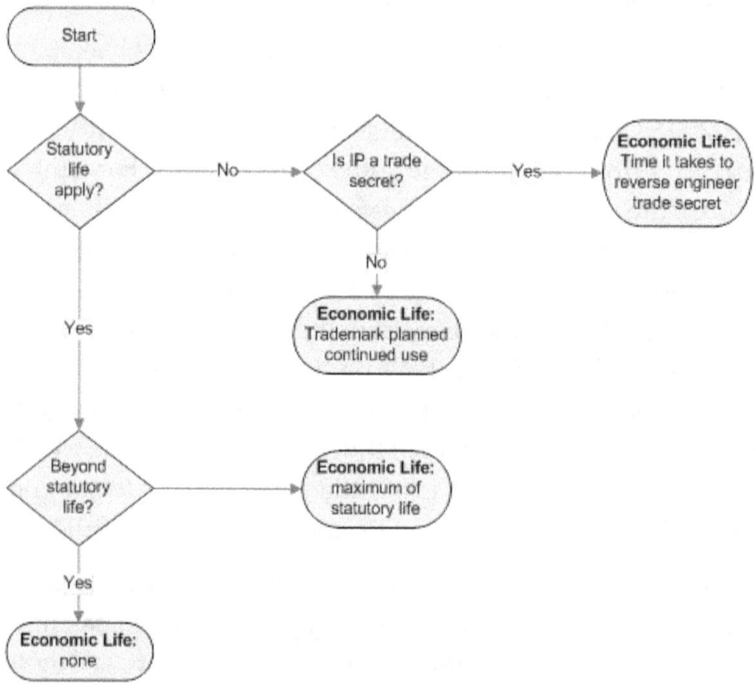

The first place to start an analysis is with the IP's statutory life, since IP protection ends with the statutory life of the IP (i.e., a patent owner cannot enforce an expired patent). If the IP is past its statutory life, the question of economic life is moot, as the IP accounts for no enforceable value proposition. The next question to ask is whether the IP can maintain utility and value up until the end of its statutory life, with the current IP owner. That answer also likely depends on the nature of the IP. If the IP supports a high-value product that has low marginal costs of production (e.g., a pharmaceutical patent), then the IP's economic life will likely extend until the statutory boundary. If not, then the economic life is likely shorter.

Estimating a Trademark's Economic Life

A brand's value does not decay over time. Oftentimes, brands get stronger the longer they exist because the public becomes more aware of the brand. For example, the Cisco brand had little power in 1984. Fifteen years later, for a short while, the market valued Cisco as the most valuable company in the world. Trademarks can also lose their value quickly, as examples in this guide have already demonstrated (e.g., Michael Vick, Wendy's, Taco Bell). These two facts make estimating the economic life for trademarks difficult, requiring the consideration of other factors. These factors include:

- *Trademark age:* New trademarks will likely command little value compared with older trademarks.
- *Market dynamics:* Trademarks will tend to have more value in highly competitive, fluid markets that comprise otherwise undifferentiated products.
- *Brand change history:* Evidence of brand updates and refreshes may give indication of brand value. If an IP owner notices fluctuations in branded product or service revenues that correlate with brand modifications, then those fluctuations may give indication of brand importance.
- *Risk:* While counterintuitive, aside from market premiums, trademark-associated impairment risk is likely the most important factor in a trademark valuation.

From a practical perspective, an IP valuation analyst may assume a perpetual economic life for a trademark or a shorter economic life if the trademark owner states that it will retire a brand in the near future. While such a statement may seem brash, the reality is that the economic life for a trademark is less important than the risk associated with it. Consider the following aspects of this example:

- Annual incremental economic income attributable to the trademark of $1,000,000;
- A brand economic life that can range between 0 and 50 years with a most likely life of 15 years (giving it a nominal life of 22 years);
- A discount rate of 30% that can vary with a sigma of 5% over a normal distribution; and
- A 0% annual market growth that can range between -2.5% and 2.5%.

The nominal present value for these conditions (treating the $1,000,000 as an annuity paid over the economic life of the brand) is $3,322,955. Simulating the uncertainty in the initial estimating assumptions for the brand life, discount rate, and growth 10,000 times, a regression analysis of the resulting values suggests that the risk is the most important value driver of the three. A regression analysis of the economic life and sales market multiple yielded the coefficients shown in Exhibit 48.

Exhibit 48. Regression Sensitivity for Present Value of Brand/B6

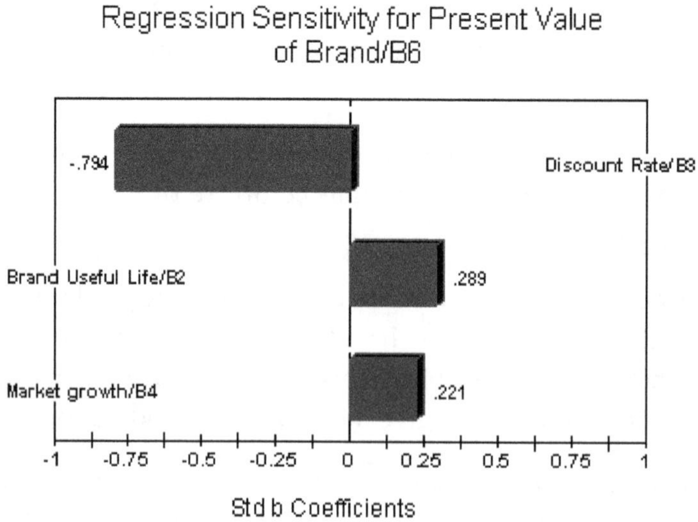

As the exhibit suggests, the discount rate and its associated uncertainty is more important than the economic life of the brand. In fact, it is almost three times more important than the brand economic life. The point is the IP valuation analyst should not worry too much if there is uncertainty surrounding the economic life of the trademarks. It is quite a bit less important than assessing the risk associated with the trademark's future cash properly. The valuation analyst should spend the time to assess IP risk properly and the result will likely have greater precision.

Estimating a Copyright's Economic Life

As a copyright typically will have a long statutory life, it mirrors the problems inherent in trademark economic life estimation. Fortunately, for the IP valuation analyst, given that a copyright's statutory life is so large for all but the smallest discount rates, the contribution on a present value from later years will be immaterial to the overall value. This makes the analysis somewhat easier. For example, for a 15-year annuity calculated with a 15% discount rate, the value contribution from the 15th year is only about 2% of the total value contribution, as Exhibit 49 demonstrates.

Exhibit 49. Copyright Economic Life				
Year	Cash Flow	Discount Rate	Present Value	% of Total Value Contribution
1	1.00	15%	0.87	15%
2	1.00	15%	0.76	13%
3	1.00	15%	0.66	11%
4	1.00	15%	0.57	10%
5	1.00	15%	0.50	9%
6	1.00	15%	0.43	7%
7	1.00	15%	0.38	6%
8	1.00	15%	0.33	6%
9	1.00	15%	0.28	5%
10	1.00	15%	0.25	4%
11	1.00	15%	0.21	4%
12	1.00	15%	0.19	3%
13	1.00	15%	0.16	3%
14	1.00	15%	0.14	2%
15	1.00	15%	0.12	2%
Total			5.85	100%

As with a trademark, the IP valuation analyst should consider both historic and prospective data surrounding the IP to determine an economic life for the copyright. However, the practical issues of risk assessment and the economic life considerations demonstrated with trademarks apply for copyrights as well. As such, the IP valuation analyst should spend significant time assessing the risk for future economic income attributable to the copyright and general market conditions, as these factors will have nearly three times the impact on value than the true economic life will.

Estimating a Trade Secret's Economic Life

Assuming economic utility for a trade secret (i.e., an IP owner makes money from it), the economic life for a trade secret to an IP owner is the amount of time it would take for a third party to reverse-engineer the trade secret without any assistance of knowledge (willing or via espionage) from the IP owner. Up to that point, the IP owner maintains value because the nature of the trade secret is private to the IP owner. Once a third party reverse-engineers the trade secret, the third party can exploit the IP in the market to the detriment of the original IP owner. While the original IP owner may still extract value from embodiments of the trade secret, any value no longer accrues to the trade secret, as the public now knows the content of the trade secret and can use it without recourse.

Estimating the economic life for a trade secret first relies on establishing the competition's impact on the economic life of the trade secret and the time it would take the competition to reverse-engineer the trade secret. The place to start this process is with the IP owner and any creators of the trade secret. The IP valuation analyst needs to understand how long it took the creators to originate the trade secret, and the trade secret's impact on overall product or service value. From there, the valuation analyst should be able to impute an economic life.

Consider an example regarding agricultural stock. SuperCow, a beef grower, has developed a genetic program over several decades to generate a pure line of beef that has a greater feed conversion ratio (i.e., total food input/total live weight of the animal) than the broader market. SuperCow can grow its cattle to mature weight for less feed cost and time, saving money and time (thereby increasing the number of processed heads for a given investment level). SuperCow spent millions to develop its genetic stock, and it took decades to create the current breeding lines it owns. SuperCow estimates that it would take at least ten years to initiate a genetic program that would even begin to rival its program; however, for a more mature program, it will likely take several decades (20+ years) to replicate. Part of this delay relates to the minimum timeline to build and perpetuate certain genetic characteristics across a line of cattle, which takes several years per cycle to complete. Next, the breeding process is one of trial and error; thus, a competitor would have to repeat this cycle over many years (as SuperCow has done) to achieve similar results. However, it would be possible to do so.

Assume that SuperCow has been working with genetics for the last 30 years and it did not experiment much with genetics before that. The competitor might be able to reproduce SuperCow's results and may be able to do it faster, given the availability of new technology. Discussions with SuperCow representatives indicate that this effort would take about 20 years in total, accounting for new technology. As such, the IP valuation analyst has a reasonable economic life of 20 years for SuperCow's trade secret-related intellectual properties. There would be no residual economic life for the trade secret, as any person skilled in the art who wanted to independently discover and develop SuperCow's trade secret could do so without penalty or threat, provided that person invested the time and resources to do so.

Survivor Curves and Mortality Models

Several authors consider using survivor curves (sometimes called an analytical method), which predict depreciation of an asset over time, as a means to predict the declining value of intellectual property over time. In one example, an author documented that the value of IP drawings might decay with the average age of the drawings and claims the method works well with IP documentation.[78] The theory behind survivor curves is to measure the mortality of the asset in question over time to gain a reasonable basis for understanding the asset's decay, and then apply that decay rate appropriately to the IP to determine the estimated remaining economic life for the IP. For example, insurance actuaries perform such analyses all the time for claims management. An insurance actuary will measure the remaining life for the population of policyholders it protects and adjust the actuary tables continually with new demographic data. With such data, the insurance actuary can predict with remarkable precision how long a given demographic will survive. Several theoretical forms represent survivor curves, including exponential distributions, Weibull distributions, and log-logistic distributions. The typical shape of a survivor curve is shown in Exhibit 50.

Exhibit 50. Sample Survivor Curves

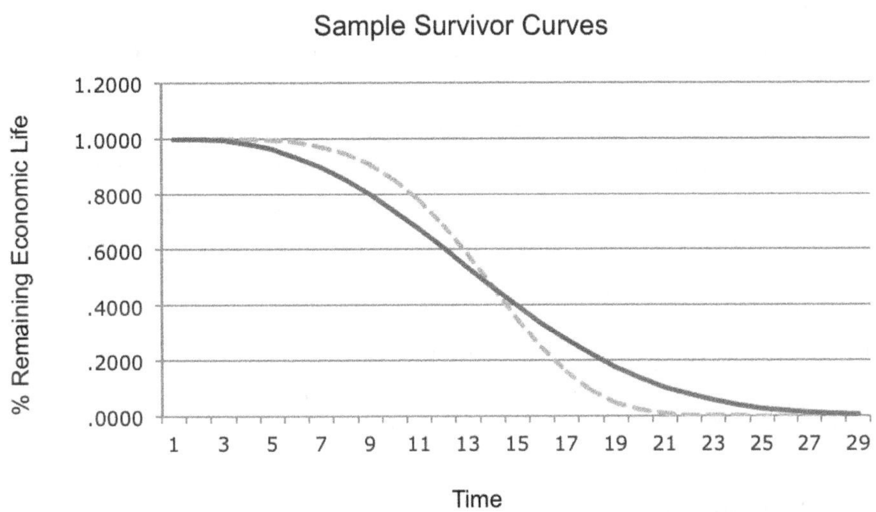

Applying survivor curves to IP valuation assignments is inappropriate for several reasons. First, IP is unique by definition, so average decay rates are not relevant proxies for a particular IP type. Suppose the Coca-Cola Co. (Coca-Cola) has many

78 Robert F. Reilly, "Intellectual Property Remaining Useful life Analysis for Bankruptcy Appraisals," *American Bankruptcy Institute Journal*, February 2005.

trade secrets that relate to marketing strategies and new products. Most have limited economic lives, as Coca-Cola changes its marketing strategies over time. However, Coca-Cola has never released its formula for its main product to the public. So the economic life for its marketing materials hardly serves as a representative proxy for all of Coca-Cola's trade secrets or its most important ones. Second, empiricists determined the shape of the typical survivor curves by taking samplings of tangible properties, such as railroad ties and telephone poles, and calculating their remaining economic lives. These tangible assets have little or no IP content and even less relevance as comparables for an IP project. An IP valuation analyst does not value a biomechanical patent using telephone poles or railroad ties as value proxies. Therefore, the concept of using a survivor curve based on telephone poles or railroad ties for an IP assignment is a poor theoretical model. Third, the survivor curves model the physical decay of assets. Physical decay has little to do with intellectual property, as already discussed in Chapter 4. Fourth, little academic research demonstrates that IP decays along any predictable means. Empirical examples in this guide have also demonstrated that value does not decay along some standard function. Eli Lilly's patent value went from $886 million to $0 with a court ruling and the tap of a gavel. Michael Vick's brand value erased within days of his indictment. Chi-Chi's went out of business quickly because of a hepatitis outbreak. It is a fundamental flaw in the theoretical model to assume that IP decays along any reasonably predictable mortality model. Fifth, courts have weighed in on the relevance of survivor curves. In *Campbell Soup Co. v. Tracy*, the valuation analyst used an Iowa curve to calculate obsolescence on a building, but failed to explain how survivor curves were relevant to the assignment of valuing a plant instead of the underlying assets in the original Iowa curve study.[79] The court disallowed the valuation analyst's testimony. While this case does not relate directly to IP, it does demonstrate that a valuation analyst needs to defend the relevance and use of such a model to have credibility.

In short, given the fundamental disconnect between mortality models and intellectual property, a valuation analyst should find little relevance in using them for IP projects as the theoretical basis for using such models is questionable.

Verifying IP Ownership

It is important for a valuation analyst to establish the ownership of the intellectual property under review, as any claims against the ownership interest by third parties may impair value. Verifying the title for assets such as real estate or automobiles is straightforward because a valuation analyst can perform a title search of the property

79 *Campbell Soup Co. v. Tracy*, 88 Ohio St.3d 473, 2000-Ohio-389.

using a variety of title search services. Further, these assets will have formal registration with government agencies. IP does not necessarily have such ownership transparency. Additional chapters explore the ownership issues specific to each IP type. However, in a general sense, the point behind the ownership question is that the IP valuation analyst must account for any factors that would tend to dilute value for the assignment. Such dilution may come in forms that lack reporting to some searchable, centralized agency, including:

- ***Title:*** Does the apparent IP owner even have title to the IP? If not, there is no value proposition to the apparent IP owner, as the owner does not own the IP. In certain cases, government databases may provide indication of the owner of record (e.g., the patent assignee database). For example, if a company owns a patent, but the USPTO does not list the company as the assignee, then under 35 U.S.C. §261 the company does not really have the ability to offer the IP in a transaction, as the company must be the assignee on record with the USPTO. Failure to be on record would void any subsequent transaction relating to the patent (a similar provision exists for trademarks under 15 U.S.C. §1060(a)(4)).
- ***Options and warrants:*** Options and warrants can have a dilutive effect on the value of IP, particularly when the IP owner must share the interest with a third party. Options and warrants may have an accretive effect on value if there are warrants or options to other IP that enables economic activity (e.g., an option to license a patent that may otherwise have blocking potential). The specifics of options or warrants are generally private to the IP owner.
- ***Reversionary rights:*** In the case of an IP licensee, does the licensee run the risk of losing the rights to use the IP in some case of nonperformance? (More on this shortly.)
- ***Royalty obligations:*** Oftentimes an IP owner may have to pay a royalty fee to another owner to avoid infringement of some prior art in the use of the owner's own IP. The royalty obligation lays an effective claim against any revenues that the IP generates.

IP owners will typically rely on various forms of documentation to support ownership claims, including inventors' notebooks, patent filings, assignment agreements, subcontractor agreements, employee agreements, buy/sell agreements, and others that may speak to the transfer or ownership of the IP. For some situations, especially related to shop rights and the employed-to-invent doctrine (more on these shortly), the IP valuation analyst may find it necessary to work with legal counsel to establish the ownership.

Commissioning Independent Counsel Review

Intellectual property deals with a set of legal rights that the valuation analyst must understand because legal interpretations may have a material value impact, as many of the examples in this guide demonstrate. However, an IP valuation analyst generally does not have a formal education in law. Thus, it is likely the valuation analyst will not be able to render what may amount to a legal opinion. For many IP valuation assignments, the issue of legal status of the IP is straightforward, presenting little uncertainty. For example, if a company has a license to reproduce and sell copies of an artist's painting, then no need exists for a complex legal analysis. However, if the nature of the assignment revolves around a complicated patented invention with many claims in a crowded space, it is important that the IP valuation analyst rely on the skills of qualified legal counsel as appropriate to understand the legal landscape. Some legal issues pertain to simple housekeeping, common across all IP types, which can affect value, which this chapter covers. Later chapters cover specific considerations that may influence different IP types.

Common housekeeping items include the following:

- Is there good recordkeeping for all inventions or discoveries?
- Are there any reversionary rights in IP-related contracts?
- Are all contracts executed?
- Are there good contractual administration procedures in place?
- Are rights assumed under shop rights or the employed-to-invent doctrine?
- Is it easy to design around the IP?
- Is it easy to detect infringement?

Recordkeeping

Establishing the date of the invention or discovery is important for helping to assign the priority of the discovery, especially in a contested situation, such as a patent interference hearing or litigation.[80] The quality of the inventor's recordkeeping can

80 Note that as of the time of this writing, the U.S. Congress has passed the America Invents Act, which moved the United States from a first-to-invent patent system to a first-to-file patent system, matching most of the rest of the world. Thus, the importance of the engineering notebook to establish priority is of lesser importance.

make or break a case. Practically, the issue of recordkeeping is more important with IP still in the trade secret or patent application stage, as issues of interference and establishing priority of who originated an idea first become important. The primary means that an inventor has to document a discovery is with an engineering notebook.

An engineering notebook is a bound notebook that inventors use to record ideas, inventions, trial and error process records, observations, and all work details necessary to explain the invention. While a complete overview of engineering notebooks is beyond the scope of this guide, it may be important for the IP valuation analyst to review the engineering notebook to ensure that it documents the invention process properly. Certain items a valuation analyst will look for regarding inventions include the following:[81]

- Complete and exact details of the invention and the date of conception;
- Details for how the inventor reduced the invention to practice (this may not be applicable for truly early-stage technologies covered by trade secrets);
- Details regarding the structure and operation of the invention; and
- The description and results of a process of experimentation regarding the invention.

As the engineering notebook may serve as evidence in litigation, it is important for the inventor to record all entries in ink. Further, the inventor must sign and date all original concepts, data, and observations and have a witness also sign the notebook, attesting to the claims by the original inventor. An engineering notebook filled out properly will lower the risk associated with defending the discovery of any invention. Thus, an IP valuation analyst who reviews or samples content from an engineering notebook and finds general conformance could reasonably attribute a lower risk to the invention. An IP valuation analyst reviewing an engineering notebook containing haphazard documentation of the invention may reasonably attribute a higher risk to the invention, as establishing the date of the discovery and invention would be in question. Of course, an IP valuation analyst may also attribute a higher risk to the invention with the lack of an engineering notebook altogether.

Practically speaking, the IP valuation analyst may not have access to the original inventors or their engineering notebooks for patent valuation assignments. Moreover, review of an engineering notebook becomes less important as a patent ages, as the

81 Engineering Notebook Guidelines, Bookfactory, October 2008.

probability for an interference hearing diminishes. However, proper documentation for trade secrets would remain important, despite the age of the invention, especially if few people know about it. For example, if an engineering notebook describes a chemical formula, and the inventor is no longer available to the company, the engineering notebook may be the only means the company has to reproduce the formula.

Reversionary Rights

An IP licensing contract typically would grant permission to a licensee to exploit the IP and pay the licensor a reasonable royalty rate. For example, a licensor executes an exclusive license agreement with a licensee, allowing the licensee to practice a patented invention in exchange for a royalty. For the duration of the license agreement, the licensor cannot license the rights to practice the invention to another licensee because of the exclusivity. However, a licensor would be remiss not to include a reversionary right, in case the licensee does not perform in accordance with the license agreement. A reversionary right is a return of the rights to the licensor by the licensee, typically for nonperformance by the licensee (i.e., the licensee promises to achieve a given royalty payment level and fails to do so). Reversionary rights are common in IP licensing contracts and are a common defense mechanism by a licensor to ensure that the licensor does not lock up a valuable asset in a nonperforming license agreement. Though the form of reversionary rights can vary depending on the creativity of the negotiation among the licensor and licensee, revisionary rights certainly can have a value impact.

Consider an example where a patent licensor has licensed an IP exclusively to a licensee. That licensee fails to perform, per the terms of the license agreement (e.g., the licensee fails to achieve an agreed sales volume). Under the reversionary rights clause in the licensing contract, the licensor would cancel the exclusive license with the licensee for nonperformance. Quantitatively, if the licensee were generating some value from the license, that value would disappear. Further, the licensor would have to find another licensee, which would take time, and that licensee may have to integrate and market the IP before paying royalties, consuming additional time. This of course has a value impact because of the future revenue timing shifts and the loss of any existing licensing revenues. Given the value implications of reversionary rights for IP licenses subject to a valuation assignment, the IP valuation analyst may need to account for the probability of reversion for nonperformance as part of the general IP due diligence.

Contract Execution

Intellectual property valuation assignments typically have a variety of agreements associated with them that a valuation analyst must consider. IP owners may have licensing contracts with licensees, may execute subcontracting agreements that contain work-for-hire provisions, and may maintain assignment agreements between the IP owner and employees hired to help develop the IP. In addition, IP owners may subject their employees to non-disclosure and non-competition agreements to help protect the confidentiality of the IP, and prevent employees from taking that knowledge to competitors. The absence of these contracts can have a serious negative value impact, such as the lack of all employees executing non-disclosure agreements impairing trade secret value.

Oftentimes, companies may not have the entire administrative house in order. Thus, the need to execute all relevant contracts relating to the IP, while obvious, does not occur sometimes in practice. Thus, it is important for the IP valuation analyst to verify the status of important contracts that can influence IP value. Failure to do so may lead the valuation analyst to render an improper value conclusion, especially if there is some point of contention regarding the contracts. For example, if an employee does not execute an assignment agreement with a company regarding a patented invention, the company cannot legally use the patent in a transaction without consent of the employee.

Contract Administration

Related to proper contract execution is proper administration for all IP-related contracts. IP contracts, particularly licensing contracts, typically require periodic maintenance to ensure that all parties to the agreement are fulfilling their respective responsibilities. This maintenance typically includes:

- Reporting of all IP-related revenues (for a book publisher, this may be the number of copies of books sold and the selling price per book);
- Remittance of periodic royalty payments, typically on a quarterly basis;
- Verifying that the licensee is using the IP in a manner specified within the contract (e.g., marking patent use conspicuously, using brands in accordance with marketing standards, etc.); and
- Noting whether the licensee is policing the market and notifying the licensor of possible infringement activities.

While none of these factors will likely solely destroy patent value, proper contract administration can reduce the associated risk that a licensee would underpay the licensor. Any risk reduction would have an inverse impact on value, thereby preventing otherwise possible value impairment. It is important for the IP valuation analyst to understand the nature of any contract administration procedures to ensure that adequate administrative procedures are in place. A company lacking proper contract administration procedures may put at risk future cash flows. This drives a lower value.

Shop Rights and the Employed-to-Invent Doctrine

Best practices dictate that a company has all employees and independent contractors who participate in the creation of IP execute agreements assigning all rights to the IP to the company. Further, best practices dictate that the employees and independent contractors also indicate via executed agreements cooperation in any further IP prosecution efforts. However, many companies do not follow best practices. Oftentimes an IP valuation analyst may come across a company that does not have all such agreements in place, particularly start-up companies. As ownership rights to the IP typically vest with the creator, this creates a possible encumbrance on the IP, possibly impairing value. In extreme cases, the IP creator could petition a court for an injunction limiting the company from using or selling any instances of the IP to third parties. At the very least, it may cause the valuation analyst to assess a higher risk for the IP, or include increased costs for legal defense. Both situations impair IP value.

Companies have some relief absent a formal assignment agreement with the IP creators, in the form of shop rights and in the employed-to-invent doctrine. Shop rights provide an employer with a limited right to use an invention, but shop rights would exist only when the employee used company resources (materials, supplies, time) to create the invention. The employed-to-invent doctrine stems from a U.S. Supreme Court decision from 1890,[82] which stated that employers might have an interest in the creative products of their employees. Various court cases have suggested that the following questions are relevant to a company receiving a favorable ruling regarding the employed-to-invent doctrine:

- Did the company hire the creator for the express purpose of creating the IP?
- Did the creator use the company's supplies to facilitate the creation of the IP?

82 *Solomons v. United States*, 137 US 342 (1890).

- Did the company pay the creator for the work performed?
- Did the company pay for the registrations for the IP (e.g. patent registration fees)?
- Did the IP contain any co-inventors that would indicate participation by the company?

Depending on the answers to these factual questions, the company may retain ownership of the IP; however, qualified legal counsel is best equipped to make any such determination. It may be necessary for the IP valuation analyst to discuss this issue with the company's legal counsel to assess the risk, if any, of the company not being able to exploit the IP due to possible ownership conflicts.

Design-Around Risks

A key driver for the value of intellectual property is whether a third party can design around the key protections for the IP, while retaining the benefits of the IP (e.g., a patented invention), and if so, at what cost. This applies primarily to patents. For example, patents where claims are hard to circumvent are generally more valuable than patents where it is easy for a third party to design around the patents' claims. However, copyright law does not allow for easy circumvention of the IP via design-around strategies, as is more common in patent law. In accordance with 17 U.S.C. §106(2), the owner of the copyright has the exclusive right to authorize one "to prepare derivative works based upon the copyrighted works." Thus, any party that makes unauthorized extensions of an author's works may collide with the original copyrights. Trademark law does not allow for easy circumvention either. Trademark owners can pursue companies that create or use marks confusingly similar to theirs, making design-around unsustainable. There is no design-around risk for trade secrets. A trade secret owner has no monopolistic protection. Thus, a trade secret owner has no enforcement mechanism to protect a design. A valuation analyst must consider possible value impairment if it is easy for a third party to circumvent the IP.

To aid in the discussion and analysis of design-around risk, the recurring example in this section will use a patent co-invented by the author. The patent of interest is U.S. patent #6,907,445. It describes a software program that abstracts communication to several classes of onboard vehicle networks (primarily based on J1708 and J1939 protocols), making it easier for a software programmer who writes embedded vehicle software and off-board diagnostic tools (e.g., service tools, testing fixtures) to interact in a consistent way with components sitting on the networks. Examples of components that sit on those networks include engine and transmission controllers. Think of the invention described by the patent like a universal translator. You ask the software a question such as, "how fast is the engine spinning?" and it will figure out the way to ask the engine controller using either J1708 or J1939 protocols, relieving the software programmer of having to know details about each vehicle protocol. Primary companies interested in this technology may be those that manufacture vehicles or accessories that utilize J1708 and J1939 protocols, which includes less than 10 OEM truck manufacturers and several Tier 1 and Tier 2 suppliers to those OEMs.

Several factors go into a design-around risk assessment. First and perhaps most obvious: does the market care about the IP, making a design-around effort worthy to pursue? If not, then a competitor would not even bother to practice the invention, because the market would find little value in a copy of the invention for sale. In the case of the subject patent, the details of this operation are of no consequence to the vehicle operator. The vehicle operator merely wants to look down at the tachometer and see the engine's speed—he or she really does not care which vehicle network the display uses to get such information. For that matter, the average vehicle operator may not even be aware of the presence of a computer network in the vehicle, let alone the existence of a J1708 or J1939 protocol.

If the market does not care about the patented invention, the IP valuation analyst would need to gain a reasonable understanding of the probability of a competitor wanting to design around the patent. In the case of the subject patent, using the claimed invention will likely provide little direct benefit to any competitor. The competitor would not only have to author the abstraction layer, which would take engineering time, it also would have to author the appropriate software to communicate with the vehicle computers. Any value from the claimed invention would accrue to the software development teams at competitors that would potentially be able to author software more quickly and bring the product to market more quickly, at less cost. However, for such a circumstance to occur, the competitor would need to believe in a tangible benefit of using the exact specification of the invention in its own implementation. Given the limited situations where it would be beneficial to use an abstraction layer to communicate with vehicle networks in a consistent manner, such a situation is not likely.

Suppose designing around an IP, like a patented invention, has a value. The next step for the IP valuation analyst is to understand how easy it would be to do. The analyst will base this understanding on his or her own comprehension of the IP, on discussions with people who have special knowledge of the IP (e.g., an IP owner's technical staff), and on discussions with legal counsel. If a patent's claims describe an invention in a manner making it easy to avoid both literal infringement and infringement under the doctrine of equivalents (more on this in Chapter 6), then the patent would have little value, as a competitor could replicate the invention's utility without infringing on the original invention. In the case of the subject patent, the claims are sufficiently narrow to make design-around relatively easy to perform. For example, claim 5 of the patent describes a translation system that describes the calling of a remote device (e.g., an engine computer) through a software object representing a network interface. This is relatively easy to avoid programmatically, as one can use a software object model that does not use a software object to represent a network interface.

Lastly, intellectual property possesses an even higher-level risk that those already discussed—the threat of a competitor using less functional alternatives if they cannot use the IP under license. If the licensee deems the costs and hassles of licensing the IP to be excessive for the value the licensee receives, the licensee will cease to pursue an IP license and will instead pursue other options, albeit with inherent drawbacks and/or disadvantages as compared to licensed IP. Practically, companies make these types of managerial decisions whenever enforcement actions initiate. Such a situation impairs value for the IP owner because, with aggressive enforcement, the IP owner may lose any possibility for economic activity altogether, as licensees that switch to alternative technologies would no longer create an actionable cause, nor would the licensee have any reason to pay the IP owner. If the IP is weak and offers little product value in the market, the risk of this occurring could be high.

Infringement Detection

A key driver for the value of intellectual property is the ability to detect infringement. Fundamentally, IP is a legal right that requires enforcement by the IP owner, and the IP owner must be able to police the market to detect instances where people use the IP without authorization or payment. IP where it is easy to detect infringement is more valuable than IP where it is not easy to detect infringement. This is because it may be less costly to detect infringement and it may be easier to prove under dispute with the infringing party. IP where it is difficult to detect infringement is worth less because there may be excess costs associated with infringement discovery and defense in disputes. For example, it is easy for Nike to detect infringement, sue a shirt company that makes knockoffs of their best-selling golf shirts, and win. It is much more difficult for Qualcomm to reverse-engineer the software code in a competitor's cellular device to detect infringement of Qualcomm's software-related patents. Despite its importance, IP valuation analysts often overlook infringement in IP valuation assignments, and little in current literature speaks to the value implications of infringement detection.

Infringement detection varies with the different forms of intellectual property. For patented inventions, it may be as simple as purchasing a copy of the suspected infringing product and performing a competitive tear-down analysis to see if the product uses an embodiment of the invention (e.g., buying a truck and taking it apart to see if it infringes on a patent for a fuel tank mount). For software programs, infringement detection ranges from difficult to easy. For Internet-based software programs, infringement detection is easy because the nature of the technology lends itself well to detection of possible infringement with minimal effort. The nature of HTML documents is that the downloaded content of many implementations includes all of the relevant source code to practice an invention. This provides much of the requisite visibility to reverse-engineer how a web page implements a possible invention. However, infringement detection of a patented invention in compiled object code would be much more difficult and may have to rely on induction instead of direct evidence of infringement.

Infringement detection is different for copyrights. Consider the case of a portfolio of published books, short stories, and plays, all protected under copyright law. First, one could merely make copies of the books and independently sell unauthorized copies. The ability to detect such infringement activity, particularly in foreign territories, is difficult; however, if there were sufficient volume to make infringing activity economically worthwhile, the chances of detecting infringement increases dramatically. Next, one could create derivative works and sell those works without authorization. Again, the ability to detect such infringement activity is difficult, regardless of the country of origin, until of sufficient commercial quantity that it would increase the probability of infringement detection. Finally, one could plagiarize the original book. Detection of plagiarism is difficult, though if an author were to maintain a unique writing style, those skilled in the identification of literary works should be able to detect such plagiarism without undue effort, particularly if the infringing work were to reach mainstream appeal. For example, guitarist Joe Satriani sued the British band Coldplay for plagiarizing Satriani's song "If I Could Fly" with their hit "Viva La Vida." Significant airtime afforded to Coldplay's tune made it easier for Satriani to detect the potential infringement.

When considering the value impacts of infringement detection and enforcement, the IP valuation analyst has to include the weight and contribution of the various items that are generating economic activity. For example, if books comprise the majority of the revenues that generate economic activity for an IP portfolio, then infringement detection is easier for these assets and enforcement for these assets is easier as well. This would indicate a lesser chance of infringement impairing the primary economic-generating capability of the IP. However, other items in the IP portfolio, such as the rights to short stories and plays, might generate random royalties of nominal amounts. Enforcement of such infringement would be difficult and costly, with some infringement costs exceeding actual licensing royalties paid. Thus, the IP owner needs to exercise balance, and it is important for the IP valuation analyst to understand both the balance and the impact of infringement detection.

Another important factor in infringement detection is jurisdictions where infringement may occur. If an IP owner generates all revenue in the United States, detection infringement may be relatively straightforward. The IP owner would likely have ready access to the infringing products, and could initiate court action to enforce its intellectual property with relative ease. Contrast that with an IP owner who generates a substantial amount of revenue from a global IP exploitation strategy occurring in many countries and spanning many languages. Detection in foreign jurisdictions is much more difficult to perform, as the infringing products may require translation (e.g., infringement of a book written in English by a copy translated to German). Detection may require actual travel to the country where the infringing activity occurs, and enforcement may require prosecution in foreign courts, which can be costly. Additionally, the IP owner must deal with any overriding potential geopolitical problems as well. For all of these reasons, infringement detection for IP in a foreign jurisdiction may carry with it more difficulty and higher risk.

The IP valuation analyst would account for the ease or difficulty in infringement detection by modifying the rate used to discount future free cash flows. IP where it is easy to detect infringement would command a lower discount rate. IP where it is difficult to detect infringement would command a higher discount rate.

Reviewing Enforcement History and Ability

It is one thing to own intellectual property, which, depending on the IP type, one can sometimes acquire for a relatively low cost. It is another thing altogether to be able to defend it in the market. A key driver for the value of IP is the propensity or willingness of the IP owner to defend it in the market against attack. For example, if a company owns a patent, but it does not pursue infringers aggressively, then the patent may be worth less because infringers would have no reason to pay royalties or cease and desist from infringing on the patent. An IP valuation analyst must calculate possible value impairment if a company demonstrates a tendency not to defend its IP in the market.

IP enforcement has a positive relationship with value. Those who defend their IP in the market will generate a higher IP value than those who are lax in IP defense. Any enforcement activity, from sending out threatening cease and desist letters to potential infringers, to full-scale initiation of legal action against an infringer, has bearing on IP value. When evaluating an IP owner's ability to defend the IP, the IP valuation analyst should be able to answer the following questions:

- Does the IP owner have an enforcement history?
- Does the IP provide enough economic incentive to infringe, despite the risk of liability?
- Does the IP owner have the resources to handle the cost of a potentially expensive litigation?
- Does the IP owner have the will to defend the IP in the market?
- Are there any willful lapses in enforcement?
- Who are the potential infringers?

Enforcement History

A clear indication of an IP owner's willingness to defend its IP is its prior history in, and degrees of, doing so. An early-stage start-up company will not generally have an enforcement history given the firm's age. A large Fortune 500 company will generally have a very strong IP enforcement history. An IP valuation analyst will be interested in knowing all details about any prior enforcement activity, including the nature of the enforcement activity (e.g., was the IP owner sending out threatening letters or filing lawsuits?) and any outcomes. For example, Monsanto has a very aggressive history of enforcing its family of patented Roundup Ready seeds. Despite how easy it is for a farmer to reuse Monsanto's seeds across growing seasons, he or she must sign an agreement stipulating to not reuse seeds and submit to inspections by Monsanto personnel. Monsanto has gone as far as initiating patent infringement suits against farmers who reuse seeds across multiple growing seasons. Monsanto also went so far as to sue and prevail against farmers who had unknowingly grown varieties of its patented products in Canada.[83] For this reason, Monsanto has been able to protect the economic income associated with its patented seeds very well.

83 *Monsanto Canada Inc. v. Schmeiser*, 1 SCR 902, 204 SCC 34 (2004).

An enforcement history, or lack thereof, may be reason for the IP valuation analyst to consider possible value impairment in the form of a higher risk assessment or a lower overall target market penetration. Thus, it is important not only for the IP valuation analyst to understand the IP owner's enforcement history, but also to understand whether that enforcement history helps preserve IP value.

Economic Incentive

An IP owner must consider a balance when enforcing its rights. On one hand, the IP owner wants to demonstrate a strong enforcement history, so that means the IP owner chases every possible lead of infringement and asserts his or her rights. Practically, this can be very costly. Consider the example of a book publisher that will own the copyright or have a right to reproduce the copyrighted work of an author. The book publisher theoretically should pursue every instance of non-fair use infringement. That means that every time someone makes a copy at a photocopy machine in a non-fair use instance, the book publisher should be initiating enforcement action, including sending out cease and desist letters and/or initiating legal actions. Operationally enforcing such a policy would be an enormous endeavor. It is so easy to reproduce the book that it would be impossible for the publisher to monitor all possible instances of infringement. Next, enforcing IP ownership rights can create a public relations nightmare. For example, the heavy metal band Metallica was very vocal in its opposition to online music sharing sites, particularly Napster, and faced a fan and public relations backlash. The public did not approve of the Recording Industry Association of America's prosecution of homemakers, college students, and dead people for copyright infringement with file sharing software such as Napster, Morpheus, or Grokster. Lastly, economically, some IP-rights enforcement strategies can be a disaster. Suppose it costs $250 to send a cease and desist letter, but the contribution margin to the publisher for a book's sale is $15. Economically, the publisher lost $235.[84] If repeating this strategy several thousand times, especially for small-time infringers and/or publishers, the publisher will be out of business quickly.[85]

On the other hand, the IP owner can pursue only those infringement actions that will have the strongest cases and generate the largest judgments or settlements. This removes the risk of incurring substantial economic losses chasing economically unprofitable enforcement activity. However, allowing some infringement to

84 This is assuming that the book publisher does not recover statutory damages, which, depending on the aggressiveness of the publisher and the ability of the infringer to pay, may make such an activity economically more rewarding.

85 This underscores a serious problem for the entertainment and publishing industries in enforcing copyrights for recorded movies and books.

go unchecked because it is economically impractical can create problems for the defense of more serious infringement actions (more on this shortly).

Costs of Litigation

IP litigation is remarkably expensive, consisting of obvious direct costs such as outside legal counsel costs, expert witness fees, and discovery expenses.[86] The American Intellectual Property Law Association (AIPLA) tracks the various costs for lawsuits pertaining to both copyright infringement and trade secret misappropriations. Through Association Research, Inc. (ARI), AIPLA produces an annual volume titled, "AIPLA Report of the Economic Survey" (the Survey), where it publishes its findings. The Survey organizes the data by litigation type (e.g., patent, copyright, trademark, trade secret), by litigation size (e.g., < $1M in damages, $1M-$25M in damages), by the type of law practice (e.g., 1-5 attorneys, 6-75 attorneys, 76 or more attorneys), and by the location of the firm (e.g., New York City CMSA, Chicago CMSA, Central States, etc.).

For each category of data, the Survey provides the number of cases in the sample size, the mean legal costs, the first quartile (25%), the median (50%), and the third quartile (75%). The Survey also provides data to account for the size of the firm litigating the case. In fact, the size of the law firm has a material impact on the costs of pending litigation. Next, it is important to consider the stage of litigation. While trial statistics vary by jurisdiction, only a few IP cases ever get to trial. Thus, an IP owner may at least incur expenses up until the completion of discovery.

Suppose there is a case centered on an IP infringement and approximate damages may be about $5 million. Within the $1 million to $25 million damages bracket for firms with 76 or more attorneys, the median cost for litigation to the end of the discovery phase in a copyright infringement suit is $500,000. Within the $1 million to $25 million damages bracket for firms with 76 or more attorneys, the median cost for litigation to the end of the discovery phase in a trade secret misappropriation suit is $750,000. Naturally, to go to trial, costs increase. Within the $1 million to $25 million damages bracket for firms with 76 or more attorneys, the median cost for litigation to the end of a trial in a copyright infringement suit is $1,000,000. Within the $1 million to $25 million damages bracket for firms with 76 or more attorneys, the median cost for litigation to the end of a trial in a trade secret misappropriation suit is $1,200,000. Even for mature companies, such costs can seem daunting. Thus, it is important for the IP valuation analyst to understand if a company can fully

86 "Patent Litigation: Is it Worth the Expense?," *Genetic Engineering & Biotechnology News*, Mary Ann Liebert, Inc., Volume 26, No. 7, April 1, 2006.

capitalize any enforcement activity. Companies that have a strong balance sheet will have the resources to defend their IP.

If a company does not have the resources to fund a protracted IP litigation directly, it could use third party investors or contingent-fee patent litigation law firms to help defray the direct costs of litigation. With a third party investor, the investor provides the capital to pay a law firm to litigate the IP case. The IP owner splits any proceeds from the case with the investor. With a contingent-fee law firm, the firm itself puts forth the capital to fund the litigation, taking its fees from any eventual proceeds. While contingent-fee service providers can cost more as a percentage of any eventual total proceeds, the defense costs would be nonexistent to the IP owner unless the IP owner wins a case at trial, or settles. In such a situation, the IP owner would then pay legal fees from the balance of the judgment or settlement it receives. If a company employs such strategies, it provides a reasonable basis for the IP valuation analyst to believe that the IP owner has sufficient resources available to enforce its IP in the market.

Enforcement Lapses

An inconsistent enforcement history riddled with lapses in enforcement can create problems when an IP owner truly means to prevent unauthorized IP use in the market. For example, if an IP owner guards trade secrets with non-disclosure agreements, but does not enforce its non-disclosure agreements uniformly across all employees, a court may find that the IP owner was not serious about protecting its trade secrets. Thus, if the IP owner does not enforce the terms of a non-disclosure agreement against a first employee, but does enforce the terms against a second employee, the IP owner may have diminished the ability to enforce the terms of its non-disclosure agreement with the second employee.

Potential Infringers

The kinds of potential infringers can have an impact on the probability of the IP owner prevailing in an enforcement action. The calculus is paradoxical. It should be easier for an IP owner to defend the intellectual property against a smaller infringer; however, a smaller infringer will likely have limited resources for a judgment or settlement. On the other hand, it will be more difficult for an IP owner to defend the intellectual property against a larger infringer; however, a larger infringer will likely have deeper pockets for a judgment or settlement. While a case should stand on the merits, litigating the case may take more resources than an IP owner has, thereby making an enforcement action difficult against a larger infringer.

Next, it is important to know the representative population of potential infringers. If enforcement action requires suing a large number of potential infringers (e.g., people who illegally download music files) that will take substantial resources to identify, the IP owner will have an increased risk of value impairment because of the enforcement costs. However, if the enforcement requires action against a limited set of competitors that are identifiable with relative ease, then the prospects for initiating action are more favorable to the IP owner.

Performing Market Analysis

Several important facts must emerge from a market analysis for the intellectual property. First, what is the state of the current relevant industry? How big is it? Is it growing or shrinking, and by how much? Second, what is the status of the current competitive environment? How large are competitors? What market power do they possess? Third, how does the product stack up against competing products? (Chapter 6 presents more on this, regarding patent utility.) How much market share will the IP capture in the market? How quickly will the market reasonably adopt the technology? All of these are factors that can drive IP value. The next sections explore several of these factors.

Market Adoption

Market adoption can be difficult to model, depending on the type of intellectual property. In general, it is easier to capture for products that offer some form of utility, such as patented technologies, over something more discretionary, such as a book. The rate of market adoption has an important value impact. Products that achieve quick and rapid market adoptions are more valuable than products that have slower market adoptions.

Exhibit 51. Five-Year Market Adoption Rate

	Year 1	Year 2	Year 3	Year 4	Year 5
Market free cash flow	100,000,000	100,000,000	100,000,000	100,000,000	100,000,000
Ending market share of net free cash flow	5,000,000	5,000,000	5,000,000	5,000,000	5,000,000
Market adoption	20%	40%	60%	80%	100%
Realized market share of net free cash flow	1,000,000	2,000,000	3,000,000	4,000,000	5,000,000
Present value of net free cash flow	**6,892,800**				

Exhibit 52. Four-Year Market Adoption					
	Year 1	Year 2	Year 3	Year 4	Year 5
Market free cash flow	100,000,000	100,000,000	100,000,000	100,000,000	100,000,000
Ending market share of net free cash flow	5,000,000	5,000,000	5,000,000	5,000,000	5,000,000
Market adoption	33%	50%	75%	100%	100%
Realized market share of net free cash flow	1,666,667	2,500,000	3,750,000	5,000,000	5,000,000
Present value of net free cash flow	8,539,733				

For example, suppose a company launches a product in the market and it anticipates achieving 5% market share of a $100 million free cash flow-generating market by the end of Year 5, in a linear growth model.[87] That means the company will achieve 20% of its ultimate free cash flow in Year 1, 40% in Year 2, and so on. The present value of the free cash flow is $6,892,800 using a 25% discount rate, as Exhibit 51 demonstrates.

However, suppose a company can achieve the same ultimate market share in four years instead of five, as Exhibit 52 demonstrates.

In that situation, the present value of the free cash flow is $8,539,733, or $1,646,933 higher, attributable to the faster market adoption rate. Thus, the market adoption rate has a material impact on the value of IP. The following IP-specific examples will help illuminate the issues.

Copyrighted Books

The market adoption rate for copyrighted works is important. Unlike IP valuations that focus on the selling of a product, which may generate some utility for a business or consumer, the competitive forces for a book author's works are more complex. First, people who seek to read J.K. Rowling's Harry Potter series of books will buy her books. Purchasing books from John Steinbeck or William Faulkner will not suffice. This eradicates competition through substitute products, as there are no substitute products for Rowling's works if one wants to read her works. Second, books, particularly for pleasure reading, represent discretionary expenditures. This can have an impact on the rate of market adoption driving book purchases. Content aside, in good economic times, a reader may decide to purchase the book. However, in tough economic times, the reader may instead check out the book from the local library, thereby avoiding the purchase cost of the book. Third, books compete with new

87 That is, the market will generate $100 million in free cash flow, of which the subject company would capture 5% of that, or $5 million.

authors and new media forms constantly. Furthermore, for a well-published author like Rowling, each new publication competes with her older novels as well. Fourth, revenue erosion is possible through new forums for selling copies of Rowling's works on the secondary market (e.g., Amazon.com marketplace), which is a marketplace that did not exist in broad form only a few years ago. This can put downward pressure on the volume of books that publishers sell. In fact, Standard & Poor's notes that used book sales have affected sales for college publishers,[88] though this applied to college textbooks more than to general consumption books like Rowling's. Fifth, new technologies either may serve to protect and possibly enhance the revenue-generating ability of the IP or may make it easier to pirate book copies. As book sales drop off, audio book sales fill in the gap. Online dissemination has increased risk of sales erosion, where readers share electronic or pirated copies of books.

Adding to the complexity equation for copyrighted items is the fact that many books lack a dedicated marketing program to drum up support. Thus, the IP valuation analyst must look to other publicity means to predict future market sales. For example, empirical analysis may suggest a book's revenue relates directly to the prevalence of the author's name in the press, through paid speeches, book reviews, exposure on a best seller list, political commentary, and other mediums. The IP valuation analyst could then perform a news search and perform a time series match against historical revenues to determine any link between revenues and media hits. If such a relationship could demonstrate explanatory power between revenues and media hits, the valuation analyst might then be able to extrapolate the findings into book revenues based on the historical interest in the author as represented by media hits.

Patented Technology

The market adoption rate for patented technology is arguably easier to model than for other IP types. First, the patent generally will represent something of utility, creating or replacing an existing solution in the market. Thus, since the patented invention carries with it functional benefits, more information is available regarding the technology and how the market may perceive the value of it. If a company comes out with a new engine technology that can reduce a vehicle's gasoline consumption by 30%, the market movement toward that product and a market adoption will likely be quick. Contrast that with a book, which is subject to the tastes of the reading public at the time. An author could create the greatest story ever written for a genre; however, if consumer tastes differ, then the story could be a flop on the market.

88 Standard & Poor's Industry Surveys, Publishing Industry Survey, Standard & Poor's Corp., September 2007, p. 12.

Oftentimes, an IP valuation analyst will look both to empirical market analysis and to theoretical models to model the market adoption for a technology. While a valuation analyst has several adoption models to use, beginning with the Bass model in 1969, the examples in this section will use the Fisher-Pry adoption model. The Fisher-Pry model is particularly useful for estimating the adoption rates and diffusion for new technologies, particularly when new displaces old because the new technology is technically and economically superior, as is common under a patent valuation.[89]

The general shape of the Fisher-Pry model is as follows:

Exhibit 53. Fisher-Pry Model

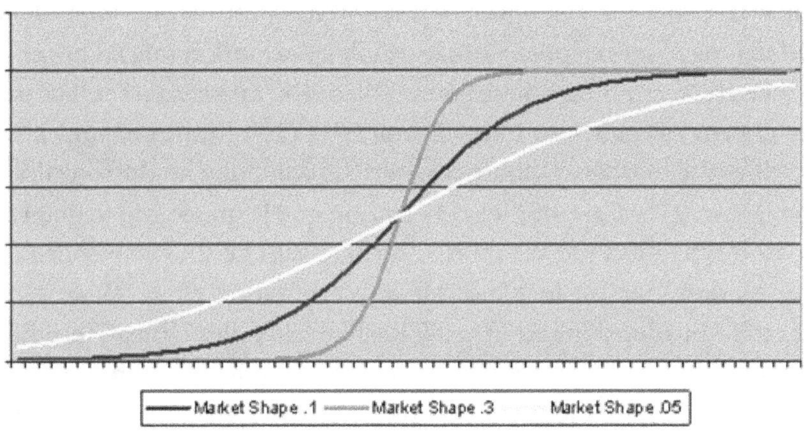

As the shapes of the adoption rates indicate, the general adoption level is a sigmoid curve (also known as an "S" curve, so named because of its shape). The adoption curve describes a slow initial market acceptance, indicated by the relatively flat areas of the left side of the curve. What follows next is a rapid adoption; the market adopts the technology at an increasing pace. This creates a sharper growth through the middle of the curve. Finally, the market adoption rate slows, as initial market momentum wears off and the market matures. This is where the adoption curve levels off on the right side.

Empirically, these models are remarkably predictive for true market adoption rates. Hundreds of technologies have followed a Fisher-Pry adoption rate. Examples of such new-for-old replacement technologies are as follows:[90]

89 IP valuation analysts have several different market adoption models to use for an IP valuation assignment. Key factors that may cause an IP valuation analyst to use one valuation model over others include the nature of the technology and its location in the market.

90 Lawrence K. Vanston and Ray L. Hodges, "Technology Forecasting for Telecommunications," Technology Futures, Inc., 2004.

- Steam power for sail power;
- Diesel engines for steam locomotives;
- Jet aircraft for piston aircraft;
- Turbojets for reciprocating engines;
- Airplanes for passenger trains;
- Plastics use versus metal use in cars; and
- Disk brake systems for drum brake systems.

Two major components drive the shape of the Fisher-Pry model. The first is a market shape, which controls the steepness or shallowness of the curve. Smaller market shapes lead to longer, more spread-out technology adoption rates. The second is the point at which the technology penetrates 50% of the target market. For example, if a company expects to generate unit sales of 50,000 by Month 60 and it expects to penetrate 50% of the market at Month 30, then the valuation analyst would use a 50% penetration factor of 30. This market penetration rate is important to determine how compressed or expanded the actual market rate will be. In the Fisher-Pry sample chart, lower market shape values indicate a more shallow market shape, representing a longer market adoption rate (e.g., VCRs, like the yellow line in the chart), while higher market shape values indicate a more steep market shape, representing a faster market adoption rate (e.g., MP3 players, like the magenta line in the chart).

Exhibit 54. VMWare Market Adoption Curve

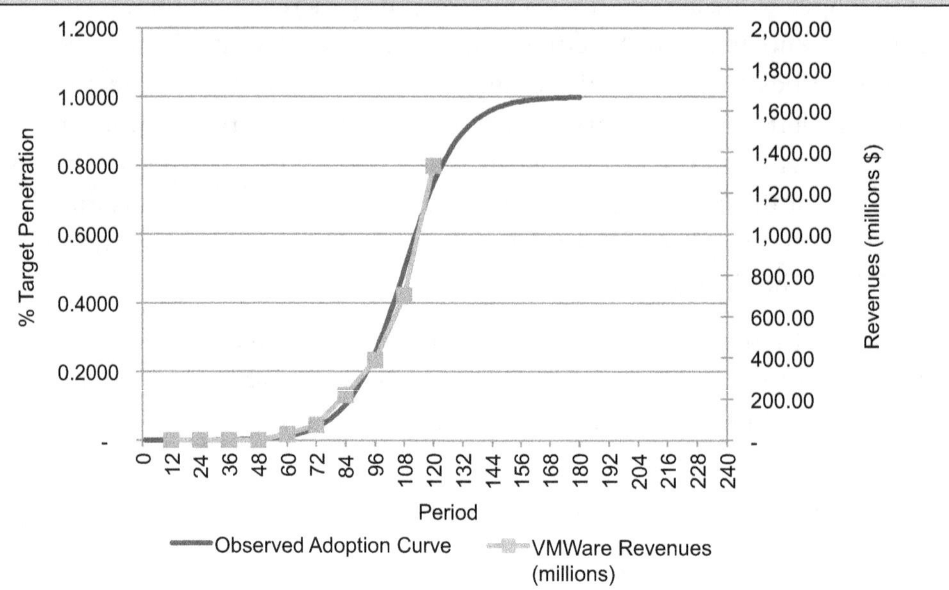

IP valuation analysts can generate a meaningful forecast of value using the Fisher-Pry model by calibrating it with empirical market adoption data if available. Without empirical data, IP valuation analysts instead look to proxy products in the market, using the shapes of those market adoption rates as proxies for the adoption rate of a technology under question. For example, consider a new, patented technology that will compete in the computer virtualization market (whereby a single server computer can run several instances of operating system server software, thus making system administration easier and reducing hardware costs). For this assignment, the valuation analyst uses VMware, a market leader, as a proxy product to estimate the adoption rates for the patented technology. An analysis of VMware's revenues since its inception yields a remarkably strong relationship for market adoption using a Fisher-Pry curve, as Exhibit 54 demonstrates.

Though VMware has existed since 1998, VMware's revenues, signified by the red diamonds in the chart, did not really start to take off until the 2002 timeframe (Months 48-60). The rate of market adoption of the VMware products accelerated by 2003, no doubt in part because of EMC, Inc.'s purchase of VMware. As the graph for VMware revenues demonstrates, the market has adopted VMware products along a curve with remarkable correlation to the Fisher-Pry theoretical model. As such, an IP valuation analyst may reasonably assume the adoption of new virtualization technology may follow a Fisher-Pry adoption curve and use that empirical adoption curve in modeling the revenue growth for the new, patented technology.

Exhibit 55. Actual Neulasta Revenue Curve

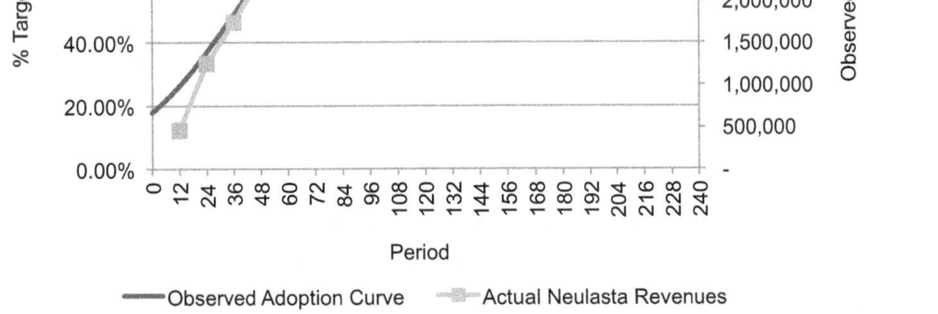

These trends apply only to software technologies, although many product adoptions follow similar trends. For example, Exhibit 55 captures the market adoption of the drug Neulasta.

Exhibit 56 captures the growth in cellular telephone subscribers in the U.S.

Exhibit 57 captures the growth in automatic transmissions in the U.S. market.

Exhibit 56. Observed Cell Subscriber Growth

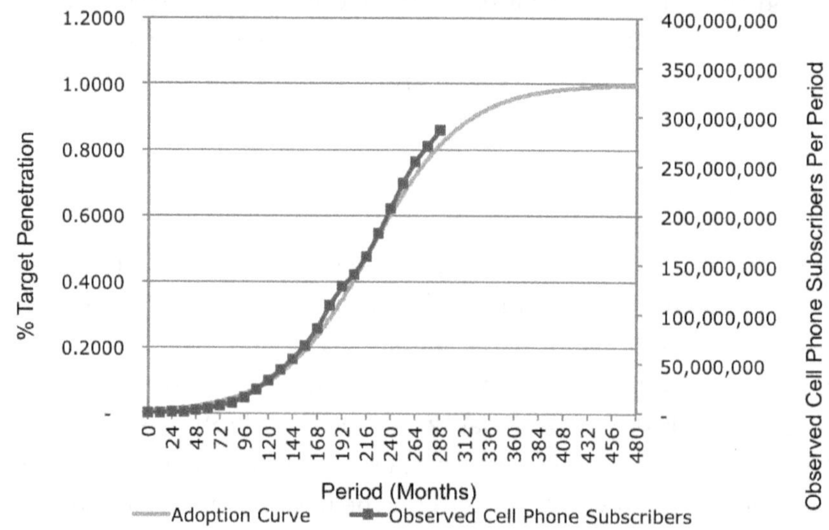

Exhibit 57. Automatic Transmission Market Adoption Curve

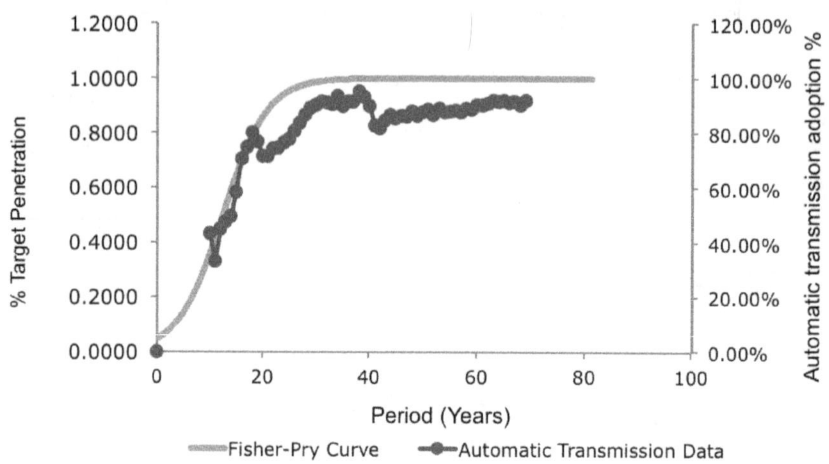

Thousands of products follow similar market adoption trends. The IP valuation analyst can use these trends to generate defensible revenue and market adoption forecasts in valuation models where significant uncertainty may otherwise exist.

Market Acceptance

Market acceptance drives intellectual property value. Market acceptance occurs when end users of the IP report feelings of satisfaction with the product and indicate a demand for additional products in the marketplace. Prior to that level of market acceptance, a willing buyer uses the relevant technology from another vendor if possible. The IP valuation analyst will be interested not only in direct sales, but also in any licensing or other negotiations that may ultimately provide indication of economic activity.

The impact is immediate—IP whose embodiment has generated economic activity (i.e., revenue) is worth more than IP whose embodiment has yet to generate any economic activity because the monetization risk is lower. Instances of economic activity demonstrate that the IP owner has overcome significant hurdles to prove utility in the IP's embodiment to a disinterested third party. One cannot deduce the same from IP that has yet to generate economic activity.

Other factors that may drive market acceptance include buyers' purchasing habits. Does the IP sell in a market where other attributes, such as brands or distribution channels, are important? Is there a long buying cycle (e.g., government contracts) or is there a short buying cycle? Each has a value impact, both in terms of risk and in terms of when the IP generates free cash flows. Next, is the buyer situation conducive to a transaction, or are there external factors that can destroy a deal, such as office politics, incumbent providers, or high switching costs? Each of these factors will create negative pressure on the market to accept and purchase embodiments of the IP, thereby impairing value. For example, a hospital incurs significant switching costs and technical risk to remove an incumbent electronic medical record system and replace it with another one, amounting to literally tens of millions of dollars. The switching cost and risk increases the value of being an incumbent electronic medical record vendor for a large number of hospitals. The IP valuation analyst needs to gain a clear understanding of these impacts, so that the valuation model can reflect them correctly.

One way an IP valuation analyst accounts for market acceptance in the IP valuation assignment is to model market acceptance explicitly in the shape of the market adoption curve or captured market share. Another way the IP valuation analyst accounts for market acceptance in the valuation assignment is by modifying the discount rate. If a given IP exhibits market acceptance, the IP valuation analyst may use a lower discount rate, but if the IP has not exhibited market acceptance, the analyst would likely use a higher discount rate. The difference in the discount rates varies depending on the IP's current development stage, regulatory approval requirements, and others. Typical discount rate variances between stages can be 10% or more. For example, venture capital markets consider product stage when selecting an appropriate discount rate. Exhibit 58 shows discount rates, by development stages, used by venture capitalists.[91]

Exhibit 58. Discount Rates by Development Stages

Development Stage	Discount Rate
Seed Financing	80%+
Start-Up	50%-70%
First Stage	40%-60%
Second Stage	30%-50%
Bridge Financing	20%-35%

As the exhibit demonstrates, IP that is already on the market in an expansion phase would warrant a discount in the 20%-35% range. Technology in a start-up or idea stage, without any proven market acceptance, would warrant a discount rate in the 50%-70% range, as it maintains a higher risk profile because the market has yet to demonstrate any utility in the IP at all when it finally reaches the market.

Evaluating the Regulatory Environment

Oftentimes, the regulatory environment can affect value of intellectual property. IP that serves heavily regulated industries may experience adverse value impacts, as regulation may defer future cash flows to some faraway point in the future. Alternatively, heavy regulation may enhance value, particularly if it creates barriers to entry that afford existing market participants quasi-monopolistic attributes.

The FDA's Center for Devices and Radiological Health (CDRH) is responsible for regulating firms that manufacture, repackage, re-label, and/or import medical devices sold in the United States. U.S. manufacturers must comply with the following requirements, as detailed on the FDA website and summarized here:[92]

91 William Sahlman and Daniel R. Scherlis, "A Method for Valuing High-Risk, Long-Term Investments," Harvard Business School Publishing, Boston, 1987.

92 Overview of Device Regulation, http://www.fda.gov/MedicalDevices/DeviceRegulationandGuidance/Overview/default.htm, accessed on July 5, 2011.

- *Establishment registration under 21 CFR §807:* Manufacturers of medical devices must electronically register their establishments with the FDA and pay an establishment registration fee, unless the FDA grants a waiver. Verification of registration information occurs annually between October 1 and December 31.

- *510(k) under 21 CFR §807 subpart E:* If a medical device requires the submission of a 510(k), a corporation cannot commercially distribute the device until the corporation receives a substantial equivalence letter from the FDA. Most Class I devices and some Class II devices are exempt from the 510(k) submission.

- *Premarket approval (PMA) under 21 CFR §814:* Products requiring PMAs are usually Class III high-risk devices or devices not found to be equivalent substantially. The PMA process is more involved than a 510(k) process and includes supporting the device's claims with clinical data.

- *Investigational device exemption (IDE) under 21 CFR §812:* To support a PMA application or a 510(k) submission to the FDA, a company performs a clinical study to collect safety and efficacy data relating to the medical device. Before a study can begin, the FDA and an Institutional Review Board (IRB) must approve clinical studies where the medical devices pose a risk of harm to the public. The IRB must approve non-significant risk devices before the study can begin.

- *Good manufacturing practices (GMP) under 21 CFR §820:* This medical device regulation includes requirements related to the methods, facilities, and controls used for designing, purchasing, manufacturing, packaging, labeling, storing, installing, and servicing. Manufacturing facilities undergo FDA inspections to assure compliance with the quality system requirements.

- *Labeling under 21 CFR §801:*[93] Labeling regulation includes labels on the device as well as descriptive and informational literature that accompanies the device.

- *Medical device reporting (MDR) under 21 CFR §803:* A company must report incidents to the FDA, where a device may have caused a serious injury or a death. Additionally, a company must also report to the FDA

93 http://www.fda.gov/MedicalDevices/DeviceRegulationandGuidance/Overview/default.htm, accessed on July 5, 2011.

certain medical device malfunctions. The MDR regulation is a mechanism for FDA and manufacturers to identify and monitor significant adverse events involving medical devices. The regulation's goals are to detect and correct problems in a timely manner.

IP valuation analysts may account for value impacts for products that fall within the FDA's jurisdiction using several different methods. Specifically, the valuation analyst can account for the timing and costs associated with the clinical trials process, and integrate those cost and timing constraints into the valuation model. Exhibit 59 captures timing and costs that one may expect to model for a drug development engagement:[94]

The valuation analyst would construct a model to account for the timing and costs associated with the regulatory approval process directly in the valuation model.

Exhibit 59. Timing and Costs for Drug Development

Development Phase	Minimum Duration	Maximum Duration	Minimum Cost	Maximum Cost
Clinical phase I average monthly duration	18	22	$1 million	$5 million
Clinical phase II average monthly duration	24	28	$3 million	$11 million
Clinical phase III average monthly duration	28	32	$10 million	$60 million
New drug application average monthly duration	16	20	$1 million	$3 million
Nominal starting revenue month	96	114	$15 million	$79 million

94 Boris Bogdan and Ralph Billiger, *Valuation in Life Sciences: A Practical Guide*, Second Edition, Springer-Verlag, Berlin 2008, p. 18.

Chapter 6
Patent Due Diligence

Patent valuation is hard, in part because patents are complex things. Some believe patent documents are the most complicated legal documents that exist.[95] Key problems with patent valuation include a lengthy and complex application process and technical, commercial, and legal uncertainties, both during that application process and with subsequent patent enforcement activity.[96] Further, as a patent represents a legal right, some may argue that the true value of a patent remains unknown until there is a legal challenge and a court decision regarding its value.[97] At that time, a full legal test of the patent's strength will result in either a court decision or a cash settlement for infringement.

Patent value depends on the party exploiting the patent. The value of a patent to Eli Lilly and Co. may be much higher (or lower) than it would be to Pfizer Inc., particularly if the patent offers complementary features or blocks value to a competitor. For example, a patent for a central nervous system (CNS) stimulant may be of low value to a startup company, which lacks the infrastructure and resources to exploit the patent to its full potential. This patent would command a lower value than if Lilly owned it, as Lilly already has a product that competes with CNS stimulants, Strattera, in the market and deep experience in marketing such therapies.

95 Andy Gibbs, "Application of Multiple Known Determinants to Evaluate Legal, Commercial and Technical Value of a Patent," Working paper, 2005, p. 2.

96 Robert Pitkethly, "The Valuation of Patents: A Review of Patent Valuation Methods With Consideration of Option Based Methods and the Potential for Further Research," Saïd Business School, University of Oxford, March 1997, p. 2.

97 Duncan Stewart, "Value Is Not So Patently Obvious; A Patent Is Worth What a Court Says It Is," *Financial Post Investing*, April 12, 2007.

Recall that the patent valuation analyst measures the future incremental economic income a patent owner can generate (by fully exploiting the invention described by the patent's claims) against other solutions in the market that lack patent protection. A patent may not be of value for a product that generates value from other sources, such as brand reverence, time to market, and others. Thus, an incremental analysis may yield little to no economic value indication—an outcome that the IP valuation analyst may expect, since a patent is not always valuable. What's more, a patent may not be of value to competitors, even if it has determinable economic benefits. For example, suppose that a software company developed a patented solution to streamline the manufacture of automobile engines, increasing plant yield and lowering costs of having to repair engines failing quality checks. Honda installs the technology in an engine manufacturing plant and saves $4 million per year. Yet this solution may be of limited value to other engine makers because internal politics among stakeholders at the other manufacturers prevents installation of the technology, despite its determinable economic benefits. As ludicrous as this scenario may seem, it happens.

In performing the due diligence in a patent valuation, the IP valuation analyst has to gain confidence that the patent is going to persist through various challenges that may arise. Challenges may occur as a matter of patent law or through other administrative or technical means (e.g., design circumvention) that the valuation analyst must understand and account for properly in the valuation conclusion. Several complications appear along the way. First, an IP valuation analyst generally does not have a formal education in law, so likely will not be able to render what may amount to a legal opinion regarding a patent's legal status. However, the valuation analyst has to evaluate the possibilities of challenges that may impair the patent's value, as has been shown to happen in several examples in this guide.

Second, the valuation analyst must maintain an understanding of changes in patent law and any possible valuation impacts over time. For example, will the U.S. Supreme Court's decision regarding injunctive relief in *eBay v. MercExchange, LLC* put downward pressure on patent valuations because the patent holder has a potentially higher bar to reach in order to satisfy the requirements for a permanent injunction? While the IP valuation analyst may not have the requisite training to opine as to the legal probability of this strategy, he or she must at least understand the implications of the decision on value, particularly if a monetization strategy includes using a threat of injunctive relief to assist with licensing negotiations. The loss of injunctive relief takes a big stick away from the patent owner; for instance, it is harder to compel a third party to pay a higher royalty rate without the injunctive threat.

As part of the patent-specific due diligence, the IP valuation analyst needs to gain an understanding of the impact of the following:

- What is the status of the invention?
- What is the status of the current art and industry on value?
- What is the patent's utility or value proposition?
- What is the patent quality?
- What is the patent age?
- Is the administrative house in order?
- What are the effects of any possible blocking patents?
- What is the status of any active legal actions?
- Are there any outstanding contractual provisions that may affect value?

The answers to these questions can mean the difference between a patent that has a strong value proposition and one that has no value proposition. Moreover, the IP valuation analyst must perform this analysis for each patent under review. Thus, the IP valuation analyst looking at a portfolio of patents should perform the same due diligence for each patent in the portfolio. While such a complete analysis can become expensive for the patent owner, it is the only way that an IP valuation analyst can reach a defensible conclusion as to the value of each patent. An exception to this rule may apply for patent continuations or patent clusters where entire value relates to a single product. In such cases, product sales that include embodiments of several patents under review would represent the value proposition of all of the patents collectively.

The Invention Status

Under 35 U.S.C. §112, the inventor must specify the patent such that it describes the invention and the manner and process of making it in full, clear, concise, and exact terms. The specification requires the inventor to disclose how to make and use the invention and to disclose the best mode contemplated. The inventor must explain these requirements in such a manner that any person of ordinary skill in the art would be able to reproduce the invention. That said, the USPTO does not require that an inventor or patent owner *prove* that the invention described by the patent actually works, that one can manufacture it, that the market will find utility in the invention, or even that the invention operates within the limits of science.[98] As such, it is entirely possible for one to own a patent on an invention that one could never make or market. Thus, manufacturability and marketability have value impacts that the patent due diligence would take into account. A patent whose embodiment works is worth more than a patent whose embodiment one only supposes will work. Instances of working intellectual property demonstrate that the inventor has overcome scientific and technological hurdles and can prove that there is some utility to the patent beyond mere speculation. A patent whose embodiment one only supposes will work carries a higher risk profile, of course, than a patent for a reduction to practice that is functionally and economically superior to market alternatives.

For example, suppose that an inventor develops a technology that would render a computer running the Microsoft Windows operating system impervious to program crashes, regardless of the source. However, the implementation of the invention requires modifying part of the low-level kernel within the Windows operating system. While the patent may appear to work on paper, it would be very difficult to implement and test, as Microsoft does not make its source code available to the public for general modifications. Thus, the inventor does not have any meaningful way to test the technology. Further, if the invention is specific to the Windows operating system, the inventor may have effectively limited any monetization strategy to a single potential prospective buyer or licensee, namely Microsoft. Such circumstances have a value impact; the risk associated with the technology working is greater here than where one has reduced an invention to practice and can prove that it works.

The status of an invention does not only relate to whether the technology can work by reducing it to practice, but also to whether one can exploit it profitably. Suppose that company NewCo developed an enzyme-based technology that converts cellulose biomass (e.g., switchgrass, corn stover) into ethanol. NewCo applies for, and receives, a patent. The science is solid and works in the lab environment. The technology appears promising, as the ethanol producer can use any generic, readily available cellulose-based feedstock instead of the corn used in traditional ethanol plants. However, there is a problem with execution and scalability. Current large-scale technologies require a cooking and fermenting process that takes twice as long as traditional corn-based ethanol plants. Thus, a nameplate ethanol plant that generates 50 million gallons per year will generate only 25 million gallons of ethanol per year using the cellulose-based feedstock. At the 25-million-gallon level

98 An example to consider in this regard is U.S. patent #3,626,605, "Method and Apparatus for Generating a Secondary Gravitational Force Field," which partially describes part of a warp drive for the Enterprise starship from the television series *Star Trek*.

and the current rack price for the fuel, the plant operator will not get enough of a contribution margin to cover the fixed costs of production and generate an economic profit. Thus, the plant is economically obsolete despite having a patent that covers the invention.

To solve this, suppose the company scales the plant large enough so that it can generate an economic profit, perhaps at 75 million gallons in capacity. Several problems arise with feedstock availability, in this case the switchgrass and corn stover (i.e., the stalks left over in a field after a corn harvest). First, in order for the plant to generate a steady supply of feedstock, travel over great distances will be required to acquire enough cellulose biomass to make the fuel. This travel consumes energy and impairs the economics of using a cheaper feedstock. Second, collection and shipment of the feedstock takes energy. Third, the farmer must replace the nutritional value of the corn stover or switchgrass in the field with chemicals or other supplements to maintain proper soil conditions for the next growing season, costing the farmer more money and more energy. Fourth, biomass such as switchgrass and corn stover is not as dense as corn, so one ships a lot of air-moving feedstock from the source to the plant, again sapping efficiency in the energy balance (unless one pelletizes the switchgrass, which requires further capital equipment and energy). Fifth, unlike corn, switchgrass and corn stover will decompose if not used readily, unless treated chemically, which increases costs. This type of analysis gets right to the heart of the value proposition for the patented technology. As the circumstances suggest, while the biologic cellulose-to-ethanol technology may appear promising, one may not practically generate economic profit from it, destroying any possible value proposition.

It is one thing to have a patent that may offer limited value to the owner. It is quite another to have a patent that provides utility that is functionally and economically superior to competing solutions on the market. This distinction is important enough that the IP valuation analyst should seek to discover exactly where in the spectrum the patent under review resides in order to account for the risk and value impacts appropriately.

Current Art

The state of the current art provides an important backdrop for an IP valuation analysis. A patent that serves in a crowded space (i.e., there are many patents in the field) may have a limited claims scope just to receive approval. Next, the patent may apply in an industry that does not traditionally depend on patents to create value. Academic research has explored this issue and found that industries, with the exception of the chemical and pharmaceutical industries, rely on mechanisms other than patents, such as secrecy or time to market, to exclude competitors from using a given product.[99] Lobbying efforts tend to reinforce this view, with technology companies such as Microsoft and IBM lobbying for shorter patent durations, while pharmaceutical companies lobby for longer patent durations.[100]

For example, consider Exhibit 60, which demonstrates the top 15 patent classes with the lowest amount of activity based on original patent classification between 1977 and 2006.[101]

Next, compare those results to Exhibit 61, which demonstrates the top 15 patent classes with the greatest amount of activity based on original patent classification between 1977 and 2006.[102]

As one may infer from the patent statistics data, the historical significance of patents in the industry is important. For example, Patent Class 79, Button Making, captures

Exhibit 60. Top 15 Patent Classes with Lowest Activity

Patent Class	Patent Description	Patent Count
276	Typesetting	1
199	Type Casting	2
258	Railway Mail Delivery	2
D00	** Design Classification Undetermined **	2
278	Land Vehicles: Animal Draft Appliances	5
79	Button Making	8
314	Electric Lamp and Discharge Devices: Consumable Electrodes	8
147	Coopering	9
163	Needle and Pin Making	15
231	Whips and Whip Apparatus	18
245	Wire Fabrics and Structure	26
1	** Classification Undetermined **	28
291	Track Sanders	32
234	Selective Cutting (e.g., Punching)	43
142	Wood Turning	59

99 Bhaven Sampat, "Determinants of Patent Quality: An Empirical Analysis," Columbia University, September 2005, p. 6.

100 James E. Malackowski and Jonathan A. Barney. "What Is Patent Quality? A Merchant Banc's Perspective," Colloquium on a Comprehensive Approach to Patent Quality, Fédération Internationale des Conseils en Propriété Industrielle, Amsterdam, June 8-9, 2007.

101 Patent Counts By Class By Year Report, United States Patent and Trademark Office, 2006.

102 Patent Counts By Class By Year Report, United States Patent and Trademark Office, 2006.

Exhibit 61. Top 15 Patent Classes with Greatest Activity		
Patent Class	Patent Description	Patent Count
514	Drug, Bio-Affecting and Body Treating Compositions	76,644
428	Stock Material or Miscellaneous Articles	56,336
438	Semiconductor Device Manufacturing: Process	55,027
435	Chemistry: Molecular Biology and Microbiology	49,599
257	Active Solid-State Devices (e.g., Transistors, Solid-State Diodes)	46,898
424	Drug, Bio-Affecting and Body Treating Compositions	41,910
73	Measuring and Testing	39,016
123	Internal-Combustion Engines	35,167
430	Radiation Imagery Chemistry: Process, Composition, or Product Thereof	34,369
439	Electrical Connectors	32,003
250	Radiant Energy	31,793
359	Optical: Systems and Elements	30,387
D06	Furnishings	29,231
370	Multiplex Communications	29,037
29	Metal Working	28,869

patents associated with the manufacture of buttons. The value contribution of a patent for button making is likely low, as button making is an industry not typically represented by patents, perhaps for many reasons. Buttons have been around for centuries and work well in their current form, requiring little further innovation. Further, because buttons have been around for a long time, statutory protection for the method of making a button would have long expired. Lastly, buttons are a relatively cheap, high-volume, low-margin, commodity product. Patent protections in this industry would have to create substantial manufacturing efficiencies in order to be valuable. This would be difficult as input costs drive a high degree of the cost in button manufacturing and are unavoidable regardless of the exact manufacturing method.

Patent count statistics for certain patent classes do change in response to new advancements in technology and industry practices. For example, in total, the statistics indicate that Patent Class 514, Drug, Bio-Affecting and Body Treating Compositions, had the most patents during that time, indicating both a crowded space and a perception of patent importance in that industry. This class covers pharmaceuticals, which is an industry dominated by large, complex patent cases. Economic evidence does suggest that patents in Class 514 can be quite valuable. For example, Eli Lilly registered its second patent in the Prozac case (#4,626,549) under Class 514; as

Exhibit 62. Top Five Patent Classes		
Patent Class	Patent Description	Patent Count
514	Drug, Bio-Affecting and Body Treating Compositions	89,707
438	Semiconductor Device Manufacturing: Process	75,177
257	Active Solid-State Devices (e.g., Transistors, Solid-State Diodes)	67,008
428	Stock Material or Miscellaneous Articles	64,032
435	Chemistry: Molecular Biology and Microbiology	61,157

explicated in Chapter 3, the economic impact of losing that protection was greater than $886 million. However, that class had the most patents issued between 1977 and 2010, as Exhibit 62 shows.

The data suggests that additional competitive pressure and importance in the Semiconductor Device Manufacturing: Process, Active Solid-State Devices, Multiplex Communications, and Telecommunications patent classes led to a change in significance over time.[103] The impact of current art may appear in the ultimate competitive market share that an embodiment of the invention achieves. A strong invention with a defined and distinguishable set of features will have a higher probability of market success. Inventions in a crowded space may have a higher probability of impairment due to blocking patents, possibly leading to wholesale market nonperformance.

Even within patent classes, the concentration of activity can vary. Exhibit 63 captures a listing of the top 25 companies that received patent grants within Patent Class 257 between January 1, 2006 and September 30, 2011.

As the data suggests, there is remarkable concentration of patent ownership within patent class 257. Further, several key players dominate the space, namely Micron Technologies, Inc. and Samsung Electronics Co., Ltd. Thus, an IP valuation analyst analyzing a new technology within Patent Class 257 may have to consider the prospects of one of these larger players claiming patent infringement (or acquisition interest) if the patent subject to review gains market traction.

The practical application of the current art boils down to risk assessment for monetization problems that would relate to the space. Patents that fall within a crowded space may have greater value compared to those in a less crowded space, as patents may be more important in those industry segments (except in the case of category-defining patents). However, a crowded space also increases the chances that an invention may infringe on another patented invention in the process, or it

103 For example, Patent Class 239, Whips and Whip Apparatus, likely gets little attention today because people have not been concerned with buggy whips since the invention of the automobile.

Exhibit 63. Patent Class 257 Ownership

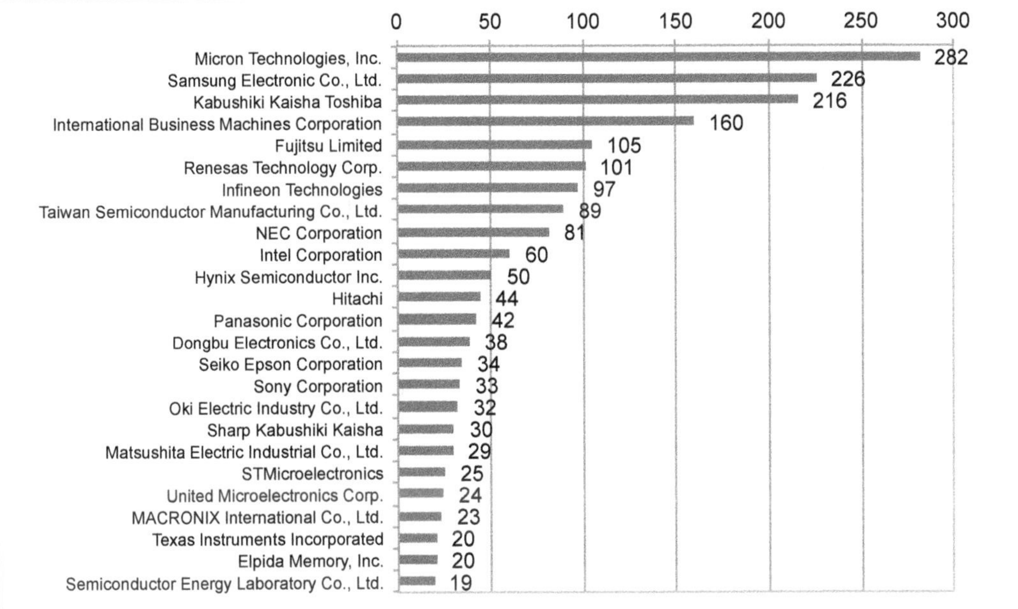

will have a very narrow claims scope, limiting the patent's utility. The IP valuation analyst should consider the ramifications of current art and its impact on value in a crowded space. Where appropriate to the engagement, the valuation analyst should consult with competent legal professionals for additional guidance as to the state of the current art.

Patent Utility

Patent utility gets to the heart of the invention. Does the invention provide some utility that the market perceives as advantageous over other alternatives? These advantages may appear in the forms of greater functionality, lower cost, faster processing, lower capital requirements, less resource consumption, reduced waste, higher yields, greater uptime, greater efficiency, and others. These advantages translate into a value proposition for the buyer, hence for the patent. If the market views a given product embodiment of a patent as superior in features, performance, and value, it pays to receive those benefits. If the market views competitive offerings as easy substitutes with low switching costs, this will threaten the value of the incremental benefits offered by the patented invention, forcing vendors to compete on price alone.

For example, consider an invention that improves the operating and handling performance of lawn mowers. For such an analysis, the patent valuation analyst should identify competitive products that may affect sales of the patented invention in the market. The competitive analysis should identify a list of directly competitive products, as perceived by the patent owner as well as the valuation analyst's own independent research. Next, where possible, the IP valuation analyst must seek to understand how the market perceives the importance of various product features. For example, suppose the IP valuation analyst reviews market literature and hosts discussions with distributors and mower users, and from that research establishes the following as decisional factors for lawn mower buyers:

- Design features;
- Compactness;
- Productivity;
- Ease of operation;
- Market perception;
- Cost;
- Reliability; and
- Customer service and support.

The patent valuation analyst then assesses the impact of these decisional factors that the market values using a multifactor decision model, which is a common way to evaluate comparative technologies in an objective manner.[104] The valuation analyst ranks these decisional factors in terms of importance to the market, and then assigns each mower individual scores within each category. The IP valuation analyst then uses the sum product of all decisional factors to arrive at a final mower "score." This allows the valuation analyst to benchmark the subject patented mower invention against competitors' product offerings. Such a process offers a framework for objective competitive analysis. While score rankings in these analyses are somewhat subjective, since the IP valuation analyst assigns the factors that formed the basis of the final score, the valuation analyst develops the score rankings using objective research of the relevant markets. It is important to realize that while the IP valuation analyst may incorporate sufficient logic into the product comparison matrix, the matrix retains a subjective characterization of the products that may not serve as an authentic ranking for purposes beyond a patent valuation (i.e., it is not likely an appropriate, statistically valid survey of the end mower buyers). Yet the subjectivity

104 The reader will find an excellent overview of multifactor decision models in Chapter 5 of Richard Razgaitis' book, *Valuation and Pricing of Technology-Based Intellectual Property,* John Wiley & Sons, 2003.

may not diminish the impact of comparing the technologies side by side, which may illuminate any value proposition associated with the patented invention.

Exhibit 64 demonstrates the ranking of various mowers against the patented invention.

Exhibit 64. Ranking of Various Mowers Against the Patented Invention

	Design Features			Compactness			Productivity	Ease of Operation	Market Perception		Cost	Reliability	Customer Support and Service		Overall Score
Value to buyer (1 to 10)	5			6			10	5	7		10	10	10		
Make	Engine HP	Weight (lbs)	Power/ Weight Ratio	Length	Width	Height	Speed	Steering mechanism	Consumer Review	Review Ranking	MSRP (61"deck)	Warranty terms	Dealer Network	Customer Financing	
Exmark Laser Z	27	1360	0.0199	82	73	58	10	Twin Lever	Best in class perception. No reliability issues. Excellent handling. Top notch accessories	A-	$8,799	2 year limited	Over 1200 dealers	Company financing program	
Scag Wildcat	27	1210	0.0223	83	73	54	10	Twin Lever	Not Available		$9,299	3 yr on cutter deck, 2 yr on components		Available via partnership	
Scag Turf Tiger	27	1350	0.0200	87	63	56	10.5	Twin Lever	Perceived inferior to Exmark, Toughest product, Stress cracks on deck after extended hours. Length of the machine causes handling problems, Top notch accessories	B+	$9,499	3 yr on cutter deck, 2 yr on components		Available via partnership	
Hustler Super Z	27	1212	0.0223	82	61	54	16	Twin Lever	Cutting quality compromised, Reliability issue with heat causing burnt turf, Excellent hill ride and highest speed, Vacuum bag undersized for more than 52" decks	B+	$10,599	2 year limited	5 dealerships in NE and KS	Company program as well as additional dealer programs	
Deere Mid Z	25	1298	0.0193	79	74	52	9	Twin Lever	Product perception in line with brand image. Vacuum system weak. Good handling on hills	B+	$10,349	3 yr on cutter deck, 2 yr on components	20,000 dealer outlets within and outside of US	Comprehensive commercial and consumer financing plans	
Toro Z 74283	27	1250	0.0216	80	70	55	10	Twin Lever	Good maneuvering, high out quality	N/A	$8,799	2 year limited	Comprehensive US and outside network	Company financing program	
Invention	27	1190	0.0227	80	61	48.5	10	Steering wheel	Cutting quality, accessories and comfort ranked high, noise level perceived lower than competition, zero turn speed faster than competition, heavily built so high reliability perception	N/A	$9,397	5 yr limited warranty	Over 55 dealerships represent Gizmow	None	
Exmark Laser Z	1.99			2.99			5.00	2.50	6.30		5.60	7.00	7.50		39
Scag Wildcat	2.23			3.17			5.00	2.50	4.90		5.35	7.00	5.00		35
Scag Turf Tiger	2.00			3.38			5.25	2.50	4.20		5.25	7.00	5.00		35
Hustler Super Z	2.23			3.84			8.00	2.50	2.80		4.70	5.00	5.50		35
Deere Mid Z	1.93			3.41			4.50	2.50	4.90		4.83	7.00	10.00		39
Toro Z 74283	2.16			3.37			5.00	2.50	4.20		5.60	5.00	7.00		35
Invention	2.27			4.38			5.00	4.00	4.20		5.00	5.00	7.00		37

The following is a summary of the feature-by-feature comparative analysis:

- ***Design features:*** The IP valuation analyst reviews the product design based on the engine horsepower and the equipment's total weight and, using these two parameters, calculates the engine power-to-weight ratio for all the competing products in the market. A higher power-to-weight ratio is a desirable attribute for the end user and thereby commands a higher score. All the competing products have comparable engine powers and vehicle weights, so one can argue that neither of these two attributes earns a product a distinctive advantage over another. These attributes are expected requirements and the lack thereof may adversely affect a product's sales. The valuation analyst ranks the importance of design features to a buyer at a value of five, on a scale of one to 10.

- *Compactness:* The compactness of a product appeals to the end user because it may lead to better maneuverability of the mower. Using mower dimensions to calculate vehicle volume, the IP valuation analyst assigns this compactness factor an importance ranking of six. The valuation analyst then uses the reciprocal of each mower's overall volume to arrive at its score, thereby ranking smaller-volume mowers at higher scores. The mower with the patented invention under review achieves the highest score.

- *Productivity:* Productivity is one of the most important attributes for a mower buyer. A vehicle with a high safe operating speed translates into a higher turf-processing rate, as measured in terms of acres per unit time. This is also a key determinant for commercial customers, since the rate of turf processing translates directly into a higher revenue model. The IP valuation analyst therefore assigns this decisional factor the highest ranking of 10 for value to the buyer.

- *Ease of operation:* Ease of mower operation is of value to the buyer. Difficult-to-operate machines present a learning curve associated with safe and effective operation. For a business, the span of this learning curve correlates directly with revenues. In this comparison, the IP valuation analyst assigns a ranking of five to the ease of operation factor.

- *Market perception:* Mowers sell in a fiercely competitive market, and buyers seek a lot of independent advice through product review forums on the Internet and trade publications. Certain websites dedicated to the lawn and garden industry have carried out detailed surveys along with rankings of products on the market. Products that have limited consumer review exposure perform at a major disadvantage to others in the market. The valuation analyst assigns market perception an importance ranking of seven.

- *Cost:* Product cost is an important parameter, as it governs decisions to rent the equipment versus buying it. In this mower comparison, the IP valuation analyst assigns cost a ranking of 10 for value to the end buyer. The valuation analyst uses the reciprocal of each product's published manufacturer suggested retail pricing benchmark cost, which produces higher scores for mowers with lower costs.

- *Reliability:* The buyer may not be price sensitive, perhaps preferring instead a reliable product. The premium price ought to impart a high-quality experience for the end user with a trouble-free experience. Warranty terms reflect manufacturers' intelligent assessment of product strengths and weaknesses and the costs associated with backing their designs over time, so the IP valuation analyst uses warranties offered by the manufacturers as a benchmark of the quality perception of these competing products. The IP valuation analyst assigns a ranking of 10 for the reliability factor.

- *Customer support and service:* Mowers are expensive machines subject to high wear applications. The price point for high-end mowers is well above others in the market (e.g., manual operation mowers, low-end products), so one may reasonably conclude that after-sales support and financing is of paramount importance to the buyer. The IP valuation analyst assigns the customer support and service factor an importance ranking of 10.

The IP valuation analyst weights the scores in the individual categories based on the importance ranking, and then adds them together to arrive at an overall product score. In this example, Exmark and Deere products have higher scores based on their success in the industry, stronger brand perception, vast support networks, and favorable pricing. The patented invention embodiment under review appears to be at or below par with the rest of the product portfolio in the model. Though the product containing the differentiating patented invention scores consistently high on the technical attributes of the product, perhaps confirmed through independent market research, it falls short in aspects of brand strength, dealer network and support services, and price, which the market tends to value more than the utility provided by the patented invention. That said, improvement in these areas would likely propel the patented invention to become a leader of the pack. However, until such time, the IP valuation analyst may assess a higher risk for the patented invention because, based on factors important to the relevant market, the patent owner clearly has some challenges to overcome before being able to monetize the invention.

As the example demonstrates, understanding the utility of the patent in the realm of the competitive target market is important in a patent valuation engagement. Overstating the invention's utility can lead to overvaluation of the patent, just as understating the invention's utility can lead to undervaluation of the patent. It is critical for the valuation analyst to benchmark the invention's utility against other offerings in the competitive market to avoid a material error in the value conclusion.

Patent Quality

Patent quality is a subjective but important measure in a valuation engagement. Given the sheer quantity of patents that the USPTO awards annually, and the fact that relatively few ever generate economic income (measured several ways, including comparative product market searches, actual patent transaction counts, or patent abandonment rates), the IP valuation analyst must understand the true qualitative aspects of the patent. Delivery of the resulting patent quality opinion is not always the easiest information to offer. Inventors may treat their inventions like new babies, and few inventors like to hear that they have ugly babies.

Smart professionals who work with patents regularly can actively disagree on what constitutes a quality patent. Statisticians may look to certain patent attributes, such as word counts, forward and backward citations, patent renewal rates, and other factors to judge patent quality. In fact, several automated patent valuation and rating algorithms derive from this basic premise. Attorneys who prosecute patents may view quality patents as those that have the broadest claims and the cleanest prosecution histories, including a low number of office actions and low or no file wrapper estoppels.[105] Some attorneys may favor a strong interaction with the USPTO, arguing that the broad claims that survive many rounds of battle with the USPTO will generate a higher quality patent, as the resulting patent claims survived a more rigorous review.[106] The patent litigator may not care about any of these factors, instead focusing on a fact pattern that will create the most convincing argument for a court and a jury. Therein lies part of the problem in defining the subjective attribute called patent quality. Some scholars suggest that patent quality relates to those patents deemed valid if tested in court.[107] Given that most patents never reach a point of litigation, such definitions remain theoretical academic pursuits, as few will ever be able to test a patent's true quality without litigation.[108] Thus, it becomes imperative to gain an understanding of patent quality using other means. Two mechanisms help in gauging patent quality.

105 Amir H. Raubvogel, "Assessing Patent Value," Fenwick & West, LLP, 2004.
106 Sharon M. Webb, "Patent Pitfalls for Early Stage Investors," *Venture Capital Journal*, November 2004.
107 Bhaven Sampat, "Determinants of Patent Quality: An Empirical Analysis," Columbia University, September 2005, p. 6.
108 Sharon M.Webb, "Patent Pitfalls for Early Stage Investors," *Venture Capital Journal*, November 2004.

First, the IP valuation analyst can consider the opinion of qualified patent counsel regarding the quality of the patent's construction. Patent construction relates to how well the patent describes the invention with a specification, which describes the structure and invention itself. In describing the invention, the inventor must use precise and exact terms. Under 35 U.S.C. §112, the inventor must specify the patent such that it describes the invention and the manner and process of making the invention in full, clear, concise, and exact terms. The specification requires the inventor to disclose how to make and use the invention and the best mode the inventor contemplated for carrying out the invention. The inventor must explain these requirements in such a manner that any person of ordinary skill in the art would be able to reproduce the invention. The law places several burdens on the inventor and each of these burdens provides an opportunity for the inventor to make a mistake during the prosecution of the patent. Moreover, the patent must describe the invention when reduced to practice (i.e., the embodiment of the patent differs from the patent's claims).

A mistake in patent construction could be very costly. If the USPTO finds that the inventor violated the four terms, then it could reject the awarded claims, thereby rendering the patented claims unenforceable. The invention would then transition to the public domain and competitors could practice the invention without recourse from the patent owner. Naturally, this has a value impact. A rejection of key patent claims may render the patent worthless. A legal issue may impair value, so the IP valuation analyst might consider checking with legal counsel to gauge the probability of value impairment for a violation of 35 U.S.C. §112. The valuation analyst should account for any value impairments by increasing the discount rate used to determine the present value of the patent's future cash flows.

A second emerging method of evaluating patent quality is to use patent scoring systems to help assess the relative strengths of patents. Patent scoring systems use empirical, regression-based models to define correlations that may indicate higher quality patents. Some of these models study patent renewal rates as an indication of patent quality; a reasonable businessperson would only renew a patent that generates economic value.[109] Others look at various components in the patent's construction, seeking to discover correlations that may give rise to a high-value probability. Patents that score higher would tend to have a higher patent quality, thus, a higher result-

109 This premise has its limitations. Companies may hold many patents as a basis for cross-licensing and to help reduce litigation risk. Thus, companies may continue to maintain low-quality patents just to keep active patent counts high, thereby invalidating models based on renewal rates. Further, technical obsolescence may make patent maintenance a non-issue since the patent owner would be maintaining a patent that no longer had any relevance in the market.

ing value. For example, one study found that patents tend to have a higher value if they list several inventors or have at least one foreign inventor.[110] Academics and valuation professionals have studied other factors as well, some of them listed in Exhibit 65, with the rationales for considering them as they relate to patent quality.[111]

Exhibit 65. Factors Influencing Patent Quality

Factor	Influence	Rationale
Did an attorney or a patent agent prosecute the patent?	Patent strength	A patent attorney may better understand how to construct claims that will withstand litigation.
How many independent claims are there?	Patent breadth	Independent claims provide the bedrock for patents, describing the foundation for the claimed invention. The greater the number of independent claims, the broader the typical patent.
How many words are in each independent claim?	Patent strength	Statistical evidence suggests that patents with fewer words have higher correlations with patent renewals.
How many dependent and independent claims does the patent contain?	Patent breadth	Patents with more dependent and independent claims describe more potential inventions and variations.
How many backward citations are there?	Patent breadth	Statistical evidence suggests that patents with more backward citations have a narrower focus, and might generate a lower value proposition in the market.
How many forward citations are there?	Patent strength	Statistical evidence suggests that patents with forward citations generated follow-on inventions that might generate a higher value proposition in the market for the original patent (e.g., the patent may have blocking value on later patented inventions).
How many inventors are there?	Patent strength	Statistical evidence suggests that patents with more inventors are more complex and have a lower tendency to survive challenges.
Are there any patent assignments?	Patent interest	Statistical evidence suggests that patents assigned to companies within the USPTO's assignee database may have a greater chance of licensure as opposed to those held by sole practitioners.
Are maintenance fees paid?	Patent interest	Statistical evidence suggests that companies that pay recurring maintenance fees on existing patents find value in them—to the extent that they spend dollars to keep them active.

The benefits of these criteria are that they provide a somewhat objective framework

110 Dominique Guellec and Bruno Van Pottelsberghe de la Potterie, "Applications, Grants and the Value of Patent," Economics Letters 69(1), 2000.

111 Of course, many other factors exist that practitioners may argue increase patent quality.

for ranking patents, much like a multifactor decision model measuring patent utility. Patents that tend to have many of the attributes associated with valuable patents would receive a high ranking whereas patents that do not exhibit many of these attributes would receive a lower ranking. For example, suppose that Patent A has a rank of 100 and Patent B has a rank of 131. Patent B, having a higher index value, would be the higher quality patent.

The current state of the art has few publications that seek to verify the precision of these models yet. Part of this relates to the proprietary nature of the models, which scholars have not academically validated. Further, these models have questionable utility in a microeconomic sense for the same reasons that the market approach fails to account properly for value. Econometric models based on linear regression, averages, and the central limit theorem cannot represent the unique attributes of patents, which describes inventions that are unique by definition. Further, patent scores have little meaning in an economic sense; if Patent A ranks 100 and Patent B ranks 131, what does this mean in terms of value? With a lower patent ranking, Patent A should have a lower value—how much lower should the value of Patent A be? The magnitude of the value difference likely varies based on micro- and macroeconomic conditions, the utility of the invention, the company marketing the invention, and other exogenous factors. Patent A may be worth $50,000 less than Patent B if both relate to support structures for backpacking equipment, but the value difference in a pharmaceutical product may be quite a bit higher, as the market dynamics differ so much.

Yet even with the highest quality patent, with the highest patent score, supported by the most ideal patent prosecution history, and ideal fact patterns and broad statistical support, if the market does not believe the invention provides utility superior to other market solutions, then the patent may have little value. Thus, while patent quality is an important metric and one an IP valuation analyst should use to assess risk, patent quality is but a small part of the larger patent valuation engagement.

Patent Age

Typically, patents with long remaining economic lives are worth more than patents with shorter remaining economic lives, yet there are always exceptions to this basic axiom. For instance, the patents surrounding Prozac were very valuable, even though they had less than two years' statutory protection remaining. Many patents that retain most of their statutory life have little or no value. Chapter 5 covered much of the territory on the remaining economic life of a patent.

Important to the IP valuation analyst considering a patent's age are any adjustments to the patent's original term. As discussed in Chapter 5, under 35 U.S.C. §154(a)(2), the statutory life for a patent is 20 years from the earliest effective filing date claimed by inventors, or 17 years after the issue date for patents filed before June 8, 1995. However, under certain circumstances, the USPTO may extend the term for a patent to account for delays that occurred during the processing of the initial patent application. The purpose of the patent term extension is to guarantee prompt responses by the USPTO and to limit patent pendency to no more than three years. Under 35 U.S.C. §154(b)(1), the USPTO will extend the term for a patent one day for each day after the three-year pendency period. For example, the USPTO has three years to award or reject a patent application, which is 1,095 days (not accounting for leap years). If it took the USPTO 1,200 days to award the patent, then the USPTO would extend the patent term by 105 days[112] to account for the delay. The IP valuation analyst should consider the effects of any patent term adjustments, as these might extend the protection period for the patent beyond the nominal statutory provision. An extended protection period can increase the patent's value, as the patent owner would have that many more days of exclusivity in the market. In particular, software

Exhibit 66. Patent Classes With the Longest Patent Pendency Periods

Main Patent Class	Patent Count	Average Days' Pendency	Minimum Days' Pendency	Maximum Days' Pendency	Standard Deviation
930	1	2,330	2,330	2,330	-
506	106	2,124	397	4,851	810
725	1,299	2,116	141	6,322	1,120
718	650	1,933	265	3,924	528
237	16	1,931	1,041	2,934	544
69	6	1,876	1,135	2,360	478
717	2,115	1,876	281	4,281	474
705	6,802	1,873	83	5,122	897
79	1	1,873	1,873	1,873	-
715	3,027	1,843	247	4,996	669
719	764	1,834	284	4,372	552
203	59	1,834	449	3,562	525
380	1,065	1,826	169	5,852	681
463	1,465	1,820	257	4,435	642
504	135	1,817	158	4,543	721
606	2,813	1,815	224	5,797	616
426	759	1,813	140	4,253	652
726	2,546	1,782	136	4,151	591
383	104	1,774	540	3,156	538
314	1	1,770	1,770	1,770	-

112 1,200 days—1,095 days = 105 day patent term extension.

patents commonly have patent term adjustments that exceed a year or more, as the average pendency for a software patent exceeds four years.

Patents in certain classes have a longer pendency than other patent classes. Exhibit 66 is a sampling of the patent classes with the longest patent pendency periods (i.e., the number of days between when the patent owner filed the patent application and when the USPTO issued the patent) for patents issued between 2009 and 2011.

As the data suggests, it may take quite a while to receive an issued patent in Patent Class 930 (peptide or protein sequence), 506 (combinatorial, chemistry technology: method, library, apparatus), or 725 (interactive video distribution systems). In each of these classes, the average pendency period was nearly six years![113]

Patents that typically have a shorter pendency period include design patents. In fact, Exhibit 67 is a sampling of the top 20 patent classes with the shortest patent pendency periods, for patents issued between 2009 and 2011. Interestingly, the patents with the shortest pendency periods belong to design patents, which are relatively easier to prosecute than utility patents. The first non-design patent class that appears is a

Exhibit 67. Top 20 Patent Classes With the Shortest Patent Pendency Periods

Main Patent Class	Patent Count	Average Days' Pendency	Minimum Days' Pendency	Maximum Days' Pendency	Standard Deviation
D09	1	189	189	189	-
D03	1	201	201	201	-
D7	1	364	364	364	-
D10	1,168	369	98	4,771	248
D 7	2,094	372	81	1,938	206
D 2	1,803	382	60	2,100	250
D28	483	384	95	1,719	243
D99	106	384	113	956	170
D26	1,899	386	105	2,307	247
D11	948	387	102	1,608	229
D20	258	393	110	1,350	220
D34	469	401	92	3,665	254
D22	438	401	126	2,077	222
D23	2,039	407	82	1,840	245
D16	791	407	106	1,410	204
D21	1,332	412	81	2,660	218
D 6	2,648	414	83	2,097	242
D 8	1,876	418	74	2,836	238
D13	2,131	424	89	2,545	261
D6	1	425	425	425	-

113 For example, the average pendency in Patent Class 725 was 2,116 days, which is about 5.8 years.

plant patent class at #37, followed by electrical connectors (Patent Class 439) at #39.

The USPTO can shorten patent term extensions as well. Under 35 U.S.C. §154(b)(2), the USPTO can reduce the term of the patent adjustment. The USPTO would do so if it were to find the patent applicant unresponsive to providing reasonable efforts to conclude the processing or examination of a patent application. Thus, if the patent applicant is slow to respond to patent notices, the USPTO can adjust the patent term downward one day for each day the patent applicant delays a response. Thus, if the patent applicant were 30 days slow in filing a response, the USPTO could reduce the patent's term by 30 days. Building on the example four paragraphs back, if the USPTO extended the patent by 105 days, but then found the patent applicant slow to respond by 30 days, the USPTO would then reduce the patent term extension from 105 days to 75 days.[114] This would of course shorten the statutory life for the patent, which the IP valuation analyst must consider, as it can have a value impact.

The Administrative House

Proper patent administration can make or break a patent's value. The first due diligence step that the valuation analyst must consider is the true status of the patent. A client may ask an IP valuation analyst to value a patent in several stages including the following:

- Pre-provisional filing;
- Provisional filing;
- Formal patent application filing;
- Patent publication; and
- Patent award.

The valuation analyst must understand that until the USPTO grants a patent, the patent applicant has no enforceable legal rights under patent law.[115] Naturally, this has a value impact and it is the first thing a valuation analyst needs to understand in the engagement. A patent application, particularly if not yet published with the patent office, remains a trade secret with a prospect of protection under trade secret law. The due diligence associated with trade secret protection differs materially from a patent engagement. However, as a patent application transitions from a

114 Original 105 day extension—30 days due to patent applicant non-responsiveness = 75 day patent term extension.

115 Sharon M. Webb, "Patent Pitfalls for Early Stage Investors," Venture Capital Journal, November 2004.

non-published trade secret to a protected patent, certain due diligence procedures begin to overlap. Further, certain due diligence procedures the valuation analyst would perform go by the wayside (e.g., status of non-disclosure agreements, which is irrelevant for patents that require full disclosure about the claimed invention). However, the valuation analyst must then perform different due diligence procedures (e.g., verifying patent status).

If the patent issues, the next step the valuation analyst must ensure is that the patent owner is current with all patent maintenance fees. Under 35 U.S.C. §41(b), government protections afforded to a patent are in force as long as the patent owner is current with patent maintenance fees. A patent owner who fails to pay patent maintenance fees abandons the patent and tenders it to public domain, meaning that anyone can practice the invention described in the patent without actionable cause by the patent owner. A reasonable businessperson would not pay a patent owner a license fee for something that remains in the public domain. Thus, the patent owner must maintain protection for a patent to retain any value related to the patent.

Patent expirations due to maintenance fee non-payment are common. For example, Exhibit 68 captures a sampling of the top 20 companies that let patents expire between 1980 and 2011.

Patent maintenance fees are due for patents along this schedule:

- 3 years and 6 months after the patent grant (42 months after the patent grant)
- 7 years and 6 months after the patent grant (90 months after the patent grant)
- 11 years and 6 months after the patent grant (138 months after the patent grant)

If the patent owner fails to pay the requisite maintenance fees, the patent expires after a six-month grace period, unless the patent owner petitions for reconsideration by the USPTO and can show that any delay in paying maintenance fees was unintentional or unavoidable as determined by the USPTO (the patent owner has 24 months to do so). However, if the USPTO refuses to reinstate the patent, the patent expires at the end of the six-month grace period. For example, suppose a patent owner misses the first patent maintenance fee at Month 42 after the patent award. The patent owner has six months to make this payment and patent protection continues as if the patent owner never missed the payment. If the patent owner misses this window, the

Exhibit 68. Top 20 Companies That Let Patents Expire Between 1980 and 2011	
Company	**Patent Count**
International Business Machines Corporation	2,112
Sony Corporation	938
Kabushiki Kaisha Toshiba	661
Intel Corporation	546
Matsushita Electric Industrial Co., Ltd.	433
Fujitsu Limited	416
Samsung Electronics Co., Ltd.	399
Agilent Technologies, Inc.	386
Koninklijke Philips Electronics N.V.	365
Hitachi, Ltd.	298
Siemens Aktiengesellschaft	197
Pioneer Corporation	184
Delphi Technologies, Inc.	172
Robert Bosch GmbH	172
Hitachi Global Storage Technologies Netherlands B.V.	167
Renesas Technology Corp.	150
General Electric Company	147
Nokia Corporation	146
Lear Corporation	142
NEC Corporation	140

patent owner has 24 months after the six-month grace period to petition the USPTO to have the patent reinstated. If the patent owner misses the deadline, the patent expires and in the process destroys any remaining value proposition attributable

Exhibit 69. Top 10 Patent Reinstatements Reported by the USPTO	
Company	**Patents Reinstated**
Intel Corporation	30
Samsung Electronics Co., Ltd.	7
The Regents of the University of California	6
Powerchip Semiconductor Corp.	6
DPHI Acquisitions, Inc.	6
Viciciv Technology	5
Wind River Systems, Inc.	4
Sensys Medical, Inc.	4
iPolicy Networks, Inc.	4
The United States of America as represented by the Secretary of the Navy	4

to the patent. While rare, large companies with sophisticated IP operations still make mistakes. Exhibit 69 captures the top 10 patent reinstatements reported by the USPTO, after receipt of maintenance fee payments, based on maintenance fee events between 1980 and 2011.

Companies rarely receive patent reinstatements. In fact, over the course of 31 years, empirical evidence suggests that patent reinstatements occurred for only 556 patents across 442 different companies. What is more common is that companies miss paying their maintenance fees and then must pay surcharges because of late payments. This rate of occurrence is high for universities. In fact, nine of the top 20 organizations that paid surcharges for missed patent maintenance fee payments are universities, as Exhibit 70 captures.[116]

Exhibit 70. Top 20 Organizations That Paid Surcharges for Missed Patent Maintenance Fee Payments

Organization	Surcharge Incidence
Cornell Research Foundation, Inc.	24
The Regents of the University of California	24
Luxtera, Inc.	19
Cascade Microtech, Inc.	16
The Trustees of Columbia University in the City of New York	14
The Johns Hopkins University	12
Board of Trustees of Michigan State University	12
Board of Regents, The University of Texas System	11
Borealis Technical Limited	9
Diaperoos, LLC	8
ZeniTech LLC	8
California Institute of Technology	8
Proton Energy Systems, Inc.	8
Stereo Display, Inc.	8
University of Southern California	8
Raze Technologies, Inc.	8
Quallion LLC	8
Trex Enterprises Corp.	8
University of Virginia Patent Foundation	7
New Jersey Institute of Technology	7

116 When considering the top 100 organizations, the number reduces to 34, which still does not reflect well for universities. While the surcharges can be low, having to pay them indicates possibly inefficient patent management. The IP valuation analyst should evaluate whether to account for any increased monetization risk or ownership costs associated with poor patent administration.

After considering patent maintenance fees, the IP valuation analyst must verify that the USPTO reflects the active status of the actual patent owners. Companies do not create inventions captured by patents—people do. Under 35 U.S.C. §261, patents have attributes of personal property. Patent applications, issued patents, or fractional interests thereof are assignable in law. Assignments occur by executing an instrument (e.g., assignment agreement) in writing. Further, 35 U.S.C. §261 indicates that an "assignment, grant or conveyance shall be void as against any subsequent purchaser or mortgagee for a valuable consideration, without notice, unless it is recorded in the Patent and Trademark Office within three months from its date or prior to the date of such subsequent purchase or mortgage." This means that for a patent to be valuable to a company, the company must be the assignee of record with the USPTO; failure to be the recorded assignee would void any subsequent transaction relating to the patent. This can create patent value impairment. For example, suppose a company seeks to sell a patent for $1 million; however, the assignee database at the USPTO does not list the company as the assignee of the patent. Accordingly, the company does not truly own the rights to the patent, so it does not have a patent to sell. The value of the patent to that company would be zero. If the patent contains multiple inventors, each inventor must assign his or her interest in the patent to the company. Failure by the IP valuation analyst to verify proper ownership of the patent may lead to an improper value conclusion.

Another important factor in patent valuation due diligence is the IP valuation analyst ensuring that all contact information for the patent owner is current with the USPTO. While a seemingly insignificant factor, the USPTO will send administrative notices to patent owners regarding patent maintenance fees and other items. For example, in the Manual of Patent Examining Procedure (MPEP), §711.03(c) states the following:

> [W]here an application becomes abandoned as a consequence of a change of correspondence address (the Office action being mailed to the old, uncorrected address and failing to reach the applicant in sufficient time to permit a timely reply) an adequate showing of "unavoidable" delay will require a showing that due care was taken to adhere to the requirement for prompt notification in each concerned application of the change of address (see MPEP §601.03), and must include an adequate showing that a timely notification of the change of address was filed in the application concerned, and in a manner reasonably calculated to call attention to the fact that it was a notification of a change of address. The following do not constitute proper notification of a change in correspondence address:

(A) the mere inclusion, in a paper filed in an application for another purpose, of an address differing from the previously provided correspondence address, without mention of the fact that an address change was being made;

(B) the notification on a paper listing plural applications as being affected (except as provided for under the Customer Number practice - see MPEP §403); or

(C) the lack of notification, or belated notification, to the U.S. Patent and Trademark Office of the change in correspondence address.

If the patent owner is unresponsive to USPTO notices, such as for payment of maintenance fees, that may impede the patent owner's ability to correct administrative problems when the patent owner finally realizes a problem exists. This may permanently impair patent value. For example, Apple Computer, Inc. transferred 984 patent properties to Apple Inc. on April 24, 2007 according to the assignee database at the USPTO. In fact, Apple Computer, Inc. changed its corporate name to Apple Inc. Thus, Apple Computer, Inc. had to register name changes via assignments recorded by the USPTO to clean up the administrative house. That said, Apple Inc. still has patents that issue under the name Apple Computer, Inc. For example, U.S. patent #7,962,637 issued on June 14, 2011 and listed Apple Computer, Inc. as the primary assignee. However, the USPTO's assignee database showed that Apple Computer, Inc. assigned this patent to Apple Inc. on January 9, 2007. Thus, an IP valuation analyst valuing U.S. patent #7,962,637 would need to verify whether Apple Inc. was the eventual owner instead of Apple Computer, Inc. in order to confirm that the contact information was in order.

While company name changes occur, there are many examples where patent prosecutors enter improper contact information. In fact, spelling errors permeate patent applications and issued patents. Spelling errors are common among patent owners, patent assignees, patent inventors, patent prosecutors, even the cities where patent owners reside. For example, between 2006 and mid-2011, one patent prosecution firm had its name listed 28 different ways across the more than 400 patents it prosecuted.

While the prosecuting firm likely intended to file most patents under a single name, it succeeded in doing so only 78.69% of the time. This problem is not unique to that particular firm or even patent agents in general. For example, between January 1, 2010 and June 30, 2011, patent prosecutors misspelled the name Indianapolis: Idianapolis, Indianpaolis, Indianpolis, and Indiapolis.[117]

117 Some patent prosecutors even erroneously associated cities such as Bangalore, India, and New Delhi, India, with the state of Indiana! There is no city named Bangalore within the state of Indiana.

Thus, if the USPTO were to send a notice to Indiapolis and the U.S. Postal Service was not able to deliver the mail, the patent owner who listed Indiapolis as the city name would miss the mailing.

Blocking Patents

At the most basic level, a patent is nothing but a legal right to exclude others from practicing an invention. This is a double-edged sword. While a patent does allow the inventor to prevent others from practicing its invention, the patent does not provide the owner with a right to practice the invention, which is important for the IP valuation analyst to consider in a patent valuation. This deserves restatement to make it abundantly clear to the reader:

A RIGHT TO EXCLUDE IS NOT A RIGHT TO PRACTICE!

This creates an interesting potential debacle for a patent owner. If a patent owner goes through the time, administrative burden, and financial cost to receive a patent that, in the course of practicing the patented invention, infringes on another company's patent, the patent owner may effectively be "blocked" from monetizing the patent. This has a value impact: if the patent owner cannot monetize the patent, the patent may hold little value. At the very least, the blocking may require the patent owner to pay a reasonable royalty rate to the owner of the blocking patent. This royalty rate impairs value, since the royalty payment represents a cost against revenues generated by the patent. In the worst case, the blocking patent's owner may refuse a license, thereby removing the possibility of taking a product to market. The patent owner would then have to engineer a solution that does not infringe—or abandon any infringing activity altogether. A blocking patent is more likely to affect a patented invention that resides in a crowded space (i.e., many patents exist in the relevant industry or technology area), as opposed to an invention in a space that has limited prior art or references.

An IP valuation analyst has several ways to objectively assess the risk of blocking patents and appropriately account for the risk in the value opinion. Common methods at a valuation analyst's disposal for evaluating the impacts of a blocking patent include:

- Reviewing the results of a freedom-to-operate search; and
- Reviewing a declaratory judgment of noninfringement.

Freedom-to-Operate Search

The first method an IP valuation analyst has to assess the risk of blocking patents is to review a formal legal opinion, usually by the client's counsel or independent patent counsel, regarding the ability to practice the invention. Known commonly as a "freedom-to-operate search," it represents a legal opinion as to the freedom to practice a patented invention without infringing on another company's patents.

The IP valuation analyst (or the client) can contract with a law firm to perform a search in the market for potentially blocking patents. This involves the law firm searching the space of available patents for those that closely resemble the patent under review, interpreting the claims of patents found during the search that may relate to the new invention, and then interpreting the claims of the found patents against the new invention's claims to find possible overlap. The result of the freedom-to-operate search is a memorandum describing potential blocking issues that may create potential infringement if the inventor were to practice his or her invention. The freedom-to-operate memorandum will typically provide a summary of the patent under review, a searching methodology, search results, and a claims analysis comparing patents the legal counsel determines might create possible infringement for the new invention.

The freedom-to-operate memorandum will discuss literal infringement of a patent's claims and infringement known under the "doctrine of equivalents." The valuation analyst wants to gain confidence that infringement will not occur under either condition. Under literal infringement, one has a product (i.e., practices the new patented invention) that would infringe the claims of a blocking patent as specified exactly in the blocking patent's claims. For example, consider a company that owns a patent for a piston-driven device that relies on magnets to move objects in a conveying system.[118] Further, suppose the piston cylinder contains a pair of sealing rings that each has a lip on one side, which would prevent impurities from getting into the piston assembly. Under a literal infringement, the new invention would consist of a piston cylinder that contains a pair of sealing rings, each having a lip on one side.

Infringement under the doctrine of equivalents occurs when one manufactures a product or practices a new patented invention and does not literally infringe on a blocking patent's claims; however, the differences between the new product as implemented and the invention described by the blocking patent are so insignificant as to render the end products functionally equivalent. In the case of the piston assembly, consider again the sealing rings. In the new design, the practitioner used a single

118 *Festo Corp. v. Shoketsu Kinzoku Kogyokabushiki Co.*, 535 U.S. 722 (2002).

sealing ring with two lips, one on each side, instead of using two sealing rings, each with a lip on one side. While the practitioner may not literally infringe the blocking patent's claims, as that invention required two sealing rings, each with a lip on one side, the practitioner's design may infringe under the doctrine of equivalents. If a freedom-to-operate search yields potential blocking patents, the IP valuation analyst needs to understand the value impacts of such a finding. Further, a legal review by competent patent counsel may discover that a patent may not infringe a blocking patent due to file wrapper estoppels,[119] which may prevent certain arguments under the doctrine of equivalents. Legal counsel has the proper qualifications to make such a determination, which a valuation analyst should consider in assessing risk associated with the patent under review.

A freedom-to-operate memorandum provides the IP valuation analyst with objective evidence as to the limits, if any, for the patent owner to practice the invention. The valuation analyst can then adjust the value opinion to account for any possible value impairments related to any limitations. For example, consider a novel technology that modifies the surface of a medical implant with an antibiotic drug to provide for better integration with body tissues, hence better efficacy. A freedom-to-operate search finds that coronary stents represent a crowded space, where several large companies have been coating coronary stents with drugs for many years and have many patents protecting these concepts. Thus, the patent owner would likely have little freedom to practice the new invention in the coronary stent market. As a result, the valuation analyst would impair the value of any products incorporating the patented technology for coronary stents, either adding in the payment of a reasonable royalty rate or considering the impacts of complete market exclusion and the generation of no revenue. However, the freedom-to-operate search identifies little overlap in the market for orthopedic implants such as for knees, hips, and shoulders. Thus, the patent owner could practice the invention of a drug-coated knee, hip, or shoulder implant without the claim of infringement from a competitor or any royalty obligations if the USPTO were to find such an invention patentable.

Ideally, the IP valuation analyst will be able to review a memorandum from a freedom-to-operate search for each patent under review; however, in practice this is rare because freedom-to-operate searches can be quite expensive, exceeding $50,000, depending on the nature of the invention. Many companies may not choose to fund a freedom-to-operate search, especially if the patent owner has a portfolio

119 A file wrapper estoppel (also called a prosecution history estoppel) occurs when a patent applicant narrows a clamed invention during the patent prosecution phase to overcome a rejection by the USPTO for a claimed invention. The file wrapper estoppel precludes the patent owner from claiming a broader claims' interpretation after the patent issues.

of patents the IP valuation analyst is to consider. Many early-stage companies may not have the resources to do so. Next, a freedom-to-operate search is a judgment by a qualified person in the legal profession; however, it is an opinion. Finally, the freedom-to-operate search does not represent a guarantee of a legal outcome, as a court may issue a finding contrary to freedom-to-operate opinion issued by legal counsel.

Declaratory Judgment of Noninfringement

Another tool the IP valuation analyst has to assess the risk of blocking patents is a review of any declaratory judgments of noninfringement. A declaratory judgment is a court decision in a civil case that instructs parties on their rights and responsibilities, "without awarding damages or ordering them to do anything."[120] It helps parties to dispute and resolve an uncertainty without some serious legal problem in the future, such as a patent infringement action. Thus, if a patent holder wants to remove the uncertainty surrounding a potential infringement finding for a blocking patent, the patent holder may petition a court for a declaratory judgment of noninfringement. If the court were to issue a ruling that no infringement exists, then the patent holder could practice the invention it patented without the risk of an infringement action by the potential blocking patent holder. From a value perspective, if a patent owner receives a declaratory judgment from a court that its patent does not infringe on a potentially blocking patent, then the IP valuation analyst will not have to consider any royalty cost or other blocking factors that would prevent the patent owner from practicing the invention.

The good news with a declaratory judgment of noninfringement is that the decision is unequivocal.[121] Thus, the IP valuation analyst has little uncertainty about economic risk attributable to the blocking patent, and the valuation analyst can account for this risk reduction accordingly in the valuation model. The problem with a declaratory judgment is that it affects only blocking patents within the scope of judgment. Thus, if the new patent resides in a crowded space, potentially blocked from several patents, but the declaratory judgment considers only one of those blocking patents, the practitioner still has a problem practicing its invention. The benefit of the freedom-to-operate search is that it would identify a broad spectrum of possible blocking patents.

120 www.nolo.com, accessed on June 8, 2008.

121 One can appeal the decision of the court, but that is immaterial for the purposes of the discussion here. Until appealed, the outcome is still final.

Status of Active Administrative or Legal Actions

Somewhat paradoxically, the more valuable the patent, the more it is open to third party attack using administrative or legal actions to find the patent invalid.[122] Third party attacks arise in attempts to demonstrate to the USPTO or a court that key patent claims are invalid or unenforceable, with the ultimate goal of an administrative finding or a judgment rejecting key patent claims awarded previously. If one were to attempt to invalidate a patent, the burden of doing so in a federal district court action rests on the party seeking a declaration of invalidity or unenforceability. Third parties may also request an ex parte reexamination by the USPTO for any patent, or an inter partes reexamination for patents awarded after November 29, 1999.

The status of any pending administrative or legal actions surrounding the patent under review should be of considerable interest to the IP valuation analyst. Under 35 U.S.C. §282, a patent is presumed valid and each claim is separately presumed valid. Therefore, the outcomes of any administrative or legal actions surrounding an issued patent may give rise to reconsideration of some or all of the patent's claims, thereby directly affecting the value proposition associated with the patent. Administrative actions may arise in several forms, including:

- Reexaminations by the USPTO;
- Pending declaratory judgments of invalidity or unenforceability; and
- Potential infringement lawsuits.

The outcomes of a reexamination by the USPTO, a declaratory judgment hearing, or an infringement suit can either protect or annihilate patent value. If the reexamination process confirms that a patent is valid, then that confirmation preserves patent value. If the USPTO rejects the patent's claims in whole or in part, that finding can destroy all value (all claims rejected) or impair value substantially (some claims rejected). The same holds true for a declaratory judgment of invalidity or unenforceability. A ruling to the favor of the patent holder will tend to preserve value, whereas a ruling against the patent holder will tend to destroy value. With respect to potential infringement lawsuits, a finding of infringement (perhaps from a blocking patent) at the least may require the IP valuation analyst to account for a reasonable royalty expense.

122 "Study on Evaluating the Knowledge Economy—What Are Patents Actually Worth?" European Commission, Directorate-General for Internal Market, May 9, 2005, p. 17.

Reexaminations

A patent owner is at risk that a third party may request one or more reexaminations with the USPTO in an attempt to invalidate one or more of the claims of its patent. A reexamination is a request to the USPTO to review any claim of a patent based on prior art from patents or printed publications that the requester believes may have a bearing on the patentability of the claims that the USPTO already awarded. If the USPTO determines that a patent claim warrants a reexamination due to a substantial new question of patentability, it will conduct reexamination proceedings, the results of which may be to affirm the original decision of a claim's patentability, or to reject the original decision of a claim's patentability. A patent owner desires an affirmative ruling, as a rejection of the original claim would remove claim protection, potentially impairing or erasing value for a given patent.

Patent law provides for two types of patent reexaminations: an ex parte reexamination and an inter partes reexamination. The key difference between them is that for an ex parte reexamination, the requester makes the request to the USPTO and the USPTO manages all communication with the patent owner for the patent under review. The requester's involvement ends before the first office action.[123] With an inter partes reexamination, the reexamination requester remains involved in the case.

The scientific nature of the patented invention may provide insights into the potential for challenges. For example, a trend has emerged whereby ex parte reexaminations of patents in the chemical discipline have remained steady from 2003-2007, whereas patent filings in the mechanical and electrical disciplines have more than doubled over the same period.[124] Thus, it may be more difficult for a patent owner to defend patents in the electrical or mechanical disciplines because of the increased incidence of ex parte reexaminations of patents in those disciplines.

The risk of a reexamination request increases if the patent owner follows an aggressive enforcement strategy. Given the relatively low cost of requesting a reexamination (one source indicates a total cost of less than $50,000[125]) companies may find a high value proposition in challenging a patent through reexamination, particularly if faced with onerous royalty commitments or the threat of an injunction. The USPTO's Performance and Accountability Report for Fiscal Year 2010 presents the following statistics for ex parte reexaminations, shown in Exhibit 71.

123 Joseph D. Cohen, "What's Really Happening in Inter Partes Reexamination," *Journal of the Patent and Trademark Office Society*, 2005, p. 3.

124 USPTO's Performance and Accountability Report for Fiscal Year 2007, Table 13A.

125 Joseph D. Cohen, "What's Really Happening in Inter Partes Reexamination," Journal of the Patent and Trademark Office Society, 2005.

Exhibit 71. Ex Parte Reexaminations					
Ex Partes Activity	2006	2007	2008	2009	2010
Total requests filed	511	643	680	658	780
Total determinations on requests	458	594	666	614	662
Total requests granted	422	575	626	574	606
Requests known to have related litigation	229	369	316	372	347
Percentage related to litigation	45%	57%	46%	57%	44%

And the same USPTO report offers the statistics in Exhibit 72 for inter partes reexaminations.

Exhibit 72. Inter Partes Reexaminations					
Inter Partes Activity	2006	2007	2008	2009	2010
Total requests filed	70	126	168	258	281
Total determinations on requests	47	119	150	229	231
Total requests granted	43	118	142	218	224
Requests known to have related litigation	32	81	115	220	196
Percentage related to litigation	46%	64%	68%	85%	70%

As the data suggests, an increasing number of reexaminations originate from a related dispute on patentability. The statistics surrounding success in reexaminations should be of importance to the IP valuation analyst performing a patent valuation. The USPTO report gives the statistics in Exhibit 73 for ex parte reexaminations.

Exhibit 73. Ex Parte Reexaminations		
Ex Parte Cases	2010	%
Affirmed	3565	49.0%
Affirmed in part	1044	14.0%
Reversed	2158	30.0%
Dismissed/Withdrawn	180	2.5%
Remanded	365	5.0%

As the data demonstrates, a patent claim under an ex parte reexamination statistically has a 49% chance of affirmation (i.e., the breadth of the patent's claimed inventions remain intact), 52% including cases dismissed. However, it has a 14% chance of only partial affirmation, and a 30% chance of complete reversal. On an expected value basis, if a patent claim is under review in an ex parte reexamination with the USPTO, the expected value may be as high as 44% that the USPTO would reject a key patent claim. Thus, a patent nominally worth $100 that is in the midst of an ex parte reexamination would have an expected value of $51.50 after accounting for the probability of a rejection of a key patent claim.

For inter partes reexaminations, the statistics are even more in favor of the petitioner. One author tracked the results of 83 inter partes reexaminations and found that the USPTO confirmed all patent claims were novel in only 1% of the patents.[126] It rejected and cancelled all claims in 71% of the patents, and required claim changes in 28% of the patents.[127] Thus, on an expected value basis, a patent stands to have a higher impairment (at least 71%) if a third party requests an inter partes reexamination of the patent under review.

Given that the USPTO grants most ex parte and inter partes reexamination requests, and given the reversal rate for key patent claims, the chances of patent value impairment once a reexamination process begins is high. As a result, if the USPTO grants a reexamination request, the patent owner may feel increased pressure to negotiate a deal, even if it is less favorable to the patent owner than it otherwise would be. This may lead to a lower patent value. When the USPTO grants a reexamination request, the patent owner has an increased risk that there will be no future cash flows attributable to the patent under review. The IP valuation analyst performing a patent valuation should explicitly account for such probabilities in the valuation model.

Declaratory Judgments of Invalidity or Unenforceability

While declaratory judgments can be of use to a patent owner, reducing the risk associated with a royalty or injunction relating to a blocking patent, they can be disastrous to value when the patent under review is the subject of a declaratory judgment of invalidity or unenforceability. Recall that a declaratory judgment is a court decision in a civil case that instructs parties on their rights and responsibilities to help parties dispute or resolve a legal uncertainty. Author Richard Stim identifies circumstances that may give rise to a declaratory judgment of invalidity:[128]

- The USPTO did not discover or properly analyze relevant prior art references that affect the novelty or nonobviousness of the invention;
- The invention does not or will not work;

126 Joseph D. Cohen, "What's Really Happening in Inter Partes Reexamination," *Journal of the Patent and Trademark Office Society*, 2005.
127 *Id.*
128 Richard Stim, *Patent, Copyright, and Trademark: An Intellectual Property Desk Reference*, 9th ed., Nolo, Berkeley, Calif., 2007, p. 130.

- The disclosure of the invention in the patent application contains insufficient information to teach an ordinary person skilled in the art to build the invention;
- The patent claims are vague and indefinite;
- The USPTO issued the patent to the wrong inventor;
- Antitrust violations occurred; and
- Other facts may exist that invalidate the patent retroactively.

Stim further identifies the circumstances that may give rise to a declaratory judgment of unenforceability:[129]

- False marking an invention, such as marking a product with a patent number that does not apply to the product;
- Illegal or unfair licensing practices;
- An extended delay in bringing the infringement lawsuit to the detriment of the defendant (also known as laches); and
- Fraud on the USPTO, such as failing to include a pertinent prior art reference in the patent application.

Under such situations, a third party asks a court to declare the patent under review unenforceable or invalid. At the most basic level, there is a binary outcome: the patent is invalid or unenforceable,[130] or it is valid and enforceable. The patent owner loses any protection on the invention if the court finds the patent invalid or unenforceable. As a result, a reasonable businessperson could practice the invention without paying a patent owner because there would be no actionable cause by the patent owner. Thus, no value would accrue to the patent. If the court rules the patent to be valid and enforceable, the patent owner would retain patent protection, and may have actionable cause if one were to practice the invention without authorization.

The IP valuation analyst must understand the status of any pending declaratory judgments of invalidity or unenforceability, because the risk of an adverse outcome can destroy any value associated with the patent. The place to start with such an assessment is the patent owner's legal counsel. Quantifiably, the valuation analyst will typically increase the risk associated with future cash flows attributable to the patent under question. For example, Company A has a patent that it projects will

129 *Id.*

130 The case of a valid patent found to be unenforceable is moot, as the patent owner has no reasonable means to generate revenue attributable to the patent under this scenario.

generate $1,000,000 in free cash flow per year for 10 years, all attributable to the patent. Using a discount rate of 25% to account for the risk attributable to the patent, the value of the patent might be $3,570,503.[131] Company A learns that a third party has petitioned a court to find its patent invalid. While the petition may not change Company A's free cash flow projections of $1,000,000 for 10 years, it does change the risk associated with those cash flows, a risk the valuation analyst estimates will add 10 points to the discount rate. Thus, the value of the patent might be $2,715,043,[132] representing an impairment of $855,460[133] after accounting for the additional risk associated with the pending hearing.

Infringement Actions

The IP valuation analyst must gain a good understanding of the disposition of any pending legal actions associated with a blocking patent that would impair the value of a patent under review. If no existing or anticipated legal actions exist, then the valuation analyst would make no adjustments to account for possible impairment. However, if legal action is pending or already under way, the valuation analyst needs to assess the risk and magnitude associated with any infringement-related impairment.

The place to start with such an assessment is the patent owner's legal counsel, who will know the status of any pending litigation and perhaps even the estimation of the odds of prevailing. While ideal to rely on the opinion of another counsel not associated with the patent owner to gain a truly independent perspective on the owner's chances of prevailing on the issue, the patent owner may not be willing to incur additional expense to gain a higher level of credibility by using a truly independent party to provide that opinion.

If the owner of the infringed patent receives an injunction, the injunction may have a catastrophic value impact. For example, in 2007 F. Hoffmann-La Roche, Ltd. (Roche) received FDA approval for a new anemia drug, Mircera. However, Roche could not sell Mircera in the United States because a court found that Mircera infringes on several patents owned by Amgen, Inc. Amgen was unwilling to allow Roche to sell Mircera, even after Roche offered to pay Amgen a 20% royalty on gross revenues. The IP valuation analyst needs to understand the status of any such actions in order to find a reasonable determination of impairment, if applicable. In the case of Mircera, if Amgen had agreed to Roche's proposed royalty terms, the valuation

131 This is calculated by valuing an annuity of $1,000,000 for ten years at a 25% discount rate.
132 This is calculated by valuing an annuity of $1,000,000 for ten years at a 35% discount rate.
133 $3,570,503 - $2,715,043 = $855,460.

analyst would have had to include an expense item for any revenues associated with Mircera. In reality, a U.S. Court of Appeals upheld a preliminary injunction barring Roche from selling Mircera in the U.S. market.[134] This effectively destroyed any value proposition for Mircera in the U.S. market, though Roche had already launched Mircera in markets outside of the injunction jurisdiction, selling actively in Sweden, Germany, Spain, Switzerland, and the United Kingdom.

Outstanding Contractual Provisions Affecting Value

In addition to any benefits or restrictions imposed by law, companies may seek to engage in terms that may affect the value of patents through contracts. The nature of these contractual terms may seek to enhance the value proposition for the patent owner, particularly in licensing situations. For example, Company A has a patent it licenses on an exclusive basis to Company B. Under the license, Company A has contractually limited its ability to monetize the patent to the efforts put forth by Company B. If Company B failed to put forth an effort to generate value from the patent, Company A would have a patent and a license agreement that is effectively worthless. However, suppose Company A makes it a requirement that Company B meet certain performance criteria as a condition of maintaining the exclusivity provision within the license. Now Company B has an incentive to monetize the patent because otherwise it would lose the exclusivity to the patent. Other forms of contractual terms that may drive value include the following:

- Rights to practice an invention in certain markets;
- Rights to practice an invention in certain geographic regions;
- Minimum licensing payments, which provide a floor on the associated patent value; and
- Terms that may extend the economic life for a technology beyond statutory boundaries (e.g., Company B must pay royalties on all patents under license from Company A until the last patent in Company A's portfolio expires, thereby extending the economic life for Company A's patents that expire sooner than the last patent).

Naturally, the forms and structures of terms that may enhance or destroy patent value are as many as there are creative lawyers and negotiators in the market. The point is that the IP valuation analyst needs to be aware of and consider the impacts of all of the applicable terms on value.

134 http://www.amgen.com/media/media_pr_detail.jsp?releaseID=1208431, accessed October 10, 2008.

Chapter 7
Copyright Due Diligence

There is not much information in professional or economic literature on copyright valuation. Much of the literature focuses on patent valuation despite the fact that copyright litigation is more prevalent than patent litigation.[135] One may only guess as to why this is the case. Perhaps the breadth of copyright protection, which spans many disparate forms ranging from bronze sculptures to books, from movies to architectural drawings, and from music to computer software, makes a comprehensive valuation process appear difficult to apply in practice. Each copyright type, in and of itself, could fill a chapter on comprehensive due diligence procedures.

Copyright valuation carries with it a nuance that adequate due diligence procedures must address. Some considerations apply directly to all intellectual property types (see Chapter 5); however, many concepts merit little consideration in copyright valuation. For example, copyright law may forbid the concept, such as the design-around of a copyright, because any attempts to design around the copyright would generate a derivative work, which the copyright owner would also own. Alternatively, some attributes of a copyright valuation engagement may have a minimal value impact, as is the case when considering a long economic life in deciding a risk-appropriate discount rate, as the length of the economic life generally is immaterial after about 20 years.

Copyrights carry other unique qualities. Unlike patents or trademarks, in many copyright forms it may be easy for an infringer to create a copy of a copyrighted item with the click of a mouse or the transfer of a file. This is especially true with the

135 William M. Landes, and Richard A. Posner, *The Economic Structure of Intellectual Property Law*, The Belknap Press of Harvard University Press, Cambridge, Mass., 2003, p. 5.

prevalence of copying technologies such as computer scanners, digital cameras, recording equipment, and computer software, which make manipulation and transfer of copyrighted works instantaneous and practically or economically undetectable. The infringer can thus receive the benefits of a copyrighted item, such as listening to a song or viewing a movie downloaded illegally from the Internet, without incurring the economic costs for access to the song or movie from the copyright owner. Moreover, the infringer may continue to enjoy the use of the copyrighted item indefinitely without detection, as the incremental costs to copy the item may be inconsequential or undiscoverable.

Contrast this fact pattern with that of a patent, which requires an infringer to reduce the invention to practice before receiving economic benefits from the invention. In such cases, the infringer has to expend much effort beyond a mere click of a mouse or transfer of a file to enjoy the benefits of the protected intellectual property. If the invention were of a mechanical nature, the infringer would have to create the parts, assemble them, and incur the attendant costs before enjoying the benefits of the invention.

An IP valuation analyst focuses copyright due diligence on several distinct areas:

- Verifying the nature of the copyrighted material (i.e., does a copyright protect it?);
- Verifying the nature of the rights to value;
- Consideration of administrative issues that can impair copyright value;
- Special considerations for software; and
- Special considerations for semiconductor designs or masks.

The following sections explore these concepts further.

Nature of the Copyrighted Material

In general, copyright protection under 17 U.S.C. §102(a) includes the following works of authorship:[136]

- Architectural works;
- Dramatic works, including any accompanying music;

136 Note that the definition of authorship is inclusive of any expressive work of creation beyond writings.

- Literary works;
- Motion pictures and other audiovisual works;
- Musical works, including any accompanying words;
- Pantomimes and choreographic works;
- Pictorial, graphic, and sculptural works; and
- Sound recordings.

Copyright law requires that a creator of a copyrightable work satisfy several requirements.[137] First, the work must be original and not a copy of some other work (e.g., a copy of the Bible). Second, the creator must fix the work in some tangible medium of expression. That is, the creator must put it onto some physical object. If the work were a book, the tangible medium of expression would be the book's pages. If the work were a song, the tangible medium of expression may include sheet music or a CD containing an MP3 of the recording. If the work were a sculpture, the tangible medium may be marble or bronze. Lastly, the work must have some creativity and not represent a mere, mundane regurgitation of some other work. For example, one author notes that a telephone white page directory is not likely creative, as it involves some nondiscretionary alphabetic listing of telephone numbers.[138] However, a custom layout of a telephone yellow page volume with customer ads arranged to maximize the visual impact of the ads to a reader may exhibit originality and creativity, making it more likely to have copyright protection, though an IP valuation analyst should rely on qualified legal counsel to make such a determination.

For music, the nature of the copyrighted material can take several forms. A musician who composes a song and affixes it in a tangible medium has protected the sheet music, lyrics, song structure, and so on. However, the *sound* of the song is another distinct right that also receives copyright protection. The song's sound covers the musical arrangement as well as the way the song sounds. The sound can vary based on a variety of factors, including instruments selected, time signature used, venue, reverb, effects, and many others. The combinations of sounds one could use to represent the same song are literally infinite.

For example, Bob Dylan originally penned the song "All Along the Watchtower" and recorded it himself in 1967. Dylan received a copyright for both the song and his

137 Richard Stim, *Patent, Copyright, and Trademark: An Intellectual Property Desk Reference*, 9th ed., Nolo, Berkeley, Calif. 2007, p. 186.
138 *Id.*

recording of it. In 1968, the Jimi Hendrix Experience recorded a cover of the same song and released it on its Electric Ladyland album. The Jimi Hendrix Experience version of the song received its own copyright protection, as it had a different arrangement and sound from Dylan's original recording, though the Jimi Hendrix Experience did not maintain copyright to the original music, lyrics, and so on. Many other artists have covered the song as well, including Dave Matthews, the Grateful Dead, John Mellencamp, Vertical Horizon, Prince, Government Mule, and Neil Young. In each instance, the artist provided the arrangement of, and sound for, the original song that Dylan penned. Of course, each of these arrangements and sounds has its own value. The covers of Dylan's song by both Matthews and the Jimi Hendrix Experience have much greater commercial penetration; thus the covers by these bands are more valuable than the version that Prince played at the 2007 Super Bowl halftime show.

Issues rarely arise in the identification of the copyrightable asset an IP valuation analyst must consider, and most copyrights fit the aforementioned framework. However, sometimes a client may misunderstand the applicability of copyright law, which can affect the scope of a valuation engagement. Under 17 U.S.C. §102(b), copyright law specifically excludes ideas, procedures, processes, systems, methods of operation, concepts, principles, or discoveries. However, copyright law protects the *expression* of such items, but not the item itself (which patents and trade secrets usually protect). Thus, an IP valuation analyst cannot value a process or idea under copyright law since no such protection exists. A client who hires a valuation analyst may not always know the distinction, so the IP valuation analyst must clarify any such discrepancies as those discrepancies may affect the client's expectation of a final deliverable work product.

Like patents, there are varying degrees of copyright strength. The public might consider some copyrights strong (i.e., broad) or weak (i.e., very narrow). A strong copyright typically means that there is much original expression in the work, such as a sculpture, painting, or new song. A thin copyright typically refers to a work that consists of little original expression, such as a book to teach general accounting processes, a history textbook, or a telephone book. In each of the latter examples, which one might consider factual works (more on factual works shortly), it will be easier to reproduce the essence of the work without direct infringement. Moreover, given their nature, thin copyrights might have a greater scope of fair use than with other works (more on fair use shortly). In short, thin copyrights are generally worth less than stronger copyrights, much as weaker patents are worth less than stronger patents. It is important for the IP valuation analyst to gauge the strength of the copyright (potentially with the help of outside legal counsel) in order to associate an appropriate risk and discount rate for it in the valuation engagement.

Verifying the Nature of Rights to Value

Copyrights represent an established bundle of rights. Each right may have its own value proposition. The IP valuation analyst must determine which set of rights is the focus of the engagement. The rights may take several forms, including the following:

- The right to sell the work;
- The right to display the work;
- The right to make copies of the work; and
- The right to make derivative works of the original.

The methods that the IP valuation analyst uses and the magnitude of the value proposition will generally vary based on the nature of the right under consideration. For example, consider the case of an author who owns a copyright on a manuscript. The author creates a manuscript and licenses the right to make copies of the manuscript, display it, and sell it in the open market to a book publisher in exchange for a defined financial arrangement including a running royalty based on book sales. The manuscript generates revenue and net income as follows:

Item	Amount
Revenue	$1,000,000
Author Royalties	($150,000)
Operating Expenses	($600,000)
Net Income	$250,000

What is the value? It depends. If the valuation analyst were to value all rights associated with the copyright, then the value would focus on the total $400,000 that represents a combination of net income generated and the royalties paid to the copyright owner, who is the author in this case, from sales of the manuscript in the market. Assuming a practical perpetual economic life and a discount rate of 20%, the value of the copyright would be $2,000,000.[139]

If the IP valuation analyst were to value the rights to the author alone, perhaps for a tax issue or for a loan collateralization, then the value would focus on the $150,000

139 $400,000 / 20% = $2,000,000.

in royalties paid to the author. Assuming a practical perpetual economic life and a discount rate of 20%, the value to the author would be $750,000.[140] The value to the author would include only the author royalties because that is the only income flowing through to the author. Net income from book sales of $250,000 flows through to the book publisher and the associated rights would be worth $1,250,000 to the publisher, assuming a practical perpetual economic life and a discount rate of 20%.[141] As the example demonstrates, the value of the copyright will depend on the perspective of the interested party. Thus, the IP valuation analyst needs to understand the nature of the rights to value in order to render a value opinion consistent with those rights.

Administrative Issues That Can Impair Copyright Value

Several administrative issues can have an impact on copyright value. Some are obvious, such as who owns the copyright, and partially covered in Chapter 5. Others are not so obvious, yet they can have a material value impact. For example, a copyrighted work that is easy to duplicate in an undetectable fashion, such as a music CD, may be worth less than one that is difficult to duplicate in an undetectable fashion, such as the bronze sculpture of the "Charging Bull" sitting in the financial district in lower Manhattan. In that situation, creator Arturo Di Modica sued Wal-Mart in 2006 for selling unauthorized images of the bull in photographs and lithographs. He was able to detect these unauthorized copies, as well as unauthorized copies generated by seven other defendants that he sued, with relative ease. The following are some of the administrative issues that an IP valuation analyst should review in the course of copyright due diligence:

- Is the work registered?
- Is the work factual?
- Does fair use erode value?
- Is the work made for hire?
- Does the copyright provide notice?
- Is the copyright in the public domain?
- Is the work covered by the Visual Artists Rights Act of 1990?

140 $150,000 / 20% = $750,000.
141 $250,000 / 20% = $1,250,000.

Registration

U.S. copyright law provides for copyright protection implicitly once the author fulfills the basic requirements to receive protection (i.e., originality, fixed in tangible form, etc.). Under 17 U.S.C. §101, authors gain protection for copyrightable work at the point that it is fixed in a tangible medium. Thus, the copyright owner receives protection immediately at that point without any explicit action by a government agency. However, registration does become important with respect to copyright litigation. In accordance with 17 U.S.C. §411(a), an author may bring action against a party for the infringement of copyrighted works, but §411(b) limits such power to authors who register such works with the U.S. Copyright Office. Thus, copyright owners who wish to bring action against potential infringers must first register their works with the U.S. Copyright Office and must do it in a timely fashion. If the IP valuation analyst is valuing a copyright that is the subject of litigation, it will be important to verify the copyright's standing with copyright counsel to ensure that the copyright is going to be enforceable and will qualify for damages.

Once the copyright owner has performed a timely registration, the copyright owner has a legal presumption of validity. In cases of provable infringement, that presumption of validity may allow the copyright owner to recover up to $150,000 in statutory damages, as well as attorney fees, the impounding and/or destruction of infringing items, and injunctions. Importantly, and distinctly different from patent law, the copyright owner may not have to prove any actual monetary harm. An IP valuation analyst does not have an equivalent Panduit-type test for lost profits or Georgia-Pacific factors to consider for determining a reasonable royalty rate. However, without registration, and under most situations, the statute does not provide for remedies for infringement.[142]

Factual Works

A factual work is a copyrighted work that is an expression of something factual. Facts themselves are not copyrightable, as they represent something of truth, something that has actual existence, or a piece of information presented as having objective reality.[143] Recall that copyrightable material must be original and demonstrate some creativity. Facts do not maintain these attributes. Further, facts generally exist in the public domain. For example, this guide serves as a factual work for how to perform IP valuation. It includes a set of truths that provide a set of important considerations when performing an IP valuation engagement, such as an expired patent has no

142 Richard Stim, *Patent, Copyright, and Trademark: An Intellectual Property Desk Reference*, 9th ed., Nolo, Berkeley, Calif., 2007, p. 287.
143 http://www.merriam-webster.com/dictionary/fact, November 30, 2008.

protection and thus no intrinsic value. Thus, elements of this guide are not necessarily copyrightable material; however, the guide itself may be copyrightable, as it includes an expression of examples and concepts presented in a creative and original form. Other examples of factual works include nonfiction stories, histories, instruction manuals, trade catalogs, travel guides, and biographies.[144]

Practically, factual works may command a lower value or no value because they may be easy to reproduce. A subsequent author would only need to know about the facts and satisfy the statute (e.g., present the facts in an original and creative manner; fix them in a tangible form) and create a competing work that would maintain similar benefits to an original work. A classic example of such a scenario occurred in Kansas in the 1980s. Rural Telephone Service Co. Inc. created a phone book listing telephone numbers for customers in its servicing area. Feist Publications, Inc. used data from Rural's publication without permission. Rural sued Feist for copyright infringement. In a decision ultimately decided by the Supreme Court, the court decided that Rural's factual data did not meet the standard for copyrightable material:

> Rural's white pages do not meet the constitutional or statutory requirements for copyright protection. While Rural has a valid copyright in the directory as a whole because it contains some foreword text and some original material in the yellow pages, there is nothing original in Rural's white pages. The raw data are uncopyrightable facts, and the way in which Rural selected, coordinated, and arranged those facts is not original in any way. Rural's selection of listings—subscribers' names, towns, and telephone numbers—could not be more obvious, and lacks the modicum of creativity necessary to transform mere selection into copyrightable expression. In fact, it is plausible to conclude that Rural did not truly "select" to publish its subscribers' names and telephone numbers, since it was required to do so by state law. Moreover, there is nothing remotely creative about arranging names alphabetically in a white pages directory. It is an age-old practice, firmly rooted in tradition and so commonplace that it has come to be expected as a matter of course.[145]

For Rural, its telephone directory had little value because of the factual nature of the directory. Furthermore, it was easy for Feist to create a work that competed directly with Rural's directory in the market, reducing the value proposition for Rural to sell ads in its directory. The valuation analyst is interested in such a scenario, as the nature of the copyrighted work may have a direct value impact that the value

144 Richard Stim, *Patent, Copyright, and Trademark: An Intellectual Property Desk Reference*, 9th ed., Nolo, Berkeley, CA. 2007, p. 239.
145 *Feist Publications, Inc. v. Rural Tel. Service Co.*, 499 U.S. 340 (1991).

opinion must reflect. Practically, accounting for a value impairment associated with the copyright of a factual work occurs by either altering the demand for the copyrighted work, or increasing the risk associated with generating future free cash flows associated with the copyrighted work (see a similar example in the Fair Use Value Erosion section).

Fair Use Value Erosion

The doctrine of fair use centers on a tenet that limited copying of the expressive elements of a work is not infringement even though the copyright holder did not grant permission to perform the copying. Governed by 17 U.S.C. §107, instances of fair use of copyrighted material include "criticism, comment, news reporting, teaching (including multiple copies for classroom use), scholarship, or research." Factors important in the determination of fair use include:

1. The purpose and character of the use, including whether such use is of a commercial nature or is for nonprofit educational purposes;
2. The nature of the copyrighted work;
3. The amount and substantiality of the portion used in relation to the copyrighted work as a whole; and
4. The effect of the use upon the potential market for or value of the copyrighted work.[146]

The IP valuation analyst should consider the impacts of fair use, as fair use can have little or large impacts on copyright value. The value impact of fair use depends on the nature of the copyrighted work. Fair use can impair the value of a copyrighted work if fair use can serve as a proxy for what one would otherwise exchange for the value of the work. If a potential buyer does not make a purchase of a copyrighted work because the buyer was able to supplant the purchase with fair use of the original work, then the copyright owner loses the economic benefit of the work with respect to that potential buyer. This would then depress the value of the copyrighted work. If the work had limited economic impact from fair use, then the work would not maintain any value impairment.

Consider the concept of buying an online article from a movie critic instead of investing the time to see the movie. The critic's review, which is fair use under copyright law, may likely divulge significant portions of the movie to the public,

146 17 U.S.C. §107.

which the public enjoys without paying for access to the movie in the form of an admission ticket. In addition, the critic's rating (i.e., the number of stars the movie receives) may induce one to see the movie if the rating is high or avoid it altogether if the rating is low. Either result will have a material value impact. Higher movie ratings will generate higher movie attendance and generate a higher value, while lower movie ratings will have a correspondingly lower attendance and generate a lower overall value.

Certain copyrighted work types may have limited value impairments from fair use. For example, a software programmer who authors some software to play a video on a computer display may experience little impairment associated with the fair use of the source code to control the video playback—the public would not have access to the original source code. As such, there is no issue of fair use value erosion.

Copyrighted works that may have a higher degree of potential value impairment from fair use may include:

- Photographs;
- Dramatic plays;
- Artistic paintings;
- Cinematic movies;
- Musical recordings;
- News subscriptions; and
- Scholarly publications.

Each of these copyrighted work types are candidates for fair use because each is generally the subject of criticism, comment, news reporting, teaching, scholarship, or research, which are permissible uses under copyright law.

Practically, accounting for a value impairment associated with fair use occurs by either altering the demand for the copyrighted work or by increasing the risk associated with generating future free cash flows associated with the copyrighted work. For example, suppose that a company was planning to sell 200,000 book copies per year for five years, generating $1 in free cash flow from each copy sold. Over the economic life of the book sales, the copyright owner generates $1 million in free cash flow. Using a discount rate of 20%, the present value of the free cash flows is $598,122.43.[147] For example, suppose that the IP valuation analyst can determine

147 Calculated by taking the present value of a five-year annuity of $200,000 using a discount rate of 20%.

that fair use erodes 10% of the sales, resulting in a value impairment of $59,812.24. Alternatively, suppose that the IP valuation analyst cannot determine with a reasonable degree of precision the rate of revenue erosion attributable to fair use. In such a situation, the valuation analyst may increase the discount rate to account for the additional risk associated with generating free cash flow from the copyrighted work. No objective rule exists for quantifying the magnitude of risk that the valuation analyst may apply in such a situation. However, suppose that a survey of potential market buyers indicates that the market demands an additional 500 basis points to account for the increased risk. Then the present value of the future free cash flows is instead $537,856,[148] indicating a value impairment of $60,266.43.[149]

Work Made for Hire

The person who creates a copyrighted work is generally the author of the work and maintains ownership over the work, including all rights associated with the copyright, unless specifically relinquished. This has rather important implications for a company that wishes to monetize a copyright created by someone it hires to author a work. For example, Microsoft hires a software programmer to code device drivers for a video display. By default, under copyright law the software programmer owns the source code created to control the video display and, as the copyright owner for the source code, the programmer controls the rights to make copies of, sell, display, or make derivative works of the original source code. Thus, if the software programmer so decided, he or she could prevent Microsoft from using the source code, even though Microsoft may have paid the software programmer to create it. This has an obvious impact for Microsoft and its ability to generate value from the video display driver. If the software programmer disallowed Microsoft from using the source code, Microsoft would generate no value. At the very least, the software programmer might demand that Microsoft pay a reasonable fee to license the source code for use. Both can have a material value impact to Microsoft specifically and to the value of the copyright in general.

Microsoft's protection in such a situation against claims from the software programmer is to commission the creation of the video display driver source code under a "work made for hire" (WMFH) provision under 17 U.S.C. §101, which defines a WMFH as "a work prepared by an employee within the scope of his or her employment." This means that if an employee creates a work for an employer, the employer would own the copyright, making the verification of ownership simpler for the IP valuation analyst to perform. Microsoft's easy fix would be to ensure that the

148 Calculated by taking the present value of a five-year annuity of $200,000 using a discount rate of 25%.
149 $598,122.43 - $537,856 = $60,266.43 impairment.

software programmer was an employee of Microsoft. However, the WMFH provision between a company and its employee is not a panacea. For example, suppose an independent contractor were to create the source code. In that case, the work's creator would not be an employee and the work would not necessarily come under the first definition of WMFH. The statute, 17 U.S.C. §101, provides a second definition, allowing two parties to specifically agree that a work would still be considered under the WMFH provision. However, only works of certain types would receive such consideration under the following definition:

> ... a work specially ordered or commissioned for use as a contribution to a collective work, as a part of a motion picture or other audiovisual work, as a translation, as a supplementary work, as a compilation, as an instructional text, as a test, as answer material for a test, or as an atlas, if the parties expressly agree in a written instrument signed by them that the work shall be considered a work made for hire. For the purpose of the foregoing sentence, a "supplementary work" is a work prepared for publication as a secondary adjunct to a work by another author for the purpose of introducing, concluding, illustrating, explaining, revising, commenting upon, or assisting in the use of the other work, such as forewords, afterwords, pictorial illustrations, maps, charts, tables, editorial notes, musical arrangements, answer material for tests, bibliographies, appendixes, and indexes, and an "instructional text" is a literary, pictorial, or graphic work prepared for publication and with the purpose of use in systematic instructional activities.[150]

The two parties must agree in writing that the WMFH provision applies to the work, as long as it is one of the following:

- Specially ordered or commissioned for use as a contribution to a collective work;
- Part of a motion picture or audiovisual work;
- A translation (e.g., converting a classic book from English to German);
- A supplementary work (e.g., something prepared to go with another work created by another author, such as an introduction, forward, afterward, or appendixes in a book);
- A compilation (i.e., the collection and assembling of preexisting materials or of data that are selected, coordinated, or arranged in such a way that

150 17 U.S.C. §101.

the resulting work as a whole constitutes an original work of authorship, such as a book of stories from famous authors);

- An instructional text, such as this guide;
- A test or answer material for a test (e.g., the SATs);
- An atlas; or
- A sound recording.

Microsoft likely has all of its employees and subcontractors perform all works of authorship under a WMFH. Moreover, to the extent that the title to the works of authorship does not, by operation of law, vest in Microsoft, or to the extent that the title is not a WMFH, Microsoft would likely require its employees and subcontractors to irrevocably assign to it all rights to the title and interest to the work. Not doing so can create problems, as Microsoft may have to defend itself against a claim of copyright infringement by the work's creator.

It is crucial that the IP valuation analyst verify the ownership rights to copyrighted works. Ideally, the IP valuation analyst relies on the opinion of competent legal counsel to make a determination as to the ownership of the work if there is any potential for dispute as to whether the work classifies as a WMFH. Failure to do so may cause the IP valuation analyst to maintain an erroneous view of the company's ability to control and monetize the copyright, and it may impair value in that the IP valuation analyst has not factored in the risk of a copyright author asserting his or her rights. At the least, it may require a company to pay an associated royalty, which could also impair value. At worst, the company may not have the right to monetize the copyright in the market, removing any associated economic benefits altogether.

Copyright Notice

Historically, copyright owners had to provide notice that a particular item had copyright protection. In particular, for copyrights originated prior to March 1, 1989, the copyright owner had to provide such notice. Failure to do so would not preserve the copyright protection. This of course has a strong value impact, for without enforceability, a copyright would retain no value. Thus, the IP valuation analyst should verify the nature of the copyright notice and its potential value impacts. This is less important for copyrights originated after March 1, 1989, because those copyrights do not have a requirement to provide notice. However, a copyright owner who provides notice may have a stronger value proposition just the same.

One author notes that a copyright owner may be able to mount a stronger defense against claims of innocent infringement.[151] A claim of innocent infringement is a defense strategy by an accused copyright infringer that his or her infringement was accidental, and the accused infringer did not realize he or she was infringing the protected work. An accused infringer can mount this strategy only if the owner of the infringed work does not provide proper notice to the public for the copyright protection. Thus, providing notice can improve value by reducing the chances of impairing a possible judgment because of an innocent infringement defense.

Ease of Duplication

Copyrighted works can come in many forms. Some forms include sculptures that are large, heavy objects difficult to duplicate or are at least easier to find when duplication occurs. Others may include electronic books, computer source code, sheet music, or songs. Each of these copyright instances is relatively easy to duplicate, especially with modern technology. An infringer could duplicate an electronic book copy merely by copying it from one computer to another (assuming the duplicator did not encounter any digital rights management protections). An infringer could easily copy computer source code, whether it included direct download of all source files, the cutting and pasting of source lines into another document, or the physical reproduction of a printed version of the source code with a copy machine, which an infringer could also easily do with sheet music. In each instance, the copyright owner loses control over the work, meaning the owner could lose a potential opportunity to monetize the copyright. If a piece of sheet music sells for $4.95, the copyright owner loses the opportunity to capture that $4.95, because the infringer copied the sheet music for the cost of a photocopy. The incremental cost for copying a song is insignificant, creating serious revenue impairments, as the Recording Industry Association of America (RIAA) knows acutely from its protracted litigations over the last decade stemming from the proliferation of digital portable music players and the growth of computers with CD drives.

Of course, a natural outgrowth of a copyrighted work that is easy to duplicate is the difficulty that the copyright owner will have in detecting unauthorized duplication of the work and then the subsequent defense. Moreover, the enforcement becomes much more expensive as duplication becomes easier. For example, the RIAA initiated more than 35,000 lawsuits from 2003 through 2008 in an attempt to

151 Richard Stim, *Patent, Copyright, and Trademark: An Intellectual Property Desk Reference*, 9th ed., Nolo, Berkeley, Calif., 2007, p. 271.

combat rampant sharing of music files on peer-to-peer networks.[152] In what became an utter public relations disaster (the RIAA wound up suing the elderly, children, even a dead person), it ultimately abandoned the strategy in December 2008, but not without massive cost. Even if the RIAA spent just $10,000 on average for each action including infringement detection, discovery, and litigation, the sum total cost to the industry would be about $350 million.[153] It was a failed strategy.

The main point of these examples is this: the easier the ability of an infringer to duplicate the copyrighted work without getting caught, the greater the potential value impairment for the copyright. IP valuation analysts must evaluate the nature of copyrighted works and determine whether there is a risk for possible impairment associated with the ease of duplicating the work. The IP valuation analyst could account for this risk by lowering the projected number of forecast sales. Alternatively, the valuation analyst could increase the discount rate associated with the future free cash flows to account for a greater uncertainty surrounding the collection of those cash flows (possibly due to a reduced potential success rate).

Mechanical Rights for Nondramatic Musical Works

Under 17 U.S.C. §115, nondramatic musical works (e.g., music that does not include operas or overtures, such as rock, country, or pop songs) provide the copyright owner with economic benefits associated with the rights to reproduce the work. Known as a mechanical right, it provides the copyright owner with a compulsory, established payment for each instantiation of the song in mechanical form. Thus, every time a music publisher makes a mechanical copy of the song on a phonorecord (e.g., CD, DVD, cassette tape) or permanent digital download (e.g., download to an iPod), the copyright owner receives payment for the copy under a compulsory license. Copyright law sets forth the rate of payment that the copyright owner receives for each copy. As of this publication, the rates are as follows:

- $0.091 per phonocopy or permanent digital download for songs five minutes or less in length;
- $0.0175 per minute of playing time for songs greater than five minutes; and
- $0.24 royalty per copy for ringtones that may be used on cell phones.

152 Sarah McBride and Ethan Smith, "Music Industry to Abandon Mass Suits," *The Wall Street Journal*, December 19, 2008.

153 In reality, the RIAA has spent more than $100 million in legal services, investigative services, and other services attempting to enforce its copyrights as of the time of this writing.

Thus, a four-minute song pressed for 10,000 copies would generate a mechanical royalty of $910.[154] If the song were five minutes and one second in length, it would generate a royalty of $0.105 per copy,[155] and $1,050 for 10,000 copies.[156] If the song generated 10,000 ringtone downloads, it would generate a mechanical royalty of $2,400. Importantly, compulsory licenses apply only to nondramatic musical compositions. As such, an IP valuation analyst must consider the nature of the work, perhaps consulting with legal counsel, to determine the applicability of payments associated with mechanical rights.

The discussion of mechanical rights for copyright valuations is important for several reasons. First, one can monetize the copyrights of a recording artist's song, so long as he or she pays the recording artist a mechanical royalty, which would show up as a claim against any revenue that is the subject of the valuation engagement. Typically, one would contact Harry Fox Agency, Inc. (www.harryfox.com), a mechanical licensing, collection, and distribution agency for music publishers, to request a mechanical license and to report payments required under the license, paying royalties quarterly.

Second, recording artists may negotiate lower mechanical rates with music publishers. If this is the case, any lower mechanical rates may represent a lesser claim against the revenues generated by the mechanical copy. The value impact depends on the perspective of the party to the transaction. For example, a songwriter who agrees to a $0.05 per copy royalty impairs the value of the song with respect to mechanical rights.[157] However, just the presence of the mechanical right and its associated payment may create extra value through increased royalties, because there is a required payment to the songwriter for each copy.

Termination of Transfers

While not discussed often in valuation literature, copyright owners have the ability to terminate transfers of copyrights and licenses granted by an author unilaterally, but only if it is not a work made for hire, and the work's publication occurred after January 1, 1978. Described thoroughly in 17 U.S.C. §203, the author or surviving family members who possess greater than 50% of the ownership rights of the copyright may terminate the grant or copyright license. It is an odd statute, however, as the transfer can only occur for a five-year period that begins at the end of the 35th

154 10,000 copies x $0.091 per copy = $910.

155 5:01 rounded to six minutes x $0.0175 per minute = $0.105.

156 10,000 copies x $0.105 per copy = $1,050.

157 Of course, if the songwriter does this in order to gain access to the music publisher's distribution network, the increased publishing volume that the music publisher brings to the songwriter may erase any foregone mechanical royalty amounts.

year after the original grant or publication. For example, the author of this book transfers the copyright to the publisher in 2011. At the end of the 35th year (2046), the author could terminate the copyright transfer to the publisher. However, the author would have to exercise this termination between 2046 and 2051. Failure to execute the termination within that window would cost the author the ability to do so. Importantly, ownership of derivative works by the transferee would remain with the transferee. Thus, an author would not be able to terminate the transfer and then claim all derivative works from the transferee, even though the derivative works have a basis in the author's original copyright.

Of course, the value impact of this could materialize in two forms, which are important in evaluating copyright assets for valuation. First, the transfer to the author could be accretive, especially if there is still demand for the work (e.g., an author's classic book). Second, the transfer could be destructive, especially if the transferee is using the copyright in a line of business. For example, suppose that a major publisher is selling copies of a book that generates $1 million per year in free cash flow. If the author terminates the grant in accordance with 17 U.S.C. §203, then the publisher loses a cash flow stream. The IP valuation analyst should consider the impacts and probabilities of termination of transfers for the valuation assignment. Failure to do so may lead the valuation analyst to an incorrect conclusion as to whether the party monetizing the copyright will have the rights to do so.

Public Domain

Under copyright law, a creative work in the public domain maintains no copyright protection. Thus, the public may freely use the work. Naturally, this has a value impact that the valuation analyst must consider. There is no value proposition attributable to a copyright in the public domain because there is no actionable claim that a copyright owner can make against one who uses a work in the public domain.

A copyright can enter the public domain in several ways, including the following:[158]

- The work published before 1923;
- The work published between 1923 and 1963, but the owner never renewed it;
- The work consists of facts or ideas, which are not copyrightable since they lack creativity or originality (see discussion of factual works earlier in this chapter);

158 Richard Stim, *Patent, Copyright, and Trademark: An Intellectual Property Desk Reference*, 9th ed., Nolo, Berkeley, Calif., 2007, p. 284.

- The work published before 1978 and lacked proper copyright notice;
- The work published between 1978 and 1989 and had a defective copyright notice;
- The copyright owner placed the work into the public domain deliberately;
- The U.S. government created the work (works created by the federal government enjoy no copyright protection); and
- The creation of the work occurred prior to 1978, but publication did not occur before December 31, 2003.

The IP valuation analyst should verify that the copyright does not belong in the public domain, otherwise the valuation analyst might incorrectly assign a value to the copyright that an owner would have no legal standing to enforce.

Visual Artists Rights Act of 1990

The Berne Convention for the Protection of Literary and Artistic Works (Berne Convention), which forms the basis for copyright law to its signatories (including the United States), grants moral rights, which are a subset of the rights of creators of copyrighted works. Codified by 17 U.S.C. §106A, also known as the Visual Artists Rights Act of 1990 (VARA), moral rights provide a copyright owner with some unique attributes. Such attributes include the right to claim authorship of the work and the right to prevent the use of a creator's name with a work not originated by the creator or associated with the creator's work. They also include the ability of the creator to prevent the distortion, mutilation, or destruction of the work. The value impact is straightforward. Art protected by the VARA may tend to have a higher value for other similar copyrighted items, all else the same, as the copyright owner has an additional enforcement mechanism to extract value or damages from the copyrighted work.

Under the VARA, moral rights apply exclusively to visual arts such as sculptures, paintings, and the like. Nonvisual arts, such as computer software source code or the text of this guide, while maintaining copyright protection, do not maintain protection under the VARA. The VARA is important in the context of an IP valuation engagement, particularly if there is a chance that the asset owner may experience impairment due to violation of the VARA. A violation of the VARA may surface in physical destruction or mutilation of the copyrighted work. For example, the Gramercy on the Park condominium complex commissioned sculptor Andrew Werby to create a bronze sculpture called Spiropod to stand in front of the building.

However, the association did not contractually limit the rights of the artist regarding the sculpture. The association decided to take down the sculpture without the owner's permission, replacing it with a flagpole. In an expensive lesson, Werby sued the association under the California Art Preservation Act (similar in many respects to the VARA) and ultimately received a settlement for $150,000 for the illegal destruction of the sculpture.[159]

As the example demonstrates, when considering the value of a copyright, the valuation analyst should understand the risk of any possible future litigation relating to the VARA and account for such risk appropriately, perhaps with a higher associated discount rate for future cash flows attributable to the work. Alternatively, and what would have been beneficial for the Gramercy on the Park condominium association, the party that commissions the copyrighted work should require all rights to the work from the hired party as a hiring condition.

Special Considerations for Computer Software

Computer software is unique among IP types in that it may simultaneously receive protection under patent and copyright laws. Elements of computer software are oftentimes the subject of patents if the computer program integrates into a machine, is manufactured to perform a process, or if it manipulates data to achieve a practical application.[160] Yet copyright law also covers the *expression* of software (i.e., the actual source code in raw or compiled form) from the moment the author fixes the work in tangible form, such as saving it to a computer's disk drive or printing it in hard copy form. Ordinarily, this should not create difficulty for the valuation analyst because the scope of the valuation engagement will delineate whether the property of interest in the valuation is the copyright or the patent. Practically, the expression of a patented idea in software may be incidental to the overall value of the software program, as one of ordinary skill in the art could likely reproduce the software just by reading the patent without ever having access to the original source code covered under copyright law. Moreover, one of ordinary skill in the art could reproduce the function the software intends to serve with a different computer language, making the issue of copyright defense to the originator moot.

For example, suppose that an inventor figures out a way to add two numbers together and review their sum (assume for the example that such a concept is patentable, which in actuality it is not). An inventor reduces the invention to practice by coding

159 Mark Abramson, "Artist Nets Big Bucks for Sculpture Removal," *Oakland Tribune*, February 13, 2008.

160 "Examination Guidelines for Computer-Related Inventions, Final Version," United States Patent and Trademark Office, http://www.uspto.gov/web/offices/pac/dapp/pdf/ciig.pdf, November 30, 2008.

it in the C++ computer language, which looks as follows:

```
x = 42;

y = 24;

z = x + y;
```

The variables "x" and "y" each contain ordinal values. The computer's compiler understands that the "+" operator will take the sum of "x" and "y" and place the result in "z." The inventor receives copyright protection for all of the authored C++ source code under copyright law. However, an independent software programmer implements the same exact algorithm in assembly language for the Intel x8086 platform. The same algorithm expressed in C++ is as follows in assembly language:

```
MOV z, 0

MOV x, 42

MOV y, 24

ADD z, x

ADD z, y
```

In both examples, the variable "z" contains the value of 66 at the end of the calculation. However, the expression of how to perform that addition operation obviously varied depending on the computer language that the author used to express the algorithm. Moreover, the author could express the algorithm in C++ differently from the original work and get the same result. The following source code examples generate the same result as the first C++ example—the variable "z" will contain the value of 66, which is the sum of variables "x" and "y":

First example:

```
z = 0;

x = 42;

z += x;

y = 24;

z += y;
```

Second example:

```
int addNumbers( int firstTerm, int secondTerm)
{
    return firstTerm + secondTerm;
}
...
x = 42;
y = 24;
z = addNumbers( x, y );
```

As the example demonstrates, the analysis can become quite complex when only software source code exists, as software programmers can express their solutions to solving a given problem (i.e., authoring source code) in literally an infinite number of forms. That said, companies may avoid the patenting of software concepts due to the extended time and cost it takes to receive a patent award and the fast pace of technological change. In such situations, companies may instead rely on copyright law to protect their source code. This introduces several factors that may increase the difficulty and/or uncertainty of a valuation engagement. These factors include the following:

- The ease in avoiding infringing activity;
- The consideration of the "Rule of Doubt"; and
- The complete or partial disclosure of the source code.

Easier to Avoid Infringing Activity

Software consists of both state (i.e., data) and behavior (i.e., functions that use data). Software programmers reflect the state using data structures to represent both simple and complex concepts. For example, the computer has a means to represent an abstract object like a car with data. The data would signify the number of wheels the car has, its color, steering wheel position, heading, speed, and many other factors. The behavior of the car would represent things that the car can actually do, such as steer left, steer right, accelerate, slow down, crash, etc. The data itself is of little value in software without functions to use that data. Importantly, the copyright protects the expression of how to implement a behavior and the state. It does not protect the utility behind it. Thus, in the car example, a software designer receives copyright protection for the expression of the car in software form, primarily through source code. However, the copyright does not protect the actual algorithms or means to steer left, steer right, accelerate, or perform any of the associated behaviors of the car.

As software programmers can represent state and behavior in literally an infinite number of ways, it makes it relatively easy for another company to originate something that provides the same utility without fear of an infringement action. This reduces the potential value that may accrue to the software, since one may be able to reproduce the expression of the state and the behavior for a cost lower than what the original author may want to charge in the open market. The risk associated with future cash flows attributable to the software may also increase as well, as it may be more difficult for a company to extract value from the software due to increased competition. The potential value impairment just described is not necessarily important for some valuation engagements, particularly if the costs to reproduce the copyrighted software would include significant sums or take a company out of a competitive market for a protracted time.

For example, suppose that Company A implements a data model that describes a policy administration system in the insurance industry. Company A is the first to create a successful implementation of the system, despite significant efforts by others in the industry.[161] It may be less expensive for another insurer, Company B, to pay Company A a significant license fee for the rights to Company A's source code, as the risks and costs assumed by Company B in attempting its own implementation can be prohibitive, despite the publication of the complete model's specification.

Disclosure

Software developers who register their source codes with the U.S. Copyright Office may be reticent to provide the original source codes. One key reason for not doing so is to prevent the publication of key company trade secrets expressed in the source code that the copyright owner does not wish to introduce into the public view. Of course, another key reason to avoid full disclosure of a source code is that it would be easy for a competitor to review the registration with the U.S. Copyright Office and learn how a competitor implemented a key value-creating feature. This creates two problems for the copyright owner. First, it would be difficult to detect the copyright infringement for such activity, as already discussed in Chapter 5. Second, the complete disclosure may erase any value-creating opportunity for the original software developer. For example, suppose that Microsoft developed a means

161 Failure rates in insurance applications are high, and such failures can routinely equate to tens or hundreds of millions of dollars in cost.

to generate very large Excel workbooks that require minimal computer resources to process. Under such a situation, Microsoft may desire copyright protection for its source code, yet disclosing all of its source code would provide key competitors such as Corel (with its Quattro Pro X4 product) with intimate knowledge into how Microsoft created its high-performing spreadsheet. If Corel were to have access to Microsoft's source code, Microsoft would potentially lose the ability to generate higher revenues typically associated with proprietary products.

Fortunately for software developers, the U.S. Copyright Office does allow them to submit redacted source code (i.e., the author blanks out every other line in the source code, requiring a potential infringer to "fill in the blanks" for the redacted areas of the source code).[162] Additionally, software developers could submit compiled object code instead of pure source code to the U.S. Copyright Office. Compiled object code is a binary representation of the software generated through the compilation and assembly process associated with taking high-level computer software and transforming it to a form understandable by the computer. Compiled object code is very difficult to understand and reverse-engineer. While it is possible to reverse-engineer what the source code is doing, given the size and scale of today's complex software applications, reverse engineering software based on modifying object code is a laborious process. For example, the following are the first 32 bytes of the Microsoft Word 2003 program:

4D 5A 90 00 03 00 00 00 04 00 00 00 FF FF 00 00

B8 00 00 00 00 00 00 00 40 00 00 00 00 00 00 00

With proper documentation for a trained professional, one could deduce what was going on just in these first 32 bytes of the program. However, considering that the complete Microsoft Word program consists of tens of millions of bytes of this object code, reverse-engineering the program in any measure of time where the effort would generate reasonable economic activity is practically impossible.

While the compiled object code is difficult for a competitor to understand and reverse-engineer, the U.S. Copyright Office also finds it difficult to understand. As such, while the U.S. Copyright Office allows a copyright owner to submit compiled object code in lieu of high-level source code, the office does not take the pains to verify that the compiled object code qualifies for copyright protection. Instead, it disclaims certainty surrounding copyright applicability with the Rule of Doubt.

162 The copyright owner could petition the U.S. Copyright Office for a variance to depart from the traditional requirement for copyright registration or deposit; however, no guarantees exist that the U.S. Copyright Office would be willing to do so.

The Rule of Doubt

The Rule of Doubt is a rule under which a copyright owner does not register the source code directly with the U.S. Copyright Office in order to avoid disclosure of proprietary algorithms and/or programming conventions:

> The rule under which the U.S. Copyright Office allows object code to be deposited in connection with a computer program registration. The rule of doubt means there is an express understanding that doubt exists as to whether the code qualifies for copyright protection should litigation later occur. In essence, the U.S. Copyright Office is saying, "We will let you deposit object code, but since we can't read or understand it, we won't commit ourselves as to its copyrightability." If the registration is accomplished under the rule of doubt, the copyright owner may be unable to claim the presumption of ownership—an important benefit of registration—should the issue end up in court because of an alleged copyright infringement.[163]

The valuation analyst should consider the impact of the Rule of Doubt on potential software value, particularly if the software owner submits object code to the U.S. Copyright Office instead of high-level source code. While the copyright owner preserves trade secrets associated with the program by submitting object code, the software's creator may not have a protectable asset; thus, any resulting copyright value would be zero, since the software's owner would not maintain enforceable copyright protection.

Special Considerations for Semiconductor Designs or Masks

Semiconductors are materials that form the basis for integrated circuits, which may collectively include memory chips, microprocessors, and other similar miniaturized electronic circuits. These integrated circuits contain miniature designs of electrical circuits that form a pattern etched into silicon by sophisticated equipment to form the basis for a product. To create a microprocessor, one must first design the circuits that comprise the microprocessor. The manufacturer will then create a mask that represents the design that the manufacturer then uses to etch the circuit design into the silicon, which becomes an integral part of the final product. For the novice, a semiconductor mask is akin to a film negative. It is a two- or three-dimensional arrangement of transistors, resistors, and other electrical components that form the basis for an integrated circuit design. It provides the pattern that manufacturing equipment uses to replicate the microprocessor design for production volumes.

163 http://www.nolo.com/dictionary/rule-of-doubt-term.html.

As the electrical circuit designs represent a work of authorship, they receive protection under copyright law, specifically under 17 U.S.C. §§901-914. Codified in the Semiconductor Chip Protection Act of 1984 (semiconductor designs and masks did not receive copyright protection before this time), Congress provides protection with certain caveats:

- First, under 17 U.S.C. §905, a mask owner receives protection to reproduce the mask work by optical, electronic, or any other means; the ability to import or distribute a product that embodies the mask; and the ability to license others to exercise the owner's reproduction, importation, and distribution rights.

- Second, under 17 U.S.C. §904, semiconductor masks receive protection for only 10 years from either the date of first commercial exploitation or from the date the mask's owner registers the mask with the U.S. Copyright Office. This statutory life is much shorter than the protection duration that other copyrighted items receive, which span many decades. Thus, a valuation analyst must consider the shorter statutory life when performing a remaining economic life analysis. While it is common for some chip designs to remain in the market for many years (e.g., Motorola 68000 series processors), any applicable mask copyrights would expire while the processor still remains on the market.

- Third, a competitor may reverse-engineer semiconductor masks. In fact, under 17 U.S.C. §906(a), a person may "reproduce the mask work solely for the purpose of teaching, analyzing, or evaluating the concepts or techniques embodied in the mask work or the circuitry, logic flow, or organization of components used in the mask work . . . to incorporate the results of such conduct in an original mask work which is made to be distributed." Moreover, a person who reverse-engineers a mask work can use elements of the work without creating a derivative work, which is another departure from other copyrighted items. This makes a semiconductor mask subject to easier copying, increasing the associated risk with forecasted future cash flows that the valuation analyst might consider.

- Fourth, unlike other copyrighted works, a mask owner must register the mask with the U.S. Copyright Office within two years of the first commercial exploitation of the mask anywhere in the world. Under 17 U.S.C. §908(a), if the mask owner fails to register the mask within this time frame, the mask loses copyright protection. Thus, the mask would have no copyright value, as a competitor could use the mask's design without legal repercussion from the mask's original owner.

As the previous points highlight, the valuation analyst has to consider several key departures from existing copyright law in the evaluation of semiconductor masks. The failure to account properly for these departures, such as using the wrong statutory life or underestimating the risk from competitive products, could lead the valuation analyst to an improper value conclusion.

Chapter 8
Trademark Due Diligence

Trademarks provide a vendor with a means to identify and/or differentiate goods and services from others in the market. Trademarks apply to products. Service marks apply to services.[164] In general, trademarks reduce buyer search costs (i.e., the costs a buyer incurs to find a product or service that meets the buyer's need).[165] If a trademark has value, it will increase the free cash flow of the firm that the seller would not otherwise generate. If the trademark cannot increase free cash flow, then it may have no value to the firm. If the trademark prevents the generation of free cash flow, it may actually impair the firm's value.

Interestingly, while the U.S. Constitution maintains provisions for patents and copyrights under Article 1, Section 8, Clause 8,[166] it does not maintain provisions for trademarks. Trademarks in the United States did not maintain protection under federal law until passage of the Lanham Act of 1946.[167] Before that, trademark protection occurred at the state level. This created several problems for the trademark

164 For practical purposes, this guide uses service mark interchangeably with trademark, as is common in professional literature (e.g., few law firms advertise "service mark" law specialties, though they do advertise trademark specialties).

165 William M. Landes, and Richard A. Posner, *The Economic Structure of Intellectual Property Law*, The Belknap Press of Harvard University Press, Cambridge, Mass., 2003, p. 64.

166 "The Congress shall have power to . . . promote the progress of science and useful arts, by securing for limited times to authors and inventors the exclusive right to their respective writings and discoveries," which does not apply to trademarks since they do not constitute science or useful arts.

167 Trademarks actually fall under the jurisdiction of the Commerce Clause under Article 1, Section 8, Clause 3, which states that Congress has the power "to regulate commerce with foreign nations, and among the several states, and with the Indian tribes." An interesting side effect of this is that federal trademark law does not cover intrastate commerce, as that is a power reserved by the states. Thus, valuation analysts need to have some familiarity with both federal and state trademark laws depending on the nature of the valuation engagement and the trademark usage.

owner, which could change the trademark's value. First, the trademark owner had different rules to consider for trademark enforcement in each state, increasing costs to maintain and defend trademarks. Second, the trademark owner might not be able to use a trademark in a particular state if another business were already using that mark. For example, Waffle House Inc. is a national chain of restaurants specializing in low-cost, short-order cooked food that operates under the "Waffle House" moniker, with the following distinctive black and yellow sign:

WAFFLE
HOUSE®

Interestingly, in its federal trademark registration, Waffle House maintains registration of the trademark in the entire United States "except for the states of Indiana, Michigan, and Wisconsin, and the northeast portion of Illinois from 10 (ten) miles north and east of interstate highway 74." This is because other preexisting companies are using the "Waffle House" name in those geographic areas, and have been since well before Waffle House Inc. sought to enter those areas. Until 2005, Waffle House Inc. named stores in Indiana "Waffle Steak" because the "Waffle House" name was already in use when Waffle House Inc. entered that state. It used the following logo instead:

WAFFLE
STEAK®

Naturally, while the Waffle Steak logo has much in common with the Waffle House logo, creating a common link for the consumer, the dual trademarks and branding strategies impair the total trademark value opportunity for Waffle House Inc., as it must maintain dual sales and marketing efforts, which increase the costs associated with maintaining and using the trademarks.

Trademarks create value in any combination of the following three ways or variants thereof:

- *Lower sales and marketing costs:* Trademarks reduce buyer search costs, as buyers might not have to spend as much time finding a product that they trust—buyers trust the brand or trademark associated with the product or service. This translates directly into value for a seller of a good or service because the seller might expend incrementally fewer dollars to close a deal, compared with competitors in the market. For example, in 2008 Starbucks had 16,680 locations (i.e., company-owned stores and licensed retailers) and generated $9.94 billion from those locations.[168] That equates to average revenue per location of about $596,000. Starbucks spent $129 million in advertising, or about $7,733 per location, which is roughly 1.3% of total revenues. A typical food service industry spends 2% to 5% of total revenues on advertising. This means that Starbucks sells coffee that requires less marketing expenditures than what might be typical for local coffee retailers, because Starbucks has established a strong brand experience for its customers. Thus, Starbucks has a competitive advantage of 0.7% to 3.7% because of its strong brand.

- *Greater revenues:* Trademarks have an uncanny ability to instill value in the eyes of the buyer. This value can translate directly into the ability of the seller to charge the buyer a premium for its good or service over competitors. Recall the example from Chapter 3 in which Morton is able to charge a premium for its otherwise generic sodium chloride (i.e., salt) because Morton has built a brand in the eyes of the buyer. An attorney with a stellar reputation is able to charge a premium over other attorneys because of that stellar reputation. This can easily amount to hundreds of thousands of dollars in earnings for the attorney. Starbucks can charge much more for a cup of coffee compared to local retailers (e.g., convenience stores) in part because of its strong brand.

- *Greater market share or faster market adoption:* Trademarks can create market share for a seller, or assist the seller in getting to the market faster. This translates directly into value for a seller of a good or service because

168 2008 Form 10-K, Starbucks Corporation, November 24, 2008.

> the seller might generate an incrementally greater product sales volume, compared with competitors in the market. Again, consider Starbucks. It has greater market share in part because of its strong brand, which it calls the "Starbucks Experience." The Starbucks Experience builds product loyalty, which relates directly to Starbucks' trademarks.

For a trademark to be valuable, it must create value along the lines of at least one of these three value creation sources. The reason that young trademarks (i.e., new trademarks applied to products or services that have a relatively short history of use) do not command much value is because the trademarks do not yet create value for the seller. Young trademarks generally require significant investments in marketing to create associated goodwill, oftentimes greater than existing products that already have traction. Next, young trademarks have not yet had the time to create value in the eyes of the buyer; thus, it may be unclear (especially with introductory pricing on new products) whether the trademark creates value. Lastly, young trademarks will not command significant market share or adoption as they are new to the market and require time to build confidence and trust in the eyes of the buyer.

Some trademarks may create value by combining the three value creation sources. For example, the basic Starbucks trademark possesses this trait. Starbucks spends less than competitors do for sales and marketing costs, which creates trademark value. Yet Starbucks charges significantly more for a cup of coffee than its competitors do, which also creates trademark value. Lastly, Starbucks has significant market share and can move the market, which also creates value.

Importantly, not all trademarks will create value. Some can in fact destroy value. For example, consider the brand name ValuJet for an airline. ValuJet was an Atlanta-based start-up discount airline. Founded in 1993, with its first flight in October 1993, ValuJet grew from one plane to 51, generating $368 million in revenue in just under three years. Becoming profitable faster than any other airline had, ValuJet was also growing fast, with orders for 50 planes in 1995 and an option for 50 more. ValuJet had only one problem: a horrible safety record. ValuJet had an accident rate 14 times that of major carriers.[169] Moreover, ValuJet's founders built the airline on a fleet of aging aircraft purchased from around the world. ValuJet outsourced maintenance operations, and ongoing maintenance issues plagued the airline. The airline had five emergency landings in 1994, 57 in 1995, and 59 from January through May 1996—one almost every other day.[170] ValuJet's performance was so terrible that the

169 Mary Shiavo, "Flying into Trouble," *Time Magazine*, July 14, 2008.
170 *Id.*

Department of Defense rejected a bid from ValuJet to fly military personnel in 1995.

ValuJet's maintenance record caught up with it in a terrible way on May 11, 1996. Flight 592, en route from Miami to Atlanta, crashed in the Florida Everglades after a fire erupted in the cargo bay. The Federal Aviation Administration (FAA) suspected that the ground crew had loaded oxygen generators improperly in the cargo bay and that these generators activated in flight, leaking pure oxygen into the cabin and generating heat that ultimately facilitated a fire that brought the plane down, killing all people on board. Within weeks, the FAA grounded the airline for just over three months, forcing it to comply with a variety of maintenance and safety requirements. The impact was catastrophic for ValuJet. It lost $55 million by the time it brought in a new CEO in November 1996 and ultimately merged with a much smaller competitor, flying under its moniker AirTran. The ValuJet brand was so impaired that it actually hurt the airline to continue to operate under that name, even though ValuJet's successor AirTran was flying the same planes, with the same employees.[171] In a dramatic departure from its former larger rival, AirTran has ranked first or second in Airline Quality Rating between 2007 and 2010.[172] Southwest Airlines subsequently bought AirTran in September 2010 for $1.4 billion.[173]

In a trademark valuation engagement, the valuation analyst should consider all three of the trademark value sources to determine any possible value attributable to the trademark.

What Is Trademark Due Diligence?

Trademark due diligence is somewhat less complicated than other intellectual property types, as there are relatively fewer factors that can derail trademarks administratively. Possible due diligence activity for trademarks includes the following tasks:

- Verify the history and creation of the trademark;
- Verify the trademark registration; and
- Verify the trademark status.

171 Ironically, I wrote this section while flying on AirTran Flight 982 from Indianapolis to Fort Lauderdale. AirTran's ValuJet roots did not impair my ticket purchase. However, my safety experiences with Aeroflot airlines in Russia will keep me from ever flying with that airline again.

172 Kelly Yamanouchi, "AirTran Tops Annual Airline Ranking," *The Atlanta Journal-Constitution*, April 4, 2011.

173 Mike Esterl, "Discount Carriers Southwest, AirTran Tie Knot," *The Wall Street Journal*, September 28, 2010.

History and Creation of the Trademark

The history of trademark creation has an important bearing on the legal strength of the trademark. As is the case with other IP types, the stronger the trademark, the more valuable it is. Trademarks can receive protection under common law, state law, and federal law. The legal complexity of these differing venues makes it difficult for a trademark owner to protect a trademark. This makes it difficult for a trademark creator, because it means that the trademark creator must perform a wide-ranging search to demonstrate a good faith effort to detect potential conflicts at both the federal and state levels.

Important in the creation of a trademark is the extent to which the trademark owner seeks to discover potential conflicts with trademarks that already exist. For example, Company A decides to register trademark SuperCow associated with the selling of a dairy product. However, Company B already owns the SuperCow trademark for that purpose. Thus, Company A may not be able to use the SuperCow trademark. This is important for the valuation analyst in several ways. First, Company A cannot legally use the trademark in a manner consistent with the valuation engagement, because Company B's ownership of the SuperCow trademark blocks Company A from using the trademark. The result is simple: the trademark as applied has no value for Company A. Second, if Company A does market its dairy product under the SuperCow trademark, it may face a legal fight from Company B. This can be quite costly. Third, if Company A did market its dairy product under the SuperCow trademark, and Company B forced Company A to rebrand its product, Company A might have to expend significant sums to recall and destroy all existing products and replace them with new products under a trademark that does not conflict with Company B's SuperCow trademark. This can be quite expensive. The valuation analyst might have to consider the possibility of these costs during the valuation engagement. Naturally, such costs have a depressing value effect, as these costs match against any associated economic benefits.

For example, The Sports Authority, Inc. (TSA) sued Prime Hospitality Corp. (PHC) for both federal trademark infringement and dilution under state law over PHC's use of "Sports Authority" associated with its restaurants. TSA is a national sporting goods retailer. PHC is a hotel operator that ran eight sports-related restaurants at some of its hotels on the East Coast. The court took notice that PHC did not perform a meaningful trademark conflict search when it developed its sports-themed restaurants, and that was a factor in the court's decision.[174] While this fact alone might not cause the valuation analyst to impair a trademark's value, if the trademark were part

174 *Sports Authority v. Prime Hospital Corp.*, 89 F3d 955 (2nd Cir 1996).

of a litigation effort, the status of any prior searches might become more important. A lack of any meaningful search (i.e., a commissioned search that includes searches of federal, state, and common law trademarks) might increase the risk for the trademark to survive the litigation. The valuation analyst would then reduce the value accordingly to account for the increased risk of future free cash flows.

Recall that Waffle House has geographic restrictions on its federally registered trademarks and operated under a second trademark in Indiana for decades. The company could not operate under its preferred Waffle House moniker due to conflicts with existing businesses. Pharmaceutical companies, afraid of the limitations of using existing words to brand their existing products, generally create altogether new words to describe their products. This ensures that the pharmaceutical companies will not experience any confusion or collision with other existing brands in the market. At the very least, pharmaceutical companies will not likely come across any potential conflicts when attempting to register a new domain name for a product. Cialis, Vyvanse, and Zyprexa all had no prior existence in language. Their trademark owners made the words up. The uniqueness is important to the IP valuation analyst. Trademarks that exhibit the risks of confusion or restriction in the market are going to be worth less than trademarks that do not exhibit these risks.

The valuation analyst should consider the likelihood of potential value impairment because of collisions with the existing market. For most products, this will likely represent a de minimis value impact, as less than 0.5% of trademarks have challenges pending at any given time. However, accounting for the expected value of a potential litigation might well impair a trademark several percentage points after considering the associated costs of litigation, which can easily grow into the high six-figure or low seven-figure range.

For example, Nissan Motor Co. sued Nissan Computer Corp. in a case that garnered much public interest. In a David versus Goliath story, Nissan Motor missed registering the domain nissan.com or nissan.net during the dot-com boom. Uzi Nissan, owner of Nissan Computer, had already registered nissan.com in 1994, well before Nissan Motor. Nissan Motor refused to purchase the domain name from Mr. Nissan for several million dollars and ultimately sued Nissan Computer for trademark infringement, dilution, domain name piracy, false designation of origin, and state law unfair competition. Nissan Motor sought $10 million in damages as well as attorney's fees. Interestingly, the court noted that "Nissan" is a common Jewish/Israeli last name, a biblical term, and an Arabic word for April, and when Nissan Motor entered North America, it did so under the "Datsun" brand. Evidence also presented the fact that "Nissan" was part of the trade name of over 190 unrelated U.S.

businesses and that thousands of domain names contained the word "Nissan," yet Nissan Motor never sued any of the other businesses. Nissan Computer spent nearly $3 million litigating this case. Nissan Motor ultimately lost the case and impaired its own brand in the process with the substantial amount of negative publicity. It might well have been cheaper for Nissan Motor to pay Mr. Nissan early on, though Nissan Motor was likely betting on Mr. Nissan running out of resources to defend himself before a judgment.

Verify the Trademark Registration

As discussed in Chapter 3, trademark registrations depend on the nature of the products and markets that the trademarks represent. Thus, it is important for the IP valuation analyst to ensure that the registration matches the means with which the trademark owner is going to monetize the trademark. For example, the trademark for the word "Infiniti" applies to a variety of different products currently for sale in the market:

- Automobiles: Nissan Motor Co. has been selling luxury automobiles under the Infiniti moniker since 1987. It uses the following logo for its automobiles:[175]

INFINITI

- Heating, ventilation, and cooling (HVAC) systems: Parker Davis HVAC Systems, Inc. has been selling Infiniti HVAC systems under the Infiniti moniker since 1966. It uses the following logo for its products:

INFINITI

175 Nissan Motor Co. has 18 different trademark registrations that include auto insurance products, tools, apparel, dealership services, and even computer games.

- Computer printers: Individual Ming Xu has been selling inkjet color printers under the Infiniti moniker since 2002. Ming uses the following logo for the printers:

INFINITI

- Hair brushes and hair combs: Conair Corp. sells a professional line of hair styling tools under the Infiniti moniker. It uses the following logo for its products:

infiniti by CONAIR

There are literally scores of products registered for trademark protection using the Infiniti moniker, including golf balls, active wear, cigars and cigar accessories, and ceiling fans.

The reason the same trademark name can apply to so many different products and services is that trademark law provides only for protection within a certain class of goods or services, unless the registration would create dilution. Exhibit 74 has a brief overview of the generalized trademark classes that the IP valuation analyst must be cognizant of during a valuation engagement.

Exhibit 74. Generalized Trademark Classes

Class	Trademark Class Description
1	Chemicals used in industry, science, and photography, as well as in agriculture, horticulture, and forestry; unprocessed artificial resins and unprocessed plastics; manures; fire extinguishing compositions; tempering and soldering preparations; chemical substances for preserving foodstuffs; tanning substances; adhesives used in industry
2	Paints, varnishes, and lacquers; preservatives against rust and against deterioration of wood; colorants; mordants; raw natural resins; metals in foil and powder form for painters, decorators, printers, and artists
3	Bleaching preparations and other substances for laundry use; cleaning, polishing, scouring, and abrasive preparations; soaps; perfumery, essential oils, cosmetics, and hair lotions; dentifrices
4	Industrial oils and greases; lubricants; dust absorbing, wetting, and binding compositions; fuels (including motor spirit) and illuminants; candles and wicks
5	Pharmaceutical, veterinary, and sanitary preparations; dietetic substances adapted for medical use and food for babies; plasters and materials for dressings; material for stopping teeth and dental wax; disinfectants; preparations for destroying vermin; fungicides and herbicides

CONTINUED ON NEXT PAGE

Exhibit 74. Generalized Trademark Classes	
Class	**Trademark Class Description**
6	Common metals and their alloys; metal building materials; transportable buildings of metal; materials of metal for railway tracks; nonelectric cables and wires of common metal; ironmongery and small items of metal hardware; pipes and tubes of metal; safes; goods of common metal not included in other classes; ores
7	Machines and machine tools; motors and engines (except for land vehicles); machine coupling and transmission components (except for land vehicles); agricultural implements other than hand operated; incubators for eggs
8	Hand tools and implements (hand operated); cutlery; side arms; razors
9	Scientific, nautical, surveying, electric, photographic, cinematographic, optical, weighing, measuring, signaling, checking (supervision), lifesaving, and teaching apparatus and instruments; apparatus for recording, transmission, or reproduction of sound or images; magnetic data carriers, recording discs; automatic vending machines and mechanisms for coin-operated apparatus; cash registers, calculating machines, data processing equipment, and computers; fire-extinguishing apparatus
10	Surgical, medical, dental, and veterinary apparatus and instruments, artificial limbs, eyes, and teeth; orthopedic articles; suture materials
11	Apparatus for lighting, heating, steam-generating, cooking, refrigerating, drying, ventilating, water supply, and sanitary purposes
12	Vehicles; apparatus for locomotion by land, air, or water
13	Firearms; ammunition and projectiles; explosives; fireworks
14	Precious metals and their alloys, and goods in precious metals or coated therewith not included in other classes; jewelry and precious stones; horological and chronometric instruments
15	Musical instruments
16	Paper, cardboard, and goods made from these materials not included in other classes; printed matter; bookbinding material; photographs; stationery; adhesives for stationery or household purposes; artists' materials; paint brushes; typewriters and office requisites (except furniture); instructional and teaching material (except apparatus); plastic materials for packaging (not included in other classes); playing cards; printers' type; printing blocks.
17	Rubber, gutta-percha, gum, asbestos, mica, and goods made from these materials not included in other classes; plastics in extruded form for use in manufacture; packing, stopping, and insulating materials; flexible pipes, not of metal
18	Leather and imitations of leather, and goods made of these materials not included in other classes; animal skins and hides; trunks and traveling bags; umbrellas, parasols, and walking sticks; whips, harnesses, and saddlery
19	Building materials (non-metallic); non-metallic rigid pipes for building; asphalt, pitch, and bitumen; non-metallic transportable buildings; monuments, not of metal
20	Furniture, mirrors, and picture frames; goods (not included in other classes) of wood, cork, reed, cane, wicker, horn, bone, ivory, whalebone, shell, amber, mother-of-pearl, meerschaum, and substitutes for all these materials, or of plastics

Exhibit 74. Generalized Trademark Classes	
Class	Trademark Class Description
21	Household or kitchen utensils and containers (not of precious metal or coated therewith); combs and sponges; brushes (except paint brushes); brush-making materials; articles for cleaning purposes; steel wool; unworked or semi-worked glass (except glass used in building); glassware, porcelain, and earthenware not included in other classes
22	Ropes, string, nets, tents, awnings, tarpaulins, sails, sacks, and bags (not included in other classes); padding and stuffing materials (except of rubber or plastics); raw fibrous textile materials
23	Yarns and threads, for textile use
24	Textiles and textile goods, not included in other classes; bed and table covers
25	Clothing, footwear, and headgear
26	Lace and embroidery; ribbons and braid; buttons, hooks and eyes, and pins and needles; artificial flowers
27	Carpets, rugs, mats and matting, linoleum, and other materials for covering existing floors; wall hangings (non-textile)
28	Games and playthings; gymnastic and sporting articles not included in other classes; decorations for Christmas trees
29	Meat, fish, poultry, and game; meat extracts; preserved, dried, and cooked fruits and vegetables; jellies, jams, and fruit sauces; eggs, milk, and milk products; edible oils and fats
30	Coffee, tea, cocoa, sugar, rice, tapioca, sago, and artificial coffee; flour and preparations made from cereals, bread, pastry, confectionery, and ices; honey and treacle; yeast and baking powder; salt and mustard; vinegar and sauces (condiments); spices; ice
31	Agricultural, horticultural, and forestry products and grains not included in other classes; living animals; fresh fruits and vegetables; seeds, natural plants, and flowers; foodstuffs for animals and malt
32	Beers; mineral and aerated waters and other non-alcoholic drinks; fruit drinks and fruit juices; syrups and other preparations for making beverages
33	Alcoholic beverages (except beers)
34	Tobacco; smokers' articles; matches
35	Advertising; business management; business administration; office functions
36	Insurance; financial affairs; monetary affairs; real estate affairs
37	Building construction; repair; installation services
38	Telecommunications
39	Transport; packaging and storage of goods; travel arrangement
40	Treatment of materials
41	Education; providing of training; entertainment; sporting and cultural activities
42-45	Providing of food and drink; temporary accommodation; medical, hygienic, and beauty care; veterinary and agricultural services; legal services; scientific and industrial research; computer programming; services that cannot be placed in other classes

A person that trademarks Infiniti must register it in every class where it expects to use the trademark in order to receive protection for it. If a company does not register its trademarks for a certain class, then another company could very well register for a trademark in the class, or it might already have coverage in a certain area (e.g., Waffle House already had common usage in Indiana before Waffle House, Inc. wanted to open a restaurant there). The valuation analyst must do research. If the valuation analyst is valuing the Infiniti trademark as it applies to HVAC systems, that trademark will have a much different value proposition than it would for automobiles. Failure of the IP valuation analyst to verify trademark registrations is a material error, which could easily lead the valuation analyst to an incorrect conclusion about the value of the trademark for a particular good or service.

Verify the Trademark Legal Status

Like other IP types, valuation of a trademark includes verification of the trademark's legal status, to ensure that the trademark will have value as applied in the market. An unfavorable discovery during due diligence in the trademark's legal status may increase the risks that the trademark owner would not survive a legal attack on the mark and be able to realize future free cash flows, thereby impairing the trademark value. This verification of legal status comes in several forms that cover maintenance fees, proper ownership of record per the USPTO, pending challenges to the trademark registrations, the continued use of the trademark, and the trademark owner's provisions of notice to the public reflecting such trademark protection.

Maintenance Fees

While a trademark maintains no fixed statutory life like a copyright or patent does, 15 U.S.C. §1058(a) states that federal trademark registrations remain in force for 10 years[176] unless cancelled by the USPTO. Under 15 U.S.C. §1059(a), the trademark owner can continue to extend federal trademark protection for successive ten-year periods following the initial registration with the payment of a registration fee and the completion of a renewal application. A trademark owner who fails to pay maintenance fees abandons the trademark. This would mean that someone might be able to use the trademark for interstate commerce without actionable cause by the original trademark owner, or a reasonable businessperson would have no reason to pay the trademark owner a license fee for the trademark's use. Note that the trademark owner might still maintain trademark protection at the state level or under common law. However, the scope of that protection might be sufficiently

176 This is provided that the trademark owner executes an affidavit stating continued use of the trademark as specified in 15 U.S.C. §1058(b).

narrow, creating significant value impairment for the trademark. Thus, a trademark owner must maintain protection for a trademark to retain a value proposition. In a trademark valuation engagement, the IP valuation analyst should verify that the trademark owner is current with all requisite fees to maintain the status of registered trademarks. Failure by the valuation analyst to do so might lead to an improper value conclusion based on a fact pattern that does not match the engagement.

If the trademark owner does forget to renew the trademark registration, 15 U.S.C. §1059(a) provides the trademark owner with a six-month grace period after the end of the 10-year period to correct the deficiency. Thus, even though an IP valuation analyst may discover that a trademark owner had inadvertently let the trademark registration lapse, the trademark owner might still have time to correct the deficiency with the USPTO. In this case, the valuation analyst might rightly conclude that no value impairment exists.

Owner of Record

As with patents, the trademark valuation analyst needs to verify that the USPTO reflects the active status of the actual trademark owners. Under 15 U.S.C. §1060(a), trademarks are assignable in law. Assignments occur by executing an instrument (e.g., an assignment agreement) in writing. Further, 15 U.S.C. §1060(a)(4) indicates that "an assignment shall be void against any subsequent purchaser for valuable consideration without notice, unless the prescribed information reporting the assignment is recorded in the United States Patent and Trademark Office within three months after the date of the assignment, or prior to the subsequent purchase." This means that for a trademark to be valuable to a company, the company must be the assignee on record with the USPTO; failure by the company to do so would void any subsequent transaction relating to the trademark. As is the case with patents, this can create trademark value impairment. For example, suppose a company seeks to sell a trademark for $1 million; however, the USPTO has no record of the company as the assignee of the trademark. As the company does not truly own the rights to the trademark, it does not have a trademark to sell. Thus, the value of the trademark to that company would be zero. As part of trademark due diligence, the IP valuation analyst must verify proper ownership of the trademark in order to avoid an improper value conclusion.

Pending Trademark Challenges

Like patents, third parties can challenge a pending trademark registration for a variety of reasons, a common one being that the opposing party believes that the new trademark is likely to cause confusion with an existing trademark. This will typically occur for new trademarks that generally will not carry much value to begin with (recall that new trademarks have yet to develop the goodwill to generate economic activity). The success rate for surviving an opposition is relatively low. Between May 1999 and May 2009, the USPTO Trademark Trial and Appeal Board (TTAB) listed 1,379 different opposition cases, of which the TTAB sustained 933 oppositions. That means that a trademark registrant has about a 33.4% chance on average of surviving oppositions by registered trademark owners to a new trademark.

The IP valuation analyst should still determine if the trademark is subject to any potential opposition proceedings. If it is, then the valuation analyst should account for the probability that the opposition filing may succeed and account for the expected value of the opposition filing in the final value opinion. For example, if NewCompany has trademark "ConfusingMark," which is the subject of an opposition proceeding, then the valuation analyst could perform a valuation for the mark as if there were no opposition petition, and then account for the difference by adjusting the final value to the expected value of success surviving the opposition petition. This would have the net effect of lowering the value to 33.4% of the unopposed petition's value on average.

Continued Use

Patents, copyrights, and trade secrets do not have any explicit requirements for use of the intellectual property to preserve ongoing government protections. The company, at its pleasure, can establish vast portfolios of patents, copyrights, or trade secrets, perhaps never monetizing them, yet still preserve basic protections for the statutory or economic life of each IP type. This is not the case for trademarks, which require continued use by a company as a condition of registration under 15 U.S.C. §1051.

The continued use requirement has an obvious reason. Without the continued use requirement, people or companies would register trademarks for products or services that they never had any intention of marketing and hoard them, much in the way that cybersquatters operate today with Internet domain names. Cybersquatters are people or companies that register literally thousands of Internet domain names that derive from the goodwill associated with trademarked goods or services and seek to resell those domain names to the trademark owners. Cybersquatters capitalize on the relatively low cost of registration (oftentimes only several dollars), purchasing them with the hopes of reselling them to other companies at large profits. Companies that refuse to pay the cybersquatters then might face the cybersquatters' postings of derogatory information about the companies on the squatted websites.[177]

177 Trademark law addresses resolving issues with cybersquatting in 15 U.S.C. §1125(d).

Thus, for a trademark to maintain a value to a trademark owner, the trademark owner must attest to continued use of the mark in order to receive continued protection. Moreover, this use must constitute more than mere token activity, such as selling 10 copies of a product using the trademark to a relative across state lines. Failure by the trademark owner to confirm continued use would allow a petitioner to request that the USPTO cancel the existing registration because the registrant is violating the continued use requirement. For example, Sharkskins Surf Gear Inc. made only token sales of T-shirts with the following triangle and shark logo:[178]

Sharkskins opposed the registration of the San Jose Sharks' trademark, claiming that it infringed on Sharkskins' mark with the following registration:

Ultimately, Sharkskins not only lost its opposition to the San Jose Sharks' trademark

178 *Sharkskins Surf Gear, Inc. v. San Jose Sharks,* Trademark Trial and Appeal Board, 87,081 and 87,082, October 29, 1996.

registration, but Sharkskins lost its own trademark registration because it did not use its mark continually, beyond token use, at the time of the trademark registration.[179]

The economic impact of not using a trademark in commerce is obvious: the trademark may not command a value proposition in the market, particularly when tested. The IP valuation analyst should understand the associated usage of the trademark *at the time of registration* to gauge the likelihood that the trademark would survive any preemptory challenges by others in the market. If the facts suggest that the trademark owner was not using the trademark at the time of registration in a manner consistent with 15 U.S.C. §1051, then the trademark valuation analyst might not be able to attribute any value to the trademark, as it might not survive legal challenges. It would be wise for the IP valuation analyst to consult with legal counsel as to the probability that the trademark owner will have a protectable trademark. If the result of the legal analysis were that the trademark owner would not survive a challenge to the trademark, then the natural conclusion for the valuation analyst would be that the trademark would have no value.

Public Notice

Under 15 U.S.C. §1117(b), a trademark owner may collect treble profits or damages from infringers when the facts demonstrate that infringement was intentional. An important part of proving intentional infringement is to provide systematic notice of trademark registrations, with a "TM" mark, an "SM" mark, or the "®" mark.[180] Failure to provide notice opens the door to a claim of innocent infringement, a defense strategy by an accused trademark infringer that his or her infringement was accidental and the person did not realize he or she was infringing the protected work. As with a copyrighted work, an accused infringer can mount this strategy if the infringed work does not provide proper notice.

The value impact of failing to provide notice of a trademark registration can be large—a trademark owner might recover only one-third of potential damages because the court might not find that the trademark owner provided sufficient notice to the public regarding the trademark registration. Thus, providing notice can improve value by reducing the chances of impairing a possible judgment because of an innocent infringement defense.

179 *Sharkskins Surf Gear, Inc. v. San Jose Sharks*, Trademark Trial and Appeal Board, 87,081 and 87,082, October 29, 1996, "In view of the fact that the counterclaim for cancellation must be granted because the opposer had not used the mark in commerce."

180 Richard Stim, *Patent, Copyright, and Trademark: An Intellectual Property Desk Reference*, 9th ed., Nolo, Berkeley, Calif., 2007, p. 410.

Practically, the valuation analyst will query the trademark owner to verify that the trademark owner is providing proper notice to the public of its registered mark. The valuation analyst should inspect samples of products and marketing materials that use the trademark to ensure conformance. If the valuation analyst finds inconsistent notice associated with the trademark, it might be appropriate for the valuation analyst to impair the trademark's value by increasing the discount rate associated with future cash flows attributable to the trademark. In situations where damages might be at issue, the IP valuation analyst might not be able to account for treble damages, instead only accounting for actual damages.

Durability

A trademark's durability in the market when exposed to adverse news can help preserve much brand value. A trademark can have a remarkable ability to generate economic activity. However, a trademark represents a double-edged sword. Any trust that the market associates with a trademark can erode quickly with negative news. The market begins to associate negative perceptions with products and services associated with the trademark and switches hastily to substitute products. The more durable the trademark, the less likely the impairment of trademark value in light of negative publicity.

Historically, trademark value took a long time to develop. Oftentimes, it took years to establish public trust in a trademark to a point where the trademark owner could command abnormal profits compared against competing market offerings. Additionally, trademark impairment took longer to develop. Trademark impairment might occur with the publication of a book (e.g., *The Jungle,* by Upton Sinclair, who wrote about nauseating conditions of the meatpacking industry), with news stories (e.g., news broadcasts of Tylenol poisoning), or via word of mouth.

Today, the proliferation of social networking technologies such as MySpace, Facebook, and YouTube can grow a trademark's value instantly with the click of a mouse. The viral nature of these platforms allows for very quick dissemination of news. For example, the quickness of information dissemination elevated the unemployed Scottish singer Susan Boyle to instant fame when she sang "I Dreamed a Dream" on the British television talent show "Britain's Got Talent." In a show with a reputation for curt, honest, and sometimes demoralizing feedback, she received gushing accolades from the judges and a standing ovation from the audience. Within days of the show's airing, Boyle became a worldwide sensation. In one week, her various YouTube videos generated more than 70 million views, followed quickly with representation by publicists, invites on Larry King and Oprah talk shows, a record deal offer in the United States with Menagerie Entertainment, and predictions that Boyle could get a number one record in the United States.

Of course, technology provides for as quick, if not quicker, trademark destruction. In the same week that viral media elevated Boyle to superstardom, Domino's Pizza experienced a significant media crisis. Two employees, Kristy Hammonds and Michael Setzer, created a video demonstrating the preparation of sandwiches for delivery. The sandwich preparer, Michael, put cheese up his nose and then onto the sandwich. He also violated other health standards in the preparation of the sandwich. Kristy narrated the video. The pair posted the video on YouTube, which quickly generated more than a million views in a matter of days. Domino's experienced brand impairment from the incident as patrons switched from Domino's products to competitors' products. The incident culminated with felony warrants, pending civil lawsuits, and a personal video posted on YouTube from Domino's president Patrick Doyle outlining the steps Domino's took to correct the situation and reassure the public about its food safety. Hammond's and Setzer's actions put some 125,000 people in 60 countries that work with Domino's franchises at risk, impairing Domino's value. Since the incident began, Domino's has had to reevaluate its hiring practices, perform damage control in the market, and even create a Twitter account to respond to online comments.

Fortunately for the trademark owner, the market can have a short memory. In the 1990s, Nike earned a terrible reputation for overseas employment practices relating to child labor, forced overtime, and arbitrary employee abuse by plant managers. This affected Nike's revenues, hence, the free cash flows attributable to the Nike trademarks. With a change in company processes and a significant amount of rebranding, Nike was able to repair its image and regain growth in its free cash flows, hence, brand value.

For other products protected by trademarks that fall out of favor, the market may maintain some level of brand equity that might provide value in the hands of the right owner. For example, CVS owns the Nuprin-branded nonprescription analgesic, known commonly as ibuprofen. Marketed originally by Bristol-Myers Products, Bristol-Myers sold the defunct brand to River West Brands, who ultimately sold it to CVS. CVS generates free cash flow from the sale of ibuprofen under the Nuprin brand today. That said, some products do not maintain the same equity. Encaprin, another ibuprofen product marketed by Procter & Gamble, did not fare as well. An anonymous caller started a hoax regarding cyanide poisoning by Encaprin capsules sold in Walgreens and Kroger stores in Chicago and Detroit. The results were catastrophic for Procter & Gamble, who mothballed the product in the market after the negative reputation of the alleged tainting (which never occurred) irreparably harmed the product.

The IP valuation analyst must understand the durability of the trademark in relation to positive and negative news. Several factors are important in this consideration:

- ***Does the trademark address a single product or a family of products?*** A trademark that represents a single product carries a higher degree of volatility than a trademark that represents a family of products. This is because the trademark receives the diversification associated with a portfolio when applied to a family of products. If one product covered by a trademark disappoints the market and violates trust, such as the Ford Pinto, it may well kill that product in the market. However, the failure of the Ford Pinto may not bring down the entire Ford Motor Co. Trademarks that apply to a single product represent a single-source income stream that lacks diversification. Thus, a single-product trademark carries a greater risk than a trademark that applies to product families.
- ***Can the trademarked product or service kill the buyer or create serious financial hardship?*** A trademark that represents products or services that can kill the buyer (e.g., tainted Tylenol capsules) or create serious financial hardship (e.g., using Arthur Andersen as an auditor) might experience value impairment catastrophically. The trademark might never recover from such impairments, as was the case for Encaprin, Arthur Andersen, and the Chi-Chi's restaurant chain.
- ***Is it common for competing products or services to maintain similar negative reputations?*** Trademarks may not receive much value impairment in the event of unsatisfactory customer experiences if competing products or services maintain similar customer satisfaction levels. For example, a used car dealer with a buyer perception of being less than honest may still be able to survive because that used car dealer's competitors may also have a buyer perception of being less than honest. Thus, the lack of viable buyer alternatives may nullify any potential value impairment to the original trademark owner.

Practically, the valuation analyst may account for the probability of trademark value impairment in several ways. The trademark owner may incur additional sales and marketing expenditures to regain buyer trust (e.g., corrective advertising). This increases costs and reduces free cash flows associated with the trademark. The trademark owner may have to lower prices for the marked product or service to motivate buyers to a sale. This reduces revenues and free cash flows associated with the trademark. The execution risk for the trademark owner monetizing the trademark can increase as well. This puts upward pressure on the discount rate associated with the free cash flows derived from the trademark, which generates a corresponding value reduction.

Incontestability

Under 15 U.S.C. §1065, a registered trademark owner's mark is incontestable after five years from the registration date. This means that another trademark owner cannot dispute the trademark's registration, claiming interference for example on a similar good or service. Incontestability provides a trademark owner with a more valuable trademark, as the probability of a third party breaking the trademark exhausts. Thus, as long as the trademark owner fulfills the basic administrative functions associated with trademark ownership (e.g., continued usage, payment of maintenance fees, etc.), the trademark owner can maintain perpetual ownership of the associated trademark rights. Moreover, no third party could contest the trademark rights.

Of course, the incontestability distinction carries with it several conditions:

- There is no adverse final decision against the trademark owner's claims for the mark, which would make the issue of value to the trademark owner moot, as an adverse ruling would remove ownership and associated rights to the trademark owner.
- There is no proceeding involving the trademark's rights pending with the USPTO or in a court that is not finally disposed of, as an adverse ruling could remove ownership and associated rights to the trademark owner.
- The trademark owner must file an affidavit within one year of the five-year anniversary of the trademark's registration date stating that the trademark has been used for five consecutive years.
- The associated trademark does not refer to a product that contains the generic name for goods or services, such as aspirin, escalator, or other products that once maintained trademark protection. See the later section in this chapter on genericide risk.

For the valuation analyst, accounting for the value generated from an incontestable mark emerges in the lower risks associated with monetizing the trademark. For example, if the expected value of a new trademark application is that there is a

0.5% chance of an opposition filing and a 50/50 chance of success, then the expected value of the impairment because the market is contestable is 0.25%. For a trademark worth $10 million, that would equate to $25,000.[181]

Interference

Under 15 U.S.C. §1066, the director of the USPTO may declare that a trademark application interferes with an existing trademark, unless the mark is incontestable. The net effect for a trademark applicant is that the pending application might receive rejection from the USPTO. This issue becomes important for early-stage trademarks that a company wishes to develop into a blockbuster brand. For example, suppose that BigBrandCompany seeks to launch the BlockBuster brand for retailing prerecorded amateur videos. The director finds that the trademark application interferes with an existing registered trademark from the Blockbuster Inc. chain of retail video rental stores. BigBrandCompany would then have to change its planned branding such that it would not interfere with Blockbuster Inc.'s brand.

The trademark valuation analyst should understand the status of any interference petitions from existing trademark owners. If there is a pending interference petition, then the valuation analyst might have to account for the probability of the USPTO director declaring interference for the trademark application. The natural conclusion for the valuation analyst in such a circumstance is that the trademark in the pending application has no value for the intended goods or services, as the applicant would not be able to use the trademark without infringement.

Standards of Use

Trademarks represent consumer trust. This trust can manifest in a variety of ways, including quality expectations or taste expectations, among many others. Inconsistent quality plagues trademarks and can destroy value. Thus, trademarks police themselves. When the trust is strong, trademarks command value in ways discussed earlier in this chapter. When the trust is weak, the trademark acts like a scarlet letter, warning potential buyers of what they are getting into. For example, when Intel released the Pentium processor in 1994, it did so with a flaw in the unit's floating-point processor (i.e., the part of the processor that deals with non-integer-based math, such as real numbers) that handled division operations. The trademark "Intel Inside" quickly went from being a badge of honor in the eyes of the consumer to a warning label. Intel violated the trust the market built. It cost Intel nearly half

181 While seemingly insignificant, the sum of the various small impairments associated with a trademark value might well become material.

a billion dollars to address the problem.[182] Intel violated the trust it built with its brand and that had significant, though recoverable, impact on Intel's value.

Thus, an important part of trademark exploitation is the consistent use of the trademark in the market to reinforce consumer trust. This might include everything from white spacing requirements used in association with the mark, to colors used, to printing specifications. The inconsistent use of the mark in the market can create confusion for buyers, thereby depressing trademark value. For example, in a contemporaneous example, PepsiCo decided in 2008 that it was time to remake its iconic Tropicana brand, the largest selling brand in the refrigerated orange juice category. In what the market now calls the Pepsi version of "New Coke,"[183] PepsiCo changed the packaging for its signature orange juice blends as part of a $35 million campaign to refresh the brand.[184] The following picture demonstrates the effects of the brand refresh on the packaging:

182 "Pentium Debacle Costs Intel $475 Million," *MacWEEK*, January 23, 1995.

183 This is in reference to the decision by The Coca-Cola Co. to change the formulation of its flagship product in 1985, which various outlets consider one of the worst marketing initiatives in history.

184 Stuart Elliott, "Tropicana Discovers Some Buyers Are Passionate About Packaging," *The New York Times*, February 22, 2009.

PepsiCo moved from the product on the left, which it used for decades, to the refreshed product on the right. The thought process was to modernize the brand. In a word, it was a flop. Moreover, it underscored how companies and design agencies can misunderstand the economic power of entrenched trademarks. Though the refreshed product still bore the Tropicana name, consumers had tremendous confusion with the new campaign, likening the new logo to a cheap, generic store brand made from concentrate instead of its signature not-from-concentrate product.[185] Moreover, consumers found it difficult to distinguish the Tropicana varieties, such as the Original formulation, the Low Acid formulation, and others.

Within six weeks, PepsiCo was reverting to its old brand. While PepsiCo played the reversion to its old brand in the media as a response to loyal customers who expressed a "deep emotional bond" with the original packaging,[186] there were more practical reasons to revert that had little to do with loyal customer emotions. Tropicana sales were falling off a cliff. In a matter of 53 days, Tropicana unit sales plunged 20%, while revenue dropped 19%, or about $33 million.[187] On an annual basis, that represents an approximate $227 million revenue loss. At a 2008 profit margin of 11.89%, and a discount rate of 6.58%,[188] PepsiCo was looking down the barrel of a total brand impairment of about $41 million.[189] Second, as a premium product, Tropicana should have sold at a higher price than its competitors' products, especially concentrated products such as Minute Maid. However, retailers had to reduce the Tropicana prices just to sell the product before it went out of code. Worse yet, this occurred at a time when sales for competitors such as Minute Maid (The Coca-Cola Co.), Florida's Natural, and Tree Ripe experienced double-digit growth (though Pepsi claimed the two events were unrelated).[190]

The Tropicana example underscores an important consideration for the IP valuation analyst: namely, understanding the trust relationship between the buyer and the trademark owner. Fragility of the trust relationship and the economic ramifications on the trademark value can emerge quickly. The valuation analyst should consider the impacts of changes to the trust relationship and possible value effects. Several factors that the valuation analyst might consider include:

185 Linda Tischler, "Never Mind! Pepsi Pulls Much-Loathed Tropicana Packaging," Fast Company.com, February 23, 2009.

186 Stuart Elliott, "Tropicana Discovers Some Buyers Are Passionate About Packaging," *The New York Times*, February 22, 2009.

187 Natalie Zmuda, "OJ Rivals Posted Double-Digit Increases as Pure Premium Plummeted," *Advertising Age*, April 2, 2009.

188 A risk free rate of 2.61%, a beta of 0.56, and an equity risk premium of 7.10%.

189 $227 million revenue loss x 11.89% profit margin / 6.58% discount rate = approximately $41 million.

190 Natalie Zmuda, "OJ Rivals Posted Double-Digit Increases as Pure Premium Plummeted," *Advertising Age*, April 2, 2009.

- What were the economic effects (positive or negative) of any marketing or trademark changes or refreshes?
- What were the economic effects of any product, service, or formulation changes? For example, Hershey's replaced cocoa butter in its mass-marketed chocolates, such as Hershey's Kisses, with vegetable oil to reduce manufacturing costs. Despite howls from consumers for violating the trust relationship, Hershey's oddly saw increased revenues after the switch.[191]

The valuation analyst can reflect anticipated effects from these factors explicitly in the valuation model, either by affecting price and quantity demanded directly, by the associated costs (e.g., the cost of reprinting cartons and advertising materials for Tropicana products), or by increasing the risk, hence the discount rate, associated with future income that the trademark might generate.

Trademark Strength

Several factors drive the strength of trademarks. Recall that the stronger the trademark, the more value the trademark can command in the market. Trademark strength can manifest in several forms (i.e., a marked product commands a greater price in the market). Valuation analysts should be interested in trademark strength from the perspective of how easy it would be for a third party to challenge and defeat the mark's protections and/or derive economic benefits from the registered mark, thereby usurping economic opportunity from the trademark's owner. The IP valuation analyst should consider several factors relating to the strength of the trademark, including the type of trademark and the trademark age.

Trademark type has a specific meaning in a legal context that lends directly to trademark strength. Arising from the *Abercrombie & Fitch Co. v. HuntingWorld, Inc.* decision, these trademark types include generic marks, descriptive marks, suggestive marks, and arbitrary and fanciful marks, in what the industry knows as the spectrum of distinctiveness.[192] The following is an overview of each:

- *Generic marks:* Generic trademarks are just that: generic. They refer to trademarks to which one attempts to assign secondary meaning, though such attempts will always fail because the marks describe an entire group of products. Consumers would not be able to distinguish one product

191 Interestingly, the increased revenues for its less expensive chocolates occurred at a time of macroeconomic turmoil, which might have more explanatory power than market indifference to the cocoa butter substitution.
192 *Abercrombie & Fitch, Co. v. HuntingWorld, Inc.*, 537 F.2d 4, 9 (2nd Cir. 1976).

from another. Famous generic marks include aspirin and escalator. The valuation analyst must always conclude that generic trademarks have no value, as there is nothing protectable to consider.

- *Descriptive marks:* Descriptive marks can be valuable when they take on a secondary meaning. Ordinarily, trademark applicants cannot receive trademark registrations on descriptive items (e.g., the "Yellow" phone book). The only way that registrants can receive trademark protection is if the trademark takes on a secondary meaning (i.e., some public meaning beyond the obvious meaning of terms or images that comprise the trademark). Restaurants such as McDonald's thrive on secondary meaning for fast-food restaurants that promise a user experience, thereby preventing another person with the last name of McDonald from opening a similar type of restaurant. Such marks can become quite valuable; however, they can take decades to develop and require significant sales and marketing investment. For nascent marks, the valuation analyst should ensure that an appropriate budget of resources matches the market intent for the trademark as used in the market.

- *Suggestive marks:* Suggestive marks suggest a quality or characteristic of the good or service that it represents. The idea is to tie the good or service mark to some image in the consumer's mind. For example, Florida's Natural branded orange juice suggests a wholesome good, made from natural ingredients. Such marks can become quite valuable, and they might get that value more easily, as the chances of the USPTO classifying the registration as descriptive are lower. However, they can also take decades to develop.

- *Arbitrary marks:* Arbitrary marks are generally very strong trademarks. These trademarks tend to describe goods or services that otherwise have no relation. For example, Amazon describes an Internet retailer as well as a jungle in South America. Such marks can become quite valuable over time; however, they can also attract unwanted attention and lawsuits. For example, Apple Corps Ltd., founded by the Beatles, sued Apple Computer several times and extracted significant settlements from Apple Computer because of Apple Computer's trademark drift into the music space, which Apple Corps Ltd. owned.

- *Fanciful marks:* Fanciful marks are generally the strongest trademarks one can own. These trademarks tend to describe goods or services and likely have no other precedent in the market. Pharmaceutical companies are famous for developing fanciful marks for various goods and services that they sell. Lipitor, Clarinex, Sarafem, Allegra, and literally hundreds of other products did not generally have precedents in the market. This is advantageous in several ways. First, the trademark registrant will likely receive no oppositions from other parties because the risk of collision is low. Second, by having distinct names, the trademark registrant reduces the potential for medical errors. Third, all traditional trademark building tools are available, including sometimes tricky items such as domain names (recall the problems with nissan.com). Fourth, having fanciful trademarks reduces the probability of a lawsuit from an unrelated brand (e.g., Nissan Motor Co. and Nissan Computer Corp.). Lastly, fanciful marks can influence significant buyer demand, despite the availability of generics (e.g., Tylenol versus generic counterparts), and can create remarkable long-term value. The largest risk for fanciful marks is the risk of genericide, which happens when the public moves from using a trademark in an adjective form to using it in a verb or noun form. For example, many people "google" an item they want to search on the Internet, as opposed to using the Google search engine to retrieve the answer. Such widespread adoption and misuse can destroy the associated value with a trademark. Several well-known nouns today, such as aspirin and escalator, were trademarks to their original inventors but have since crossed over into common usage. Today, these words are generic and maintain no trademark power.

Trademark age has a positive relationship with trademark strength as well. The older the trademark, the more likely it will be stronger, as historically, trademark renewal rates averaged only about 27% between 1934 and 1999.[193] Additionally, older trademarks speak directly to the economic life of the trademark, since the trademark owners must maintain continual use of the trademarks to maintain protection.

Dilution

Recall that a trademark owner registers the trademark for a certain class of goods or services. Generally, a trademark owner cannot prevent others from using a similar mark for unrelated goods or services. However, if the trademark proves to be famous, then a trademark owner might be able to prevent a third party from using

193 William M. Landes and Richard A. Posner, *The Economic Structure of Intellectual Property Law*, The Belknap Press of Harvard University Press, Cambridge, Mass., 2003, p. 250.

the similar mark, as it might aid dilution of the primary trademark. Under 15 U.S.C. §1125, the IP valuation analyst can find the definition of famousness:

> (A) For purposes of paragraph (1), a mark is famous if it is widely recognized by the general consuming public of the United States as a designation of source of the goods or services of the mark's owner. In determining whether a mark possesses the requisite degree of recognition, the court may consider all relevant factors, including the following:
>
> (i) The duration, extent, and geographic reach of advertising and publicity of the mark, whether advertised or publicized by the owner or third parties.
>
> (ii) The amount, volume, and geographic extent of sales of goods or services offered under the mark.
>
> (iii) The extent of actual recognition of the mark.
>
> (iv) Whether the mark was registered under the Act of March 3, 1881, or the Act of February 20, 1905, or on the principal register.

Whether or not use of a similar trademark for an unrelated good or service causes dilution depends on the facts of the usage and the famousness of the original trademark. Practically, this issue might arise in valuation engagement for nascent trademarks, where the nascent trademark owners are staking out territories for goods and services. For such engagements, the valuation analyst should refer to legal counsel and cite any freedom-to-operate opinions in assessing risk for the associated future free cash flows. Naturally, the higher the associated risk of a dilution contest, the lower the value for the nascent trademark.

Counterfeit Risk

Counterfeits present value impairment risk for a trademark owner. Counterfeits are unauthorized reproductions, also known as knock-offs, of products or services represented by a strong trademark. As the trademark helps reduce buyer search costs, the counterfeit products seek to leverage the goodwill and trust that the market puts in a certain product or service. The counterfeiter does so by offering a typically similar or identical version of the product or service at a lower cost. Though not a requirement, many of these counterfeit products have inferior initial quality and inferior durability. Also, they may not work as well, they may not last as long, and they may have been constructed with inferior materials. Key benefits that accrue to the counterfeiter include lower sales and marketing costs, and potentially greater gross margins (especially in cases where the counterfeit products use lower-cost materials or lower-quality labor).

Counterfeiters target a variety of branded products including software, medicines, cosmetics, shampoos, soft drinks, tea, food, auto parts, music, apparel, and luggage—pretty much any branded consumer product. For example, Procter & Gamble owns the Gillette brand and spends millions of dollars annually to enforce its Gillette brands against counterfeit copies of its razors and replacement blades. Unsuspecting buyers of discount razor blades for Gillette's Mach3 and Fusion razor systems routinely send suspected counterfeit replacement cartridges to Procter & Gamble to hear the news that they purchased counterfeit products of inferior quality. While it is common practice for counterfeiters to sell their products through flea markets, and by word of mouth, one of the largest channels for counterfeit products is Internet retailers.

Counterfeit products can have devastating impacts on the value of trademarked products. First, counterfeits can interfere with revenues of the original products. In fact, loss of revenue is a key metric that trademark owners use to detect potential sales of infringing products. If a product had consistent sales of $10 million per month, and those product revenues dropped off $2 million with no material changes in the market (e.g., new competitors), then the trademark owner might reasonably infer that counterfeit products may be impairing trademark value. Second, buyers of counterfeit products might associate the inferior products with the quality of the trademark owner. A consumer buys inferior counterfeits of Gillette's Fusion replacement razor blade cartridges, cuts his face while shaving, and assumes that the Fusion product is inferior and no longer buys it. Thus, the counterfeit impairs the legal trademark owner's trademark value. The value impairment does not stop at lost revenues. Trademark owners must expend significant sums to counteract the effects of counterfeit products. This drives up the costs of trademark maintenance, reducing associated free cash flows, hence, value. For example, Tiffany and Co. budgeted over $14 million to neutralize the damaging effects of counterfeit products over a four-year period, or $3.5 million per year.[194] The after-tax capitalized value of these expenditures represents value impairment to Tiffany of about $14.8 million,[195] not including potential market share losses, which can exceed the $14.8 million value easily.

Certain attributes of trademarked products will increase the risk of counterfeit products, including:

194 *Tiffany (NJ) Inc. v. eBay Inc.*, No 04 Civ. 4607 (RJS) (S.D.N.Y. July 14, 2008).

195 Cost x (1—income tax rate) / discount rate = $3.5 million x (1—36.42%) / 15% = $14,834,491.

- *Costs and ease of producing the counterfeits:* Products that are easy to copy, and require little cost to do so, are more at risk for counterfeiting than products that take significant investment to copy.
- *Equity of the trademarked product:* Products that represent a significant revenue base and command significant market power are prime targets for counterfeit products.
- *High availability of distribution channels:* A counterfeit product will generate greater revenues with greater access to distribution channels for the offending products. If a vendor in China sells knock-offs of Procter & Gamble shampoo in the Guangdong Province, the counterfeit product will have one value impact. However, if the counterfeiter ships counterfeit products all over the world, generating easy sales over the Internet either directly or indirectly, that counterfeit product will have a much greater negative impact on the original trademarked shampoo.
- *Difficulty in infringement detection:* As is the case with other IP types, the harder it is to detect infringing products in the market, the greater the damage a counterfeiter can inflict on the trademark owner.
- *Affordability of the authentic products:* Products that are low cost are generally at a high risk of value impairment due to counterfeits. Rolex and Tiffany are not likely losing much in sales from counterfeit products. People who can afford a Rolex or Tiffany are not going to eBay to buy a $50 copy—they will demand certified authenticity or purchase their products from an authorized retailer. This does not mean that demand for counterfeit Rolex or Tiffany products does not exist. The buyers of the counterfeit products cannot afford the real thing and so purchase the counterfeits instead.

  For example, Gillette's Fusion replacement razor cartridges command a significant premium in the market. Yet, one may find it relatively inexpensive to produce counterfeit copies of these razor cartridges. The untrained eye would find it very difficult to discern a counterfeit copy from an original. Lastly, the Fusion replacement cartridges are affordable by a large portion of the market. It would be much more difficult for a counterfeiter to create a knock-off Bentley automobile. Complete automobiles require significant capital investment to produce, and the automobile would still likely cost tens of thousands to create even an inferior

> copy. Bentley only sells several thousand automobiles per year. Thus, the odds of a counterfeiter producing counterfeit Bentley automobiles are low because a significant revenue opportunity does not exist for the counterfeiter. Next, Bentley sells its vehicles through authorized resellers. Buyers do not flock to eBay to purchase a new Bentley, which removes a significant distribution channel for the counterfeiter. Infringement detection will be easy, as a buyer could verify the vehicle's serial number with the manufacturer. Lastly, because a Bentley is so expensive, Bentley is not going to lose sales to counterfeits. People who want a Bentley are not going to seek out Bentley knock-offs—they want the authentic product.
>
> Perhaps most interestingly, iconic trademark owner Louis Vuitton (and others) allegedly incinerates all leftover products and accessories. It does this deliberately for the same reason that one will not find an authorized or company-owned Louis Vuitton retail outlet anywhere online or in a brick and mortar location. It seeks to keep the brand exclusive. Liquidating the branded products in retail outlets at deep discounts both offends the full-price buyers and cheapens the overall emotive response to the branded goods. Thus, to preserve the emotive response to its brand, Louis Vuitton does not dispense with sales on overstocked items. It burns them instead.

As a practical matter, service marks generally maintain a lower risk of value impairment due to counterfeits than trademarks that represent products. Service marks protect services, meaning that the service provider must demonstrate competence. For example, IBM has a significant software consulting practice. It is impractical for a counterfeiter to offer a counterfeit service that will generate the typical value that accrues to counterfeiters, such as lower sales or marketing costs, or lower direct costs.

For valuation analysts, accounting for the potential impacts of counterfeits occurs in several ways. First, they might adjust the associated sales forecasts to account for potential counterfeit losses. Second, the valuation analyst might increase costs associated with trademark enforcement to include significant detection efforts, product repackaging, and buyer education campaigns. Lastly, the IP valuation analyst might increase the discount rate to account for the associated risk of realizing revenues from products with trademarks.

Market Dynamism

The dynamics of the particular market for a trademark can play an important role in trademark value. These dynamics can include the market size, the cost of information, and the cost of recognition.[196] First, the market size has a large impact on trademark value. The larger the applicable market, the larger the number of potential buyers for the products, thus, the greater the brand value potential. For example, suppose that a trademark owner earns $1 in contribution margin attributable to the trademark for a product. If the trademark owner sells 1 million units in a year, then the trademark owner will generate $1 million in that year, attributable to the trademark. If the trademark owner sells 100 million units in a year, then the trademark owner will generate $100 million in that year attributable to the trademark. The market size dictates the economic opportunity. General Electric (GE) likely has a strong brand in light bulbs that represents a significant number of units shipped annually. The GE brand for light bulbs is valuable.

The second major market driver for a trademark relates to the cost of information. The higher the cost of information relating to a product, the more difficult it is for a buyer to evaluate the product. Thus, the buyer is willing to trust the brand of the seller more. This is especially important in large fragmented markets with many vendors. For example, literally dozens of sellers make antivirus software for computers. Yet Symantec owns the antivirus market space because of its strong trademarks, even though other products might rank higher in functional tests and consume fewer system resources. The search costs for a consumer are thus high (imagine a layperson evaluating the complex technical features of a product like an antivirus system), increasing the prevalence that a trademark could prove valuable. GE commands a strong portion of the light bulb market because acquiring the information to evaluate all competing products is costly, and people trust the GE brand. Interestingly, the GE brand is less important for highly technical and functional products that it sells, such as jet engines or ultrasound machines. Buyers of these product types are highly technical users that will expend much time and energy evaluating the technical and functional merits of the products. Moreover, these buyers will demand ready access to significant information regarding the product's characteristics from GE's technical sales force. As a point of comparison, a consumer does not have general access to technical data or a technical sales force when buying a light bulb. Thus, for the jet engine or ultrasound scanner, the cost of information is lower, driving a lower potential trademark value for GE-branded products.[197]

196 William M. Landes and Richard A. Posner, *The Economic Structure of Intellectual Property Law*, The Belknap Press of Harvard University Press, Cambridge, Mass., 2003, p. 64-65.

197 Of course, these products might still derive significant value from patents and other trade secrets.

A third major market driver for trademark value relates to the cost of recognition. The more recognizable the trademark, the more valuable it becomes. The traditional direct proxy for the cost of recognition is dollars spent on marketing efforts: the greater the advertising budget, the more valuable the trademark. Internet technologies have injected an interesting wrench into this traditional train of thought. The widespread use of the Internet, the viral nature of information dissemination, and the relative speed and low cost with which one can create that dissemination has lowered the costs of recognition. Trademarks such as SouthPark and JibJab developed trademark equity very quickly, courtesy of the low costs of recognition as well as the low costs to disseminate initial offerings in the market.

Fair Use Value Impacts

Like copyrights, fair use can have a value impact for trademarks. While that value impact can be positive (e.g., the "Oprah Effect" on the interest generated in goods and services demonstrated on the "Oprah Winfrey Show"), oftentimes it might be negative. This is a function of trademark law, which states in 5 U.S.C. §1125 that third parties and news organizations can use trademarks for product comparisons, product criticisms, parodying, news reporting, news commentary, and noncommercial use. For example, a news outlet publishes a story about a woman eating a severed fingertip in chili from a Wendy's restaurant. Eventual damages to Wendy's International were $21.2 million, $500,000 to JEM Management (owner of the restaurant), and $170,605 to Wendy's employees for lost wages.[198] Despite the fact that Wendy's was the victim of a scam in this event, Wendy's cannot sue the news outlet because of the fair use permissions in 5 U.S.C. §1125.

The IP valuation analyst needs to understand the impacts of fair use on potential trademark value. Understanding the fair use value impacts begins with the valuation analyst gaining an understanding for the dynamics of the markets where the trademark owner uses the trademark. If the market dynamics suggest that the cost of information is high, the target market is large, and the costs of recognition are low, then the risk of value impairment due to adverse fair use of the product could be large.

The IP valuation analyst must also understand the dynamics of the product bearing the trademark and the impacts of fair use. For example, when an airplane crashes, the public typically does not associate the catastrophe with the plane's manufacturer. Thus, despite any news stories about a particular make and model of plane

198 http://articles.sfgate.com/2007-09-22/bay-area/17262341_1_anna-ayala-appeals-court-judge-edward-davila, accessed on November 1, 2011.

crashing, passengers will still fly on that make and model plane. In 2008, American Airlines and Delta Airlines cancelled all flights associated with MD-80 aircraft to inspect hydraulic wiring and ensure proper operation. Despite these groundings, the public continues to fly on MD-80 aircraft—and on the two airlines—regularly. Thus, in this instance, the negative publicity had little lasting impact on the overall trademarks for the aircraft (though the airlines received temporary impairments from lost revenues).

Typically, the value impacts of fair use are going to emerge consistent with a trademark's traditional value sources (depending on the nature of the fair use): revenues (lower or higher), market share (more or less), and sales and marketing costs (higher or lower). It is important for the valuation analyst to understand the nature of the fair use and to adjust the valuation model accordingly to account for possible enhancement or impairment.

Chapter 9
Trade Secret Due Diligence

Trade secrets represent valuable corporate knowledge that a company has developed or acquired, but that the public does not generally know about. The value accrues to the company because the company is able to generate additional incremental economic income from the use of the knowledge in the market. If a company is not able to generate incremental economic income from the knowledge, then that knowledge is likely of little value to the company. For example, consider a company that spends $100 per month on office paper. That purchase represents private information; however, that information is not likely valuable in most circumstances because it would be difficult to extract economic income from such information in most cases (unless you are a market researcher in the office paper market). Trade secrets will typically have the following characteristics:[199]

- They are not known outside of the particular company;
- They are valuable to the owner and possible competitors;
- They have expenditures in time, effort, and money to develop;
- They are known only by employees and others involved in the company;
- They are difficult for others to properly acquire or independently duplicate; and
- They are subject to reasonable measures to guard the secrecy of the information.

199 Richard Stim, *Patent, Copyright, and Trademark: An Intellectual Property Desk Reference*, 9th ed., Nolo, Berkeley, Calif., 2007, p. 486.

Trade secrets can represent intellectual property in a great many forms. For example, trade secrets can represent inventions that the inventor has not yet described in a patent application, a marketing strategy for a competitive product launch, or a food product's secret recipe. Because of their variety, trade secrets can provide a difficult platform to create value. Typically, trade secrets will generate incremental value in one of five ways:

- *Revenue generation:* The trade secret will provide some barrier to entry, enabling the trade secret owner to extract abnormal profits from selling a product or service in the market that uses the trade secret. For example, a company sells an effective liquid cleaner. A trade secret protects the formulation. The formulation allows the trade secret owner to generate revenues in excess of other less effective cleaners in the market, despite the fact that costs to produce the cleaner are similar to competing products. Thus, the trade secret formula allows the trade secret owner to generate greater revenue without excess cost, creating additional value.
- *Revenue preservation:* The trade secret will prevent negative information from becoming public, thereby preserving the continuance of revenues. For example, suppose ProfitableCompany protects the fact that it offered a favorable discount to a large customer. Other existing customers may want visibility into that pricing decision to use it as leverage for their own purchases from ProfitableCompany. Thus, the pricing data reflects a valuable trade secret for ProfitableCompany and is one that ProfitableCompany should guard closely to preserve revenues with existing customers.
- *Cost savings:* The trade secret will provide some advantage to the owner, creating some type of ongoing cost savings that competitors may not have. For example, SuperCow, a beef grower, has developed a genetic program over several decades to generate a pure line of beef that has a greater feed conversion ratio (i.e., total food input/total live weight of the animal) than that of the broader market. SuperCow can grow its cattle to mature condemnation weight for less feed cost. Suppose the trade secret creates an annual feed cost reduction that produces an additional $5 million in free cash flow. Suppose further that SuperCow's discount rate is 25% and the annual feed cost reduction is practically perpetual (i.e., it would take decades to reproduce the genetic program). The fact pattern just described would indicate that the present value of SuperCow's trade

secret is $20 million as it relates to feed cost savings.[200]

- *Risk reduction:* The trade secret will provide some reduction in the risk that the trade secret owner would have to incur to generate cash flows. For example, suppose that a company intends to create a new medical device that detects blood glucose in a continuous monitoring system. This device is a Class III medical device and must survive testing under a premarket approval with the FDA. A company that seeks to survive this testing, having never gone through it, is at a greater risk of failure than the company that has been through the process already. The knowledge of preparing and performing the clinical trials is a trade secret for the company. That knowledge would reduce the risk for the company of getting the product to market successfully. The risk reduction would create value. If the product's value was $12 million without the use of the trade secret, but was $21 million with the use of the trade secret, then the value of the trade secret to the company would be $9 million.

- *Time acceleration:* Trade secrets can help create value in two forms as that value relates to time acceleration. Recall that a dollar today is worth more than it is in the future because of the time value of money. Thus, a trade secret that can accelerate the time to receiving cash flow can create value for the trade secret owner. For example, if a trade secret allows a company to get a product to the market one year sooner, the value relates to this time acceleration because the company is receiving revenues sooner than it otherwise would have. Exhibit 75 demonstrates a 12-month shift in the market adoption and thus the value that the trade secret creates.

Exhibit 75. 12-Month Shift in Market Adoption

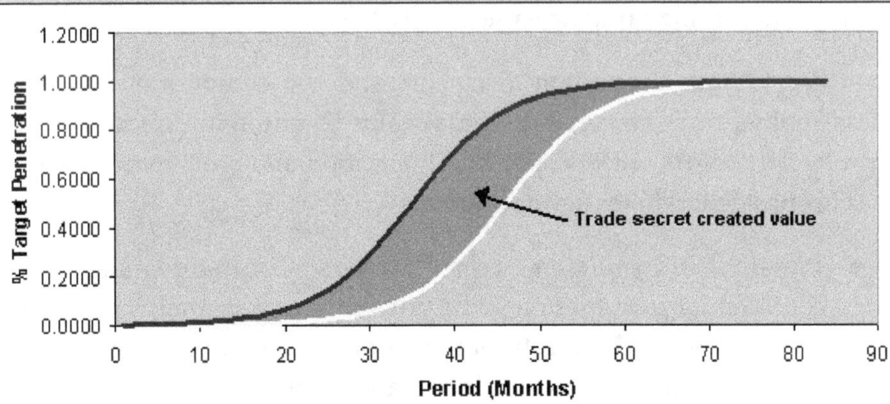

200 $5 million free cash flow / 25% discount rate = $20 million.

Alternatively, the trade secret may help the market adopt the product faster, perhaps due to a highly targeted and effective marketing program. Under this situation, the trade secret would account for the difference in the value before and after the trade secret usage, as Exhibit 76 demonstrates.

Exhibit 76. Difference in the Value Before and After Trade Secret Usage

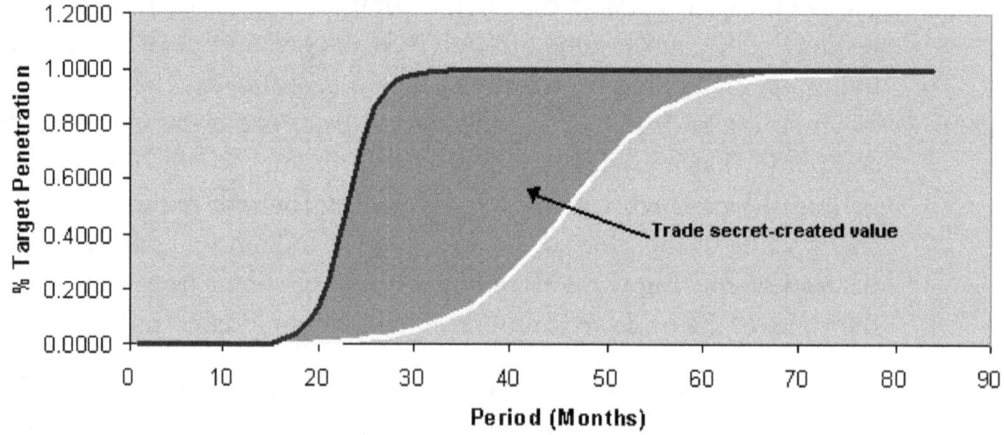

Trade Secret Value Sources

Companies traditionally protect trade secrets with non-disclosure and non-competition agreements considered under the jurisdiction of state law. Strong non-disclosure and non-competition agreements provide forceful incentives to preserve the confidentiality of trade secrets, which may improve and/or maintain value. Weak non-disclosure or non-competition agreements or lax enforcement of such agreements, such as not requiring all employees to execute them or willful inaction pursuing agreement breaches, may impair value.

It is one thing to have strong non-disclosure and non-competition agreements in place. It is another thing to generate actual value by enforcing trade secrets. Trade secret protection occurs with proper administration and enforcement of the trade secrets. This protection takes several forms:

- *Physical information access barriers:* Companies should protect confidential information with physical barriers that prevent outright access to the trade secrets. For example, a company that limits all access to its locations with walls, locks, and electronic security protocols is a good start.

- ***Limited information access:*** Trade secret strength relates directly to the number of people who actually have knowledge of the trade secret. If fewer people have knowledge of a company's trade secrets, there is less chance of an accidental or intentional disclosure. Taken to a deeper practical level, some companies run extensive background checks to verify employee credentials and limit access to trade secrets to only authorized personnel.

- ***Proper marking of confidential information:*** Knowing what constitutes a trade secret is an important aspect of trade secret protection. A trade secret owner makes such determinations obvious with conspicuous marking of all trade secret documents as confidential. Trade secret documents that lack conspicuous marking may be subject to accidental or inadvertent disclosure by employees who might not know that the documents were secret. For example, in one case, a former employee of a company disclosed that company's trade secrets to a competitor. When the company sued the former employee, the former employee pointed to language in an executed non-disclosure agreement that required the company mark confidential documents, which it failed to do.[201] It is up to the valuation analyst to inspect samples of documents covering the trade secrets to evaluate consistency of the marking policy. Shoddy or inconsistent marking of confidential documents could cloud what data is confidential to the casual observer and what data is not. This increases the risk of some possible accidental disclosure, which impairs value. To account for the value impact of such a risk, the valuation analyst might increase the discount rate associated with the trade secret's future cash flows, thereby impairing the trade secret's value.

- ***Consistent enforcement:*** Trade secret strength relates directly to consistent enforcement of non-disclosure and non-competition agreements. Companies that demonstrate consistent steps to protect trade secrets can avoid defenses of laches from infringers. A defendant in a lawsuit would claim a defense of laches when the defendant could have reasonably believed that the plaintiff was not going to protect the plaintiff's legal rights. The defendant also might present evidence of the plaintiff's inequitable enforcement of trade secrets. Any finding for the defendant would weaken the value of a trade secret, as the plaintiff would have no mechanism to receive damages for infringement.

201 *The Fox Controls, Inc. v. Honeywell, Inc.,* U.S. Dist. LEXIS 14410 (N.D. Ill, July 14, 2005).

- *Sufficient enforcement:* Trade secret strength also relates directly to sufficient enforcement of non-disclosure and non-competition agreements. Companies that demonstrate sufficient steps to protect trade secrets maintain trade secret enforceability and preserve value. Insufficient enforcement can impair trade secret value. For example, Apple Computer, Inc. (Apple) lost a trade secret case covered heavily in the media regarding its Asteroid product. Asteroid was a code name for a FireWire-based breakout box for a GarageBand product that Apple was introducing at the 2005 MacWorld Exposition for digital recording. However, Apple did not perform what the court considered a sufficient investigation of a trade secret breach or sufficient enforcement with its employees.[202] Specifically, Apple did not demonstrate that it adequately pursued various means to determine the source of the leaked trade secret. Apple did not demonstrate that it searched network logs for suspicious activity. Nor did it provide any evidence of how the person who leaked its trade secret disseminated the information (it only said the trade secret dissemination was electronic), sufficient investigation of workstation and server logs or printer logs, or any investigation regarding misappropriation through espionage (i.e., someone hacked Apple's computers to acquire the data). Ultimately, Apple not only lost the case and its trade secret protection through enforcement, but Apple had to reimburse its opponents for attorney fees exceeding $700,000.[203]

As with other IP types, the valuation analyst should consult with legal counsel to gauge the probability of value impairment due to proper administration of trade secret protections. The valuation analyst should account for any value impairments by increasing the discount rate used to determine the present value of the trade secret's future cash flows. Alternatively, the IP valuation analyst could account explicitly for the expected value of losses in the valuation model.

Trade Secret Floor Value

Recall that trade secrets have the following characteristics:

- They are not known outside of the particular company;
- They are valuable to the owner and possible competitors;

202 *O'Grady v. Superior Court*, 139 Cal. App. 4th 1423 (Cal. App. 2006), p. 60, "Apple has failed to demonstrate that it cannot identify the sources of the challenged information by means other than compelling petitioners to disclose unpublished information. This fact weighs heavily against disclosure, and on this record is dispositive."
203 Brad Stone, "Apple Rumor Site to Shut Down in Settlement," *The New York Times*, December 21, 2007.

- They have expenditures in time, effort, and money to develop;
- They are known only by employees and others involved in the company;
- They are difficult for others to properly acquire or independently duplicate; and
- They are subject to reasonable measures to guard the secrecy of the information.

That said, for a competing company to overcome the barriers imposed by these characteristics, it would have to invest both time and dollars. This creates an immediate floor on the value of the trade secret (i.e., the value cannot go lower than the floor value), if it is indeed valuable. This floor value consists of two primary components: the replacement or reproduction cost to regenerate the trade secret and the opportunity cost for the investment in time and dollars that it will take. The formula is as follows:

$$tradeSecretFloorValue = replacementOrReproductionCost + opportunityCost$$

For example, consider a trade secret for a specialty lawn care fertilizer owned by SuperGreenLawn Co. SuperGreenLawn generates $1 million annually in free cash flows attributable to its trade secrets. GreenerPastures Co. wants to reverse-engineer SuperGreenLawn's fertilizer formulation and sell a competing product in the market. In order to reverse-engineer the formulation, GreenerPastures will have to spend $150,000 in development costs to reproduce the fertilizer formulation, and it will take one year to complete the product development. After that time, GreenerPastures will enter the market, growing its market share to 40% of SuperGreenLawn's free cash flows over a two-year period. GreenerPastures has a discount rate of 30% for this project to account for the inherent riskiness associated with investments in this space.

The reproduction cost for the trade secret formulation is $150,000. At a 30% discount rate, the economic rent on $150,000 for one year (the time it takes to reproduce the formulation) is $45,000, indicating a total reproduction cost of $195,000.[204] This cost represents a value source for SuperGreenLawn. Next, since it takes GreenerPastures one year to develop the competing product, GreenerPastures is out of the market for that time. To account for this value, the trade secret valuation analyst looks at the value differential between what GreenerPastures could generate without the time

204 $150,000 initial cost + $45,000 economic rent = $195,000.

delay and the value GreenerPastures will generate after accounting for the time delay of one year to develop the product.

Exhibit 77 demonstrates the value of direct entry into the market:

Exhibit 77. Value of Direct Entry Into Market						
Greener Pastures Company	Year 1	Year 2	Year 3	Year 4	Year 5	Terminal
Free cash flow	1,000,000	1,000,000	1,000,000	1,000,000	1,000,000	
% to SuperGreenLawn Company	20%	40%	40%	40%	40%	
Adjusted free cash flow	200,000	400,000	400,000	400,000	400,000	1,333,333
Present value of free cash flows	1,096,617					

Compare that to the value of a one-year delay in the market (Exhibit 78).

Exhibit 78. Value of One Year Delay Into Market						
Greener Pastures Company	Year 1	Year 2	Year 3	Year 4	Year 5	Terminal
Free cash flow	1,000,000	1,000,000	1,000,000	1,000,000	1,000,000	
% to SuperGreenLawn Company	0%	20%	40%	40%	40%	
Adjusted free cash flow	-	200,000	400,000	400,000	400,000	1,333,333
Present value of free cash flows	824,427					

The difference attributable to the one-year delay is \$272,189.[205] As the calculation demonstrates, GreenerPastures would create an additional \$272,189 if it were able to enter the market sooner (which it cannot). Thus, this time delay creates additional value for SuperGreenLawn's trade secret. The sum of the total reproduction cost of \$195,000 and the opportunity cost due to time out of the market of \$272,189 is \$467,198. This \$467,198 represents the minimum value for the trade secret to SuperGreenLawn. Even though SuperGreenLawn generates greater value from the trade secret,[206] its trade secret has a minimum value because of the associated direct and opportunity costs for a competitor to reverse-engineer SuperGreenLawn's trade secrets.

205 \$1,096,617 - \$824,427 = \$272,189.

206 This is because SuperGreenLawn has a lower discount rate, associated with an existing and proven market product, plus a larger initial free cash flow engine.

Factors That Prolong Trade Secret Value

Certain factors can prolong trade secret value. Recall that one can destroy trade secret value by reproducing the trade secret's value proposition and exploiting it directly. Old Pet Food Co. has a special formula for a pet food product that the company protects with trade secrets and sells in the market successfully. New Pet Food Co. decides to enter that market selling a competing product. It buys Old Pet Food's product and reads the guaranteed analysis of its adult dog food product (listed in the product's label). Using that guaranteed analysis, New Pet Food hires a nutritionist and reverse-engineers the formulation of Old Pet Food's product and develops a new product in the market. In theory, this is straightforward to perform. New Pet Food could reproduce the formulation in short order (several months) and for minimal cost (several hundred thousand dollars). In practice, it will be difficult for New Pet Food to bring a competing product to the market. Several factors will make this process difficult:

- ***Difficult to reproduce:*** Trade secrets that are difficult for a competitor to reproduce will generally have a longer economic life. In the case of New Pet Food Co., if it were difficult to reverse-engineer the formulations for a competing product, it might never generate a satisfactory competing product. This increases risk associated with the reproduction effort. Companies that cannot reverse-engineer trade secrets will not be able to compete effectively in the market, even if the competing company has the resources and infrastructure to do so.

- ***High reproduction costs:*** Trade secrets that have high costs to reproduce will have a longer economic life. In the case of New Pet Food Co., in order for it to sell the product in the market, it might have to spend tens of millions of dollars to create the marketing program to launch the product. This adds to the cost of monetizing the trade secret formulation and increases the costs to reproduce it. Companies that cannot capitalize a large trade secret reproduction effort will not be able to compete, even if the competing companies had access (authorized or unauthorized) to the trade secret to do so.

- ***Long development timeframes:*** Time is a strong strategic competitive advantage for trade secrets. In order to develop an equivalent trade secret, New Pet Food Co. would have to build the product development team, generate a variety of formulations, test those formulations with pets, make formulation modifications, retest them with pets, and so on. For pet foods, it can take a minimum of 18 months to generate a new product

> from scratch. Thus, in addition to the base cost and associated risks, New Pet Food loses time in the market, which creates a time-value-of-money loss for it. For example, the delay of $10 million in value by 18 months at a 15% discount rate is $1.89 million.[207]

Other factors might also make it difficult for New Pet Food to succeed in bringing a competing product to the market. Embodiments of trade secrets that compete in industries that have high barriers to the monetization path will generally have longer practical lives.[208] In the case of New Pet Food, selling a pet food product successfully means that it has to gain access to retailers that will sell the product. This is not an easy task because the failure rates for new products are so great. In 2000 for example, 30,000 new consumer products entered the market, yet 93% of them failed to gain traction.[209] Retailers may be reluctant to commit shelf space to new products that carry a high risk of failure. This increases the barriers associated with monetizing copied trade secrets. However, these barriers do not relate to the value of the trade secrets as much as they do to the environment where embodiments of the trade secrets will compete. The trade secret valuation analyst should understand this distinction in order to consider only the trade secret's value in a valuation engagement.

Factors That Kill Trade Secrets

Several different factors can kill trade secret value because in certain situations disclosure of the trade secret is likely to occur, thus killing any secrecy associated with the trade secret. Several common situations that may arise that can impair trade secret value include the following:

- Litigation effects;
- Inadvertent disclosures;
- Trade secret agreement terms; and
- Publication as a patent or copyright.

207 This is determined by calculating the present value of an 18-month delay at 15% using a monthly compounding convention.

208 Note that the prolonged value may relate more to supplier networks, existing customers, and brands. For practical purposes, these items may be inseparable for some engagements.

209 "No More Trial and Error for New Products," press release, http://www.bases.com/news/news03052001.html, accessed March 15, 2009.

Litigation Effects

Recall that one key protective measure to prolonging a trade secret's value is to limit the number of people who have access to the trade secret. Paradoxically, enforcement of a trade secret can actually increase the risk of trade secret impairment. The reason is that the trade secret owner must disclose with particularity the trade secret during the discovery phase. This opens the opportunity for possible disclosure, either deliberately or accidentally by the opposing party. The trade secret owner can seek a protective order to limit those people who will have access to the trade secret.[210] However, the opposing party's attorneys and in-house counsel will learn about the trade secret as part of the litigation. This situation runs contrary to good practices for trade secret protection and may cause additional collateral damage from trade secret exposure.

For example, suppose that a semiconductor company sues a competitor for trade secret misappropriation. During the discovery, the defendant learns of new market intelligence that it would not have had were it not for the discovery. This discovery process and the associated new trade secret leak would not have occurred were it not for the litigation.

In a trade secret valuation engagement, the valuation analyst should perform a thorough review of all trade secret disclosures, especially in the event of any litigation, to ensure that those disclosures would not artificially depress the economic life of any trade secrets. In the event of any such limitations, the valuation analyst might limit the free cash flows considered, or increase the discount rate associated with future free cash flows, to account for the risk of possible deliberate or accidental disclosure.

Inadvertent Disclosures

Accidental or inadvertent disclosures of trade secrets can destroy trade secret value because the basic premise of value—secrecy—no longer exists. The fact that the disclosure is accidental or inadvertent is immaterial, and courts have not provided much sympathy for trade secret owners in such situations. For example, one trade secret case involved conversion of a proprietary customer list accidentally left in the memory of a computer sold at a liquidation auction. Though the plaintiff kept its originals in a locked room, the plaintiff lost its case because it did not take reasonable steps to protect the lists from inadvertent disclosure, by ensuring that the computer

210 For example, see 18 U.S.C. §1835, "In any prosecution or other proceeding under this chapter, the court shall enter such orders and take such other action as may be necessary and appropriate to preserve the confidentiality of trade secrets, consistent with the requirements of the Federal Rules of Criminal and Civil Procedure, the Federal Rules of Evidence, and all other applicable laws."

equipment did not contain copies of the trade secret.[211] The court noted that:[212]

> A customer list developed by a business through substantial effort and kept in confidence may be treated as a trade secret and protected at the owner's instance against disclosure to a competitor, provided the information it contains is not otherwise readily ascertainable . . . However, the owner is entitled to such protection only as long as he maintains the list in secrecy; upon disclosure, even if inadvertent or accidental, the information ceases to be a trade secret and will no longer be protected.

In a trade secret valuation engagement, the IP valuation analyst should perform a thorough exploration of all potential accidental or inadvertent disclosures of the trade secret to ensure that these disclosures do not invalidate the trade secret's value. In the event of any such limitations, the valuation analyst should consider limiting the free cash flows considered to only those covered before the disclosure (which might occur in a valuation where the effective date is historical). Some factors might mitigate the effects of value impairment, even in the face of an inadvertent disclosure, such as high reproduction costs, but the valuation analyst should explore this possibility thoroughly when considering how to impair the trade secret.

Trade Secret Agreement Terms

A very important part of any non-disclosure or non-competition agreement is the term of the agreement. As the term dictates the duration that the parties agree to keep information confidential (or for one party to refrain from competing against the other), the term has a direct bearing on the economic life of the trade secret. Thus, trade secret owners should push for extended terms to these agreements. For example, suppose that an employer wishes to disclose a chemical formulation to an employee. As with many employers, the employee must sign a non-disclosure agreement. The employer sets a term for the agreement of five years. In setting the agreement term to five years, the employer just potentially set the maximum economic life for the trade secret to five years. The employee could disclose the trade secret formulation after five years without legal recourse. Thus, in setting the five-year agreement term, the employer may have limited the economic life of the trade secret.[213]

211 *Defiance Button Machine Co. v. C&C Metal Products Corp.*, 759 F.2d 1053 (2nd Cir. 1985), paragraph 34.
212 *Id.*, paragraph 37.
213 The employer may have limited the economic life of the trade secret; however, other factors, such as high reproduction cost or high reproduction risk, may actually extend the economic life of the trade secret.

Also important in the consideration of a trade secret's economic life is that the valuation analyst gain an understanding of those non-disclosure agreements that may have already expired. The reason the economic life is important is that the valuation analyst must account for the possibility that some non-disclosure agreements for people who had former access to the trade secrets may have expired. If so, the trade secret owner would have no legal recourse to sue the disclosing person. The impact can be immense. A valuation analyst might presume that a trade secret had a protected life when in fact it did not.

For example, suppose TopSecretCompany hires an employee named Bob and makes Bob sign a non-disclosure agreement with a two-year term after he leaves the company. Bob leaves the company after nine months on the job. Two years after that, TopSecretCompany is still using the trade secret Bob had access to, and is generating $10 million in free cash flows from those trade secret per year. TopSecretCompany has a discount rate of 20%, and it considers its trade secret economic life to be perpetual. Thus, the trade secret value to TopSecretCompany would be $50 million.[214] At the end of the non-disclosure period, Bob decides to print the trade secret material on a billboard for the world to see. Even though other employees may still be under non-disclosure agreements, Bob is no longer under any such agreement. Thus, despite all current employees being under contract to protect TopSecretCompany's trade secrets, Bob's non-disclosure agreement sets the economic life for the trade secret, because he can disclose the trade secret without legal recourse.[215] After accounting for the true protected life of the trade secret, the total value of the trade secret was instead only $15,277,777,[216] or 31% of the original value indication, because Bob could use it two years after he left the company. Thus, TopSecretCompany experienced a value impairment of 69% due to improper construction of its non-disclosure agreement.

In a trade secret valuation engagement, the valuation analyst should perform a thorough review of all non-disclosure agreements to ensure that the agreements do not artificially depress the economic lives of any trade secrets. In the event of any such limitations, the valuation analyst should limit the free cash flows considered to only those covered by earliest agreement expiration date.

214 $10 million annual free cash flow / 20% discount rate = $50 million present value.

215 Of course, other factors might mitigate the severity of trade secret value impairment, including the costs to use the trade secret and the time it would take to use the trade secret in the market, among others.

216 This is determined by calculating the present value of a two-year $10 million annuity with a discount rate of 20% and an end of year discounting convention.

Publication as Patent or Copyright

An important tenet of any trade secret is preserving secrecy. So what happens to trade secrets that become part of a patent application or a copyright registration? The answer is simple: the trade secret loses its value. Recall that a patent requires full disclosure in order to receive the monopolistic benefits associated with the claimed invention. Thus, the disclosure associated with a patent necessarily destroys any secrecy imperative to preserving trade secret value. A similar condition exists for trade secrets that become part of a copyright registration. Recall that a copyright registration requires providing copies of the work to the U.S. Copyright Office. At that time, a disclosure occurs, destroying any of the secrecy imperative to preserving trade secret value. As discussed in Chapter 7, a company can submit software source code it deems to be a trade secret in redacted form, preventing complete disclosure of material that may still comprise a trade secret. Alternatively, the trade secret owner could register the object code for the software instead, though the trade secret owner would do so under the Rule of Doubt, as discussed in Chapter 7.

Naturally, the impact of a patent filing or a copyright registration on trade secret value becomes obvious: the trade secret no longer has value (though it may have value as a patented invention or a copyrighted work). The valuation analyst must consider the impact of any potential patent applications or copyright registrations on trade secret value and account for the value impacts accordingly in the valuation model.

Chapter 10
Discount Rate Development

Intellectual property risk is difficult to evaluate. Yet, proper risk assessment for an IP project is paramount because the primary mechanism for IP valuation depends on building income valuation models. To complete an income valuation model, the valuation analyst needs a discount rate, which is the IP risk proxy. Improper IP risk consideration can have a dramatic value impact. IP risk analysis emerges in several forms, which include the following:

- Strength of IP protections;
- Legal jurisdiction;
- Management's execution ability;
- Adequacy of financial resources;
- Economic life of the IP;
- Competitive threats;
- Contractual limitations;
- Foreign currency risks; and
- Government regulation.

Naturally, there may be other forms but this list is certainly a reasonable starting point for the valuation analyst. Prior chapters have gone to great lengths to demonstrate the value impacts of the various risks that jeopardize the future cash flows that a given IP asset may generate. The challenge of course is to evaluate these risks and integrate them into the valuation model objectively and defensibly. This chapter focuses on a means to account for risk in an objective way for IP projects.

Accounting for IP Risk

Valuation analysts use an income-based approach for most IP valuation projects. An intrinsic part of the income approach is the selection and use of a discount rate to value future anticipated cash flows on a present value basis. The magnitude of the discount rate serves as a proxy for the risk associated with receiving the future cash flows. There is an inverse relationship between risk and value. A higher risk project will have a lower value, and a lower risk project will have a higher value.

Consider the example of an asset that generates an annual payment of $1 million in perpetuity. Suppose that the value is relatively high risk and the valuation analyst uses a 50% discount rate to account for the associated risk. The value of the perpetuity is $2 million.[217] On the other hand, suppose that the same annual $1 million payment has a lower risk profile, such that the valuation analyst uses a 20% discount rate to account for the associated risk. In this case, the value of the perpetuity is $5 million.[218] Exhibit 79 captures the essence of this relationship for a $1 million perpetual annuity valued using discount rates from 4% to 125%.

As the chart demonstrates, there is a nonlinear relationship between the discount rate and the value. This means that changes in value do not change in direct proportion

Exhibit 79. Discount Rate Impact on $1 Million Annuity

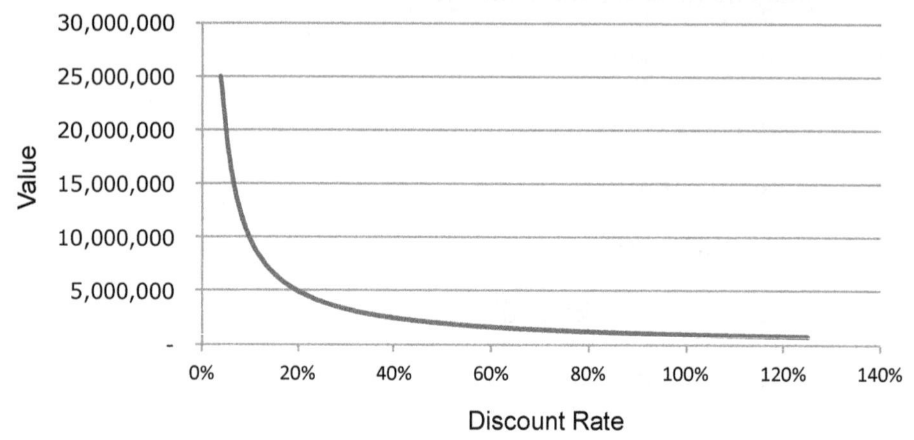

217 Recall that the present value of a perpetuity is as follows: $1,000,000 / 50% = $2,000,000.
218 $1,000,000 / 20% = $5,000,000.

to the discount rate. If a valuation analyst raises a discount rate by 5%, the value impact is not constant. Instead, it depends on the starting discount rate that the valuation analyst was adjusting and the direction of the change (i.e., lowering it or raising it from the starting discount rate). Raising the discount rate from 20% to 25% lowers the value by $1 million.[219] However, raising the discount rate from 75% to 80% lowers the value by only $83,333.[220]

Current valuation literature establishes these concepts well. For example, "the discount rate should properly reflect the risks of an investment in the forecasted profit stream."[221] However, the magic question is this: how do you determine what discount rate to use for the project? Not one major source in current literature speaks specifically as to how to do that objectively and defensibly for an IP engagement.[222] Thus, that leaves the IP valuation analyst to fall back on methods used in other valuation disciplines, such as business valuation. As a result, following current literature dutifully, the valuation analyst calculates the discount rate using either the capital asset pricing model (CAPM) or its variant the Fama-French Model, the arbitrage pricing model, the build-up method, or some other method. The bad news for the IP valuation analyst is that these methods are all woefully inadequate for estimating the discount rate of an IP valuation project for several reasons.

First, a search of the academic research yields little useful correlation between IP valuation projects and these methods, despite a substantial emphasis in current literature on using these methods for IP valuations. For example, all derivations of the CAPM derive from studying changes in stock prices for a specific company against the broader value-weighted market index, none of which deals with IP investment. Therefore, it is simply erroneous to apply a discount rate based on company market values against an IP asset, as the valuation analyst would be mixing altogether unrelated items.

Second, a company's discount rate, as calculated using any of the aforementioned methods, represents an income portfolio that provides risk diversification. That typically is not the case for an IP project. For example, Lilly sells a variety of products including Prozac, Zyprexa, Cialis, Cymbalta, and others. If Lilly loses patent protection on a single product, such as Prozac, Lilly will likely continue to be a going concern because it has diversified its operations such that any single product

219 ($1,000,000 / 20%)—($1,000,000 / 25%) = $1,000,000.

220 ($1,000,000 / 75%)—($1,000,000 / 80%) = $83,333.

221 J. Timothy Cromley, "20 Steps for Pricing a Patent," *Journal of Accountancy*, 2004.

222 For that matter, the same holds true for early-stage companies or other assets that lack a defined marketing program or distribution infrastructure.

failure will not ruin the company. Contrast that with an IP project. A patent, unless it touches several distinct markets (e.g., an adhesive works equally well in biomedical, commercial construction, and aerospace applications), represents a single-source income stream that may have no value if it fails in the market. Alternatively, consider a startup company focused on one product whose patent captures its essence. If the patented invention fails to fulfill a value proposition, the invention has no realizable value and the company that depends on that invention's value folds because of a lack of diversification.

Third, contemporary discount rate development methods lack the precision to calculate a discount rate commensurate with specific risk levels within an industry. Yet the risks associated with an IP project vary considerably based on the project's nature and the company monetizing the IP. For example, one study indicates that the cumulative success rate for an infectious disease therapy winning FDA approval for sale is 28.1%.[223] That same study indicates that the approval success rate for a respiratory therapy is only 12%.[224] Under existing discount rate methods, such as the SIC-code-based build-up method or the CAPM, the IP valuation analyst would attribute the same discount rate to each of these investments despite their grossly different success rates. This is erroneous. In fact, the infectious disease therapy has more than twice the chance of getting to market, so its risk profile is lower while its valuation is higher, all else the same. Moreover, a start-up company incurs greater risk than a mature company does to bring an equivalent therapy to the market. The discount rate should reflect this difference. Existing literature does suggest that the valuation analyst can add some "alpha" factor to the discount rate to account for the additional risk. Yet no method demonstrates an objective, empirical method to do so.[225] Thus, using existing discount rate methods, the IP valuation analyst makes what amounts to a random guess as to the possible adjustment to account for the risk differences. However, this random guess lacks both a theoretical model and any means to test the guess empirically.

Lastly, contemporary discount rate development methods that depend on stock price analysis rely on the broad presumption that stock price equates to stock value. Benjamin Graham and David Dodd first wrote about the difference between the two in their seminal book *Security Analysis: Principles and Techniques* more than half a century ago. Even if price did equal value in the long run, the CAPM expresses

223 Joseph A DiMasi, "Risks in New Drug Development: Approval Success Rates for Investigational Drugs," *Clinical Pharmacology & Therapeutics* 69, p. 301.
224 *Id.*
225 Some studies suggest adding a size premium or discount to a base discount rate to account for the relative size differences of companies in the market. Yet this data suffers from survivorship biases and brings no illumination to evaluating differences between start-up or privately held companies and mature companies.

volatility based on daily changes in the stock price that may likely have little or no correlation to value. The market created a simple example of this phenomenon with respect to Lilly's stock price when Lilly lost its second Prozac patent. The market value of Lilly, based on its stock price, fell $35 billion. However, the true economic impact for Lilly was only about $886 million or so. The valuation profession uses stock price to derive a beta using the CAPM to arrive at the value of an asset. This requires a leap of faith that stock price matches company value. It requires an even larger leap of faith to assume that stock prices match intellectual property value for diversified companies.

Deeper Analysis of Current Methods

Discount rates for most intellectual properties are not directly observable in the market. The closest analogues are early-stage companies, which typically receive venture funding and share key traits and risks[226] with intellectual properties, including the following:

- ***Lack of diversification:*** Early-stage companies oftentimes have limited capital to diversify risk among a portfolio of intellectual property investments. For example, an orthopedic company develops a replacement knee. It will barely raise enough money to capitalize that effort, let alone diversify its development efforts into other implants such as shoulders or hips. Intellectual properties share this same lack of risk diversification. The concentration of risk-adjusted returns increases the discount rate to fund those returns.[227]

  This risk pattern is quite common and the entire point of the mutual fund industry. For example, as discussed already, Lilly lost a patent it had on Prozac in 2001, costing it 15 months' exclusivity in the market. This was catastrophic for the value of the patent to Lilly. However, it did not bring down the company, as Lilly had diversification across many other products, such as its insulin products. However, contrast that with a company in an earlier development stage that lacks such diversification. La Jolla Pharmaceutical's stock cratered 90% after its lead drug candidate, Riquent, failed in a clinical trial. NASDAQ subsequently delisted La Jolla, and its stock trades are currently virtually worthless, down from split-adjusted

226 Risk is of course the important factor among venture-backed early-stage and intellectual property investments.

227 This pattern is quite common in business valuation as well, especially if the value of a business relates closely to a personal goodwill or single customers that comprise a significant portion of a company's revenues.

highs well above $4,000 per share.[228] La Jolla had no other products in its portfolio to help maintain its entity value. Intellectual properties share remarkable commonality in risk profile with venture-backed investments. Naturally, there are many other examples in the market that bolster this position.

- ***Value is inseparable:*** The value of most early-stage companies that develop patents or copyrights is inseparable from the early-stage company's intellectual property for practical purposes because of the lack of asset diversification. Thus, if the product represented by the intellectual property fails in the market (e.g., book, drug), the failure is catastrophic for the value of the intellectual property. Empirically, this is evident all the time.

A search of the academic research yields no major source in the current literature that speaks specifically as to how to calculate a discount rate objectively and defensibly for an IP engagement. Despite these challenges, valuation analysts may oftentimes state that financial theorists have generally favored the CAPM as the preferred method to estimate a discount rate.[229] However, many valuation analysts fail to acknowledge any suggestions that the CAPM is inadequate despite evidence supporting CAPM's inadequacy. For example, Eugene Fama and Kenneth French published several articles decades ago arguing that the CAPM oversimplifies a complex market and even developed another model to use instead, which many valuation analysts do not generally consider. Instead, valuation analysts spend remarkable time debating and selecting factors used to calculate a discount rate using the CAPM (e.g., is the beta right? how many years' worth of historical data is in the sample?). Following dogmatic principles about looking to the market for evidence of what appears to suggest appropriate discount rates, valuation analysts may naively ignore a basic question: does the theory match reality? Is history appropriate for *future* investments?

Fundamentally, IP risk coincides directly with industry success. This is not a concept one develops in a vacuum. Other authors have come to similar conclusions.[230] Furthermore, little data exists to suggest that contemporary discount rate development methods have relevance to IP engagements. Suppose one is developing a

228 According to data on finance.yahoo.com for LJPC.PK as of November 1, 2011.

229 The inventors of the CAPM received a Nobel Prize in economics for the creation, so it *must* be correct; so goes the thinking.

230 Terry Dorsey, "A Portfolio Model for Venture Capital Performance Measurement and Investment Selection," Polaris Group, January 2000.

discount rate for a book copyright valuation. The book sells in educational circles. How do changes in the stock price for a multibillion educational publisher relate to the risk associated with monetizing the book copyright? In fact, discount rates for the book copyright should be greater.

For example, consider the following schedule of assets a company owns. In one sense, a company is a mutual fund of independent assets comprising net working capital, plant, property, equipment, patents, copyrights, and so on. Thus, the blended discount rate for a company may be lower or higher than the discount rates for different asset classes. Exhibit 80 dictates clearly that the discount rate for intangibles is greater than for other asset types:[231]

Exhibit 80. Discount Rate For Intangibles

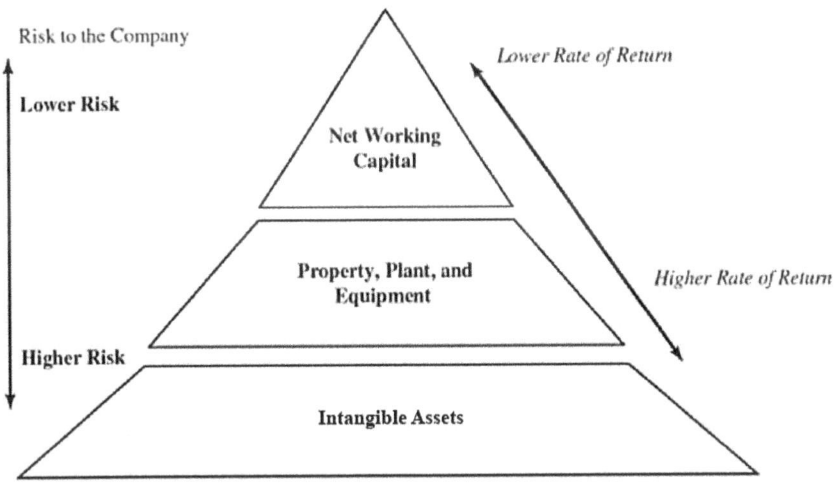

Academic research suggests that discount rate development methods employed commonly by valuation analysts are inappropriate. For example, one source states the following:[232]

> Techniques used to measure risk when investing in publicly traded securities that have a market, or traded, price are problematic when extended to private-market transactions[233]... market prices ... don't exist on the same one-year holding-period basis common with liquid assets traded in public markets. Therefore, objective

231 Shannon Pratt and Roger Grabowski, *Cost of Capital 3rd Edition*, John Wiley & Sons, 2008.

232 Note that this source focuses on venture capital investments; however, venture capital investments and intellectual properties share many similarities (e.g., lack of diversification, execution risk, market uncertainty).

233 Note that these problems are even more apparent for intellectual properties, and existing methods have even greater shortcomings than the paper's authors described.

> comparisons of risk and return relative to other public markets are difficult to justify. This problem is not unique . . . discussions like this have appeared in other fields with illiquid characteristics . . . the subjective valuation isn't a good proxy for price changes for use in a CAPM formulation and would lead to biased estimates of risk . . . most often, investments . . . are valued at cost until a 'material' event occurs that 'affects' the valuation. After another year, another valuation is performed. That valuation will be made as objectively as possible, but will be based in large part on the valuation determined in the previous year . . . it is easy to see that the valuation is largely affected by the valuation in the previous period and thus is artificially correlated with the previous valuation. In statistics, this is termed 'autocorrelation,' which creates estimation problems. More importantly, since there is no price to value . . . the value doesn't fluctuate year-to-year as a market-driven price would. This tends to lower the volatility of returns.[234]

Moreover, as discount rates are forward-looking items, this necessarily means that there are investors willing to finance the assets at a level sufficient to monetize the IP. The contemporary market certainly does not lend credence to availability of investors willing to invest. For example, in the contemporary economic climate (i.e., 2008-2011), calculated discount rates are lower because of shrinking equity risk premiums and a shrinking riskless rate. Despite this phenomenon, a credit shortage exists. Of course, a credit shortage increases the required rate of return because of basic supply and demand imbalances (i.e., investors demand greater returns because of greater perceived risks).

Other factors become important in determining a discount rate, including the target rate of return, the holding period, and associated management expenses. None of the current methods accounts for these factors. In short, it is not appropriate to use these methods for an IP-based project. Further, an alternative method exists to account for all of these considerations. The next section introduces an analytical framework that considers the relevant factors of an IP project to impute an appropriate discount rate based on empirical research.

An IP Discount Rate Estimation Model

As discussed in the prior section, existing methods for estimating the discount rate for an IP project are inadequate. Specifically, they fail to account for the following factors that are crucial in the pricing of capital costs for IP projects:

234 Terry Dorsey, "A Portfolio Model for Venture Capital Performance Measurement and Investment Selection," Polaris Group, January 2000, pp. 2-3.

- The target rate of return for the investment;
- The success rate of getting IP to the market;
- The holding period for the IP investment; and
- Associated expenses for managing the investment for the holding period.

This chapter presents a new discount rate estimation model. This new IP discount rate estimation model accounts for all of the above factors. Moreover, it works for angel investors, venture capital firms, and public and private companies. The model works for intellectual property in all stages of development, regardless of whether it is just at the idea stage or whether it is already selling in the market. The model works for every major industry and every IP type. Additionally, the model passes empirical and theoretical tests, validating the model approach. Lastly, the model is relatively straightforward, providing for simple verification of model results.

Target Rate of Return

To explain the model, one first needs to consider the nature of an IP investment. An investor invests resources in intellectual property in order to generate a return on investment (ROI). However, not all investments will generate an ROI. Some projects will fail, and the investor will lose the entire investment in the project. Other projects may meander on for years never generating outright losses, but also never achieving target return objectives. This situation is what some investors may call the "living dead." Lastly, some projects will generate successful returns well in excess of the desired target return. For example, suppose that an investor makes equal $1 million investments in three separate projects. In the first project, the investor loses the entire investment, generating an ROI of (100%). In the second project, the investor breaks even on the investment, generating an ROI of 0%. In the third project, the investor generates an ROI of $3 million, or 200%, for a cumulative ROI of $1 million (33%), as Exhibit 81 demonstrates.

Exhibit 81. Return on Investment for Three Projects

	Investment	Ending Value	Return %
Investment #1	1,000,000	-	-100%
Investment #2	1,000,000	1,000,000	0%
Investment #3	1,000,000	3,000,000	200%
Totals	3,000,000	4,000,000	33%

Thus, if the investor is to generate a target rate of return, perhaps 15% annually, the investor must account for both the expected successes and failures.

Holding Period

An investor invests $1 million into the portfolio and requires a 20% compound annual return on that money. Important in the consideration of this investment is the holding period. The longer the holding period, the longer the investment portfolio has to generate an economic return (i.e., the portfolio does not need to generate all of its returns on a compressed schedule). This holding period thus lowers the implied rate of return, which lowers the discount rate. For example, consider that an investor wishes to double his or her investment in five years. In order to meet this target, the portfolio would need to generate compound annual returns of 14.87%.[235] If the investor wants to double the investment in seven years, then the portfolio would need to generate compound annual returns of 10.41%.[236]

To understand the importance of the holding period, presume the investor will target a seven-year holding period and seeks a 20% compound annual return. This means that the investor wants to generate a 20% compound annual return on a $1 million investment and receive the proceeds at the end of Year 7. The investor would thus receive a check at the end of Year 7 for $3,583,181. Of that check, $1,000,000 represents a return of the original investment amount. The balance represents the 20% rate of return that the investor sought. In this example, the model assumes that the entire $1,000,000 investment will generate a return. However, recall that not all of the portfolio investment may generate a return, as some specific portfolio projects will fail and some will break even. Thus, capital available to generate the total portfolio return will be less than the original investment. In fact, if a company has a 20% success rate, then the expected value of the initial investment is $200,000.[237] That means that the remaining $200,000 investment must grow over a seven-year period to $3,583,181. In order to do so, that $200,000 must generate a compound annual rate of return of 51.02%.[238] This fact is the key to the discount rate model. By accounting for the expected success of the overall initial investment, and then solving for the compound annual rate of return needed to meet the target rate of return to the original investor, one can compute the appropriate discount rate to use for a project, as the following equation describes:[239]

235 This is calculated using a financial calculator with a present value of ($1,000,000), a holding period of five years, interim payments of $0, and a future value of $2,000,000, solving for the interest rate.

236 This is calculated using a financial calculator with a present value of ($1,000,000), a holding period of seven years, interim payments of $0, and a future value of $2,000,000, solving for the interest rate.

237 $1 million x 20% probability of success = $200,000.

238 $200,000 x $(1+ 51.02\%)^7$ = $3,583,181.

239 Algebraically, the investment amount is irrelevant in the discount rate calculation. The discount rate would be the same regardless of whether the investment amount was $1 or $1 billion.

$$discountRate = \left(\frac{(1 + targetRate)^{holdingPeriod}}{successRate} \right)^{1/holdingPeriod} - 1$$

Key drivers for the model include the target ROI sought, the success rate of the investment portfolio, and the holding period. Changes to any of these will adjust the portfolio's risk profile; thus, the discount rate adjusts to account for the change in the risk profile automatically.

Fortunately, much data exists in the public domain relating to holding periods. For example, empirical evidence supports that current private equity holding periods can vary. Academic research suggests that half of the deals exit by Year 6, while 76% of deals exit by Year 10, as Exhibit 82 demonstrates.[240]

The valuation analyst can use such empirical holding period data to help determine the discount rates that have a fundamental basis in reality.

Exhibit 82. Existence of Holding Periods

Investment Duration	1970-1984	1985-1989	1990-1994	1995-1999	2000-2002	2003-2005	Whole Period
2 years	14%	12%	14%	13%	9%	13%	12%
5 years	47%	40%	53%	41%	40%		42%
6 years	53%	48%	63%	49%	49%		51%
7 years	61%	58%	70%	56%	55%		58%
10 years	70%	75%	82%	73%			76%

Exhibit 83. Holding Period and Required Rate of Return

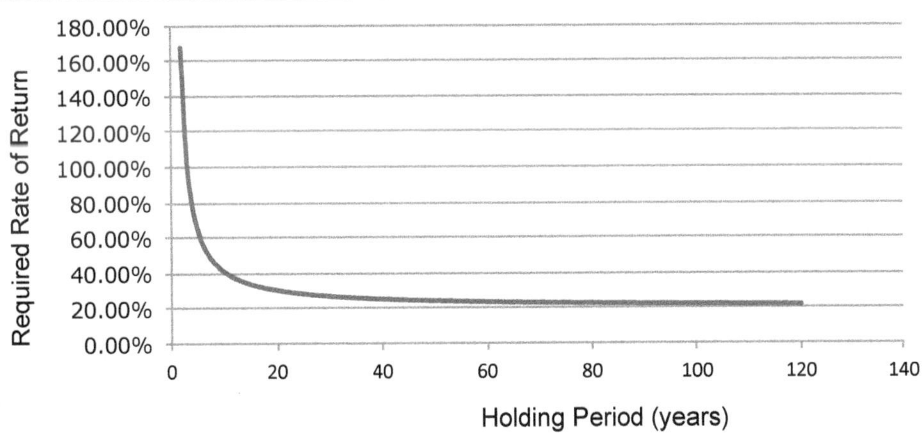

240 Steven N. Kaplan and Per Strömberg. "Leveraged Buyouts and Private Equity," *Journal of Economic Perspectives*. Volume 23, Number 1. Winter 2009..

Further, this new discount rate estimation model works well under different holding periods. Recall that the shorter the holding period, the less time available to generate a favorable return. Assuming a success rate of 20%, a holding period of five years, and a target rate of return of 20%, the model would determine a discount rate of 65.57%. If the holding period were seven years, the discount rate would be 51.02%. If the holding period were 10 years, the discount rate would be 40.95%. As the holding period extends to infinity, the discount rate of return approaches the target rate of return, as Exhibit 83 demonstrates.

Success Rates

The new discount rate estimation model works well under different success rates for projects. Recall that infectious disease therapies have an approval success rate of 28.1%. Assuming a target rate of return of 20% and a five-year holding period, the required discount rate to reach the investment objective is 54.68%. Now contrast that with the respiratory therapy, which exhibits a 12.0% approval success rate. In that situation, the discount rate rises dramatically to 83.38% to account for the increased risk that the therapy will fail to gain approval for sale in the market. The success rate bears an exponential relationship to the discount rate as Exhibit 84 demonstrates using a five-year holding period and a target rate of return of 20%.

As the chart demonstrates, the greater the success rate for the portfolio in converting the original investment to an ROI, the lower the required discount rate.

Exhibit 84. Success Rate and Required Rate of Return

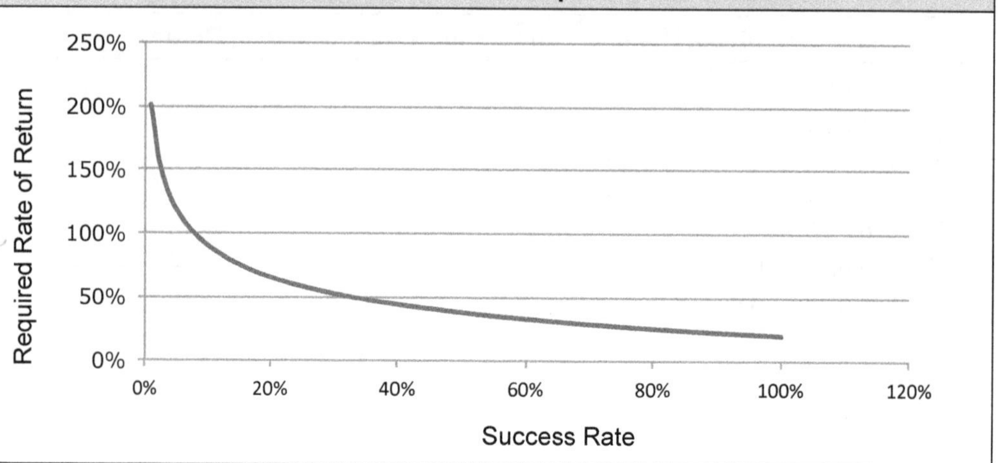

Target Returns

The new discount rate estimation model works well as the investor changes the desired ROI. Assuming a success rate of 20%, a holding period of five years, and a target rate of return of 20%, the model would determine a discount rate of 65.57%. If the investor changes the target ROI from 20% to 15%, perhaps due to a loosening credit market, then the resulting discount rate reduces to 58.67%. If the investor changes the target ROI from 20% to 25%, perhaps due to a tightening of the credit market, then the resulting discount rate increases to 72.47%. A direct linear relationship exists between the target return and the resulting discount rate, as Exhibit 85 demonstrates.

As Exhibit 85 demonstrates, investor demands for higher returns for the initial investment directly increase the discount rate.

Exhibit 85. Target Rate and Required Rate of Return

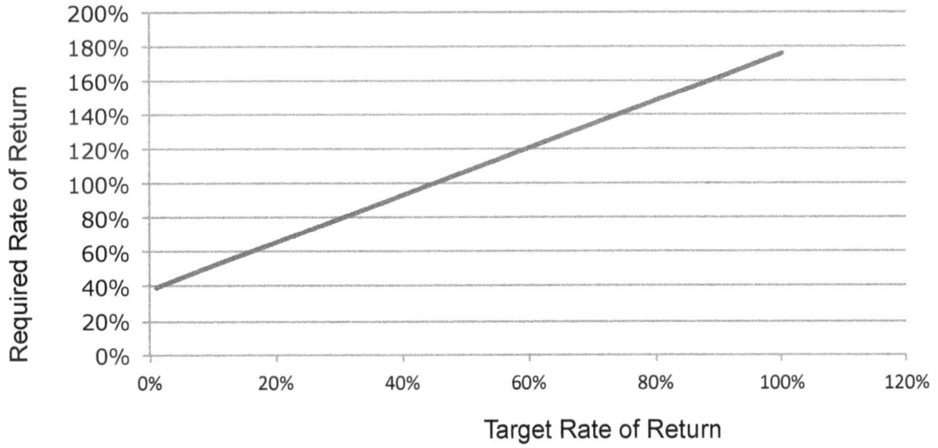

Investment Expenses

Target returns to the investor should always represent the net cash returned to the investor. Thus, any items that reduce the amount of cash that could go to the investor, such as investment expenses, represent a drag on the realized investment returns. In order for the investor to achieve target return objectives, the realized rate of return from the successful portfolio projects must be even higher to account for portfolio management fees. If the investment portfolio represented management by a venture capital firm, fees would include an annual maintenance fee, which is typically about 2%, and a carried interest (i.e., profit share of investment gains), which is typically 20% of the investment profits.

For example, suppose that a venture capitalist raises a $10 million fund, has a target rate of return of 20%, expects a 20% success rate over a five-year holding period, and operates under an arrangement that pays him or her 2% of the fund amount as management fee and a 20% carried interest. Under that target return, the investor expects to receive $24,883,200 at the end of Year 5, $10 million representing the initial investment and $14,883,200 representing a 20% annual return on the original investment over a five-year period. The venture capitalist will have to generate that return with a realized investment amount of $2 million after considering the success rate on the initial investment.[241] Since the venture capitalist will receive 2% annually to operate the fund, total management expenses will be $1 million over the life of the fund.[242] That means that the investment must then generate an additional $1 million to cover the fund's expenses and still meet the target return objectives. Thus, the $2 million investment must now generate $25,883,200 over five years. In order to do so, the venture capitalist's investments would have to generate a return of 66.88%. That return does not account for the carried interest, which is the profit component that accrues to the venture capitalist for his or her investment acumen. That carried interest is the profit component of the investment, which is $14,883.200. However, do not forget that the venture capitalist has $1 million in management fees to cover as well. Thus, actual profit that represents the basis for the carried interest is $15,883,200. To get a net return of $15,883,200 after a 20% carried interest, the model has to gross up returns and then subtract out the profit to the investor. The formula to do that is as follows:

$$carriedInterestAmount = \frac{(targetInvestmentReturn + managementFee)}{(1 - carriedInterest\%)} - (targetInvestmentReturn + managementFee)$$

$$carriedInterestAmount = \frac{(\$14{,}883{,}200 + \$1{,}000{,}000)}{(1 - 20\%)} - (\$14{,}883{,}200 + \$1{,}000{,}000)$$

$$carriedInterestAmount = \frac{(\$15{,}883{,}200)}{(80\%)} - \$15{,}883{,}200$$

$$carriedInterestAmount = \$19{,}854{,}000 - \$15{,}883{,}200$$

$$carriedInterestAmount = \$3{,}970{,}800$$

The carried interest of $3,970,800 gets added into the total returns that the $2 million investment must generate, which now is $29,854,000. In order to generate the venture capitalist's target return after accounting for management fees and the carried interest, the venture capitalist will have to generate a compound annual rate of return of 71.71% over the five-year holding period. That is, the true cost of equity for an investment by this venture capitalist would be 71.71%. Thus, a valuation analyst would use this discount rate for the valuation.

241 The $10 million fund net of the 20% success rate.

242 $10 million fund x 2% x 5 years = $1 million.

Adding management expenses into the original equation complicates the formula somewhat, but the formula is still quite usable despite this complication. Following is the revised discount rate formula, which accounts for both the recurring management fee and the carried interest amount calculated previously:

$$discountRate = \left(\frac{\begin{array}{l}(1 + targetRate)^{holdingPeriod} + \\ annualManagementFee\% * holdingPeriod + \\ carriedInterestAmount\end{array}}{successRate} \right)^{1/holdingPeriod} - 1$$

As an interesting sidebar, some venture capitalists charge higher carried interest fees. For example, Charles River Ventures charges a 30% carried interest,[243] well above the industry norm of 20%. Assuming the same success rate of 20% and a five-year holding period, Charles River Ventures increased its required rate of return from 71.71% to 75.61%, as the $2 million net invested capital must now generate $33,404,571 instead of $29,854,000.

What About Empirical Evidence of Support?

A theoretical model is only good if it models reality within some measure of error. The obvious implication is that using data based on real-world observable circumstances makes for a better approximation of true value. Proponents of the CAPM and its derivatives point out quickly that real-world data drives the results that valuation analysts use. However, as discussed already, the utility of those results for an IP engagement is dubious at best, despite their empirical roots. By analogy, one can show empirically that a Fortune 500 company has a lower discount rate that correlates negatively with the number of McDonald's Big Macs that its employees consume. However, correlation does not equal causation. Moreover, recall that IP's discount rates are not directly observable in the market. That said, this new discount rate estimation model does provide for consideration of empirical evidence to drive the ultimate discount rate in several forms.

First, from a theoretical perspective, it is simple to prove the model with simple algebra based on the inputs. If the model were wrong, then the results generated would not satisfy the target return objectives or cover the associated expenses needed to manage the investment based on the projected success rate.

243 Andrew Metrick, *Venture Capital and the Finance of Innovation*, John Wiley & Sons, Inc., 2007.

Second, the model allows the valuation analyst to set the discount rate based upon target returns of funds. When fund managers sell an interest in their fund, they typically will issue a target rate of ROI. The market that invests in that fund explicitly accepts the projected target rate of return in exchange for the investment. That target rate of return for the fund thus becomes the basis for the targeted return to use in the model. Alternatively, consider the case of a public company that makes continued investments in research and development. Using a discount rate model, such as the CAPM or information from public filings, one could determine the company's discount rate or its hurdle rate. That rate would thus become the target rate that one would use for the model.

Third, the model allows the valuation analyst to select the holding period for the investment explicitly. If the length of time for a drug to make it through a pharmaceutical's pipeline to market is 10 years, that 10-year indication is what the valuation analyst uses for the holding period for the model. If a venture capital fund projects a seven-year holding period to its investors, then that seven-year holding period should be used in the model. In both examples, the model uses empirical evidence to drive the resulting output.

Fourth, the model allows the valuation analyst to set the expected success rate for the total investment. The valuation analyst can do so using historical data from either its own investment success rate or data from the broader market. For example, recall that infectious disease therapies have a 28.1% historical success rate of making it through the clinical trials process and on to final market approval, while respiratory therapies have a 12.0% historical success rate. Empirical evidence drives that success rate statistic directly. Thus, using it would reflect empirical observation.

Lastly, the model allows the valuation analyst to account for the expected expenses associated with the investment management. For a company, these expenses would likely be zero. For a fund, they would reflect what the fund's prospectus indicates. Thus, if a venture capital fund expects a 2% management fee with a 20% carried interest, the valuation analyst can program that directly into the model. Again, this data has an empirical basis that reflects what the valuation analyst observes directly in the market.

In short, the new discount rate estimation model is a simple calculator, easily provable with algebra. Using empirically derived inputs should provide a valuation analyst with an empirically based discount rate suitable for an IP project.

Proving the Model

Discount rates developed using the model described in this chapter are greater than what many other sources may indicate. Mathematically, they have to be. For example, suppose that an investor invests in 10 deals, investing $100 per deal. Thus, the investor invests a total of $1,000. The investor desires a 20% annual rate of return on the investment. Thus, at the end of the first year, the investor wants to have a total value of $1,200.[244] The investor anticipates that the success rate for these investments will be 50%. That is, five of the deals will succeed, while the balance will not succeed at all. The model indicates that the discount rate for this investment must be 140%, as the following math demonstrates!

$$discountRate = \left(\frac{(1+20\%)^1}{50\%} \right)^1 - 1$$

$$discountRate = \left(\frac{120\%}{50\%} \right) - 1$$

$$discountRate = 240\% - 1$$

$$discountRate = 140\%$$

Naturally, this discount rate appears to be remarkably high. No company that trades on any U.S. exchange commands that type of required rate of return. Yet, Exhibit 86 demonstrates that the discount rate must be that value:

Exhibit 86. Required Rate of Return

Investment Number	Amount Invested	Successful Amount Invested	Nominal Returns @ 20%	Required Returns @ 140%	Difference
1	$100	$100	$120	$240	($120)
2	$100	$100	$120	$240	($120)
3	$100	$100	$120	$240	($120)
4	$100	$100	$120	$240	($120)
5	$100	$100	$120	$240	($120)
6	$100	$0	$0	$0	$0
7	$100	$0	$0	$0	$0
8	$100	$0	$0	$0	$0
9	$100	$0	$0	$0	$0
10	$100	$0	$0	$0	$0
Total	$1,000	$500	$600	$1,200	($600)

244 $1,000 initial investment x (1 + 20% target rate of return) = $1,200.

As the data in the table shows, the total amount invested was $1,000 across 10 deals. The investor succeeded in half of those deals, preserving $500 in capital. Recall that the investor desires $1,200 at the end of the year. Thus, the investor has to generate $700 in returns, starting with a $500 principal amount. If the investor achieved the overall target rate of return from each deal (i.e., 20%), then the investor would receive only $600 at the end of the year.[245] The $600 that the investor has is $600 short of the desired $1,200. In reality, the only rate of return that creates the ending value the investor desires is $140%.[246]

Let us revisit our book publisher example. Suppose a book publisher is interested in funding a new book copyright. It is trivial to work backwards to determine the target rate that the publisher would have to demand in order to have a 15% overall business discount rate. One of five books in the publishing arena succeeds (a 20% success rate). Considering a ten-year holding period (this is admittedly unrealistic and optimistic, as few publishers would be willing to wait that long for returns on a copyright collection), this means that the formula would look like the following:

$$15\% = \left(\frac{(1 + targetRate)^{10}}{20\%} \right)^{1/10} - 1$$

One can determine the target rate by rearranging the equation and solving for the target rate that the publisher would have to generate. The result of that activity is that the target rate is below zero. This means that the publisher would commit additional capital over the ten years and the initial investments would never generate the target returns. The result: mathematically, it is impossible for a publisher to assign a 15% discount rate to its specific investments with a published 20% success rate.[247] The publisher will never generate the returns necessary to overcome the industry-standard failure rates and will require continual new funds from investors until it can no longer raise such funds. At that point, it will likely go bankrupt or sell to a competitor at a depressed price. Thus, using a target rate of 15%, a 20% success rate, and a ten-year holding period, the discount rate has to be 35.08%. Mathematically, it can be no other value.

245 $500 successful investment amount x (1 + 20% target rate of return) = $600.

246 $500 successful investment amount x (1 + 140% target rate of return) = $1,200.

247 As an aside, the 20% success rate is consistent with success rates for entrepreneurs. Academic research suggests that first-time entrepreneurs have about a 20% success rate, while serial entrepreneurs have about a 25% success rate. Please refer to Paul Gompers, Anna Kovner, Josh Lerner, and David Scharfstein, "Skill vs. Luck in Entrepreneurship and Venture Capital: Evidence From Serial Entrepreneurs," NBER Working Paper Series, No. 12592, 2006, p. 12.

Model Extensions

The new discount rate estimation model in its basic state includes several baseline assumptions that should work well for many instances. First, the model presumes that all capital is ready for investment on the first month. This may not be true in all cases. Oftentimes investors may supply capital over several months or years. The model extends well to support this structure. The net effect of such a structure would be to lower the required rate of return for the project. For example, suppose that an investor provides $10 million in capital and seeks a ten-year holding period, a 28% success rate, and a target rate of return of 15%, with no management fees or carried interest. The discount rate is 30.57%.

Suppose, however, that the investor provides the $10 million over two years, with $5 million added in the first year and $5 million added in the second year. The net effect would be a reduction of the discount rate to 29.69%, primarily because the investments must return a lesser amount, as the second $5 million would have to cover only nine years' worth of compound annual returns at a 15% target rate to return to the investor, instead of ten years' worth. Exhibit 87 captures those cash flows and the required rate of return.

Next, the model presumes that all dividends and the return of capital occur in the last year. However, like capital infusions, extending the model to allow for a sooner return on capital is a trivial extension. For example, suppose that an investor provides $10 million in capital and seeks a ten-year holding period, a 28% success rate, and a

Exhibit 87. Discount Rate Calculation with Deferred Investment

	Year 1	Year 2	Year 3	Year 4	Year 5	Year 6	Year 7	Year 8	Year 9	Year 10
Beginning Balance	-	5,750,000	12,362,500	14,216,875	16,349,406	18,801,817	21,622,090	24,865,403	28,595,214	32,884,496
Investment	5,000,000	5,000,000	-	-	-	-	-	-	-	-
Dividends	-	-	-	-	-	-	-	-	-	-
Annual Return	750,000	1,612,500	1,854,375	2,132,531	2,452,411	2,820,273	3,243,313	3,729,810	4,289,282	4,932,674
Total Investment	5,750,000	12,362,500	14,216,875	16,349,406	18,801,817	21,622,090	24,865,403	28,595,214	32,884,496	37,817,170
Total Needed Deal Return	37,817,170									
Expected Value of Investment	2,810,000									
Necessary Rate of Return	1245.81%									
Annualized Rate (compound)	29.69%									

Exhibit 88. Discount Rate Calculation with Interim Dividend Payment

	Year 1	Year 2	Year 3	Year 4	Year 5	Year 6	Year 7	Year 8	Year 9	Year 10
Beginning Balance	-	11,500,000	13,225,000	15,208,750	17,490,063	20,113,572	17,380,608	19,987,699	22,985,854	26,433,732
Investment	10,000,000	-	-	-	-	-	-	-	-	-
Dividends	-	-	-	-	-	(5,000,000)	-	-	-	-
Annual Return	1,500,000	1,725,000	1,983,750	2,281,313	2,623,509	2,267,036	2,607,091	2,998,155	3,447,878	3,965,060
Total Investment	11,500,000	13,225,000	15,208,750	17,490,063	20,113,572	17,380,608	19,987,699	22,985,854	26,433,732	30,398,791
Total Needed Deal Return	35,398,791									
Expected Value of Investment	2,810,000									
Necessary Rate of Return	1159.74%									
Annualized Rate (compound)	28.83%									

target rate of return of 15%, with no management fees or carried interest. However, the investor receives a return of capital in Year 6 of $5 million. The net effect is that it would lower the discount rate to 28.83%. The discount rate reduces primarily because the investor would have fewer years to wait to receive the return of some capital and dividends, as Exhibit 88 demonstrates.

Additionally, the model presumes a simplified success rate over the life of the investment portfolio. However, a valuation analyst can extend this model to account for a more complex algorithm to determine the success rate and integrate that into the model accordingly. For example, suppose that the investment consists of two projects, one of a $1 million investment with a 25% success rate, and the other of a $5 million investment with a 15% success rate. The valuation analyst could then calculate and use a weighted average success rate of 16.67%, as Exhibit 89 demonstrates.

Exhibit 89. Calculation of Weighted Average Success Rate

Investment Amount	Success Rate	Weight (Investment Amount / Total Investment)	Success Component (Weight * Success Rate)
1,000,000	25%	16.67%	4.17%
5,000,000	15%	83.33%	12.50%
6,000,000		100.00%	16.67%

Back to the Roots

The new discount rate estimation model reduces to a target rate of return with perfect execution and an indefinite holding period. For example, consider again the example of an investment that has a target rate of return of 20%, a 20% success rate, a holding period of five years, and no additional management expenses. Under this example, the model would calculate a per-investment discount rate of 65.57%. Now, suppose that the investor has a 100% investment success rate instead of a 20% success rate (e.g., a drug company would bring every drug therapy it attempts to market and that product would succeed in the market). That would drive the discount rate down to 20%—the target rate of return. This makes sense because extra premium needed to account for any investment losses is unnecessary.

Now consider the original example's fact pattern again, with an investment that has a target rate of return of 20%, a 20% success rate, a holding period of five years, and no additional management expenses. This time the holding time is 500 years, which for practical purposes, is infinite. Now the discount rate is 20.39%. Notice that the discount rate is way down, though it does not erase entirely because the remainder of the investment (20% of the original principal) still must cover the 80% loss of the investment principal, which takes time. With enough time, the model would converge to the target rate of return. This demonstrates that, at worst case, an IP valuation analyst has the precision of current methods for estimating the discount rate for an IP project. However, for most cases, the valuation analyst should be able to use the new model to produce a discount rate that more closely represents the facts at hand. This should drive a value opinion of greater precision.

Real-World Examples

Applying the new discount rate estimation model in real-world examples proves to be straightforward. Two examples appear below, one to determine the discount rate for a public company, and one to determine the discount rate for a venture capital fund. Both examples are for the same project; however, the examples will show dramatically different results for each case.

Public Company

Consider the case of Eli Lilly, whose beta as of this writing is 0.84.[248] Using a risk-free rate of 2.10%[249] and a historical equity risk premium of 6.70%, Lilly's discount rate would be as follows:

248 http://finance.yahoo.com, October 8, 2011.

249 At the time of this writing this is the rate for a 10-year Treasury note.

$$discountRate = riskFreeRate + beta * equityRiskPremium$$
$$discountRate = 2.10\% + 0.84 * 6.70\%$$
$$discountRate = 7.73\%$$

Now suppose that Lilly needs to price the discount rate for a new cancer therapy that is just about to enter clinical trials. Industry statistics indicate that oncology therapies at this stage have a 15.8% success rate. Lilly expects to generate a return over a ten-year holding period. In this situation, Lilly would use a discount rate of 29.56% to value its project.

Suppose Lilly is at a drug discovery phase. Drug companies may test 1,000 compounds in order to arrive at a final marketable drug. This represents a 0.10% success rate.[250] Under such a situation, Lilly should use a discount rate of 114.95% to value its project, as it will need to generate substantial returns based on a miniscule residual investment in order to meet its target returns.

Venture Capitalist

Consider the case of a venture capitalist that generated average returns of 15.0% for the 20-year holding period. That is the target rate to use for the model. The venture capitalist is making the same type of investment in a cancer therapy as Lilly, at the same development stage. Thus, the venture capitalist investment carries the same success rate. However, empirical evidence suggests that venture capitalists have current average holding periods of eight years.[251] Next, most venture capitalists charge a 20% carried interest for their fund management,[252] a 2% annual fee, and an average fund size of $166 million.[253] In this example, the venture capitalist would use a discount rate of 48.68% to value the project. The discount rate for the venture capitalist is about 65% greater than that Lilly may use for the same project.

Suppose the venture capitalist invests at a drug discovery phase. Like Lilly, this represents a 0.10% success rate.[254] Under such a situation, the venture capitalist should use a discount rate of 179.96% for the project. The discount rate for the venture capitalist is about 57% greater than that Lilly may use for the same project.

250 1 success / 1,000 attempts = 0.10% success rate.

251 Bart Schachter and George Hoyem, "High Anxiety or Great Expectations," *Venture Capital Journal*, October 1, 2008.

252 Andrew Metrick, *Venture Capital and the Finance of Innovation*, John Wiley & Sons, Inc., 2007, p. 32.

253 National Venture Capital Association 2008 Yearbook, National Venture Capital Association, 2008, p. 9.

254 1 success / 1,000 attempts = 0.10% success rate.

Of course, the key differences between Lilly and the venture capitalist include a higher target return, a shorter holding period, management fees, and a carried interest. These factors increase the discount rate to the venture capitalist, as the venture capitalist requires a higher return to cover the venture capitalist's discount rate and expenses.

Chapter 11
Determining Royalty Rates

Multiple approaches and methodologies exist within the valuation profession for determining royalty rates. Analysts, economists, court judges, and the like have been the originators of many of these approaches. Some approaches are outright theoretically questionable and have been the focus of much litigation (e.g., 25% rule). Other approaches require a remarkable amount of work to use; however, they produce results that are auditable and defensible (i.e., have a reasonable theoretical foundation). Before getting too far into the mechanics of royalty rate calculations, it is important to understand the purpose of calculating a royalty rate in the first place.

Licensing transactions are a primary driver for royalty rate determinations.[255] With a licensing transaction, there are two parties, the licensor (i.e., the owner of the IP) and the licensee (i.e., the party wishing to receive rights to use the IP). The licensor grants the licensee rights to use some IP in exchange for economic consideration, typically in the form of royalty payments, payable by the licensee to the licensor. For a royalty rate engagement, the valuation analyst needs to determine the rate at which the licensee should pay royalties to the licensor.

The fundamental question of course is how much money does the licensee pay to the licensor for the rights? The short answer is that it depends. The longer answer is that the amount of money that a licensee should pay to a licensor depends on the circumstances of the license and the specific rights granted by the license.

255 Note that some valuation professionals may argue that core IP valuation calculated using the relief-from-royalty method also necessitates the determination of a royalty rate. However, there are fundamental abuses of the relief-from-royalty method (e.g., using a nonexclusive royalty rate to represent the entirety of rights that some piece of IP might confer) that weaken the use of the method for a core valuation engagement.

Consider a new formulation for a chemical adhesive. The primary IP consists of a patent that describes a composition of matter for the core adhesive formulation as well as trade secrets that manufacturers can use to produce the adhesive economically. This IP represents a platform adhesive technology that has applications in biomedical, aerospace, and commercial and residential construction fields of use. The value proposition for each of these fields of use is different, for several different reasons, including the following:

- *Performance:* The performance requirements for the adhesive vary by the field of use. For example, if the adhesive is part of a bandage in a biomedical field of use and the adhesive fails, then the bandage may fall off. That type of failure may be acceptable. However, in an aerospace field of use, the failure of the adhesive may cause a composite material to detach from the craft while in operation. Such a failure could be catastrophic and lead to an entire hull loss, passenger and crew death, and property destruction.
- *Regulatory pathway:* The regulatory pathway for the adhesive varies by the field of use. For the biomedical field of use, the adhesive would likely go through an approval process with the U.S. Food and Drug Administration (FDA). If the adhesive were for a bandage, then the FDA might consider the adhesive as a Class 1 device (i.e., easier approval pathway). However, if the use of the adhesive is to affix an orthopedic implant to bone in the body, then the FDA might consider the adhesive as a Class 2 device (i.e., harder approval pathway). If the field of use for the adhesive were in the aerospace market, then the U.S. Federal Aviation Administration (FAA) would require performance characteristics that may be different from other fields of use. For example, the FAA may require that any aerospace adhesive be fire resistant. In fact, Boeing had a problem with the use of an adhesive that did not self-extinguish when ignited with a Bunsen burner.[256] The adhesive's failure almost halted delivery of all commercial airplanes—everywhere![257] Flammability, while of utmost concern for aerospace fields of use, has little practical concern for Class 2 medical devices inserted into the body, primarily because there is no ignition source that originates within the body. Hence, the fire resistance may be of minimal concern to the FDA. In contrast, the

256 Weiss, Dina, "Burn Notice," Boeing Frontiers, February 2011, http://www.boeing.com/news/frontiers/archive/2011/february/i_bca02.pdf, p. 30.
257 Weiss, Dina, "Burn Notice," Boeing Frontiers, February 2011, http://www.boeing.com/news/frontiers/archive/2011/february/i_bca02.pdf, p. 30.

regulatory pathway for general commercial or residential construction applications might be trivial. As the examples demonstrate, the regulatory impact can have remarkable cost and time impacts that could serve to depress the value proposition of the adhesive in a particular field of use; hence, the eventual royalty rate.

- *Competing solutions:* The status of competing solutions in the market has an impact as well. If the incremental benefit of the adhesive is low (e.g., insignificant materials cost or labor savings), then the value proposition for the adhesive would be low too. Any eventual royalty rate might be lower.

When a valuation analyst performs an analysis to determine royalty rates, the unique facts and circumstances associated with the fields of use for the IP should always be at the forefront of the valuation analyst's mind. A credible royalty rate analysis will always include detailed consideration of the unique facts and circumstances that are the focus of any IP rights grant.

Royalty Rate Considerations

Valuation analysts should start by considering six standard factors in the development of an appropriate royalty rate determination. Sullivan describes these as follows:[258]

- *License terms:* Is the licensing agreement to be exclusive or nonexclusive? In an exclusive arrangement, the licensor assumes more risk while granting the licensee more opportunity, largely limiting potential competition; therefore, the royalty rate for an exclusive agreement is higher.

- *Competitive advantage:* The usefulness or amount of competitive advantage the technology offers to the licensee is of utmost importance. Technologies that offer a significant head start on the competition are more valuable than those that offer only opportunities for playing catch-up. Technological capabilities that will enrich the licensee firm and allow it to enhance its strategic position are the most valuable.

- *Cost savings:* If a licensee would otherwise have to create its own market position by developing around the licensor's patent, or by developing

258 Parr, Russell L. et al., Technology Licensing: Corporate Strategies for Maximizing Value, New York: John Wiley & Sons Inc., 1996, pp. 180-181.

its own technology at a significant cost, then licensing-in the technology saves the licensee money and therefore would justify paying a higher royalty rate to the licensor.

- *Legal protection:* The nature and amount of protection that a licensor offers to the licensee as part of the license agreement is a major consideration. The royalty rate will be higher for a patent proven enforceable and whose infringement is easy to detect. The licensee must be assured not only that adequate legal protection is in force, but also that the licensor is prepared to enforce and is capable of enforcing this protection against infringers.
- *Technology maturity:* Is the technology fully developed and able to be used immediately in the design or manufacture of products, or does it require further refinement or development before it can be commercially applied? Fully developed technologies command a premium over technologies that require additional development.
- *Commercial success:* Technologies proven to have marketplace appeal and to have significantly increased sales are more valuable than technologies still untested in the marketplace or those whose commercial success is not an issue.

Note that the valuation analyst should not increase a royalty rate directly based solely on these factors (e.g., increasing a royalty rate by 0.5% because of some perceived greater competitive advantage). Instead, the valuation analyst should include the impact of the aforementioned factors in the calculation of the value proposition. Doing so will provide the licensor with appropriate consideration of a pro rata share of the benefits that the IP license might create. As described later in this chapter, the calculation of the value proposition serves as the basis to which the valuation analyst applies a royalty rate.

Royalty Rate Magnitude

There is a simple corollary one can surmise from the analysis of IP licensing agreements: the broader the rights granted by the licensor to the licensee, the greater the associated royalty rate. Exhibit 90 captures the broad expression of the relationship between the magnitude of a royalty rate and the rights conferred under a particular license.

As the chart suggests, the greater the rights that the licensor grants to the licensee, the higher the royalty rate that the licensee would pay. Several general classifications describe the various forms of license types that a valuation analyst may encounter. The magnitude of the royalty rate amount varies by the license type, as Exhibit 91 demonstrates.

Exhibit 90. Rights Granted and Royalty Rate %

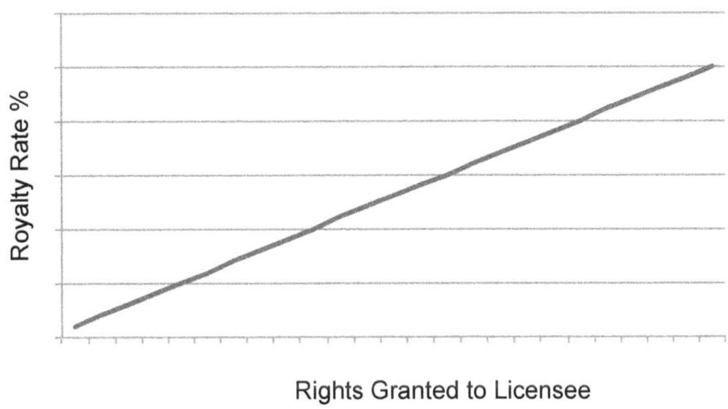

Exhibit 91. Royalty Rate Amount Varies by License Type

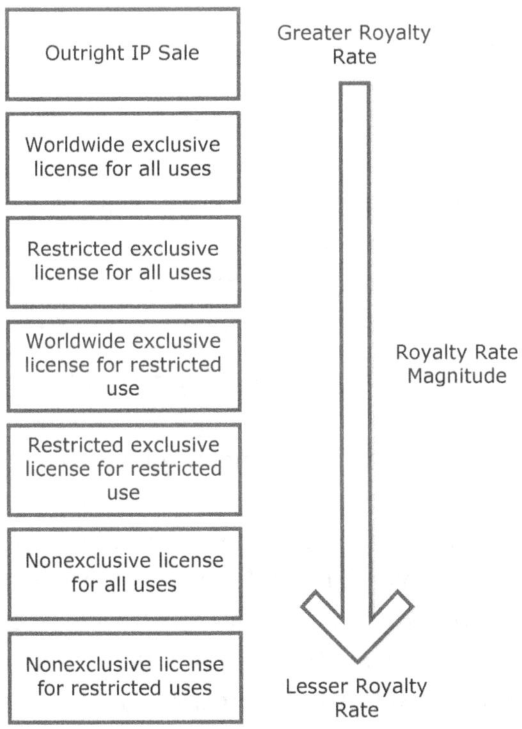

An overview of the various license types is as follows:

- *Outright sale:* With an outright sale, the IP licensee would in fact become the new IP owner; thus, the licensee (i.e., new owner) would command a royalty rate of 100% of the apportioned value creation.[259] The new IP owner would be the listed owner of record for the IP (e.g., the registered assignee with the USPTO), and the previous IP owner would no longer maintain an interest in the IP.
- *Worldwide exclusive license for all fields of use:* In the event of a worldwide, exclusive license for all fields of use, the licensor still owns the IP and remains the listed owner of record (e.g., the registered assignee with the USPTO). However, the licensor grants the rights to exploit the IP to a licensee exclusively. Thus, in the case of our adhesive example, the licensor would license all rights to the biomedical, aerospace, and commercial and residential construction fields of use to the licensee. Such a deal structure may be common with universities and other not-for-profit entities that create IP, but do not exploit the IP directly.
- *Restricted exclusive license for all fields of use:* In the event of a restricted exclusive license for all fields of use, the licensor still owns the IP and remains the listed owner of record. However, the licensor grants the rights to exploit the IP to a licensee exclusively, with certain restrictions. These restrictions can emerge in a variety of ways; however, one common form is a geographic restriction. In the case of our adhesive example, the licensor would license all rights to the biomedical, aerospace, and commercial and residential construction fields of use to the licensee in Europe, or in Japan, or in South America, and so on.
- *Worldwide exclusive license for a single field of use:* In the event of a worldwide exclusive license for a single field of use, the licensor maintains ownership of the IP and is still the listed owner of record. However, the licensor grants the rights to exploit the IP to a licensee exclusively for a particular field of use. Thus, in the case of our adhesive example, the licensor would license all rights to the IP under three separate negotiated agreements. Consequently, the licensor would execute a license in the biomedical field of use with possibly different terms (e.g., royalty rates, milestone payments) from the aerospace field of use or the construction

259 Technically, this transaction is not a license at all, so the better description for the concept of licensor and licensee is seller and buyer respectively.

field of use. Each licensee is likely a different company in this case. For example, Johnson & Johnson might be the licensee for the biomedical field of use; Boeing might be the licensee for the aerospace field of use; and AkzoNobel Coatings Inc. (maker of Liquid Nails adhesive) might be the licensee for the commercial and residential construction field of use.

- *Restricted exclusive license for a single field of use:* In the event of a restricted exclusive license for a single field of use, the licensor maintains ownership of the IP and is still the listed owner of record. However, the licensor grants the rights to exploit the IP to a licensee exclusively for a particular field of use. Thus, in the case of our adhesive example, the licensor would license all rights to the IP under three separate negotiated agreements. Consequently, the licensor would execute a license in the biomedical field of use with possibly different terms (e.g., royalty rates, milestone payments) from the aerospace field of use or the construction field of use.
- *Nonexclusive license for all fields of use:* In the event of a nonexclusive license for all fields of use, the licensor maintains ownership of the IP and is still the listed owner of record. However, the licensor grants the rights to exploit the IP to a licensee in a nonexclusive capacity in all fields of use. In our adhesive example, the licensor might execute a license with two different chemical companies to produce the base adhesive for sale—regardless of whether the field of use had a biomedical focus, an aerospace focus, or a construction focus.
- *Nonexclusive license for a single field of use:* In the event of a nonexclusive license for a single field of use, the licensor maintains ownership of the IP and is still the listed owner of record. However, the licensor grants the rights to exploit the IP to a licensee in a nonexclusive capacity for a single field of use. For example, the licensor might grant a license to both Johnson & Johnson and Medline Industries Inc. (maker of the Curad brand bandages) simultaneously.

Naturally, this framework is just a starting point for any royalty rate analysis. The nature of the IP drives the complexity of the royalty rate determination. For example, if the IP in question were a brand, and that brand generated the same economic value regardless of geographic boundary, then it may be appropriate to use a royalty rate that is the same for every market. However, if the economic environment is dramatically different from market to market, then it may be appropriate for the valuation analyst to calculate a different royalty rate for each market.

For example, consider an automotive engine technology based on a gasoline engine. Suppose that the licensor wishes to enter the Indian and Brazilian markets. The magnitude of the royalty will vary dramatically across these markets for a variety of reasons. For example, India has more than 1.1 billion people and only 11 cars per 1,000 households.[260] While the Indian market has remarkable growth potential, Indian buyers tend to be the most price-sensitive of the major auto markets, preferring quite small vehicles. The largest engines that sell in the Indian market are in the 101 kW to 120 kW range and represent only about 2% of the entire market. Those engine sizes are the equivalent of a 135 hp to 161 hp engine in the United States, which is about the size engine that one may find in any compact car. In Brazil, the story is a bit different. In Brazil, there are about 104 vehicles per 1,000 households (about five times that of India).[261] Further, Brazilians like to buy cars with larger engines than Indians do; however, more than 90% of all vehicles that sell in the Brazilian market are flex-fuel vehicles.[262] Thus, unless the automotive engine technology can work in an environment with high ethanol content in the fuel (i.e., a requirement to work properly in Brazil), then the value proposition for the technology may be suspect in Brazil. Thus, the royalty rate in each market is certain to be dramatically different for the same technology.

Common Royalty Rate Determination Methods

Common approaches that valuation analysts use to develop royalty rates include the following:

- Establishment via rules of thumb;
- Establishment via negotiation;
- Establishment via court judgments;
- Establishment via lawsuit settlements;
- Establishment via similar licensing transactions;
- Establishment via return-on-investment analysis;
- Establishment via differential analysis; and
- Establishment via analytical methods.

---

260 Haddock, Ronald and John Jullens, "The Best Years of the Auto Industry Are Still to Come," Booz & Company. May 26, 2009.
261 Haddock, Ronald and John Jullens, "The Best Years of the Auto Industry Are Still to Come," Booz & Company, May 26, 2009.
262 Beasley, Stephanie, "Brazil's Auto Industry Cruises as Economy Booms," Reuters, May 23, 2008.

There is wide disparity among the credibility of the results that each of the approaches provides. Moreover, despite the broad use of certain royalty rate approaches (e.g., 25% Rule), several have remarkable theoretical shortcomings. The following sections describe these methods and their general suitability for engagements.

Establishment Via Rules of Thumb

Rules of thumb are the lore of lazy valuation analysts. Rules of thumb make it easy for valuation analysts to distill otherwise remarkably complicated analyses into discrete, easy-to-perform calculations that render a number with supposed precision. Perhaps better represented as an abbreviation (i.e., ROT[263]), valuation analysts encounter rules of thumb every day. The capital asset pricing model (CAPM), benchmarked price-earnings ratios, and the venerable 25% Rule are all general rules of thumb that valuation analysts encounter.

The 25% Rule is the focus of this section, as this is a chapter about determining royalty rates.[264] Long used by valuation analysts,[265] it represents a relatively straightforward way to determine royalty rates with the purpose of allocating profits to a licensor. The basic mechanics are shown below.

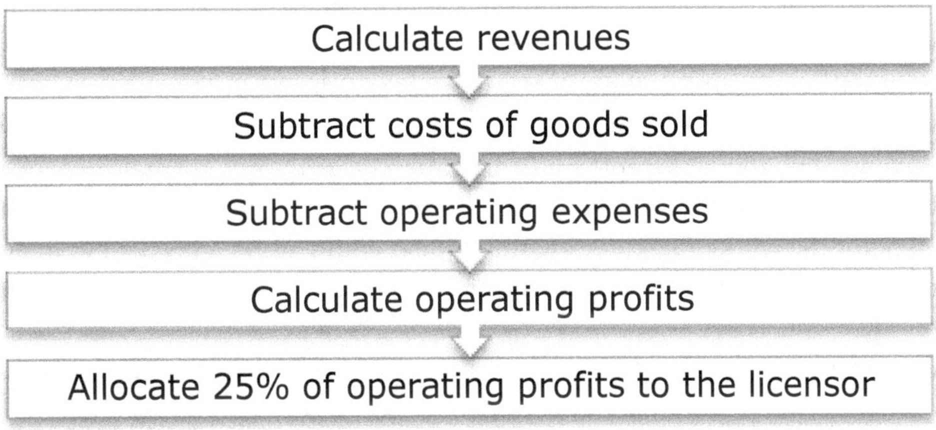

263 Perhaps ROT (i.e., meaning to decay, decompose, deteriorate, languish, etc.) is what should happen to the practices of valuation analysts that rely primarily on rules of thumb in the course of rendering professional opinions. I am glad that doctors and engineers do not make healthcare or engineering decisions based on informal and untested rules of thumb.

264 Note that I could easily make the topic of the 25% Rule a chapter in itself because there is much to discuss. I did not do so because I did not want to elevate the method to a level of importance greater than it warrants. That said, I must confess to having used the 25% Rule early in my own valuation practice. However, I stopped doing so years ago. Over time, it is my hope that the 25% Rule and other rules of thumb will be supplanted by more thoughtful and comprehensive analysis.

265 Record of the 25% Rule usage in the courts goes back to the 1930s in the United States. Robert Goldscheider, John Jarosz, and Carla Mulhern, "Use of the 25 Per Cent Rule in Valuing IP," 37 les Nouvelles, December 2002, p. 124.

One of the rule's key proponents provides an example of its application in an article from 2002.[266] Exhibit 92 provides a basis for discussion of the example from that article.

Exhibit 92. Example of 25% Rule		
Component	No Patent	Enhancing Revenue Patent
Revenues	$100	$110
Cost of Sales	$40	$40
Gross Margin	$60	$70
Operating Expenses	$30	$30
Operating Profits	$30	$40

Using this example, the total operating profits would be $40. Thus, the licensee would be entitled to 25% of these operating profits, or $10.[267] That equates to an effective royalty rate of 9.1% of the patent's revenues.[268] As the example demonstrates, the application of the method is simple. Further, the math is easy to compute and the supporting research is not hard to perform. The rule of thumb worked like a charm. However, let us explore in more detail why the results make little economic sense.

Recall from Chapter 4 that IP valuation is about incremental analysis. What is the true economic value of the enhancing revenue patent? In the example proposed by the original authors, using the patent enhances revenue by $10 per unit. How much does the licensee pay to the licensor in the example under the 25% Rule for use of the revenue-enhancing patent? The answer is $10. With incremental revenue generation of $10, and incremental costs of $10, how much profit does that leave for the licensee for the work of negotiating the license, engineering a product to integrate the inventions described in the patent, etc.? The answer is exactly $0. The math on this is clear-cut. The licensee never receives any benefit associated with use of the IP. Further, the licensor receives rewards that equal 100% of the incremental benefits created. It makes no economic sense for the licensee to execute a license with the licensor—ever. Objective analysis reveals that a license agreement negotiated using the 25% Rule has no economic substance for the licensee. Any practical, rational business professional would not undertake the efforts to negotiate a license only to receive no benefit from doing so. This is easy to prove. Suppose that a company launches a new product. It does not pay all of the profits for that new product to some third party. The company must maintain some economic benefit for producing

266 Robert Goldscheider, John Jarosz and Carla Mulhern, "Use of the 25 Per Cent Rule in Valuing IP," 37 les Nouvelles December 2002, p. 125.
267 ($40 operating profits * 25% allocation) = $10 profit allocation
268 $10 profit allocation / $110 revenues = 9.1%

the product. If the company does not gain some economic benefit for producing the product, opportunity costs would dictate that the company pursue some other market opportunity. Thankfully, the courts have stepped up in recent times to address what is a core deficiency in the method.

One of the most significant rulings regarding royalty rates since the introduction of the Georgia-Pacific factors (more on these shortly) emerged in 2011 in the court case *Uniloc USA Inc. v. Microsoft Corp.*[269] Specifically, the Court of Appeals for the Federal Circuit (CAFC) questioned the theoretical validity of the 25% Rule. While the CAFC addressed several issues in its decision, the expert's use of the 25% Rule was a primary point of discussion and the main determinant for Microsoft receiving a new trial on the damages component in the lawsuit. It is quite clear in the decision that the court was finally addressing the validity of the 25% Rule. In fact, the court announced its intentions quite early in the discussion of the damages component:

> The district court noted that "the concept of a 'rule of thumb' is perplexing in an area of the law where reliability and precision are deemed paramount."[270]

While the district court allowed the use of the 25% Rule, the CAFC made clear its intentions to address the reliability of the method. Specifically, the CAFC identified key deficiencies in using rules of thumb like the 25% Rule:[271]

- The 25% Rule fails to account for the unique relationship between a patent and a product that might embody inventions claimed in that patent. Thus, a valuation analyst using the 25% Rule makes no distinction for the importance of the patent to the product, the potential availability of close substitutes, or many other idiosyncrasies that affect practical royalty rate negotiations.

- The 25% Rule fails to account for the unique relationship between the licensor and the licensee, especially the contributions and risks borne by the licensor and the licensee.

- The 25% Rule is essentially an arbitrary shortcut and does not fit well within the model of a hypothetical negotiation.

The court further noted that it has primarily ignored the issue of the reliability of the 25% Rule in prior cases because use of the 25% Rule was not the primary focus

269 *Uniloc USA Inc. v. Microsoft Corp.*, No. 03-CV-0440 (Fed. Cir. Jan. 4, 2011).
270 *Uniloc USA Inc. v. Microsoft Corp.*, No. 03-CV-0440 (Fed. Cir. Jan. 4, 2011), p. 35.
271 *Uniloc USA Inc. v. Microsoft Corp.*, No. 03-CV-0440 (Fed. Cir. Jan. 4, 2011), pp. 38-39.

of the case (i.e., even if the use of it were improper, using something else may not have altered the valuation conclusion materially). Thus, courts have been accomplices in the proliferation of the alleged credibility of the 25% Rule, which provided some level of "cover" for valuation analysts. In the *Uniloc* case, the CAFC has put an end to this cover. The ruling from the CAFC is rather unequivocal:

> This court now holds as a matter of Federal Circuit law that the 25 percent rule of thumb is a fundamentally flawed tool for determining a baseline royalty rate in a hypothetical negotiation. Evidence relying on the 25 percent rule of thumb is thus inadmissible under *Daubert* and the Federal Rules of Evidence, because it fails to tie a reasonable royalty base to the facts of the case at issue.[272]

Any valuation analyst who takes the time to go through a thorough, fact-driven, microeconomic-based analysis to determine a royalty rate should applaud this finding by the court. Others, who rely on the 25% Rule, should find new religion. First, while proponents of the 25% Rule have over time attempted to present evidence to suggest empirical roots for the approach, such empirical studies had associated flaws that skewed the results. Specifically:

- The original 25% Rule empirical study included data from only one company, in only one general industry, based on data from the 1950s.[273] Thus, the data includes selection and sampling biases.

- The original 25% Rule empirical study covered completely different technologies. For example, personal computers did not exist at that time. Hence, the relevance of the rule to contemporary technologies is also questionable.

- Data used in subsequent studies may have autocorrelation problems.[274] Several sources confirm this phenomenon.[275] For example, a technology manager at Company A negotiates a license deal that conforms to the 25% Rule. A technology manager in Company B reads that Company A negotiated a deal that conformed to the 25% Rule in a deal. The technology manager at Company B knows and respects the technology manager at Company A. Therefore, the technology manager at Company B uses the 25% Rule in a negotiation with another company. The technology manager

272 *Uniloc USA Inc. v. Microsoft Corp.*, No. 03-CV-0440 (Fed. Cir. Jan. 4, 2011), p. 41.

273 Robert Goldscheider, John Jarosz and Carla Mulhern, "Use of the 25 Per Cent Rule in Valuing IP," 37 les Nouvelles, December 2002, p. 123.

274 Think of autocorrelation as the statistical equivalent of the self-fulfilling prophecy.

275 Robert Goldscheider, John Jarosz and Carla Mulhern, "Use of the 25 Per Cent Rule in Valuing IP," 37 les Nouvelles, December 2002, p. 127, p. 130.

at Company A applauds the move because it is "what everyone does." The results of Company B's negotiation make it into the public forum, perhaps through a regulatory disclosure. A technology publisher that developed a database that tracks the various royalty rate agreements executed by public companies finds this transaction and adds the transaction to the publisher's royalty rate database. A technology manager at Company C is a subscriber to the publisher's royalty rate database. The technology manager at Company C must research a reasonable royalty rate for a license and performs a search at the publisher's royalty rate database and reads that Company B developed a royalty rate (which really referenced a deal by Company A) that equals about 25% of Company B's licensee's profits. Company C's technology manager executes a license based on the 25% Rule license and the results of that license negotiation eventually becomes part of a public regulatory disclosure also. The database publisher detects Company B's license in the public filings and adds it to the database. Now there are several license agreements, that all seem to be independent, confirming a market view of what royalty rates should be. Yet all depend originally on a single deal negotiated by Company A. This is the problem of autocorrelation. Thus, subsequent reviews of many "independent" licensing transactions are actually quite dependent! As an aside, one should expect that licensing royalty rates derived from lookup and publication services have autocorrelation errors.

Moreover, empirical studies do not provide any accounting for royalty stacking provisions. Royalty stacking occurs when a company has to pay several different IP owners for IP licensing rights. For example, Exhibit 93 captures a summary of standards-essential patents related to long-term evolution (LTE) technologies in the field of radio and networking interfaces for cell phones, as reported to the European Telecommunications Standards Institute (ESTI).[276]

276 Stasik, Eric, "Royalty Rates and Licensing Strategies for Essential Patents on LTE (4G) Telecommunication Standards," les Nouvelles, September 2010, p. 116.

Exhibit 93. Summary of Standards-Essential Patents		
IP Owner and Licensor	Number of Standards-Essential Patents	Published Per-Handset Royalty Rate
Alcatel-Lucent	9	2.00%
Apple	0	N/A
AT&T	1	N/A
Ericsson	146	1.50%
ETRI	35	N/A
France Telecom	3	N/A
Freescale Semiconductor	1	N/A
Gemplus	1	N/A
Hewlett Packard	1	N/A
Huawei	182	1.50%
Icera	1	N/A
iCODING	1	N/A
Infineon	2	N/A
InterDigital Technology Corp	282	N/A
InterDigital Patent Holdings	155	N/A
IPR Licensing Inc.	4	N/A
LG Electronics	150	N/A
Motorola	16	2.25%
NEC	19	N/A
NextWave Wireless	0	N/A
Nokia Corporation	142	1.50%
Nokia Siemens Networks	32	0.80%
Nortel Networks	46	1.00%
NTT DoCoMo	78	N/A
Panasonic	39	N/A
Qualcomm	350	3.25%
RIM	0	N/A
Samsung	170	N/A
Siemens	11	N/A
Sony	12	N/A
Sony-Ericsson	0	N/A
Texas Instruments	26	N/A
TDF	3	N/A
T-Mobile Deutschland GmbH	12	N/A
T-Mobile International AG	5	N/A
Vodafone	0	N/A
VoiceAge	6	N/A
ZTE	0	1.00%
Totals	1,914	14.80%

As the data clearly show, some 38 different companies have declared that they own collectively some 1,900 patents related to 4G technology for cell phones. If each company were to receive value based on 25% of the operating profits of the licensee, then the royalties would likely exceed the entire revenues of the product. That is a nonsensical conclusion. As the data show, total stacked royalties amount to about 14.80% of total revenues—a number that is quite a bit less.

Despite this logical conclusion, valuation analysts have proffered untenable royalty rate conclusions. Perhaps one of the most egregious examples in recent times is the royalty rate developed by Dr. Wagner in *I4I Limited Partnership et al. v. Microsoft Corp.*,[277] a case that dealt with certain eXtensible Markup Language (XML) editing capabilities that Microsoft included into the Microsoft Word product. In his work, Dr. Wagner opined that the reasonable royalty rate was $98 per copy, quoting the infamous 25% Rule in his analysis, stating that the rule was "well recognized" and "widely used" by people in his field.[278] The foundations of this conclusion are obviously questionable. As of this writing, the retail value for Microsoft Word at various retail locations was about $110. Thus, the royalty imputed by Dr. Wagner was for just about the entirety of the program—meaning that Microsoft would not be able to sell Microsoft Word if it lacked XML editing capabilities. This was a nonsensical conclusion. While Dr. Wagner's opinion did stand, it was not for the credibility of his analysis. In that case, Microsoft failed to file a pre-verdict judgment as a matter of law (JMOL) that would have allowed the court to revisit the damages conclusion.[279] The CAFC in this case noted the following:

> Had Microsoft filed a pre-verdict JMOL, it is true that the outcome might have been different. Given the opportunity to review the sufficiency of the evidence, we could have considered whether the $200 million damages award was "grossly excessive or monstrous" in light of Word's retail price and the licensing fees Microsoft paid for other patents. . . . However, we cannot. Instead of the more searching review permitted under Rule 50(b), we are constrained to review the verdict under the much narrower standard applied to denials of new trial motions. . . . This standard is highly deferential: we may set aside a damages award and remand for a new trial "only upon a clear showing of excessiveness." . . . Under this highly deferential standard, we cannot say that Microsoft is entitled to a new trial on damages.[280]

277 *I4I Limited Partnership et al. v. Microsoft Corp.*, 2009-1504 (Fed. Cir. Dec. 22, 2009).
278 *I4I Limited Partnership et al. v. Microsoft Corp.*, 2009-1504 (Fed. Cir. Dec. 22, 2009), p. 30.
279 *I4I Limited Partnership et al. v. Microsoft Corp.*, 2009-1504 (Fed. Cir. Dec. 22, 2009), p. 36.
280 *I4I Limited Partnership et al. v. Microsoft Corp.*, 2009-1504 (Fed. Cir. Dec. 22, 2009), p. 37.

However, Microsoft did not file a pre-verdict JMOL, so the court could not revisit Dr. Wagner's damages conclusion. As an aside, the importance of the feature to Word was questionable. Microsoft released a software patch (i.e., a modification to the shipping version of Microsoft Word) to remove the feature from Microsoft Word. Importantly, sales of Microsoft Word sustained despite Dr. Wagner's conclusions, proving that the feature was incidental to the value of the product in the market.

Recall that the courts are using the *Daubert* principles (introduced in Chapter 4) to help filter expert testimony to reduce the possibility of pseudoscience, which could mislead a jury from making its way into the courtroom. These principles are as follows:[281]

- The valuation method is testable.
- The valuation method has undergone publication and peer review.
- The valuation method has an acceptable rate of error and maintenance of standards concerning its operation.
- The valuation community has accepted the valuation method.

It is clear that use of the 25% Rule satisfies several of the *Daubert* principles. Specifically, use of the 25% Rule has undergone publication and peer review. The valuation community has also accepted the valuation method. However, and as the CAFC noted, the 25% Rule is effectively not testable because of the deficiencies that the CAFC noted in the use of the method (i.e., arbitrary shortcut, ignores relationship between licensor and licensee, etc.). Second, because the use of the 25% Rule is not testable, there is no way to measure whether there is an acceptable rate of error and maintenance of standards concerning the use of the 25% Rule. Under these conditions, use of the 25% Rule should fail every time.

For the valuation analysts still unconvinced about the problems associated with the 25% Rule, the CAFC goes on to clarify its position further:

> The 25 percent rule of thumb as an abstract and largely theoretical construct fails to satisfy this fundamental requirement. The rule does not say anything about a particular hypothetical negotiation or reasonable royalty involving any particular technology, industry, or party.[282]

281 Babitsky, Esq., Steven and James Mangraviti, Jr. Esq., *Writing and Defending Your Expert Report*, SEAK Inc., Massachusetts, 2002, p. 247.
282 *Uniloc USA Inc. v. Microsoft Corp.*, No. 03-CV-0440 (Fed. Cir. Jan. 4, 2011).

Valuation analysts should heed the warning that analysis based on the 25% Rule is inadmissible under the *Daubert* principles and the Federal Rules of Evidence.

Establishment Via Negotiation

As implied by its title, royalty rates established by negotiation are determined through negotiation between licensor and licensee. In this scenario, conversations between unrelated parties arrive at a value deemed reasonable in the eyes of each party to the negotiation. Negotiated licensing agreements are often dependent upon the skill of the parties involved. As such, the same patent license can result in disparate royalty rates. Stronger negotiators may negotiate for lower or deferred royalty rate payments, while weaker negotiators may have to deal with high royalty rates and/or significant minimum royalty rate payments. Without using a formal or even informal analysis of the specific value creation afforded by the intellectual property, parties in a negotiation may negotiate royalty rates more on emotion rather than fact. As such, the resulting royalty rate agreements may be too high or too low. Moreover, it may be difficult to prove whether the arrangement is equitable to both parties. This would make it difficult to audit whether the royalty rate conclusion conforms to a particular standard of value. For example, a valuation analyst would have to prove that the conclusion is equitable to both parties in order to fulfill the criteria for the fair market value standard. The valuation analyst does not have enough facts to prove whether a deal is equitable.

Further, valuation analysts typically reference royalty rates established via negotiation on a historical and case-by-case basis. Naturally, selection and survivorship biases are an artifact of this process and can distort a resulting value conclusion. Moreover, the fields of use that were the subject of those negotiations may be

Exhibit 94. Conclusions Based on *Daubert*

Daubert Principle	Pass or Fail	Notes
Testable	Fail	One cannot test that the conclusions have a meaningful representation of the economic value apportionment. Further, different professionals can come to remarkably different conclusions based on the same fact patterns.
Peer review and publication	Pass	Various authors have published articles using prior negotiations as a basis for royalty rate determinations.
Acceptable rate of error and maintenance of standards	Fail	One cannot prove the error rate because there is no way to test the method's results.
Community acceptance	Pass	Various authors have published articles using prior negotiations as a basis for royalty rate determinations.

remarkably different. Remember that patents are unique and novel by definition and value is context-driven. Thus, any comparable negotiations may at best represent crude approximations for appropriate royalty rates.

In short, a valuation analyst cannot anticipate and calculate reasonably how multiple parties may react in a negotiation setting for a given set of IP rights. As such, it is not credible for a valuation analyst to determine a royalty rate by studying the results of prior negotiations. An audit of the approach against the *Daubert* principles yields the conclusions shown in Exhibit 94.

Establishment Via Court Judgments

Royalty rates established by court judgments are often the result of economic damages analysis. Per 35 U.S.C. § 284, a patentee is entitled to "damages adequate to compensate for the infringement, but in no event less than a reasonable royalty for the use made of the invention by the infringer." In this context, judgments can be unpredictable, may lack factual basis, and are specific to each individual case. Many courts refer to a landmark court case that established precedent for determining compensation in an IP damages scenario. The court case, *Georgia-Pacific Corp. v. United States Plywood Corp.*, resulted in Georgia-Pacific factors that valuation analysts might use to help determine possible reasonable royalty rates. These factors include the following:

- The royalties received by Georgia-Pacific for licensing the patent, proving or tending to prove an established royalty.
- The rates paid by the licensee for the use of other similar patents.
- The nature and scope of the license, such as whether it is exclusive or nonexclusive, restricted or nonrestricted in terms of territory or customers.
- Georgia-Pacific's policy of maintaining its patent monopoly by licensing the use of the invention only under special conditions designed to preserve the monopoly.
- The commercial relationship between Georgia-Pacific and licensees, such as whether they are competitors in the same territory or whether they are inventor and promoter.
- The effect of selling the patented specialty in promoting sales of other Georgia-Pacific products; the existing value of the invention to Georgia-

Pacific as a generator of sales of non-patented items; and the extent of such derivative or "convoyed" sales.

- The established profitability of the patented product, its commercial success, and its current popularity.
- The utility and advantages of the patent property over any old modes or devices that had been used.
- The nature of the patented invention, its character in the commercial embodiment owned and produced by the licensor, and the benefits to those who used it.
- The extent to which the infringer used the invention and any evidence probative of the value of that use.
- The portion of the profit or selling price that is customary in the particular business or in comparable businesses.
- The portion of the realizable profit that should be credited to the invention as distinguished from any non-patented elements, manufacturing process, business risk, or significant features or improvements added by the infringer.
- The opinion testimony of qualified experts.
- The amount that Georgia-Pacific and a licensee would have agreed upon at the time the infringement began if they had reasonably and voluntarily tried to reach an agreement.

Often the IP that is the subject of a royalty rate determination represents a technology that has limited operating history currently in the market (e.g., new technology emanating from a technology transfer office). Further, the IP owners in such situations do not necessarily have many different products that they sell or patents that they license. As such, many of the Georgia-Pacific factors are indeterminate for the purposes of many royalty rate engagements, for a variety of reasons.

First, many of these factors require access to private data made known in a litigation environment through court (e.g., discovery proceedings). Many royalty rate engagements do not allow for these circumstances. Second, judgments may carry bias from particular judges; hence, why certain districts are "plaintiff friendly," while other districts are "defendant friendly." These biases can cloud any resulting determination. Further, because of the potential for bias, different courts could render different conclusions based on the same fact patterns, further impairing the quality of the data.

Third, it may not be appropriate for a valuation analyst to consider royalty rate conclusions determined by a court as a credible proxy. This is especially true when the subject technology is different from that considered by the court. Further, the parties in the referenced cases are not by definition willing participants to the transaction, because one or both parties may be under a compulsion to act. If the value standard were fair market value, then the valuation analyst could not use prior court judgments as a proxy.[283]

Fourth, valuation analysts typically reference royalty rates established via court judgments on a historical and case-by-case basis. Naturally, selection and survivorship biases are an artifact of this process and can distort a resulting value conclusion. Finally, the fields of use that were the subject of those court judgments may be remarkably different. Remember that patents are unique and novel by definition and value is context-driven. Thus, any comparable negotiations may at best represent crude approximations for appropriate royalty rates.

In short, a valuation analyst cannot anticipate and calculate reasonably how multiple parties may react in a royalty rate negotiation setting for a given set of IP rights, using a set of transactions that were the focus of litigation as a starting point. Thus, it is not credible for a valuation analyst to determine a royalty rate by studying the results of court judgments. An audit of the approach against the *Daubert* principles yields the following conclusions, shown in Exhibit 95.

Exhibit 95. Audit of the Approach Against the *Daubert* Principles

Daubert Principle	Pass or Fail	Notes
Testable	Fail	One cannot test that the conclusions have a meaningful representation of the economic value apportionment. Further, different professionals can come to remarkably different conclusions based on the same fact patterns.
Peer review and publication	Pass	Various authors have published articles using prior court judgments as a basis for royalty rate determinations.
Acceptable rate of error and maintenance of standards	Fail	One cannot prove the error rate because there is no way to test the method's results.
Community acceptance	Pass	Various authors have published articles using prior court judgments as a basis for royalty rate determinations.

283 One may argue that a court is objective and presents what is the utmost in objective evidence. However, this argument is unpersuasive. For example, in *I4I Limited Partnership et al. v. Microsoft Corp.*, Dr. Wagner's damages calculation sustained for administrative reasons—not for objectivity or theoretical soundness.

Establishment Via Lawsuit Settlements

The roots of IP law focus on the rights of an IP owner to exclude third parties from using the IP in the market. Thus, the IP owner has the right to pursue infringers to enjoin them from infringement activity and/or to demand payment for economic damages incurred. Eventually, litigation may ensue. Oftentimes, adversaries may decide to settle open intellectual property litigation, either through payments of damages or through intellectual property cross-licensing arrangements. With this royalty rate determination method, valuation analysts seek to establish royalty rates by studying records of lawsuit settlements and using similar settlement rates to establish the basis for the intellectual property of interest. For example, Dr. Bruce Saffran sued Boston Scientific for patent infringement on his patent that describes a drug-eluting stent. Dr. Saffran won and received a damage award of $431 million plus interest. Yet, despite prevailing in court, Dr. Saffran settled for only $50 million (about 11.6% of the judgment excluding interest. In an interesting development, Dr. Saffran also prevailed for patent infringement against Cordis, a Johnson & Johnson subsidiary. In that case, Dr. Saffran received a damage award of $482 million, plus $111 million in pre-judgment interest.

As is the case with other royalty rate methods, the determination requires a formal analysis of the specific value creation afforded by the intellectual property. Failure to do this may result in royalty rate conclusions that are inappropriately too high or low. Using the results of royalty rates developed through lawsuit settlements as a proxy for some other IP inherits many of the same core deficiencies as establishing a royalty rate using court judgments as a proxy, plus several more. Specifically, many companies choose to settle to avoid the costs, hassles, and distractions of a protracted litigation effort. Perhaps the parties perceive a hanging judge or jury that might bias the outcome for political or other reasons as opposed to factual reasons and want to settle the case quickly to avoid a worse pain.

Additionally, it may not be appropriate for a valuation analyst to consider royalty rate conclusions determined by a lawsuit settlement as a credible proxy. This is especially true when the subject technology is different from that considered in the settlement. Further, the parties in the referenced cases are not by definition willing participants to the transaction, because one or both parties may be under a compulsion to act. If the value standard were fair market value, then the valuation analyst could not use prior lawsuit settlements as a proxy.

Further, valuation analysts typically reference royalty rates established via lawsuit records on a historical and case-by-case basis. Naturally, like other historical methods, selection and survivorship biases are an artifact of this process and can distort a resulting value conclusion. Moreover, the fields of use that were the subject of those settlements may be remarkably different; thus, any comparable lawsuits may at best represent crude approximations for appropriate royalty rates. Lastly, any conclusions that were a result of the settlement process might not serve as an appropriate proxy, as parties may agree on a royalty rate under duress.

In short, a valuation analyst cannot anticipate and calculate reasonably how multiple parties may react in a royalty rate negotiation setting for a given set of IP rights, using a set of transactions that were the focus of litigation as a starting point. As such, it is not credible for a valuation analyst to determining a royalty rate by studying the results of lawsuit settlements. An audit of the approach against the *Daubert* principles yields the following conclusions, shown in Exhibit 96.

Exhibit 96. Audit of the Approach Against the *Daubert* Principles

Daubert Principle	Pass or Fail	Notes
Testable	Fail	One cannot test that the conclusions have a meaningful representation of the economic value apportionment. Further, different professionals can come to remarkably different conclusions based on the same fact patterns.
Peer review and publication	Pass	Various authors have published articles using prior lawsuit settlements as a basis for royalty rate determinations.
Acceptable rate of error and maintenance of standards	Fail	One cannot prove the error rate because there is no way to test the method's results.
Community acceptance	Pass	Various authors have published articles using prior lawsuit settlements as a basis for royalty rate determinations.

Establishment Via Similar Licensing Transactions

Using this approach, a valuation analyst looks for comparable licensing transactions in the same industry and of the same relative size and form that recently occurred in the open market. The valuation analyst determines the value of the royalty rate indirectly using the comparable intellectual property transaction as a value proxy for target intellectual property. The reasoning seems logical: if the market paid $X per unit or X% of sales for rights to use or own that intellectual property once, then one would expect that the market would reasonably pay a similar royalty rate again, all else the same.

The problem with this approach is that it may not work well for calculating the true value of the royalty rate to a licensor or licensee. First, comparable circumstances rarely exist. Intellectual property and related licenses by their very nature are novel and unique. It is generally impossible for a valuation analyst to find a comparable transaction in the market for similar technologies and similar value-creating capability. Therefore, any reference to other intellectual property transactions is at best a crude method for determining an appropriate royalty rate. For example, no comparable patent exists in the market for the compound that Pfizer Inc. sells as Lipitor.

Second, as introduced earlier in this chapter, a reasonable royalty rate for an intellectual property depends on the field of use for the intellectual property to the market. As such, circumstances need to be similar to serve as a credible royalty rate proxy. Licensing a trademark for a soft drink may not command nearly the value applied to a car that it does for fruit-flavored, sugar-sweetened water. To use a soft drink brand transaction as a basis for establishing the royalty rate of a license to a car's brand is not appropriate either—the two are altogether different in their fields of use and in the general industry.

Valuation analysts often search for evidence of any comparable royalty rate or licensing transactions in publicly available data sources. For example, valuation analysts may perform searches at the Securities and Exchange Commission (SEC), reviewing filings that describe licensing transactions. Valuation analysts may also perform searches using one of several databases that exist in the market that categorize royalty rate information (e.g., ktMine, RoyaltySource, etc.). While these sources do carry autocorrelation, selection, and sampling biases, the market does not seem to indicate concern with associated statistical errors while using such tools.

In summary, we find the following deficiencies using comparable licenses as a proxy for royalty rate determinations:

Exhibit 97. Audit of the Approach Against the *Daubert* Principles

Daubert Principle	Pass or Fail	Notes
Testable	Fail	One cannot test that the conclusions have a meaningful representation of the economic value apportionment because comparative IP may not in fact be comparable.
Peer review and publication	Pass	Various authors have published articles using prior similar published transactions as a basis for royalty rate determinations.
Acceptable rate of error and maintenance of standards	Fail	One cannot prove the error rate because there is no way to test the method's results.
Community acceptance	Pass	Various authors have published articles using prior similar published transactions as a basis for royalty rate determinations.

- Nondisclosure of important licensing terms;
- Ignorance to uniqueness of IP under review;
- Reliance on historical, possibly antiquated data; and
- Presumption that the market valued IP in the comparable transactions correctly.

Additionally, the practice of studying similar licensing transactions inherits common market approach errors discussed earlier in Chapter 4 as well as selection and survivorship biases. For example, many small and private companies issue licenses that never make their way into the data sets offered by publishers.

An audit of the approach against the *Daubert* principles yields the conclusions shown in Exhibit 97.

Establishment Via Return on Investment Analysis

A valuation analyst develops a royalty rate based on a licensor's return on investment by studying the requisite risk-adjusted investment returns a licensor must receive to meet predetermined financial targets. For example, suppose an intellectual property owner spends $1 million to develop a technology. The intellectual property owner's internal hurdle rate for capital investments is 20% per year. Therefore, the intellectual property owner would command a royalty rate of $200,000 from potential licensees for each year covered by a license agreement.

The upside of the approach is that it is easy to calculate. The royalty relies not on the value of the IP license, which is difficult to measure, but the IP investment, which is substantially easier to measure. Next, the licensor receives a guaranteed and predictable revenue stream for each year the license is in force. This makes valuation of the eventual royalty stream easy to calculate as a fixed annuity. Further, as long as the licensor receives an adequate return on investment, at or in excess of its hurdle rate, then it is creating value. Thus, one may be able to make an argument that the royalty rate and subsequent royalty payments, while not optimal (i.e., perhaps the licensor leaves much money on the table), is accretive to value.

The downside of the approach is that royalty rate calculations based on a reasonable return on investment model do not consider the economic value creation for the IP. The approach inherits many of the problems associated with the cost approach discussed in Chapter 4. Thus, this method may provide substantially lower royalty rate recommendations when the cost incurred to develop the original intellectual properties is low. For example, if a musician creates a song, the cost of the song

Exhibit 98. Audit of the Approach Against the *Daubert* Principles		
***Daubert* Principle**	**Pass or Fail**	**Notes**
Testable	Fail	One cannot test that the conclusions have a meaningful representation of the economic value apportionment because development cost and the economic value are disjointed concepts.
Peer review and publication	Pass	Various authors have published articles using prior levels of investment as a basis for royalty rate determinations.
Acceptable rate of error and maintenance of standards	Fail	One cannot prove the error rate because there is no way to test the method's results.
Community acceptance	Pass	Various authors have published articles using prior levels of investment as a basis for royalty rate determinations.

creation may be insignificant. Yet, the royalty rate to license this song may be high if it is a catchy jingle or has a good hook. Next, like other cost-based approaches, this method penalizes companies that work efficiently, rewarding those that expend more, sometimes less efficiently, with greater royalty payments. The cost-based royalty artifact reinforces the wrong incentives for licensors.

An audit of the approach against the *Daubert* principles yields the conclusions shown in Exhibit 98.

Establishment Via Differential Analysis

A valuation analyst develops a royalty rate based on a differential analysis by studying market evidence for pricing action when the IP owner is a price setter in the market versus when the IP owner is a price follower in the market. The difference between the two establishes the implied royalty rate for the IP. This method is helpful for developing royalty rates for lawsuits that claim infringement where price erosion is measurable.

There are many examples in product pricing that demonstrate the efficacy of this royalty quantification method. For example, evidence of this phenomenon is also prevalent in the price differences between patent-protected pharmaceuticals and those that come off patent protection. Consider Exhibit 99 for revenues associated with Lilly's Prozac drug from Chapter 3.

As the data clearly suggest, Lilly enjoyed significantly greater revenues when it had patent protection for Prozac versus when it lost the patent protection. The difference between the two clearly indicates the value of the patent to Lilly.

Exhibit 99. Total Combined Prozac® Revenues

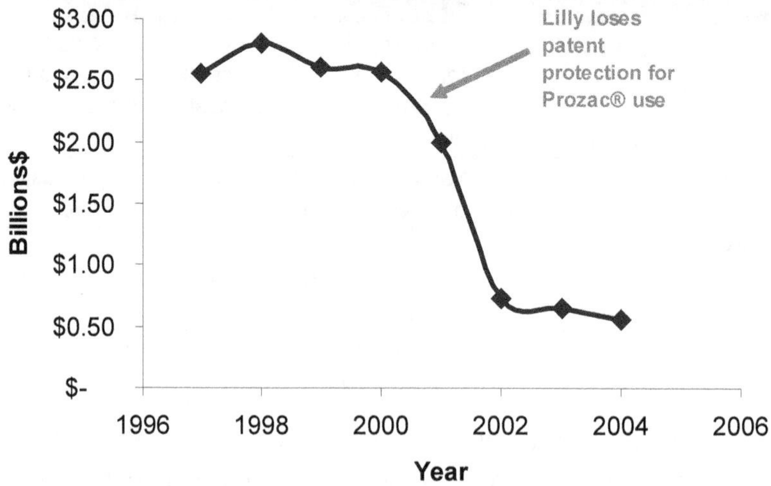

The mechanics of applying this method are straightforward. For example, suppose that a product embodies a patent. That product sells for $120 when the IP owner is a price setter in the market. At this point, the IP owner enjoys the full benefits of the monopoly that the government granted it with the issuance of the patent. A competitor enters the market with an infringing substitute and sells the equivalent product for $100. The competitor establishes the price as a commodity producer without any special advantage (except of course for the unauthorized use of the IP owner's inventions). Consequently, the IP owner becomes a price follower at $100 (i.e., the IP owner must reduce the cost of its product to stay competitive in the market). The differential analysis between the two price points suggests that the royalty is $20,[284] which equates to a royalty rate of 16.67%.[285]

As mentioned earlier, this method may be helpful in establishing royalty rates in adversarial situations. However, this method has shortcomings that may limit its utility to negotiations among friendly parties. Specifically limitations include the following:

- Pricing data may not be available—especially for pre-revenue IP, making differential analysis impossible to calculate.
- Royalty rate conclusions may be sensitive to price variance, which would lead to different royalty rate indications based on pricing differences among geographic disparities.

284 $120 price as price setter - $100 price as price follower = $20 royalty amount.
285 $20 royalty amount / $120 price as price setter = 16.67%.

Exhibit 100. Audit of the Approach Against the *Daubert* Principles

Daubert Principle	Pass or Fail	Notes
Testable	Pass	The valuation analyst can test the royalty indication directly and empirically.
Peer review and publication	Pass	Various authors have published articles using differential analysis methods as a basis for royalty rate determinations.
Acceptable rate of error and maintenance of standards	Pass	Because one can test the outcomes of the results in a manner specific to the IP under review, one can measure the associated error from the royalty rate determination and accept or reject a conclusion based upon conformance to standards.
Community acceptance	Pass	Various authors have published articles using differential analysis methods as a basis for royalty rate determinations.

- The method presumes that the IP owner does not provide a license, which is usually the case in infringement actions; however, this is not necessarily the case for negotiations among friendly parties.
- The resulting royalty rate indications can differ based on different pricing structures. For example, if transportation costs contribute to a significant portion of the cost structure, transactions with customers that are at greater distances may indicate royalty rates higher than otherwise warranted. Of course, a valuation analyst can reduce the risk of such bias by normalizing transportation expenditures or using average transportation costs instead of actual transportation costs.
- The method measures only the size of the pie, not how the pie divides among parties. Thus, while the method is helpful in quantification of the value proposition, it fails to help allocate the value proposition among friendly parties.[286]

An audit of the approach against the *Daubert* principles yields the conclusions shown in Exhibit 100.

Establishment Via Analytical Methods

A valuation analyst develops royalty rates using analytical methods based on the intellectual property's value proposition and the economic activity that it generates in the market. Using this method, the valuation analyst studies the prospective parties in the value chain to determine the value attributable to each party and allocates the value using a profit split method.

286 The method is still quite useful in allocations among adversaries, because the IP owner would retain 100% of the pie; thus any allocation activity would be moot.

Using the profit split method, a valuation analyst studies the exact value proposition of the intellectual property in a market context. This market context is typically the use of the licensed intellectual property for a specific purpose. The profit split method apportions value according to the value created by the licensor and licensee relationship. There may be multiple business entities in the value chain for the IP. In such a scenario where there are multiple entities, the valuation analyst attributes value accordingly based on the relationship between these entities.

The profit split method requires a study of the specific creation and allocation of value for each intellectual property. This method provides the most precise indication for what might constitute a reasonable royalty rate because it allows the valuation analyst to account for all of the various factors that courts and other professionals have deemed important and crucial to performing a royalty rate determination credibly. Specifically, the profit split method allows the valuation analyst to:

- Account for the unique attributes of the IP.
- Map how the IP brings value to a particular product or service.
- Outline the importance of the IP to the particular product or service. For example, does the product fail in the market without a particular patent (e.g., pharmaceuticals), or are there non-infringing substitutes that may also make a product work (e.g. cell phone).
- Account for the relative differences in risk borne by the licensor and licensee.
- Account for the specific licensing terms that a valuation analyst can only quantify for with an incremental analysis.
- Account for increased revenues or cost savings generated by the IP.
- Account for specific legal protections shared by the licensor and licensee (e.g., patent defense or patent enforcement).
- Account for changes in technology maturity over time.
- Account for the chance for commercial success for the IP under license.
- Test whether there is an economic substance to the resulting royalty rate determination.

- Use a method that generates a result that is consistent theoretically. Thus, IP rights grants that are broader and include more territories may command greater royalty rates than IP rights grants that are narrower and may have territorial restrictions. Because the valuation analyst calculates the impact of rights and territories directly in the analysis, the resulting royalty rates reflect the accretive nature of these additional rights and territories.

In summary, credible use of an analytical method for royalty rate determination should prove a basis for a hypothetical negotiation and a level of due diligence that is not deemed by any reasonable audience to be a "shortcut." Lastly, credible use of the analytical method for royalty rate determination should be able to withstand attacks for nonconformance to the *Daubert* principles.

Analytical Royalty Rate Determination Process

As previous examples in this chapter demonstrate, determining a royalty rate can be a very fact-specific activity that requires a remarkable amount of research and consideration. In order to withstand what may be a blistering attack of a royalty rate determination, the valuation analyst has to do the necessary homework to understand the nature of the rights granted, the economic value of those rights, and how much of that economic value should divide between the licensee and the licensor.

Specifically, a typical royalty rate determination should follow a framework similar to the chart in Exhibit 101.

Exhibit 101. Royalty Rate Determination

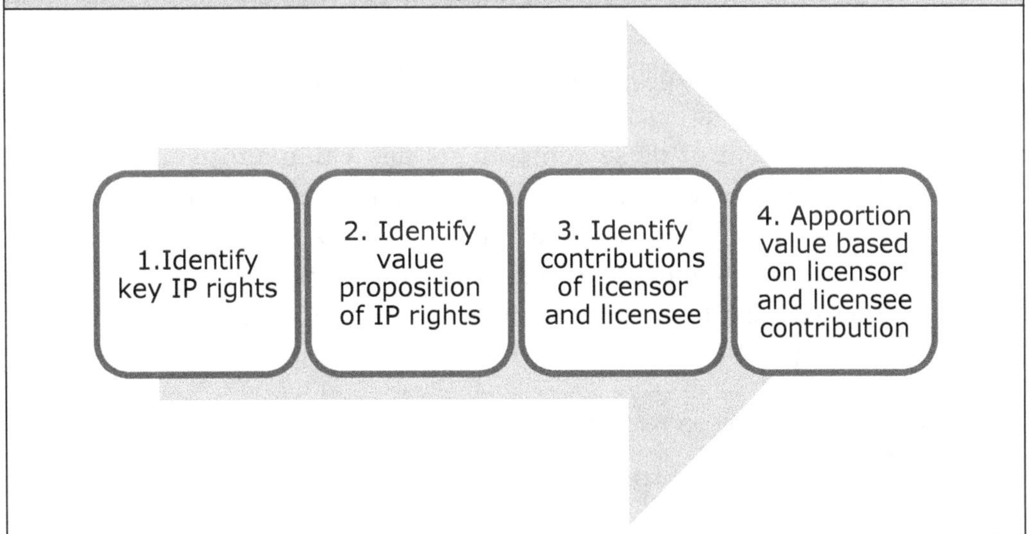

The various steps in the process are as follows:

- ***Identify key IP rights:*** In determining a reasonable royalty rate, the valuation analyst first considers whether there is even a basis to negotiate a royalty rate. To do that, the valuation analyst should determine the key rights that are subject to the royalty rate analysis. This includes understanding all fields of use, geographic restrictions, exclusivity restrictions, and others. These key rights will form the basis for the value proposition analysis that occurs next.
- ***Identify value proposition of IP rights:*** The valuation analyst determines the actual micro-economic value proposition associated with the rights afforded by the license grant. This is not a time to be lazy, and there are no shortcuts. The valuation analyst must, within some measure of reasonable effort, look to quantify the economic impacts of the IP rights grant. For example, suppose that one is valuing the rights to use a brand in a particular geographic market. The valuation analyst would have to determine the amount of value associated with that brand in the particular market. Unless the market were similar to others where a royalty rate is already known (that in and of itself can be a substantial amount of microeconomic analysis), the valuation analyst must establish the value proposition. For a brand, this means understanding any pricing premium, potential market share gains, the velocity of these market share gains, and potential cost savings associated with use of the brand in the market.
- ***Identify contributions of licensor and licensee:*** The contributions that the licensor and licensee bring to the licensing transaction should have a material impact on the magnitude of any royalty rate determination. The licensor naturally owns the IP rights; however, the licensee brings value to the table, usually through execution prowess (e.g., manufacturing capability or expertise), sales and distribution channels, or working capital. Each of these components has value and is an important determinant in ultimate market success. If one party contributes more to the overall success, then that party should reap more of the rewards.[287] Thus, the valuation analyst must identify what both the licensor and licensee bring to the transaction in order to apportion the contributions in an equitable manner.

287 Note that this is the basic theory behind the use of the 25% Rule, whereby the licensor of the technology commands about 25% of the economic benefits generated from some IP, with the balance going to the licensee. The problem with the 25% Rule is that it is a clumsy instrument and lacks a fundamental theoretical basis (e.g., what if it should have been the 33% Rule, the 20% Rule, or the 18.45334877589% Rule—each may be equally valid and we have no way of proving or disproving it)

- *Apportion value based on licensor and licensee contributions:* The apportionment of the value is the easiest part of the royalty rate determination. It builds on the identification of the rights granted in Step 1, the quantification of the value proposition of those granted rights performed in Step 2, and the allocation of the value to the licensor and licensee based on the contribution analysis performed in Step 3. Thus, suppose that the valuation analyst determines that a set of rights consists of an exclusive license for a food brand for the United States for a corn chip (Step 1). The value proposition for this brand equates only to incremental premium pricing that yields 28% per bag sold (Step 2) on a product that wholesales for $2.69 per bag. The valuation analyst identifies that the licensor brings 20% of the incremental economic substance of the transaction while the licensee contributes the remaining 80% (Step 3). Thus, the royalty rate payable by the licensee to the licensor in this case would be 20% of the 28% pricing premium.[288] The 28% wholesale price premium is worth $0.7532 per bag,[289] meaning that the licensor would receive a royalty payment of $0.15064.[290] Because of the pricing premium, the wholesale price of the bag of corn chips rises to $3.4432.[291] Thus, the eventual royalty rate, expressed as a percentage of the price of the bag of corn chips is 4.375%.[292]

Calculating the Value Proposition

Once the valuation analyst understands the nature of the rights granted in a license, the next step in any royalty rate analysis consists of understanding the value proposition of the IP rights grant. The value proposition drives the purpose and magnitude of an economic transaction involving the IP. Further, a valuation analyst looking to the market for indications of possible value needs to understand the depth and breadth of the IP in order to perform a competent comparative analysis. Thus, it is necessary to understand the value that the IP creates in remarkably detailed and specific ways.[293]

As you may recall, IP must have a sustainable value proposition to find market success. Typical drivers for a value proposition include better efficacy, lower cost,

288 20% * 28% = 5.6%

289 $2.69 * 28% = $0.7532

290 $0.7532 * 20% = $0.15064

291 $2.69 * 1.28% = $3.4432

292 $0.15064 / $3.4432 = 4.375%

293 It may be quite common for a valuation analyst to hear from an IP owner about the "value" of some particular IP. However, if the IP owner or valuation analyst cannot articulate, in precise terms, the actual value creation, then the IP may have little basis for establishing a royalty rate.

or easier product use. A product's value proposition may emerge in several forms. First, the product may contain additional features that give it more utility compared with competing solutions. Common examples of that utility may be that the product may provide more features than competing products; that the product is easier to use (requiring less time to operate); that the product may require fewer third party licenses to use; that the product better integrates with existing tools. Second, a product could create the same utility for lower acquisition or operating cost, lowering the total cost of ownership. Third, a product could possess some additional feature (e.g., patent protection) that would allow one to generate excess profits due to the monopolistic nature of the IP. The ultimate measure of this value is free cash flows.[294]

For example, suppose that a university spins out R&D Company that develops a vaccine to help a farmer increase the yield of beef cows. R&D Company wishes to license this vaccine to Drug Company. Drug Company in turn wishes to sell this vaccine directly to Livestock Farmer through an animal health subsidiary. Exhibit 102 captures the supply chain for this treatment:

Exhibit 102. Vaccine Supply Chain From Development to Drug Company to Farmer

Possible value streams for this vaccine include the following:

- Greater livestock weights (more meat to sell);
- Reduced livestock mortality (greater number of head to sell); and
- Reduced growing costs (e.g., increased feed conversion ratio, or FCR).

The quantification of the value proposition is not too difficult in this example. For example, suppose that the market value for the average cow at condemnation is $1,100. If clinical trials show that the vaccine lowers premature cow mortality by 20%, and market evidence suggests that 5% of all cows die due to disease,[295] then the vaccine preserves a net 1% of the cows. Thus, the vaccine creates about $11 per

294 If the valuation analyst cannot reduce the value proposition to a quantifiable, credible representation of positive free cash flows, then the value proposition may be indeterminate.

295 All of these numbers have a factual basis one can research and confirm.

Exhibit 103. Summary of the Total Value Proposition of the Vaccine	
Value Source	**Amount**
Reduced Mortality	$11
Improved Condemnation Weight	$110
Lower Feed Costs	$20
Total Value Creation	$141

head in value.[296] Next, suppose that the vaccine creates better health outcomes for the cows, helping improve weight gain by 10%. The value of this weight gain is about $110 per head.[297] Lastly, suppose that improved feed conversion reduces the cost to feed each cow by $20. The summary of the total value proposition of the vaccine is shown in Exhibit 103.

As the data suggests, the total value creation is $141. This $141 becomes a value basis that the valuation analyst will allocate to all parties within the value chain. Recall that the value chain includes R&D Company, Drug Company, and Livestock Farmer. Drug Company should capture some portion of all of these value streams, and R&D Company should capture an equitable portion of Drug Company's share.

Suppose that Drug Company performs market research and determines that Livestock Farmer is interested in buying the vaccine, but only if the vaccine increases the value per head by $50. The price elasticity of demand suggests that nothing below $50 per head is worth it to Livestock Farmer to buy. Thus, Drug Company knows that it will be able to command about $91 of the total $141 in value creation, because it will give $50 in value to Livestock Farmer.

Drug Company has gross margins of 80%. Thus, Drug Company generates $72.80 in gross profit from the $91 in revenue by selling the vaccine. This $72.80 becomes the basis that R&D Company uses for a royalty payment. Note that this view (i.e., the use of gross profits as opposed to operating profits) differs substantially from what other authors may have presented. Yet there is a reason for doing so, which will become clear after determining the contributions of the licensor (R&D Company) and the licensee (Drug Company). Specifically, the determination of licensor and licensee contributions account for which party pays all or some part of the operating expenditures. Thus, the royalty rate provides the mechanism to account for operating expenditures explicitly. If the value basis were operating profits, then the valuation analyst may double-count the benefits that the licensee brings to a

296 $1,100 value per head * 1% = $11.
297 $1,100 value per head * 10% weight improvement = $110.

transaction. Consequently, gross profits provide the more appropriate value basis, as there is no risk of double-counting.

Determining Licensor and Licensee Contributions

A licensor and a licensee share in value equity created through a license arrangement. Since the licensee assumes certain aspects of risk vacated by the licensor, the licensee would reasonably have greater upside potential for the highly profitable case of technology adoption and proliferation. Projected profits should divide according to the investment risk interface as realized by the licensor and the licensee. If the deal were a pure "joint venture," then the profits fairly divide on a 50/50 basis. If one party absorbs more risk, then the projected profits shift to favor the risk-taking party. This is the challenge: how does the valuation analyst determine in a credible, defensible way the amount of profit shift between the parties?

The approach described here is to allocate the value among the parties (in this case, the licensor and the licensee) based on each party's total contributions to value creation. For example, suppose that the following factors are what an industry analysis suggests is crucial to the success of monetizing the vaccine in the marketplace:[298]

- *IP rights:* IP rights typically vest with the licensor, shifting the profit allocation to the licensor's favor. However, the licensor may not always be the prevailing party. For example, the licensee might grant a cross license to the licensor, thus offsetting any profit allocation to the licensor.
- *IP enforcement:* Depending on the IP type, it may be necessary for the licensee or licensor to patrol the market and enforce IP rights to preserve IP value (e.g., prevent counterfeits). Depending on the IP type, IP enforcement can be quite expensive. Thus, a portion of the profit allocation shifts to the party providing IP enforcement.
- *IP defense:* Recall that IP defense can be expensive. It is possible that IP defense can easily exhaust nominal royalty streams paid to licensors.[299] Thus, a portion of the profit allocation shifts to the party providing IP defense.
- *IP commercialization:* It is one thing to prove that IP works well in a lab environment. It is another to show that it works in a commercial setting. For

298 Naturally, the valuation analyst can consider other factors that are industry specific. That is the beauty in this analytical model—the valuation analyst can customize it to meet the specific needs of a licensing transaction or industry.
299 The author has observed this firsthand.

example, suppose that a vaccine derives from a small-molecule chemical process. A large pharmaceutical company may have the institutional knowledge to scale the chemical process to industrial production levels, thus making any value realization possible. In this case, a portion of the profit allocation shifts to the large pharmaceutical company, as it is the party that can commercialize the IP. IP commercialization activities may also include bringing the vaccine through the regulatory pathway. This profit allocation may cover costs incurred for ongoing research and development activities to scale the core IP (but not to develop new IP), as well as regulatory approval expenditures.

- *Manufacturing:* Typically, a licensee is the one that is going to have the manufacturing capability to bring the IP to the market. As a result, a portion of the profit allocation shifts to the party providing the manufacturing capability. This profit allocation may cover indirect expenses like depreciation and allocated interest on capital equipment to produce the vaccine.

- *Sales and marketing:* Many excellent products and services may fail in the market because of ineffective sales and marketing expenditures. Therefore, sales and marketing efforts are an intrinsic part of successful IP exploitation. As a result, a portion of the profit allocation shifts to the party providing the sales and marketing capability. This profit allocation may cover indirect expenses like sales salaries and commissions and marketing expenditures to bring awareness of the vaccine to Livestock Farmer.

- *Distribution:* Order fulfillment is another important component in the cycle of developing and selling the vaccine. Consequently, a portion of the profit allocation shifts to the party providing the distribution and order fulfillment capability.

- *Working capital:* Lastly, the party that provides the working capital may incur capital charges to provide financing to enable ultimate exploitation of the IP in the market. As a result, a portion of the profit allocation shifts to the party providing the working capital.

Given equal weighting for each factor, the licensor and licensee would receive credit for those components for which each party provided material support. Thus, in the vaccine example, suppose that R&D Company provides the IP (without any reciprocal IP rights grants), the IP enforcement, and the IP defense. Exhibit 104 captures the possible weighting.

Exhibit 104. Allocating Value Based on Contributions					
Factor	Weight	Licensor Contributions	Licensee Contributions	Licensor Allocation	Licensee Allocation
IP Rights	12.50%	X		12.50%	
IP Enforcement	12.50%	X		12.50%	
IP Defense	12.50%	X		12.50%	
IP Commercialization	12.50%		X		12.50%
IP Manufacturing	12.50%		X		12.50%
Sales & Marketing	12.50%		X		12.50%
Distribution	12.50%		X		12.50%
Working Capital	12.50%		X		12.50%
Total Allocation	100.00%			37.50%	62.50%

In this situation, the licensor might provide for IP contribution and IP defense, and the licensee might provide the balance of the value creation in the transaction. Under this algorithm, the licensor receives 37.50% of the total gross profit as a royalty, with the balance remaining with the licensee. Thus, in the vaccine example, with gross profits of $72.80, the R&D Company would receive a payment of $27.30 from Drug Company. Drug Company would retain the balance of $45.50. As a percentage of total revenue to Drug Company, Drug Company will pay R&D Company using a royalty rate of 30.00%.[300]

Suppose that R&D Company provides only the IP rights, while Drug Company takes care of all IP enforcement and defense related matters. In this case, R&D Company's allocation is only 12.50% of the total gross profits. The other 25% of the gross profit allocation would vest with Drug Company to cover what might be a costly IP enforcement and defense strategy. Thus, the royalty to R&D Company would instead be $9.10,[301] or 10%[302] of the total revenues to Drug Company. What happens if the R&D Company and Drug Company share in expenditures of a certain class, such as IP commercialization? In that case, both parties would receive equal credit (i.e., 6.25%) of the gross profit allocation. As is obvious, the valuation analyst has a much greater ability to alter the royalty rate allocations based on facts that are specific to the particular licensing transaction versus other royalty rate development methods.

300 $27.30 royalty to R&D Company / $91.00 revenue to Drug Company = 30.00%.
301 72.80 * 12.50% = $9.10.
302 $9.10 / $91 = 10.00%.

Analytical Method Attack Points

Naturally, no valuation method is perfect. The analytical method discussed in this chapter is also open to various attack points. The following is a description of common attack points:

- *Difficulty of detailed analysis:* As several of the examples demonstrate, performing a detailed analysis using an analytical method is difficult. A thorough royalty rate determination can easily consume 80 hours or more to assemble the various data points and perform the calculations. This is especially true if there are several intermediaries in the value chain. Thus, a royalty rate analysis developed using analytical methods can be quite costly in comparison to one compiling a set of licenses captured within a published database.
- *Equal allocation of factor weighting:* In the example model presented, each of the factors received equal weighting. Thus, the implicit assumption in equal weighting is that all components require the same level of expenditures, time, and so on. This attack point is easy to neutralize. In fact, the model supports custom weightings that might vary by industry. For example, equal weighting is appropriate for a company in the durable goods industry, but inappropriate in the semiconductor industry. This may be because the semiconductor industry has greater emphasis on research, development, and IP defense expenditures. In such a situation, the valuation analyst can alter the weighting to increase the allocations to those factors such as research and development investment. A valuation analyst that adjusts the weightings to reflect industry-specific expenditure levels would remove any biases that might otherwise alter the royalty rate conclusion.
- *Dearth of available data:* Especially for novel or category-creating platform technologies, there may be little available information that valuation analysts can reference directly and incorporate into an analysis. This is usually the case—especially for pre-revenue products. Value creation data may not be available. There is uncertainty as to how the market may adopt the technology. The technical risks may be unprecedented. Despite this lack of information, the valuation analyst must still generate credible results. Doing so requires the valuation analyst to continually review and refine the royalty rate model, oftentimes in concert with the client.

- ***Value creation and market response calculations:*** At some point, the valuation analyst needs to know what the end customer is willing to pay for access to the licensed IP. From there, the valuation analyst can work backward through the supply chain, apportioning revenues to the various supply chain participants, in order to get to the total value apportioned to the licensor. If the valuation analyst estimates a substantially different market response, then the royalty rate conclusion may be incorrect.
- ***Variance sensitivity:*** The royalty rate result may be sensitive to variance associated with the imputed value creation and market response. Fortunately, using statistical simulation methods (perhaps with a tool like @Risk or Crystal Ball), the valuation analyst can understand the impact of the variance on the resulting royalty rate determination and refine the analysis with additional research as warranted.
- ***Findings disagreements:*** For all of the potential clarity and precision that the analytical approach brings, the licensor and licensee may just refuse to agree with the findings. This may be especially true if the results present a view that is adverse to a particular party's economic standing in the transaction. For example, some technology managers may be constrained by corporate policy from paying a royalty rate in excess of some predetermined level.[303] Alternatively, a licensee may not want to

Exhibit 105. Audit of the Approach Against the Principles

Principle	Pass or Fail	Notes
Testable	Pass	The valuation analyst can test the value proposition and apportionment assumptions directly and empirically, calibrating the model to account for variances that occur outside of statistical and observable norms.
Peer review and publication	Pass	Various authors have published articles using analytical methods as a basis for royalty rate determinations.
Acceptable rate of error and maintenance of standards	Pass	Because one can test the outcomes of the results in a manner specific to the IP under review, one can measure the associated error from the royalty rate determination and accept or reject a conclusion based upon conformance to standards.
Community acceptance	Pass	Various authors have published articles using analytical methods as a basis for royalty rate determinations.

303 For example, a client once said to me something to this effect: "I see what you have done. It is thoughtful, well documented, and you clearly defend it well. However, we have an informal corporate policy that we will never pay more than 5% for a technology license."

hear that the royalty rate the licensor seeks is lower than what the licensee envisioned.

None of these attack points is a showstopper. In fact, with a credible analysis, the valuation analyst can show, with data, that the analytical approach produces a result that fulfills all of the *Daubert* principles. For example, a valuation analyst can measure the error rate of the individual drivers important in the royalty rate conclusion. If one driver is off by an order of magnitude, the valuation analyst can respond as to whether the difference really matters because the valuation analyst can measure the impact directly.[304]

An audit of the approach against the *Daubert* principles yields the conclusions shown in Exhibit 105.

304 I was able to defend a value conclusion against a "spirited" attack in court once because the opposing counsel spent a disproportionate amount of time arguing about one value driver out of more than 50 different value drivers. I was able to show mathematically that the importance of the particular value driver in question was so low that, even if the driver were off by a factor of 1,000%, it would not have had a material impact on the resulting value conclusion. After hearing this, the opposing counsel changed the line of questioning altogether.

Chapter 12
Case Study in IP Valuation

This chapter presents a real-world example in celebrity valuation originally offered by several academic professors. This analysis made international headlines and generated several media inquiries for the professors. This chapter also includes a critical analysis of that valuation to demonstrate key concepts that make IP valuation difficult, especially when looking to the market for guidance. The chapter closes with several examples of how a valuation analyst may approach a similar valuation engagement in a manner that may withstand a critical review.

A Poor Example of Celebrity Valuation

In November 2009, Tiger Woods was the focus of an international media storm relating to marital infidelities. Fallout erupted with several of Woods's sponsors. In January 2010, two professors at the University of California-Davis (U.C.-Davis) published a paper claiming that the scandal had reduced shareholder value between $5 billion and $12 billion. The authors go to great lengths to show statistical correlations between data points to render their conclusions. However, a deeper analysis of their methods yields several significant shortcomings.

Celebrities typically create value in one of three ways (or variants thereof):

- *Lower sales and marketing costs:* For example, Starbucks spends 1.3% of total revenues on sales and marketing while competitors spend between 2% and 5% of total revenues on equivalent expenditures.
- *Greater revenues:* For example, Starbucks sells a $1 cup of coffee for $2.

- *Greater/faster market adoption:* For example, Starbucks sells some 4.5% of total coffee in the United States including home brews, which is a much larger amount than other coffee vendors sell.

If celebrity value cannot achieve any of these outcomes, then the celebrity brings limited value for the product or service in question. Thus, if the Woods scandal had any true impact on the value of Woods's sponsors, then any one of the sponsors would experience excess sales and marketing costs (e.g., costs to change advertising, which may be true), reduced revenues, or shrinking market share.

First, the U.C.-Davis study performs no meaningful analysis of any of these phenomena. For example, consider some of Woods's sponsors. While there are costs to Accenture to change advertising, has Accenture lost a deal because of its association with Woods? Has Nike experienced lower demand for Air Jordan shoes and Umbro gym shorts because of its association with Woods? Has Tag Heuer lost watch sales to Rolex or Movado because of its association with Woods? Have any of these vendors cut prices to generate demand because of lackluster sales resulting from their association with Woods? Without answers to such questions, valuation analysts, or academics, cannot opine on the true economic value impacts.

Second, the "market value" of a company is a misnomer when looking at public stock markets, especially as it relates to intellectual properties. Many factors tend to obfuscate the true value of intellectual properties, the least of which includes antiquated accounting standards that lack a fundamental recognition of intellectual property value. Thus, the balance sheets of most companies do not reflect any intellectual property assets they have acquired through their own development efforts, distorting the market's perception of value associated with intellectual properties. For example, it is remarkably difficult to find banks that will collateralize intellectual property.

Third, it is likely that the U.C.-Davis study inappropriately applies multiple regression methods to a problem that cannot be determined using such methods. For example, using the multiple regression methods from the U.C.-Davis study, one can show empirically, and with statistical significance, that a Fortune 500 company has a market value that correlates directly with the number of McDonald's Big Macs that its employees consume. Does this mean that valuation analysts should value companies based on this type of analysis? In a rather amusing April 2009 study, Marco Hickey correlated U.S. stock market returns to certain phases of the moon using multiple regression analysis.[305] Of course, the point of these examples is this:

305 http://www.scribd.com/doc/17522003/The-US-Stock-Market-Correlated-With-the-Phases-of-the-Moon, accessed on May 11, 2011.

correlation does not equal causation.

Classic finance literature teaches that the value of an asset is the risk-adjusted present value of the future economic returns one generates from employing that asset over its economic life. Empirically, the market value of public companies bears little resemblance to this principle. Otherwise, companies would never trade above their risk-adjusted intrinsic value. Empirical evidence suggests that this is certainly not the case, or speculative investment bubbles would not exist. In short, the price of a company's shares in the public markets has frustratingly little to do with the underlying value of the assets.

A simplified look at the reasonableness of the U.C.-Davis study's claims proves the disconnected nature of the price of a company's share of stock and the underlying asset value. A $5 billion to $12 billion loss in market value should represent the permanent loss of capitalized free cash flows to the sponsor's shareholders. A price to free cash flow ratio of 10 (indicating a discount rate of 10%) would mean that Woods's sponsors collectively lost between $500 million and $1.2 billion in incremental free cash flow per year because of association with Woods ($5 billion times 10%, $12 billion times 10%). At generous free cash flow ratios of 10% of revenues, that means that these companies would have collectively lost between $5 billion ($500 million divided by 10%) and $12 billion ($1.2 billion divided by 10%) in incremental revenues because of their association with Woods. These losses are permanent, not transient. This conclusion is nonsensical.

Basic research into the fundamental economics of Woods's sponsors proves it. Nike, one of his largest sponsors, generated $19 billion in revenues as of May 31, 2009. Much of that revenue occurred outside of the United States in countries that may be indifferent to Woods's infidelities. Further, much of that revenue had nothing to do with Woods. For example, per the annual report of Nike, Nike Golf, a division of Nike most closely associated with Woods, had fiscal 2009 revenues of $648.3 million, or about 3.3% of Nike's total. At Nike's cumulative net income margin, the profit from Nike Golf is likely about $50 million. As Nike sponsors 19 professional golfers, it is certainly unreasonable to attribute all of the $50 million to Woods's activity. Even if Nike thought Woods brought value to its other product lines as well, Nike would have to report permanent free cash flow losses of hundreds of millions of dollars, which would indicate billions of dollars of lost revenues.

These billions of dollars in lost revenues did not occur. According to Nike's 2010 annual report, Woods does not even draw a mention in the entire document. Moreover, while Nike Golf did experience a slight revenue drop to $638 million (down about $10 million, or 1.5%), there is no evidence to suggest that the revenue drop relates at all to the Woods incident.[306] Nike attributes the decrease in revenues to general reductions in discretionary consumer spending (Cole Haan, another division of Nike, had revenue drop by a similar percentage). Further, revenues associated with the two quarters nearest to Woods's incident were actually greater than the prior two quarters.[307] Lastly, revenues in Nike Golf dropped 11% between 2008 and 2009, before Woods's incident. Perhaps the most compelling statement in the entire filing refutes any notion of what the U.C.-Davis study claims:

> Moreover, a significant portion of our revenue is not derived from futures and advance orders, including at-once and close-out sales of NIKE footwear and apparel, wholesale sales of equipment, Cole Haan, Converse, Hurley, Umbro, Nike Golf, and certain retail sales across all brands.[308]

A similar result comes from another sponsor of Woods, Electronic Arts (EA). A substantial portion of EA's revenues emerges from blockbuster titles such as *Rock Band, Rock Band 2, Madden NFL*, and the *Need for Speed* series. The *Tiger Woods Golf* product is but a fraction of the total revenue contribution to EA. For example, when *Tiger Woods PGA Tour 10* launched in June 2009, EA sold 272,400 copies of it. At a suggested retail price of $59.99, that represents revenues of $16.3 million. Annualized over a year (which is generous as the launch month is generally higher than later months), total revenue nets out at about $196 million. EA runs at a loss at the time of this writing (EA has in fact lost more than $2 billion since 2008). Thus, a generous free cash flow allowance of 10% would net EA about $19.6 million—and that is assuming that EA could not sell the game using any other pro such as Phil Mickelson, Steve Stricker, Zach Johnson, or others instead of Tiger Woods.

Fourth, the wholesale comparison of Nike or EA to their publicly traded competitors inherits several common failings, which include the following:

- ***Fallacies of comparability:*** With respect to intellectual property, comparable transactions in the market are rare. Therefore, any reference to other intellectual property transactions is at best a crude value approximation. For example, consider a market-based approach

306 Nike Inc., Form 10-K, July 20, 2010, p. 38.

307 *Id.*, p. 22.

308 *Id.*, pp. 4, 13.

where the IP valuation analyst must normalize the comparables and the subject intellectual property to value. How does that occur? Current literature does not provide an objective method for comparing a company's intellectual property portfolio to others in the market. Nobody recommends performing a trademark search for each company to compare the size of the intellectual property portfolios. Not that such methods would likely provide meaningful results (what if a company owns one valuable trademark but another company owns 100 poor ones?), but the general profession lacks methods to determine comparability objectively. Several of the following key attributes must be very close for a comparison to be meaningful: the remaining economic lives; free cash flow generation potential (which can be difficult to determine for novel products); the timing of the products in the market; and the risk associated with the subject intellectual property and the comparable intellectual property.

- ***The market does not understand IP valuation:*** Dissecting the broad financial market indicates a population that may have little understanding of the intellectual property valuation process and requisite considerations. While the market is composed of smart people, the market's intelligence does not focus on intellectual property valuation (hence the explanation for any value change). Here is the point: if the market is so poor or inexperienced at valuing intellectual property, how can an IP valuation analyst possibly rely on the market and still generate a credible value indication, particularly when performing any of the common market IP valuation approaches such as comparing profits, residual incomes, or business enterprise value? This is where reality and theory clash. The market is not good at valuing intellectual property. It is inappropriate to rely on market indications of intellectual property value, especially by people who are not skilled or educated at valuing intellectual property in the first place. Market participants enter the market routinely with imperfect information. These market participants drive prices sky high. Market participants also leave the market irrationally and abnormally, depressing market transaction prices. For example, literature suggests that the market can indirectly reflect the value of intellectual property, as would be seen by studying changes in the market value of companies, as one might do in an event study like that performed by U.C.-Davis. However, in practice, this method is poor at best. For example, one may infer with an event study that the market value of the Prozac patent to

Eli Lilly was $35 billion, because Lilly lost approximately that much in market value on the day it lost its Prozac patent protection. However, the market overreacted in a tremendous way, as the true economic impact to Lilly was about $886 million for the 15 months of exclusivity it lost, or about 1/40th the impact indicated by the event study. Further, the market simplifies many complex considerations with assumptions about risk, timing, and other intrinsic value drivers. One only needs to look at the contemporary economic climate for substantial evidence to support this assertion.

- *The portfolio effect:* As discussed earlier, comparable transactions in an intellectual property valuation engagement may represent a portfolio of intellectual property with a set of conditions that are unique (e.g., strong reversionary rights, preferential rights to derivative inventions, etc.). It is rare to find stand-alone comparable intellectual property transactions that do not include other bundled tangible or intangible assets, or similar contractual arrangements. Other factors may tend to exacerbate the portfolio effect as well. First, intellectual property valuation literature mentions little about researching the trademarks for comparable companies to determine if the size and economic power of the trademark portfolios is comparable and what any possible effects on market value would be. This is not necessarily a bad thing, as little academic research exists to suggest that such a method works and that any value conclusion would be reliable. Second, trademark quality is a very important factor in an IP portfolio analysis. A company that owns one strong trademark may be worth more than a company that owns 100 weak ones. Pepsi has 598 registered live trademarks that could affect its market valuation (e.g., think back to the Tropicana rebranding fiasco in January 2009 that cost stockholders tens of millions of dollars). As the entire Gatorade family represents less than 7% of the retail value of Pepsi's products, Gatorade sales would have to utterly crater by billions of dollars to support the U.C.-Davis study's contention of value destruction.

Further, the U.C.-Davis study assumes that companies and products are generally the same across the board and serve as effective substitutes, which runs contrary to the basic nature of celebrity value. For example, trademarks represent exclusive rights that are unique by definition (i.e., no comparable). There is no comparable for the Tiffany & Co. Blue Box, the Louis Vuitton bag, or the Nike Air Jordan shoes. As such, it is an incorrect theoretical model to state that one trademark is comparable to another, as doing so would run contrary to the USPTO's finding that the trademark is unique and warrants protection for a given class of goods or services. Most importantly, this incorrect theoretical model ignores the requisite microeconomic analysis necessary to opine about the associated value losses related to Woods. For example, Nike may be more valuable than Reebok or Adidas for certain products (e.g., golf), but not all products (e.g., soccer). The methods employed in the U.C.-Davis study fail to account for the company-specific analysis routinely required in celebrity valuation engagements of any sort.

The U.C.-Davis event study also includes survivorship biases that may artificially inflate the significance of their regression coefficients. For example, at the very least, the study did not perform any analysis of competing sponsors to determine if events surrounding their sponsored athletes may have had an impact on the market value of their firm. There may well be dozens of exogenous factors that drive the differences the U.C.-Davis study attempts to capture, such as the effects of algorithmic trading activities (on any one day greater than 50% of trading activity may be algorithmic and automatic), shareholder composition, industry-specific market conditions, or basic financing limitations. The relative inexperience of the market in valuing intellectual properties, the shortcomings in the academic peer review process (i.e., there are few academics that have any tangible experience in intellectual property valuation), and the herd mentality of the market buyers and sellers calls into question the basic premise for the study.

Based on these considerations, the conclusions of the U.C.-Davis study are meaningless in the context of true IP value and lack any theoretical or practical grounding in reality. Further, a deeper analysis of the study's methods suggests that the U.C.-Davis study's conclusions do not bring additional clarity to the issue and may be outright incorrect by a wide margin. Moreover, it is trivial to discredit the methods employed by the U.C.-Davis professors under a *Daubert*-type analysis by simple back-testing of the conclusions. As the data suggest, Woods's sponsors exhibited little revenue impairment associated with Tiger Woods's personal issues. In this example, the academic economists at U.C.-Davis, whom did not have any apparent tangible experience in intellectual property or celebrity valuation engagements, rendered conclusions that are wholly impeachable.

A Credible Approach to Celebrity Valuation

Literature establishes that damage components can include a combination of lost unit sales, lower unit sales prices, higher costs (such as increased marketing or legal costs), and/or lost sales on ancillary products. The components that comprise the damages that an IP valuation analyst might consider for a credible analysis of the impact Woods had on his sponsors are shown below:

- ***Cost to cure brand impairment:*** If the publicity associated with Woods's infidelities casts a negative view on the stability, security, and integrity of the Nike brand, Nike must repair that damage. An industry-accepted way to estimate the value of the brand impairment is to value the cost to cure the brand impairment. To help restore confidence in the stability, security, and integrity of Nike products and services, Nike might consult with a public relations agency to perform an independent assessment of the brand impairment to Nike and to create a campaign to repair the reputation damage (Nike did this). The tangible result of these public relations activities would be to persuade the public and the target markets for Nike products that the Nike brand is indeed strong by continued association with Woods. If the full economic costs of this campaign (i.e., including capitalized opportunity costs on dollars spent performing these corrective actions) were $10 million, then Nike would have incurred a value impairment of $10 million.

- ***Cost of permanent income losses or deferrals:*** Suppose that the publicity associated with Woods's infidelities has caused Nike to lose sales to competitors either temporarily or permanently. The main driver of this phenomenon is that customers would not want to buy products from Nike anymore because of the association of the Nike brand with Woods. In this situation, Nike incurs temporary or permanent cash flow losses because Nike loses the customers, as captured in Exhibit 106.

Exhibit 106. Impact of Celebrity Brand Impairment on Cash Flow

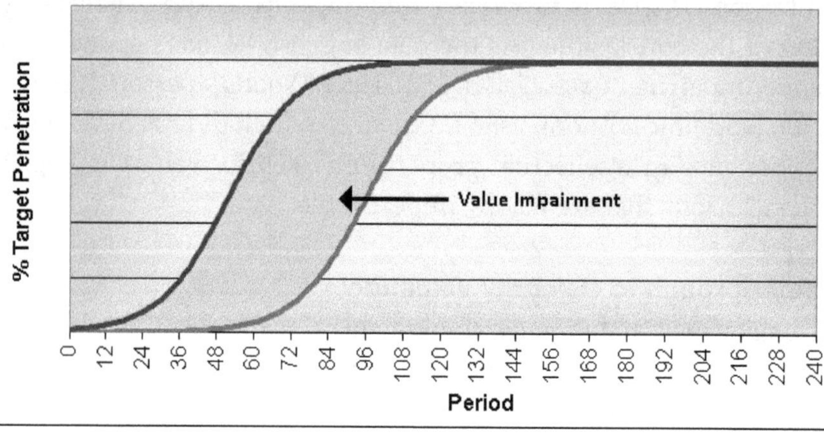

The chart demonstrates a time delay that will defer cash flows Nike would have enjoyed sooner. The shaded area represents the value impairment that Nike might incur. This impairment occurs because Nike cannot enjoy the benefits of the cash flows that it would have generated sooner (i.e., the leftmost line in the chart curve) than what Nike can enjoy now (i.e., the rightmost line in the chart curve). Recall that a dollar today is worth more than it is in the future because of the risk-adjusted time value of money.

A valuation analyst would have to use the income valuation approach to quantify any permanent revenue losses that Nike would have suffered. The valuation analyst would have to build two discounted cash flow models to capture the magnitude of the damages. The first discounted cash flow model would capture the present value of the free cash flows that Nike may likely have generated were it not for any impairment associated with Woods. The second discounted cash flow model would capture the present value of the free cash flows that Nike may likely have generated as well. However, it would have deferred a portion of those free cash flows to account for the time lag it would have taken for Nike to cure any impairment that it suffered because of Woods's actions. The value of the damage that Nike may have incurred is the difference between the value indications of the first and second valuation models.

Chapter 13
Managing an Engagement

There is an inherent flow to managing an IP valuation engagement. It starts with the sales process (which can vary from organization to organization and is beyond the scope of this book) and ends with the delivery and support of any resulting valuation report. The typical valuation engagement may follow the process outlined in Exhibit 107.

Exhibit 107. Typical Valuation Engagement

The following sections provide an overview of each of these activities.

Project Preparation

The purpose of the project preparation in the IP valuation process is to prepare the team that is going to perform the valuation engagement by outlining project expectations. A project kickoff meeting should be the first task in the project preparation; this meeting pulls together all members of the team that will work on the engagement to discuss it in detail. The project kickoff meeting is an important part of the valuation engagement because it may help set the tone and direction for the engagement. Typical items that should be discussed in the project kickoff meeting include the following:

- *Valuation project type:* In the project kickoff meeting, the project manager explains to the team the type of project the team will perform. Is it a non-certified valuation calculation, an appraisal that conforms to the Uniform Standards of Professional Appraisal Practice (USPAP), a Rule-26 compliant report, or something else? The project type may dictate the process that the engagement team uses to execute the project and produce any eventual work product.

- *Value standard:* The project manager explains to the team the value standard for the engagement (e.g., fair value, fair market value, etc.). While there is little initial difference in IP valuation engagements based on the value standard (e.g., the IP due diligence procedures are identical regardless of the value standard), downstream activities such as market research, valuation modeling, and valuation reporting will depend on the value standard.

- *Key project dates:* The project manager reviews key project dates so that the valuation team understands when items are due.

- *Project schedule:* The project manager reviews the project schedule with the team to confirm team member tasking and to discuss critical path items in the schedule that may affect the timing of any project deliverables.

- *Team availability:* The project manager needs to understand the availability of the team members slated to work on the project. Valuation analysts typically work on several projects at a time. Thus, team availability constraints imposed by unrelated projects and general team availability (e.g., vacations, personal time) may have a schedule impact. The project manager needs to understand team members' availability at the start of the engagement in case availability constraints would warrant changes to the project team, engagement tasking, or the project schedule.
- *Engagement tasking:* The project manager reviews key engagement tasking with the team. Following this project kickoff meeting, the team should have a clear understanding who performs IP due diligence, who performs market research, who performs valuation modeling, who performs peer reviews, and so on.

Initial Due Diligence

Initial due diligence is the part of the engagement process where the valuation analyst gains a reasonable understanding of the intellectual property to value. Performing initial due diligence is a customer-facing activity. The valuation analyst meets with the customer to review the IP, seeking to gain a reasonable understanding of the following:

- IP to review;
- Status of IP rights;
- IP development costs;
- Target markets for the IP;
- Competitive landscape for the IP; and
- Forecast economic expectations for the IP.

A typical initial due diligence meeting may take one to three days, depending on the nature of the intellectual property and the number of contexts to consider for the IP.[309] Typical activities that an IP valuation analyst must perform during the initial due diligence engagement phase include the following:

309 IP valuation is context driven, especially for platform technologies like a chemical formula or a semiconductor manufacturing process. The same chemical formula may have a different value proposition depending on the target markets for the formula. Thus, the formula may have a high value in a biomedical application and a low value in an aerospace application. The valuation analyst must understand all valuation contexts for an engagement and review each with the customer during the initial due diligence part of the process.

- *Prepare meeting questionnaire:* A valuation analyst needs a questionnaire to use as a guide to execute the initial due diligence meetings with the customer. This questionnaire is not necessarily comprehensive, as many due diligence items do not apply for many valuation engagements. Rather, the purpose of the questionnaire is to serve as a guide for the valuation analyst to ask probing questions about the IP.

- *Schedule the meetings:* The valuation analyst should dispatch with IP due diligence early in the engagement as due diligence drives a substantial amount of downstream analysis activity. This activity consists of scheduling the customer meetings, arranging requisite travel, and so forth.

- *Perform initial due diligence:* During initial due diligence, the valuation analyst will meet with the customer to learn about the IP. This consists primarily of walking the customer through the meeting questionnaire, reviewing product demonstrations (if applicable), and collecting relevant valuation materials.

- *Send out open action items:* As is oftentimes the case, a valuation analyst will not be able to address all items during the initial due diligence meetings with the customer. Thus, it is important for the valuation analyst to record all open action items and present them to the customer after completion of the initial due diligence meetings.

- *Catalog any materials received from customer:* An initial due diligence meeting may provide a valuation analyst with a set of materials that may include financial schedules, legal agreements (e.g., license agreements), market research, and others. The valuation analyst should catalog these materials (e.g., perhaps in an online system such as Microsoft's SharePoint) so that others on the engagement team can access them.

IP Analysis

IP analysis is the next step in the IP valuation engagement process. During this step, the valuation analyst must generate a complete, comprehensive understanding of the intellectual property. This includes understanding the use of the IP in the market currently, the chain of ownership for the IP, any claims against the IP, the administrative status of the IP (e.g., are patent maintenance fees current?), the IP owner's litigation record and resources, and the current development status of the IP.

- *Review IP with customer's IP counsel as appropriate:* Oftentimes, the customer's IP counsel will have specific knowledge about the structure of the IP in question, which may help the valuation analyst focus the analysis effort. For example, if the IP in question were a patent, the IP counsel may be able to explain why the patent's claims have a certain structure or breadth. While customers may not always be willing to let the valuation analyst speak to the IP counsel (mostly because of the corresponding attorney cost), the valuation analyst should always attempt to do so.

- *Verify current ownership/title of IP rights:* Perhaps one of the most interesting circumstances of 2009 is the role that the U.S. Treasury played as an owner in rights associated with intellectual properties. On August 27, 2009, the Treasury became one of the largest creditors in an IP portfolio owned by GM Global Technology Operations, Inc. Citibank, N.A. maintained a security interest in this IP portfolio as well. Thus, anyone valuing technology associated with the GM portfolio would have to know about these two security interests in order to come to a correct value conclusion. Note that if the valuation analyst is reviewing a portfolio of 50 patents, then the valuation analyst has to check the status of each patent in the portfolio. While it can be a significant labor burden to verify the proper ownership of IP rights, doing so is necessary in the due diligence portion of the engagement process to avoid coming to an improper value conclusion.

- *Review non-disclosure and non-compete agreements:* Intellectual property that is valuable because of secrecy (e.g., trade secrets, business strategies, licensing partners) requires proper coverage with non-disclosure and non-compete agreements. The valuation analyst should plan to review a sampling of such agreements to evaluate possible value risk.

- *Review employee ownership transfers:* Employees create intellectual property; companies do not. Thus, the valuation analyst must review transfer agreements that move an employee's IP interests to the company. Note that if the valuation analyst is reviewing a portfolio of 50 patents, then the valuation analyst has to check the status of each ownership assignment for each inventor for each patent in the portfolio. For example, if a company has two patents, one with four listed inventors, and one with five listed inventors, then the valuation analyst should verify the recording of nine assignments with the USPTO (one assignment for each listed inventor on each patent).

- *Verify contact information for IP is current in government registration systems:* The valuation analyst must verify that all contact information and company name information is current with any government registration systems. Note that if the valuation analyst is reviewing a portfolio of 50 patents, then the valuation analyst has to check the contact information of each patent in the portfolio.
- *Verify associated maintenance fee status:* The valuation analyst verifies with the USPTO that the patent owner is current with all patent maintenance fees due for each patent. Note that if the valuation analyst is reviewing a portfolio of 50 patents, then the valuation analyst has to check the maintenance fee status of each patent in the portfolio.
- *Establish the statutory expiration date of the IP:* The valuation analyst verifies the statutory expiration of the intellectual property, accounting for term extensions as appropriate in the case of patents.
- *Verify appropriate marking and notice as appropriate:* The valuation analyst verifies recommended marking of all products or services that bear protection. For example, if the IP is a patent, the valuation analyst needs to verify that the product that embodies the inventions claimed within the patent has a marking providing public notice of the patent.
- *Verify customer's litigation history with IP and general IP defense strategy:* The valuation analyst verifies the customer's IP litigation history and general IP defense strategy.
- *Verify additional claims against IP value (e.g., royalties due to third parties):* The valuation analyst verifies any other claims that may arise against IP value. These may include third party royalty agreements, judgments, etc.
- *Discuss ways to identify infringement of the IP in the fields of use:* The valuation analyst reviews with the customer ways to identify possible infringement of the IP.
- *Discuss possible design circumvention:* The IP valuation analyst discusses ways that a possible competitor may design around key IP protections, if applicable. For example, if the IP were a patent that describes a means to affix a fuel tank to a truck frame, then the valuation analyst would discuss other ways that truck manufacturers may affix fuel tanks to truck frames in a way that does not infringe the patent, but may provide for similar utility.

- Identify development timeline: The IP valuation analyst confirms the amount of time (typically in months if the valuation model uses a monthly time scale) until product is ready for sale in the target market. As product delays can have a value impact (see Chapter 4), the valuation analyst confirms any development schedules and associated time variances.

Market Analysis

Once an IP valuation analyst understands the intellectual property, the valuation analyst then needs to understand where the IP fits within the broader market. This is the function of the market analysis piece of the IP valuation engagement. Importantly, a valuation analyst cannot begin market analysis until having a complete understanding of the IP under review. For example, a purpose of the market analysis is to evaluate a given IP asset against possible competing alternatives in the market. The valuation analyst would not be able to perform this analysis competently without first understanding the IP well. Market analysis for an IP project may include the following activities:

- *Develop value proposition for the patent:* Intellectual property must have a sustainable value proposition to find market success. Typical drivers for a value proposition include better efficacy, lower cost, or easier product use. A product's value proposition may emerge in several forms. First, the product may contain additional features that give it more utility compared with competing solutions. Common examples of that utility may be that the product: provides more features than competing products; is easier to use (requiring less time to operate); may require fewer third party licenses to use; and better integrates with existing tools. Second, a product could create the same utility for lower acquisition or operating costs, lowering the total cost of ownership. Third, a product could possess some additional feature (e.g., patent protection) that would allow one to generate excess profits due to the monopolistic nature of the IP.

- *Identify sustainable competitive advantages for the IP:* For IP to retain value, it is imperative that the IP maintain certain sustainable competitive advantages against competing alternatives. Without these sustainable competitive advantages, market forces would erode any economic power of the IP and drive a lower value. Typical sustainable competitive advantages may include strong IP protections, high switching costs, the status of any research & development efforts, strategic partners, product efficacy, and so on.

- ***Identify key risks associated with the IP:*** All IP exploitation strategies have associated risks. The IP valuation analyst identifies key risks associated with the IP in relation to the market and competing alternatives. Typical key risks may include development timelines, undercapitalization, the potential to circumvent the IP protections, time to market, and others.

- ***Establish the size of the target market for the IP:*** The valuation analyst establishes the size of the relevant market where the IP may find use. For example, if the IP relates to a patent for online advertising, then the valuation analyst may need to understand the size and market dynamics of the online advertising marketplace.

- ***Identify key competitors for the utility provided by the patent:*** The competitive market has a material impact on value. If the market views a given asset as superior in features, performance, and value, it pays a premium to receive those benefits. If the market views competitive offerings as easy substitutes with low barriers to changing, then this phenomenon will threaten the value of the asset, forcing vendors to compete on price alone. This can place downward pressure on the value of an asset. The valuation analyst gains a reasonable conclusion about the state of the competitors in relation to the value provided by the IP under review.

- ***Identify appropriate market adoption proxy:*** As appropriate, the valuation analyst develops appropriate proxies for the IP in the market. This is especially important for nascent technologies that are category-defining (i.e., a brand new category of products in the market) and lack a strong historical revenue or earnings record.

- ***Identify and evaluate the regulatory environment:*** Oftentimes, the regulatory environment can affect value. Intellectual property that serves heavily regulated industries may experience adverse value impacts, as regulation may defer future cash flows to some faraway point in the future. Alternatively, heavy regulation may enhance value as well, particularly if it creates barriers to entry that afford existing market participants quasi-monopolistic attributes. The valuation analyst gains an understanding of the regulatory environment where the IP may find use in the market.

- ***Establish economic life for IP:*** An important value driver for any intellectual property is the economic life over which the owner could exploit the IP. The economic life has a direct relationship to value. IP with a longer economic life has a higher value than similar IP with a shorter economic life, all else the same.

- *Identify historical pricing for competing solutions in the market:* Despite what IP owners may claim, all IP has price competition against prior goods or services. For example, a remarkably large number of patents describe inventions included in cellular telephones. Yet, the world operated just fine without cellular telephones; hence, while all cellular telephone technology may be novel, it might only find market success when the value proposition exceeds that of existing market solutions. With this step, the IP valuation analyst benchmarks the value proposition against competing market alternatives.
- *Review any existing market response:* The valuation analyst reviews any evidence (e.g., product reviews, customer reviews, etc.) that suggests that the utility provided by the IP has any favor within the market. Positive or negative reviews may give rise to the valuation analyst adjusting valuation models to account for such reviews and possible demand or margin impacts. For example, if a review claims a product costs too much, then it may be appropriate for the valuation analyst to model a possibly lower product price in the revenue model.

Valuation Modeling

Once a valuation analyst understands the legal status and the market for the intellectual property (i.e., the qualitative measures), he or she needs to pull all of these together into a valuation model (i.e., the quantitative measures). This is the function of the valuation modeling in an IP valuation engagement. Importantly, a valuation analyst cannot begin valuation modeling until having a complete understanding of the IP under review and the market where the IP deployment occurs. For example, a purpose of the valuation modeling is to quantify the revenue potential for a given IP asset against possible competing alternatives in the market. The valuation analyst would not be able to perform this analysis competently without first understanding the possible demand and associated pricing. Valuation modeling for an IP project may include the following activities:

- *Develop the project discount rate:* The valuation analyst develops a risk-appropriate discount rate for the valuation engagement. This is perhaps one of the most important aspects of the valuation modeling process, as an inappropriate discount rate may render any eventual forecast, no matter how precise, invalid.

- *Develop the economic life for the IP:* The valuation analyst determines the remaining economic life for the IP. If it is a patent, this may be the remaining statutory life for the patent, but it does not have to be.
- *Develop the market adoption curve:* The valuation analyst models what a reasonable market adoption curve may be for the IP. To do this, the valuation analyst gains a strong understanding of the IP and possible proxies to use in the market for a suitable market adoption curve.
- *Design and develop the demand forecast:* The valuation analyst models what the demand may be for the IP. Such an effort may typically build upon the development of a market adoption curve.
- *Design and develop the revenue forecast:* The valuation analyst models what the revenues may be for a demand forecast. The difference between a revenue forecast and a demand forecast may be subtle. The demand forecast indicates the number of units that may sell. The revenue forecast is what ties the demand forecast to dollars.
- *Design and develop the expense forecast:* The valuation analyst models what the expenses may be for a revenue forecast. The valuation analyst matches the requisite expenses incurred to generate the revenues in the forecast. The expense forecast includes direct and indirect expenditures as well as any capital expenditures and any associated depreciation or amortization expenses.
- *Integrate forecasts into a master valuation model:* In this step, the valuation analyst integrates all forecasts into a master valuation model.
- *Review demand, revenue, and expense forecasts with the customer:* The valuation analyst reviews the demand, revenue, and expense forecasts with the customer, tweaking items as necessary to reflect an execution path that may be achievable within industry norms.
- *Identify and specify simulation parameters for key value drivers:* As appropriate, the IP valuation analyst identifies all valuation model drivers that may require sensitivity analysis and/or simulation testing. Concurrent with this process, the valuation analyst also defines the ranges for the value drivers, typically based upon empirical market evidence.

For example, if the price per bushel of corn varies between $2 and $6, then the valuation analyst would bound the per-bushel corn pricing to the observed data points (i.e., allow corn prices to vary between $2 and $6 per bushel).

- *Perform simulations and test conclusions for reasonableness:* In this step, the valuation analyst performs all sensitivity analyses and tests the value indications for reasonableness, perhaps based on industry norms.

Valuation Reporting

Valuation report writing is the last major element of the process in an IP valuation engagement. The valuation analyst pulls all of the due diligence, IP analysis, market research, and valuation modeling into a comprehensive, cohesive work product. The report writing process typically consists of the following steps:

- *Author general report content:* In this step, the valuation analyst writes the report. Note that this occurs after all IP review is complete, after all market research is complete, and after all valuation modeling is complete. The valuation analyst will not have enough information to produce a final report until all previous steps are completed. Report length varies and many factors contribute to the length of a report, including the writing ability of the valuation analyst, the complexity of the IP, the number of markets or fields of use considered, the complexity of the valuation model, and others. Typical self-contained reports that conform to the USPAP typically will exceed 50 pages or more.[310]

- *Perform editing of integrated valuation report:* In this step, a peer of the valuation analyst performs an independent review of the report to ensure that it conforms to established standards.

- *Integrate findings from report editing process:* In this step, the valuation analyst integrates any suggested edits from the peer review process.

- *Perform final review of the work product:* In this step, the valuation analyst performs a final review of the report and valuation models, performing a final consistency check of each.

- Produce final report work product: The valuation analyst produces a final report, which may include hard-copy printed versions of the report and

310 The author has produced work products in excess of 1,000 pages per copy. While review of such a work product can be tedious, such review is necessary to ensure work product integrity and quality.

supporting valuation models, or soft-copy electronic versions of these. In the case of a work product used in conjunction with a legal proceeding, the valuation analyst may have to mark the work product as confidential and/or an attorney work product.

Project Support

Project support varies by engagement. Some customers may never call again because the report satisfied a particular purpose and there is no longer a need for any project support (e.g., an acquisition where the seller hires the valuation analyst to provide a value of the IP to ensure the seller is receiving a fair deal). Other customers may require ongoing support, including availability of the valuation analyst to answer questions, availability of the valuation analyst to testify in any legal proceedings, and so forth. While it is difficult to know the depth and breadth of such project support initially, valuation analysts commonly address post-project support on an hourly basis or as part of a support level included in the original engagement description.

Chapter 14
Auditor's Review Guide

Today's financial auditor has much to deal with. As the auditor renders an opinion as to whether the audited financial statements fairly reflect the historical state of the company, the value of the company's intellectual property, which is an asset to the company, can be a major component in that opinion. The auditor's role is not a trivial one to fill. In addition to the myriad new developments in general accounting practices and fraud detection, the auditor must now consider inherently complex, hard-to-value assets, such as a company's IP portfolio. As such, the financial auditor may be subject to errors and omissions liability in trusting an independent appraisal performed by a third party at face value. It is not enough for the auditor to know that an independent person or entity opined on the value. Rather, it is important for the auditor to know if there is a basis to accept a value opinion as credible in the first place. This chapter provides a basic guide that an auditor may use to determine whether the data collection, valuation methods, data analyses, and value conclusions are sufficient for inclusion in an IP valuation report.

Analyzing the Analyst

The background of the valuation analyst is paramount in IP valuation engagements. It is not enough to have a valuation firm with a strong brand create and deliver a valuation report and for the auditor to rely on that brand alone. The auditor needs to understand the qualifications of the valuation analyst who actually performed the work on the report and how those qualifications relate to the engagement. This is especially important if the report relates to patents or trade secrets of a scientific nature. The valuation analyst must demonstrate to the auditor that he or she has the education, capacity, and scientific understanding regarding the IP to perform an adequate review of the technology. Much in the same way an auditor would cringe at the thought of a chemistry major—with no formal training in accounting—handling the day-to-day operations of a billion-dollar company, the auditor should cringe when the valuation analyst cannot demonstrate relevant competence to perform the engagement. In short, the auditor should not rely on the resulting value opinion.[311]

While the former paragraph presents a controversial view, there is precedent in the IP service sector for such iconoclastic thought. For example, companies do not hire pure financiers or accountants to prosecute patents. In fact, they cannot. Patent attorneys and patent agents must hold baccalaureate degrees in science or engineering disciplines to sit for the patent bar. For example, the USPTO requires that the candidate have a bachelor's degree in a recognized technical subject. The General Requirements Bulletin for Admission to the Examination for Registration to Practice in Patent Cases Before the USPTO lists recognized technical subjects for a bachelor's degree as follows:[312]

Biology	Pharmacology	Electrochemical Engineering
Biochemistry	Physics Engineering	Engineering Physics
Botany	Textile Technology	General Engineering
Computer Science	Aeronautical Engineering	Geological Engineering
Electronics Technology	Agricultural Engineering	Industrial Engineering
Food Technology	Biomedical Engineering	Mechanical Engineering
General Chemistry	Ceramic Engineering	Metallurgical Engineering
Marine Technology	Chemical Engineering	Mining Engineering
Microbiology	Civil Engineering	Nuclear Engineering
Molecular Biology	Computer Engineering	Petroleum Engineering
Organic Chemistry	Electrical Engineering	

In the same way as the patent office requires fundamental scientific education for its practitioners, IP valuation analysts should hold a baccalaureate degree in a science- or engineering-related discipline as well; the valuation analyst must be capable of describing the science that underlies the assets, which creates the utility that benefits the licensors of the technology. Only in this way can the valuation analyst properly value the technology.

311 The author recognizes this to be a controversial position that many current IP practitioners who lack formal scientific backgrounds would dispute vigorously.

312 www.uspto.gov/web/offices/dcom/olia/oed/grb.pdf. Note that an applicant can have a degree in some other subject; however, the applicant must still demonstrate formal education in the sciences.

That is not to say that the valuation analyst or valuation team must not have proper accounting and financial education. Such backgrounds are important as well (particularly finance), as value development centers on concepts deeply rooted in those disciplines. A valuation analyst who has a pure scientific background but lacks the acumen to work with state-of-the-art finance tools is equally incompetent. As such, the auditor should also question a report's integrity when the valuation analyst lacks properly demonstrated competency in finance and accounting.

Of course, many IP valuation engagements do not require a scientific understanding. For example, there is little applied science in the development of brands and trademarks or copyrights for a bronze sculpture or a song. Thus, the educational requirement for performing those engagements would rely less on science and more on the specific talents important in that subject matter. For example, for a brand valuation, the valuation analyst should demonstrate competence in marketing.

Analyzing the Due Diligence

After analyzing the valuation analyst, the auditor needs to analyze the level of due diligence. The auditor looks at several distinct areas of the IP due diligence process. The auditor needs to verify that the valuation analyst has provided proper consideration of IP due diligence items. Chapter 5 of this guide covers many important due diligence items that warrant consideration. Important questions that the auditor should ask include the following:

- ***Did the valuation analyst review the IP?*** The report must demonstrate to the reader that the valuation analyst actually reviewed and understood the nature of the IP.

- ***Did the valuation analyst verify statutory registration, if applicable?*** The report must demonstrate to the reader that the valuation analyst actually verified registration with the proper government authority, if applicable, as failure to do so can affect value catastrophically.

- ***Whom did the valuation analyst interview to understand the IP?*** The report must demonstrate to the reader that the valuation analyst interviewed the appropriate people who have knowledge of the IP. For example, if a valuation analyst is considering a patent, but does not interview the patent's inventors, that should raise a red flag to the auditor. Of course, many patent valuation projects involve patents that have changed owners several times and the original inventors may no longer be relevant. However, the valuation analyst must at least demonstrate consideration of the inventors, as the inventors are particularly relevant in understanding functional differences between the claimed invention and current market alternatives.

- *Did the valuation analyst use the appropriate valuation approach?* The report must demonstrate to the reader that the valuation analyst used the correct valuation approach for the engagement. Recall that IP engagements focus on incremental benefits; thus, the valuation analyst should use an income-based approach for most engagements.

- *Did the valuation analyst focus appropriately on the future value of the IP?* Recall that IP valuation is a forward-looking concept. Thus, the report must demonstrate to the reader that the valuation analyst properly considered the probability of future events, while at the same time not relying too much on historical performance, especially if market conditions have changed dramatically.

- *Did the valuation analyst have independent legal counsel review any IP protections?* Recall that the valuation analyst typically will not have sufficient legal training to render opinions as to the strength of the IP's protections. While not imperative (many clients do not want to incur the additional expense to have independent legal counsel review their IP protections), the valuation analyst should articulate any consideration of using external counsel to review the strength of any IP protections.

- *Did the valuation analyst interview company management?* It is perplexing that some valuation analysts will generate IP valuation reports without ever speaking directly with the management responsible for monetizing the IP. The valuation analyst must understand exactly how the company will monetize the IP. The report must demonstrate to the reader that the valuation analyst has interviewed company management.

- *Did the valuation analyst perform a meaningful market survey?* The report must demonstrate to the reader that the valuation analyst performed a credible market survey. It is not enough for an analyst to cut and paste an industry overview from Yahoo! Finance into a report.[313] The valuation analyst, especially regarding items of utility such as patents, must perform a market survey that evaluates a technical and economic value proposition of the IP. The valuation analyst must then reflect that value proposition appropriately in the valuation model.

- ***Did the valuation analyst build and include a copy of the valuation model?*** If the auditor seeks to validate any calculations in the valuation report, the valuation analyst should include a copy of the valuation model in the report. While valuation analysts may not want to provide auditors with a copy of the actual spreadsheet that contains the model, the valuation analyst should provide enough detail and clarity in the valuation model so that the auditor can reproduce the mathematical results.

Report Boilerplate

When analyzing the valuation report, the auditor should ensure that the report contain all of the standard boilerplate consistent with valuation reporting standards. The report must state an effective date for the report (i.e., the date of the report printing) as well as the effective date of the value conclusion. Consistent with business valuation engagements, a clearly written purpose is essential for the IP valuation report. The purpose does not need to be long, but it should state each purpose the valuation report intends to serve comprehensively. If more than one purpose exists, then the auditor should verify that the report expresses each purpose clearly and distinctly so readers know there are multiple purposes for the report.

The report must state the intended users of the report. Additionally, the report must state who any other readers or users of the report may be. This requires the valuation analyst to forecast who may have in interest in the IP and who may, because of that interest, read the content and conclusions in the valuation report. Naturally, it is impossible to forecast all possible users or readers of the IP valuation report. However, it must be clear that the valuation analyst has carefully considered possible readers or users and that the report lists these individuals or entities and the nature of their anticipated interest. This includes explicit technical descriptions of what assets the opinion covers, including which particular markets the opinion covers.

313 The author has actually witnessed such work in reports from several large, well-known, well-branded firms with international valuation practices.

Of course, to authenticate the validity of the report, the valuation analyst (or each valuation analyst if multiple analysts participate in the engagement) must sign the report. The signature authenticates the work performed by the valuation analyst and is fundamental in transforming the report into a formal document.

Economic Conditions and Nature of the Industry

Certain economic indicators have less impact on the value of a particular IP portfolio. So which economic indicators are germane to the valuation? The answer to this question is tricky, but there are some general guidelines. First, for the most part, the macroeconomic indicators include historical consumer confidence, interest rates, inflation rates, employment rates, currency exchange rates, housing starts, job growth, worker productivity, and wage growth. Depending on the industry, these may or may not influence the IP valuation. Critically, if the valuation analyst includes an economic indicator, he or she must articulate why and how that indicator makes a difference in the value assessment. Second, many IP types may generate value that differs from the macroeconomic cycle. For example, IP that creates energy cost savings may receive more attention and value in locations where energy cost is high. In addition, if a valuation analyst excludes a widely published economic indicator, then he or she must provide reasons that justify this exclusion. In summary, the auditor should expect certain levels of flexibility when addressing the credibility of an IP valuation report when it comes to macroeconomic indicators.

Ultimately, the market drives IP value. Intellectual property that has a large and credible applicable market is worth more than IP that has limited market applications. A valuation analyst must consider the relative size, growth, and trends in the target markets for IP to determine whether credible market opportunities exist for value. Another important value driver is the state of the current market. Growing markets generally will support the notion of long-term value, while shrinking markets can indicate little long-term value prospects. An adequate market analysis does not consist of parroting economic trends from the prior economic quarters. Value is a forward-looking concept, and the future is where the valuation analyst should be looking. Where is the market going in three years? What is the effect of attrition or obsolescence on the asset? What is the anticipated market response to the substitution effect of other products? A credible valuation report will speak materially to these issues.

The competitive market has a material impact on value as well. If the market views a given piece of intellectual property as superior in features, performance, and value, it pays a premium to receive those benefits. If the market views competitive offerings as easy substitutes with low barriers to changing, then this phenomenon will threaten the value of the IP's incremental benefits, forcing vendors to compete on price alone in a commodity market. This places downward pressure on IP value. It is not enough for a valuation analyst to mention competitors in passing in a valuation report. A valuation analyst must evaluate the competitive technologies feature by feature (perhaps in a multifactor decision model or market survey) to ascertain the IP's advantages and reflect any advantages as appropriate in the valuation model.

IP Utility

The valuation analyst must clearly describe the property and the underlying protected assets. Through the description, the reader must become confident that the valuation analyst has strong, detailed knowledge about the relevant IP, especially if it is technology based. The report must make clear that the valuation analyst has the necessary education, capacity, and scientific understanding regarding the technology to be able to forecast the utility the technology will provide the world. After all, utility creates value and science creates the utility. If the reader does not gain an appreciation that the valuation analyst has a deep working knowledge of the relevant technology, then a gap exists, calling into question the credibility of the valuation analyst and the resulting report.

Government Protections

For the intellectual property to retain value, the IP must maintain certain sustainable competitive advantages (e.g., patent protection). Without these sustainable competitive advantages, market forces erode any economic power of the IP and drive a lower commodity value.

One key driver for IP value is the ability to detect infringement. IP is more valuable in situations where it is easy to detect infringement (because it may be less costly to detect infringement and it may be easier to prove under dispute with the infringing party) than in situations where it is not easy to detect infringement. IP with difficult detection of infringement is worth less because there may be excess costs associated with infringement discovery and defense in disputes. For example, it is easy for Nike to detect infringement, sue a shirt company that makes knockoffs of Nike's best-selling golf shirts, and win. It is much more difficult for Qualcomm to reverse-engineer the software code in a competitor's cellular device to detect infringement of Qualcomm's software patents. A credible valuation report will consider the effects of infringement detection and speak to the corresponding value effects. The valuation analyst should include in the report a detailed, systematic method for assessing the ability of the owner of the IP to police possible infringement.

Another key driver for IP value is the ease with which a third party designs around the key protections for the intellectual property. For example, patents with claims that are hard to circumvent are generally more valuable than patents where it is easy for a third party to design around the patent's claims. The valuation analyst should write a detailed section on design-around attributes of the subject IP and assess a quantified level of design-around directly built into the valuation model as one of the many independent variables affecting the fair market value. The valuation analyst must also consider possible value impairment if it is easy for a third party to circumvent the intellectual property's protections. As another example, companies that maintain trade secrets, yet have loose confidential and non-compete provisions for employees, inherently impair the value in the trade secrets. A credible valuation report will consider the effects of design circumvention and speak to the corresponding value effects.

A third driver for IP value is the propensity or willingness of the IP owner to defend the intellectual property against attack in the market. For example, if a company owns a patent, but it does not pursue infringers aggressively, or its balance sheet lacks the financial resources necessary to do so, then the patent may be worth less because infringers would have no reason to pay royalties or cease and desist from infringing on the patent. The valuation report should address this game-theoretic perspective formally.[314] The auditor should look to see that the valuation analyst considers possible value impairment if a company demonstrates a tendency not to defend its IP in the market.

Functional Realization

Related to the concept of utility, the valuation analyst must rigorously challenge the hypothesis that the underlying technology will actually work. Using scientific- and engineering-related education and experience, the strong IP valuation analyst will offer concrete examples of how or why the technology will suffer from risk of operation, as well as how and why the technology will work at all. Again, without the proper educational background, this sort of challenge will be difficult for many valuation analysts. For example, auditors of the IP valuation report should look to see if the valuation analyst included a section that discusses "challenges" or "risks" to the technology. Auditors should also check the curriculum vitae of the valuation analyst to ensure that the valuation analyst has a science or engineering degree, in addition to a degree in business or finance. Any discussion within the body of the report should describe the actual, physical, electromechanical, chemical, biological, or

314 Oftentimes valuation analysts will use real option models to account for such considerations.

software challenges inherent to the invention and exactly the plan the owners of the technology may employ to overcome such challenges. The valuation analyst should transform these challenges into a risk assessment during the valuation process.

Demand Analysis

Not to belabor the obvious, but market acceptance, which drives demand, drives IP value. Market acceptance occurs when end users of the technology report feelings of satisfaction with the product and indicate a demand for additional product in the marketplace. Prior to that level of market acceptance, a willing buyer uses the relevant technology from another vendor, if possible, or does nothing (i.e., status quo, which is one of the largest competitive threats to new products). Intellectual property whose embodiment has generated economic activity (i.e., revenue) is worth more than IP whose embodiment has yet to generate any economic activity. Instances of economic activity demonstrate that the owner has overcome significant hurdles to prove utility in the embodiment of an invention to a disinterested third party. One cannot deduce the same from IP that has yet to generate economic activity. A credible valuation report will speak materially to this consideration and demonstrate a realistic demand analysis based on historical performance and other indicators of future cash flows.

Financial History

If the valuation is for a going concern with considerable intellectual property or is for IP with a proven historical earning record, then historical financial statements may be available. The auditor should look to see that the valuation analyst considered these financial statements to help develop the valuation conclusion. History is sometimes an indicator of the future, although there are obvious limits to this cliché. If the technology has not yet been exploited, then historical financials are clearly not available. Further, if the market is changing (as markets always do), then history may in fact be a poor indicator of value. In either case, the valuation analyst is responsible for the development of forecasts or projections. If historical financials are available, the valuation analyst should use them. If the valuation analyst does not use them, this is a red flag. Also, if the client has provided forecasts, the valuation analyst should use this information carefully. In fact, the auditor should consider it a red flag if the valuation analyst takes such forecasts and uses them in his or her analysis without any modification based on engineering economic analysis. The valuation analyst must perform engineering economic analysis and derive his or her own forecasts of cash flows used to value the IP. Historical financial information is one of many sources to help a valuation analyst understand a reasonable forecast of the future.

Chronology

Timing for revenues associated with IP valuations drive a large amount of IP value. It will take a commitment of time for a company to realize the economic value from IP through the company's efforts, sometimes called marketing, preproduction, or start-up time. Up-front time will include necessary preparations by the company to create the product, to prepare materials and extend marketing efforts, to hire additional staff to handle further development, to grow sales, and others. This time has a value impact, as it defers cash flows the company will ultimately generate from the IP. Factors such as revenue and expense recognition policies can change the timing of cash flows that a company generates. This timing has an inverse value impact. Revenue recognition policies that are aggressive on the front end of a project will generate a higher value, as the company receives use of cash sooner rather than later. Yet such policies may be unrealistic in the market. Conservative revenue recognition policies generate lower values when the company defers cash flows until later periods, which are worth less because of the time value of money. The auditor should look to see that the valuation analyst provides adequate consideration of revenue recognition policies and time in the value opinion and that such policies do not conflict with broader accounting standards.

Royalty Rate Analysis

Intellectual property, by definition, is unique. Thus, when IP sells or is licensed, it is serving a purpose to a constituent that is unique. The utility is unique, the way the benefit is realized is unique, and the invention (for patents) is unique. For trademarks, the mark itself must be unique as well. All this talk of uniqueness begs the question of why the valuation analyst would consider looking at the economics of other technologies if the comparability is apparently low. The answer is that the valuation analyst should look at databanks of royalty rates. While it is true that the technology may be unique, the utility may be unique, and the invention or mark may be unique, the economic problems these properties attempt to solve are mostly not unique. Further, the industries in which such properties transact often treat "similar" technologies in similar economic ways. In fact, the valuation analyst should assess the royalty rate analysis with as much rigor as was used in the understanding of the protected technology itself. Detailed descriptions of the comparable royalty rates and underlying technologies should be provided, and the valuation analyst must make a compelling case as to why each license transaction is used as a comparable technology to the subject IP. Again, it should be apparent to the reader that the valuation analyst is a scientist or engineer, as others may not have the competence to make such assessments.

Valuation analysts typically use two methods to calculate the net present value of intellectual property. First, the valuation analyst may choose to forecast cash flows, which would arise from the direct exploitation of the protected asset. Second, the valuation analyst may choose to value the likely royalty seen from a license agreement to a third party who would exploit the asset. Generally, the engagement may call for the analysis of one or both of these methods. For the direct exploitation model, the valuation analyst should provide considerable detail to support several particulars:

- *Revenues:* Revenue forecasts should have grounding in a reasonable analysis of likely pricing and volume estimates. Important components allowing the valuation analyst to have a basis for a strong, sensible revenue forecast include price growth; demand analysis; and market size, growth, and penetration.
- *Fixed costs:* Fixed costs forecasts should have a basis comprising the likely financing of the required plant, property, and equipment necessary to produce the invention at the appropriate volumes.
- *Variable costs:* Variable costs include labor, utilities, travel, and other non-fixed business costs. The valuation analyst must spend considerable time thinking about the fixed-variable cost mix that would reflect the IP owner's ability to secure assets, gain financing, and survive a start-up period.
- *Timing:* Timing of costs and revenues forecasts must have some reasonable explanation surrounding them.
- *Cash flow:* The valuation analyst is responsible for using the revenue and cost structures developed from the rigorous understanding of the science, engineering, and economics of the invention to forecast likely cash flow numbers. The concept of remaining economic life is relevant to the period of the cash flow projection.
- *Risk level:* The valuation analyst must offer a well-described, comprehensively articulated defense that inures to the IP. The risk level must be persuasive and should fit industry expectations, the risk profile of the actual invention, and the profile of likely adoption in the marketplace versus available rival products and substitutes that are currently available.

Income Approach Using Reasonable Royalty Method

Remember that IP valuation is about incremental economic analysis. Thus, the auditor should review work by the valuation analyst to delineate the profit from an operation that is attributable to the IP from the profit that accrues due to management, customer relationships, margin on materials, and others in an IP valuation engagement. If such delineation does not occur, it is possible to introduce bias into any value opinion, as a valuation analyst would attribute an abnormally low or high amount of cash flow to the IP. That said, for some IP types, the IP might constitute the entire basis for the profit-creating engine. In such a situation, the valuation analyst may reasonably accrue all profit to the IP. There are several ways to segregate such value (e.g., profit split), and the valuation report should present to the auditor in clear form the consideration of value segregation of the IP from the product or service that embodies it.

Consideration of Cost Approach

Generally, the cost approach to valuation is not useful in IP valuation. However, if the valuation analyst finds a particular case compelling for the use of the asset approach, then the valuation analyst should do so with very well written supporting analysis. A lack of historical cash flows is not a sufficient reason to rely on the cost approach of valuation. In such case, any value conclusion derived via the cost approach might well constitute valuation malpractice, as already discussed in earlier chapters. The cost approach generally describes the cost of the invention inasmuch as it actually costs to produce, which has little to do with future cash flows. It is common in many cases of IP valuation for the valuation analyst to reject the cost approach. However, when a valuation analyst does choose to employ the cost approach to value IP, the valuation analyst must specify careful reasoning, consistent with modern and accepted standard practice and theory in financial economics, for its use in the report. The auditor should assess such use on a case-by-case basis, and the auditor may do well to hire a third party IP valuation analyst for such a critique.

Use of Market Methods for IP Valuation

Intellectual property is unique and novel by definition. As such, an auditor should test and question the wholesale use of certain market-type approaches to perform IP valuations. These methods consist generally of comparing the financial performance of companies that own IP against those that do not, with the difference supposedly being attributable to IP ownership. However, there is little academic research suggesting that the explanation of the difference is true with some reasonable degree of confidence. Second, ownership of IP cannot explain an abundant amount of exogenous variance using such methods, especially when compared against traditional market indices. In fact, such methods can sometimes yield a negative value indication, meaning that owning the IP in fact hurt the firm. Such outcomes can be nonsensical. The valuation analyst must accentuate with specificity why a market-based approach is appropriate and why other methods are not.

Use of Valid and Reliable Inferential Statistics

Oftentimes in IP valuation, a valuation analyst considers certain statistics and parameters for analysis. The valuation analyst may use simulation tools that generate thousands of data points from a model containing 15 or 20 independent variables or more. In such cases, the valuation analyst will likely encounter statistical or econometric issues such as heteroskedasticity, skewness, multicollinearity, or nonrandom sampling. Other issues threaten the validity of results as well. Generally, the use of large amounts of data in formulating valuation conclusions requires a level of statistical and mathematical reasoning that transcends well beyond the capabilities of the traditional CPA. In fact, this analysis has quite little to do with accounting, and plenty to do with mathematical logic. Knowing when to deduce and when to infer comes from a background in science, engineering, math, econometrics, or statistics. The auditor should check the valuation analyst's curriculum vitae to ensure the valuation analyst's capabilities are sufficient; otherwise, it is questionable whether the valuation analyst has the skills to make IP value judgments when using certain types of data.

Repeatability

Key parts of the valuation process should be obvious so that one skilled in the art could reasonably reproduce the same results given the same inputs. As such, the valuation analyst must state and quantify all assumptions and describe all methods, tools, and analytical processes transparently. The valuation analyst must describe, in detail, all data collection methods. The disclosure of the entire series of data collection methods, data analysis methods, and inferences made must occur without opacity so that other valuation analysts may be able to repeat the study for reliability purposes. Without such transparency, the valuation report cannot stand on its own, and the conclusions are drawn into question. With considerable sums of money oftentimes at stake, the report must stand on its own and be repeatable.

www.ingramcontent.com/pod-product-compliance
Lightning Source LLC
LaVergne TN
LVHW062113200926
848484LV00007B/1653
* 9 7 8 1 9 3 5 0 8 1 6 0 9 *